D0960770

Berlin Rising

By the same authors

Operation Lucy
Colonel Z
The Deadly Embrace
Kristallnacht
The Fall of Berlin

By Anthony Read (with Ray Bearse)

Conspirator: Churchill, Roosevelt and Tyler Kent, Spy

BERLIN RISING

Biography of a City

Anthony Read

and

David Fisher

W. W. Norton & Company
New York   London

Copyright © 1994 by Anthony Read and David Fisher

All rights reserved

First American Edition

Printed in the United States of America.

Manufacturing by the Haddon Craftsmen, Inc.

ISBN 0-393-03606-5

W. W. Norton & Company, Inc.
500 Fifth Avenue, New York, N.Y. 10110
W. W. Norton & Company Ltd.
10 Coptic Street, London WC1A 1PU

1 2 3 4 5 6 7 8 9 0

CONTENTS

KEY TO ILLUSTRATIONS

AKG: Archiv fur Kunst und Geschichte, Berlin
LBS: Landesbildstelle, Berlin
Ullstein: Ullstein Bilderdienst, Berlin

ACKNOWLEDGEMENTS

We would like to acknowledge the help, advice and hospitality of many Berliners, among them:

Federal President Richard von Weizsäcker, a former governing mayor of the city, for his enthusiasm for our project;

Herr Eberhard Diepgen, the present governing mayor of Berlin, for his encouragement and practical help;

Götz, Freiherr von Coburg and Herr Herbert Segal of the Presse- und Informationsamt des Landes Berlin, for their support in our researches;

Frau Gisela Höppner, Herr Brodersen, Herr Jahnke, and all at the Verkehrsamt Berlin, for their assistance and good humour in putting up with our increasingly impossible demands – and for an unending supply of passes for Berlin's excellent public transport system;

Frau Friede Springer and Herr Reiner Laabs of Ullstein, for allowing us access to the late Axel Springer's marvellous Zille collection;

Herr Herbert Ernst of the Zille Museum, Berliner Flohmarkt, Bahnhof Friedrichstrasse, whose enthusiasm for Zille proved to be infectious, and whose knowledge was hugely helpful;

Dr Barbara Schönefeld of the Polizeihistorisches Sammlung of the Berlin Polizeipräsident for her patience in looking out so much material for us, in particular details of the Ringvereine;

the staff of the Bildarchiv of the Landesbildstelle, the Archiv für Kunst und Geschichte and Ullstein Bilderdienst, for invaluable assistance with our picture research;

Bruce Anderson, a New Zealander who stopped off in Berlin for a few days' holiday 20-odd years ago, fell in love with the place and stayed, and whose knowledge of the city is truly encyclopaedic;

Maria Gräfin von Maltzan, a Berlin legend in her own right, for being her impossible self;

Walter Lassally, who has lived in England since before the Second World War, but who still keeps a suitcase in Berlin, who first introduced us to the city he loves;

Herr Heinz Gutknecht, Frau Martina Anders, and the staff of the Hotel Metropol, Friedrichstrasse – Ossies one and all – for their kindness and courtesy and the hospitality of their excellent hotel;

Frau Dagmar Dominke and the manager and staff of the Hotel President, An der Urania – Wessies all – who run one of our favourite hotels;

Herr Willi Weiland and his staff at the Hotel Inter-Continental, Budapesterstrasse, for their courtesy, kindness and hospitality.

Many others kindly offered assistance which we were not able to make use of: Herr Alfred Schönemann of the Berlin Dom (Hilton); Herr Michael Osterlitz, Forum Hotel; Herr T. Wachs, Maritim Grand Hotel; Herr Güthoff and Frau Susanne Winde of Novotel-Berlin, Siemensstadt; Frau Martina Kaslitz of the Palast Hotel; Frau Barbara Lotte, Hotel Savoy; Frau Inge Gedel, Hotel Unter den Linden; and Herr Peter Elser, of Hecker's Deele.

We would also like to thank the staffs of the London Library, the Goethe Institut, London, and Diss, Eye, Norwich and Maidenhead Public Libraries, for their patience and assistance.

Lastly, we would like to express our gratitude to our wives, Rosemary and Barbara, for putting up with our frequent absences and our preoccupied presences.

Central Berlin 1945

To Daisy, Elliot and Jack: the future.
May they come to enjoy Berlin as much as we do.

CHAPTER 1

Eagle versus Bear

O N T H E E V E N I N G O F 9 November 1989, television sets all over the world were tuned to one of the greatest spontaneous happenings of the twentieth century. Countless millions in Europe, North and South America, Australasia, Asia, Africa, all watched with amazement as a young man with a knapsack on his back climbed on to the top of the Berlin wall from the eastern side, directly in front of the Brandenburg Gate. As he strolled nonchalantly to and fro along that concrete monstrosity, they waited breathlessly, hardly daring to believe that the border guards were not opening fire. But, incredibly, he was soaked, not shot – the worst the guards could offer was a half-hearted drenching from a couple of water hoses. Soon, they gave up even that. Within minutes, the young man was joined by hundreds of others from east and west, dancing, singing, embracing, in a celebration that echoed around the globe.

At one astonishing stroke, before the politicians of either side could react, the young people of Berlin had made history. They had declared the cold war unofficially over. The world would never be the same again. True, there had been signs of change for some time: President Gorbachov had promised Glasnost and Perestroika in a

Soviet Union that was already crumbling, and shortly before the wall walk he had let it be known that he would not intervene militarily to prop up the East German regime. The Hungarians had opened their borders, and East Germans had begun flooding into the west through Austria. There had been massive demonstrations in Dresden and Leipzig. But it was Berlin that the world had been waiting for. Berlin, the living symbol of the division between east and west, was where it mattered.

For more than a century, Berlin has exercised a strange fascination for the rest of the world – when US President John F. Kennedy declared '*Ich bin ein Berliner*' on 26 June 1963, he could not have produced the same effect by claiming to belong to any other city. Over the years, the world has seen Berlin as the symbol of militarism and imperialism, bloody revolution, hyperinflation, the wildest excesses of the Twenties, the terrors of totalitarian rule by both left and right, the horrors of total war and the miracle of regeneration.

But the story of Berlin goes back much further than those hundred years. Every city is unique, of course, but Berlin has always been a singular city, even when divided. It has grown that way through an eventful history that few other cities could hope to match.

The story of Berlin is the story of its people, a people largely composed of successive waves of immigrants. Dutchmen, Frenchmen, Huguenots, Jews, Italians, Poles, Scots, Silesians, Galicians, Saxons, Pomeranians, Prussians, Lithuanians, Russians and God knows what else – rucksack Berliners, they were called – all poured into what was for a long time little more than a malodorous garrison town. There, they were transformed by the *Berliner Luft*, the special Berlin atmosphere, into something rich and strange. It has been said that no one is born a Berliner; everyone has to become one. You breathe in the air, which has been described as being as addictive as cocaine or alcohol, and tune in to the fast *Berliner Tempo*, and are transfigured.

The special quality that marks out a Berliner from any other German is mostly an attitude of mind, the underdog's subversive sense of the fundamental ridiculousness of those above him. Like Noël Coward's natives, Berliners have often found their rulers and supposed betters 'a source of much hilarity and mirth'. Humour and grumbling are traditionally two of the safety valves available to the powerless, and

2

both are deeply ingrained in the Berlin psyche. Berliners are possibly the world's greatest grumblers, and their humour is the blackest to be found anywhere. Over the centuries, they have needed both in full measure, as the city has been dominated by the presence of armed troops, whether Prussian, Swedish, French, Russian, British, or American, and ruled by men who were either mad, bad or incompetent, and often a combination of all three.

No matter their origins, each new generation has absorbed existing characteristics: the modern Berliner's habit of puncturing pomposity with irreverent nicknames – the ruined Kaiser Wilhelm Memorial Church is 'the hollow tooth', for example, and the ultra-modern Congress Hall 'the pregnant oyster' – dates back in an unbroken line to at least the early fifteenth century. When their first Hohenzollern ruler, whom they dubbed '*Eisenzahn*', 'Iron-tooth', built the first Schloss in the little city in 1448, they swiftly named it the '*Zwingburg*', 'Coercion Castle'. Even then, they understood that no dictatorship is ever benevolent.

Austrians and Bavarians are famous for their *Gemütlichkeit*, one of those untranslatable words meaning charm, cosiness, sentimentality. The word used for Berliners is *Schnodderigkeit*, brashness, cockiness. Anyone who is in doubt about what that means has only to watch a Berliner on his own turf, be he barman or market trader or simply a man entering his local *Kneipe*, the traditional Berlin corner pub. He steps with a strut, like a slightly muscle-bound James Cagney, proclaiming himself cock of the walk. Not surprisingly, he has his own unique dialect: *Berliner Schnauze*, 'Berlin gob', or *Berlinisch* as it is more politely known. A combination of Low German, Saxon, French and even some Yiddish, its vocabulary is coarse, caustic and earthy – just like those who use it.

Dr Goebbels, Nazi Party boss of Greater Berlin for 19 years, despaired of Berliners. He thought them rude, cynical, churlish and hopelessly unsatisfactory representatives of Nazi ideology. They were not German thoroughbreds, but mongrels set down in the bleak, sandy Prussian plain, only too ready to bite the hand of anyone who tried to stroke them.

Bismarck and Hitler both hated Berlin. So, too, did Konrad Adenauer, first German chancellor after the Second World War. Like Goebbels a Rhinelander and a Catholic, he regarded it as alien, hostile and ungodly, 'a Babylon amid the northern steppes'. Some things, it seems, never change. On the other hand, the spirit of the city has got under the skin of countless thousands of more sympathetic souls, whose devotion is neatly described by a well-used phrase: they 'always keep a suitcase in Berlin'.

Berlin came late to the ranks of the great cities. Unlike London or Paris or Rome, which had all enjoyed metropolitan status for several centuries, Berlin did not become what the Germans know as a *Weltstadt*, 'world city', rather than a *Grossstadt*, 'big city', until late in the nineteenth century. At the beginning of that century it had been little more than a provincial state capital, one of no fewer than 390 in the German empire (the number was reduced to 39 after 1803). Although Berlin already had over 170,000 inhabitants by 1800 – of whom more than 25,000 were military personnel – it had only in the preceding few decades become more important than Weimar, Dresden, Cologne, Frankfurt-am-Main, Munich or several others. As a city, it still could not rank itself alongside imperial Vienna.

In the following 70 years, however, Berlin exploded. It outstripped all its rivals to become the capital of a united Germany in 1871, its population rocketing to 826,000. Over the next 20 years this figure more than doubled to nearly two million, and by the beginning of the First World War in 1914 it had doubled yet again to make Berlin the sixth-biggest city in the world, with almost four million inhabitants. During the period between the two world wars it continued to expand, despite the mass exodus of Jews and anti-Nazis, adding another half million souls by 1939.

This phenomenal rate of growth gave Berlin the same sort of brash vitality as New York or Chicago. It produced the industrial and commercial drive that made Berlin the powerhouse not only of Germany but also of continental Europe. And the first taste of political freedom after more than 700 years of repression created a sudden explosion of artistic energy. For one glorious decade, the so-called Golden Twenties, the city became the world centre of the avant-garde. Theatre, film, painting, music, architecture – suddenly it was all happening in Berlin. But it did not last long. The darkness soon closed in again. Berlin's grim past was not so easy to shake off.

Berlin started life in the twelfth and thirteenth centuries as a remote frontier town and trading post in what has been described as the

'Wild East', far out on the great plain of northern Europe. This was the Mark Brandenburg – '*Mark*' is basically the same word as the English 'march', meaning a border region – a 10,000-square-mile (26,000 square kilometres) wilderness of sand and scrub, swamp and forest in the farthest corner of the Holy Roman Empire. The Mark, newly conquered by Albrecht the Bear, was the empire's defence zone against marauding tribes of Slavs, and even against the Mongol horde, who were still sweeping westward at the time: they took Moscow and Kiev in 1240, then rampaged through Hungary, Poland and Silesia before suddenly pulling out of Europe following the death of their leader Ogodai Khan, son of the great Genghis.

The largest and most important city in the Mark was Brandenburg itself, the seat of the bishopric. But Albrecht and his family, the Askaniers, chose to live in a fortress on a secure island site where the rivers Spree and Havel meet at Spandau. Some 18 miles further east at Köpenick, where the Spree is joined by the Dahme, they built a second fortress. Both are still standing, their original timber and earth construction replaced between the thirteenth and sixteenth centuries by more permanent red brick structures – stone was always in short supply in the sand and marshlands of the Mark.

Almost exactly halfway between the two Askanier strongholds, a group of fishermen had settled on an island in the Spree, their simple huts huddled into a protective square like a train of Conestoga covered wagons. They called the place Cölln – probably from the old German *Collen*, meaning a hill or mound rising from the water. Another group of settlers, meanwhile, had built their homes on the north bank of the river directly opposite, creating a separate village which became known as Berlin, probably from a Slavic word meaning a swamp, marsh or wallow. The first recorded mention of either settlement was in 1237, but men had already been living on the site for well over 100 years by then, and there are relics of several bronze age settlements nearby.

Initially, the two communities were quite separate; indeed, they were even in different provinces of Brandenburg: Cölln was in Teltow and Berlin in Barnum. Considering the possible origins of the names, they may well have come from two different tribes, one Germanic, the other Slav, making Berliners mongrels from the start. In any case, the racial mix was fostered by Albrecht and his successors, who brought in settlers from as far afield as Utrecht, the Rhineland, Holland, Zeeland and Flanders, to colonize the territory and encourage trade. More new blood was provided by Saxons and Slavs from further east. The first Jews were living in Berlin towards the end of the thirteenth century.

Before long, the two villages were linked by a mill dam across the river, the Mühlendamm – the name now belongs to a bridge on the same spot – and in the best frontier tradition they erected a stockade around themselves for protection. In due course, the Berliners dug a wide moat around the north-eastern side of their settlement, joined to the river at either end, so their village, too, became an island.

The twin villages, positioned almost in the centre of the Mark, provided a convenient staging post for the knights of the Teutonic Order in the great '*Drang nach Osten*', the drive to the east, which Hitler was to emulate 700 years later. These brave and brutal warriors, survivors of the Third Crusade to the Holy Land, were

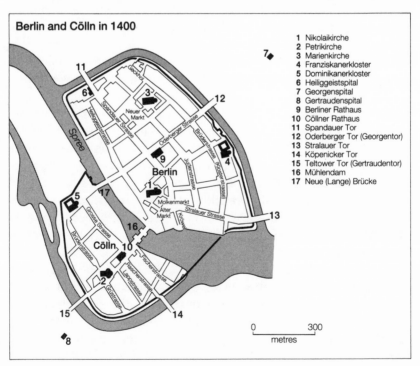

Berlin and Cölln in 1400

1 Nikolaikirche
2 Petrikirche
3 Marienkirche
4 Franziskanerkloster
5 Dominikanerkloster
6 Heiliggeistspital
7 Georgenspital
8 Gertraudenspital
9 Berliner Rathaus
10 Cöllner Rathaus
11 Spandauer Tor
12 Oderberger Tor (Georgentor)
13 Stralauer Tor
14 Köpenicker Tor
15 Teltower Tor (Gertraudentor)
16 Mühlendam
17 Neue (Lange) Brücke

0 ___ 300
metres

charged by the emperor with the mission of imposing Christianity on the heathen tribes of Prussia, the territory beyond Brandenburg and Pomerania bordering Poland and the Baltic. But they were largely financed by the Hansa merchants of north Germany, who wanted the eastern Baltic opened up for trade in valuable commodities like timber, resin, furs and grain.

The landless knights were quite happy to carry the cross to the heathen, and to regard baptism as a convenient symbol of submission – *Tod oder Taufe!* (Death or baptism!) was their war cry. But once they had subdued the natives, they carved up the territory between them and stayed on to become the *Junkers*, colonial lords of vast feudal estates. The grand master of their order became the ruling prince of Prussia, answerable in theory to the Holy Roman Emperor in Vienna. Those conquered Slavs who had not managed to escape to the east became the landless serfs of this master race, living like cattle and treated like cattle. And so the essential elements of the character of Prussia were laid down from the beginning. But in those early days, Brandenburg was not Prussia.

As the twin villages grew into small towns, the Berliners started a market for milk and dairy products on their side of the river, and the inhabitants of Cölln established a fish market on theirs – the sites are still known as the Molkenmarkt and Fischer Insel today. Soon, the mill dam linking them was supplemented by a bridge – known for centuries as the Lange Brücke (the Long Bridge), now called the Rathausbrücke (town hall bridge). Together, the dam and the bridge created the basis of Berlin-Cölln's early prosperity, forming a junction between two ancient trade routes: east–west by water to the Elbe, Hamburg and the North Sea, and north–south by land between the Baltic and the Erzgebirger (ore mountains) of Bohemia, beyond which lay Prague, a major trade centre since the tenth century.

Because the Mühlendamm blocked the passage between the upper and lower Spree, river craft had to stop and unload their cargoes in Berlin-Cölln. Before they could reload them into vessels on the other side, merchants and skippers were obliged to offer their wares for sale in the market for several days, and to pay tolls, market taxes and customs dues to the margrave. Since the margrave also received a tax on all grain ground in the water-powered flour mills alongside the dam, Berlin-Cölln soon became one of the ruler's main sources of revenue. The Askanier family still lived in their castle at Spandau, but were represented in the twin towns by a governor known as the Schultheiss – a name used today by the city's largest brewery.

During the second half of the thirteenth century, the villages blossomed rapidly into twin towns. Two churches, the Nikolaikirche (St Nicholas's) alongside Berlin's Molkenmarkt and the Petrikirche (St Peter's) at the other end of the Mühlendamm in Cölln were both built around 1250. In Berlin a second church, the Marienkirche (St Mary's) was built about ten years later. All three were destroyed by bombs during the Second World War, but the Nikolaikirche and the Marienkirche have both been totally restored. The Marienkirche, where Johann Sebastian Bach once played the organ, now forms part of the modern Alexanderplatz complex; the Nikolaikirche, with its distinctive twin spires, stands at the heart of a painstakingly reconstructed 'old quarter'.

There were Franciscan monks in Berlin from the earliest recorded times – by 1250 their monastery was already the provincial chapter for Saxony. Their church, the Klösterkirche, was also destroyed during the Second World War, but the old monastery is remembered today by Klösterstrasse. The Dominicans, meanwhile, set up house in Cölln, on Bruderstrasse. The first hospitals appeared around this time – the Heiliggeistspital (Holy Ghost hospital) just inside the Spandau gate, and the Georgenspital (St George's), a leper house, some little way outside the Oderberg gate. A third, the Gertraudenspital, followed some years later across the southern arm of the Spree from Cölln; its site is commemorated in today's Berlin by Spittelmarkt, at the end of Leipzigerstrasse, and by the Gertrauden bridge and Gertraudenstrasse. Another religious order, the mysterious Knights Templar, set up their cloister about two and a half miles south of Cölln. The Templars are long gone, but the name of their headquarters, the Tempelhof, remains.

The citizens of Berlin-Cölln, however, were more concerned with trade than with prayer. There were soon thriving guilds of ships' captains, merchants and tailors – who later joined forces as the Merchant Taylors, with links to the English company of Merchant Adventurers, formed to develop the export of cloth to Europe. A Berlin family named Brügge – either because they came from Bruges or because of their connections with it – headed the importers of

Flemish cloth. At the same time, weavers started producing cloth in Berlin itself, the modest beginnings of a textile industry which in later centuries was to become the biggest in Germany.

Mushrooming into something of a boom town, Berlin-Cölln swiftly became one of the leading trading partners with Hamburg, the value of its shipments surpassed only by those of Ghent, Utrecht and Lüneburg. At 4,569 silver marks, Berlin-Cölln's overall trade with Hamburg in 1290 was more than double that of all the other towns in the Mark put together. The principal exports were timber, especially cut oak, and grain from the fertile fields of Barnum and Teltow – the grading 'Berlin Rye' has been the highest standard of quality in Hamburg since 1288. Both were exported to Flanders and even to England. In 1274, the master carpenter from Norwich cathedral was buying timber from Berlin, no doubt in order to repair the damage caused when angry citizens attacked and set fire to the cathedral two years before. The twin cities were also the main trading centre for fish for the interior.

The first written record of Jews living in Berlin – and, incidentally, the first record of discrimination against them – comes in a guild document dated 1295, when weavers were forbidden to buy yarn from them. In fact, their presence was vital to a trading community, because the church had introduced a ban on Christians lending money for interest. The Jews, with their long experience in money-lending, thus became the only source of finance for most of the city's merchants. As in most European cities of that era, the Jews were confined to one street. Judenstrasse still exists, starting alongside the Red Town Hall and running between Klösterstrasse and the Mol-kenmarkt. But they were not allowed to bury their dead in Berlin-Cölln; the nearest Jewish cemetery was in Spandau, nine miles away, where the fortifications offered some protection against desecration.

Growing affluence brought with it the need for greater security, and the two towns decided to unite for their mutual defence. For a start, they built up a stronger wall around themselves, the remains of a small section of which can still be seen today in Littenstrasse. In 1307, they merged their administrations under the Berlin name, with a new town hall symbolically situated in the middle of the bridge; it was painted red, decorated with elaborate wood carvings, and topped with ornate turrets. For their coat of arms, they chose

9

the Berlin bear rampant, with the eagle of Cölln and Brandenburg guardant, in a subsidiary role.

The union proved to be a wise move. During the fourteenth century, after the ruling Askanier family died out, the Mark passed through the hands of a succession of different margraves. None of them showed much interest in governing it. The dusty plains became desolate badlands, terrorized by robber barons and rogue knights who preyed on travellers and local inhabitants alike. Behind its fortress walls, and with the added security of the river Spree and the deep moat, Berlin usually managed to fight off their attacks – though it was burned to the ground in 1380.

Unlike other, often larger towns in the region, Berlin managed to hang on to its independence. In 1391 it became a self-governing city within the empire, eligible to become a member of the Hanseatic League, the association of mercantile free cities that flourished throughout northern Europe from the fourteenth to the sixteenth centuries. This was a privilege that should have guaranteed Berlin's steady development as a centre of commerce under a solid and prosperous middle class. But it was not to be.

At the beginning of the fifteenth century, the Mark Brandenburg was given by the Emperor Sigismund to the wealthy Burgrave of Nuremberg, Friedrich von Hohenzollern, who had financed his election to the imperial throne. At the same time, and for the same services rendered, Friedrich was elevated to the rank of *Kurfürst*, one of the seven elector princes responsible for choosing the emperor. The Berliners, who were leading a confederation of Mark towns trying to bring the robber barons under control, were delighted when Friedrich rode into his new territory and imposed his authority on the barons and knights with the help of a brand-new weapon, a massive siege gun called 'Foul Grete', which could demolish their castle walls. But the Berliners were not so pleased when Friedrich's son and successor, Johann the Alchemist, decided to subjugate their city, too. Their resistance was spirited enough to deter Johann, who withdrew to his fortress at Spandau.

Johann was succeeded by his brother, Friedrich '*Eisenzahn*' (Irontooth), a much more determined character. In 1442, taking advantage of the grievances of merchants and tradesmen against the city magistrates, he persuaded them to invite him in to defend their interests and settle the dispute. Once in, he stayed, deciding to make the town his official residence. It was the end of Berlin's independence, and the beginning of 477 years of autocratic Hohenzollern rule.

Harshness and ruthlessness were to be the hallmark of the Hohenzollerns in their treatment of Berlin from the very beginning. Irontooth started by separating Berlin and Cölln again, no doubt working on the principle of divide and rule. He demolished their city walls and fortifications, leaving them defenceless. He then seized a large area of Cölln, where he proceeded to build himself a palace, the notorious 'Zwingburg'. The Berliners were deprived of all their former liberties. They were forced to surrender control of their city council and their courts to the elector. All association with other cities was forbidden, putting an end to Berlin's membership of the Hanseatic League. Shortly afterwards, most other forms of association, both private and public, were banned.

The Berliners, however, were not prepared to give up their independence so easily. In 1447–8 their indignation boiled over in a revolt, dubbed the 'Berliner Unwillen' by the chroniclers. They drove out the elector's officials, burned his books and documents, and looted the chancellery. They opened the mill dam and flooded the land on which he was building his Zwingburg. They put up a strong palisade to replace the old city wall which he had demolished, and re-established their joint administration in the town hall on the Long Bridge.

Friedrich's response was entirely in character: he sent in the troops. Led by 600 heavily armoured knights, they soon put a bloody end to the rebellion. The eagle had triumphed conclusively over the bear, and in case the Berliners had not yet got the message, Friedrich imposed a new coat of arms on the city. In this one, the Brandenburg eagle was rampant, its claws sunk into the back of the couchant Berlin bear. It would be hundreds of years before the bear was allowed to stand alone again on the city's crest, and until 1875 it continued to wear a slave collar.

The eagle was to fly over the castle, and the palace that replaced it, until 1918 when Berlin was finally released from the Hohenzollern yoke. Even then the city was to enjoy a respite of less than 15 years before the eagle returned in a still more oppressive form, perched above a swastika. Those 15 years were the only time between 1448 and 1990 when the city was not housing a sizable garrison of troops, either those of its rulers or of conquering armies. For more than 500 years, Berliners were forced to kowtow to anyone wearing a uniform, and particularly a military uniform. Civilians, no matter how rich or clever or exalted, were regarded as a lesser species whose primary duty and principal function was to serve and support the army.

When it came to choosing garrison troops, the Hohenzollerns were not fools; few if any of the soldiers were themselves Berliners, apart from the aristocratic officers. They did not trust local men to guard them. In truth, the garrison was there to protect the ruler from the ruled.

Because of the constant presence of troops in their midst, the Berliners have only twice staged actual revolts against their oppressive rulers since the Unwillen of 1448: once in 1848 as part of the nationalistic fervour that was erupting throughout Europe, and again in 1953, against the communist regime of Walter Ulbricht in East Berlin. Both uprisings failed. There was an actual revolution in 1918, it is true, but that was part of the general chaos at the end of the First World War, and the last of the Hohenzollerns had already fled by the time the fighting started.

The arrival of Friedrich Iron-tooth's court, coupled with withdrawal from the Hanseatic League, changed the city's prime function from trade to administration, marking the beginnings of the huge bureaucracy that would flourish there in later centuries. The divided city (technically, it was Berlin-Cölln again, but for convenience we will go on calling it simply Berlin) sank into the stagnation of a provincial backwater on the fringe of European civilization. While cities such as Bruges and Ghent flourished with populations of over 50,000, Cologne with over 35,000, and several other German cities easily topping the 25,000 mark, Berlin had scarcely 7,000 inhabitants. About 400 of them were court employees and another 400 the elector's soldiers. Many of the rest were farmers, who brought their sheep and cattle back to their stalls inside the city every night: for the next 200 years, the unpaved streets were filled with chicken coops, cowsheds and steaming dungheaps.

The Renaissance which swept through Europe during the fifteenth and sixteenth centuries left Berlin virtually untouched. The

Hohenzollerns showed little interest in any of the arts and sciences. Until 1506, there was not one single high school in the entire Mark Brandenburg – and when the first university was eventually built, it was sited in Frankfurt-an-der-Oder rather than in Berlin, in order to avoid contaminating the court. At a time when Shakespeare and his fellow playwrights were delighting the citizens of London with their sophisticated dramas, barely 100 Berliners could read or write. Anything to be printed had to be taken to other, more advanced cities, such as Leipzig in Saxony.

Having successfully avoided the intellectual infection of the Renaissance, the Hohenzollerns also did their best to avoid the spiritual dangers of Luther's Reformation. The peasants' uprising which erupted throughout the rest of Germany in 1524 never touched the Mark – maybe because there were few peasants there, only landless serfs. Elector Joachim II procrastinated as long as he could, breaking with Rome but claiming that the church in Berlin and the Mark would be 'neither Papist nor Wittelsbergian, but truly catholic'. It was the citizens of Berlin and Cölln who finally made up his mind for him, joining together in February 1539 with an urgent petition requesting that their churches should become Lutheran that Easter. Joachim agreed, and promptly seized the opportunity to enrich his treasury by appropriating all church lands and property.

With all this new wealth at his disposal, Joachim decided to build himself a fine new hunting lodge in 1542 on the eastern side of the Havel lake amid the dense pines of the Spandau forest. Over the entrance door he had an inscription carved, 'Zum Grünen Wald' (To the Green Wood), from which the lodge took its name, Jagdschloss Grunewald (for some reason, the umlaut accent over the letter u was dropped). Where the route from the city to the Grunewald (as that part of the forest was soon called) passed over marshy ground that bogged down carriage wheels and horses' hooves, Joachim had a long causeway of logs – a *Damm* – laid down. It became known as the Kurfürstendamm.

At the beginning of the seventeenth century, while the rest of the empire was ravaged by the Protestant–Catholic conflict of the

Thirty Years' War, Brandenburg in general, and Berlin in particular, remained an island of peaceful tolerance. As a perfect example of the relaxed approach to religion that could then only be found in his state, and which has since always been a feature of life in Berlin, Elector Joachim Friedrich declared that the religious freedom he had granted to his subjects also applied to himself and his court. On Christmas day 1613, he and some 55 courtiers switched to the Reformed, Calvinist faith. His wife, like the majority of Berliners, stayed Lutheran.

Joachim Friedrich's successor, Georg Wilhelm, managed to keep out of the Thirty Years' War for another ten years, by sitting on the fence like Joachim II a hundred years before. When the war eventually engulfed Brandenburg, Georg Wilhelm, one of the weakest of all the Hohenzollern rulers, fled to Königsberg in East Prussia, which he had inherited in 1618 as a dukedom under the Polish king. The governor he left in charge of the Mark, Graf Adam von Schwarzenberg, panicked and took refuge in Spandau, leaving Berlin to its own devices.

In 1628, the Bohemian General Wallenstein appeared outside Berlin at the head of an imperial Catholic army. The Berliners threw open the gates, and invited him in. With typical Berlin bloody-mindedness, they had always refused to have anything to do with the war, declaring it to be a matter for noblemen. In 1630, however, Wallenstein was dismissed by the emperor, and left for home. The Swedish Protestant army immediately invaded the region, devastating the countryside and wasting its towns. Magdeburg, 88 miles from Berlin, was sacked and virtually all its 40,000 inhabitants massacred. When the Swedes captured Spandau, Berlin opened its gates once again and made the Swedish King Gustav Adolf, who was married to the elector's daughter, no less welcome than they had Wallenstein.

The Berliners managed to avoid being slaughtered by the Swedes, but were ruined by having to pay a ransom of 300,000 gold thalers to the imperial army, and then having to feed and house Gustav Adolf's troops. Roaring inflation led to a collapse of the currency, and as if that were not enough, three successive outbreaks of the plague wiped out half the population. Desperately, they appealed to their absentee elector for help. 'Pestilence, arson, robbery, and extortion,' they reported, were leading people to 'slash, drown, or hang themselves to end their lives'. But the only thing Georg

Wilhelm could do for them as he cowered in the safety of Königsberg was to die. In 1640, he finally obliged, clearing the way for the start of a new era.

CHAPTER 2

Cabbages and Kings

T HE STORY OF MODERN BERLIN – indeed, of modern Germany – begins with Georg Wilhelm's 20-year-old son and heir, Friedrich Wilhelm, who earned himself the sobriquet 'The Great Elector'. The inheritance he came into could hardly have looked less promising: the whole of the Mark Brandenburg was in ruins and all his best estates had been either sold or mortgaged. In Berlin the population had been reduced to less than 6,000 near-destitute survivors. At least half the buildings had been burnt down or had fallen down, and a third of those that were left were uninhabitable. When he returned to the city in 1643, the young elector's own palace was in such a dangerous condition he dared not go inside. While it was being repaired, he had a modest new palace built in the small village of Potsdam, on the Havel lake about 18 miles south-west of Berlin, away from the noise and smells of the city and a safe distance from any further outbreaks of the plague.

The peace treaty that ended the Thirty Years' War, however, brought considerable territorial gains for Brandenburg. New lands granted to the elector included the eastern half of Pomerania and the bishoprics of Magdeburg, Halberstadt, Minden and Kammin.

Together with the recently inherited duchies of Prussia in the east and Jülich and Cleves on the Rhine, these more than doubled the size of his possessions. Brandenburg was still insignificant in comparison with the Habsburgs' Austrian dominions, or even with Bavaria and Saxony, but the expansion provided the base on which the Great Elector and his successors could build their own empire.

More immediately, however, Friedrich Wilhelm was faced with the task of rebuilding his capital. While his father had skulked in Königsberg, the young prince had been sent to Leiden University, in Holland. There, he had been impressed by the dynamism and prosperity of the spotless Dutch cities, then at the very centre of world commerce. He became a Calvinist, married the sensible Dutch Princess Louise of Orange, and returned to Berlin determined to recreate it as another Amsterdam or Antwerp.

Friedrich Wilhelm started as any Dutch burgher would have done, by ordering the twin cities to be cleaned up: 'Pigsties, stables and all other places offering a similar stink are to be removed from public streets!' he ordered. Each household was to hang a lantern outside at night, to light the streets. He issued citizens with free wood and other materials to rebuild their homes, cutting down the trees in front of his palace and elsewhere to help provide timber. On 5 March 1686, no doubt mindful of the damage caused to this precious resource, he issued an edict that no couple could be married unless the bridegroom could produce a notarized statement that he had planted at least six fruit trees and six young oaks; for winter weddings, the groom was allowed to deposit a sum of money as a guarantee, which would be returned when he presented proof of planting in the spring.

But most important of all, the new elector imported fresh blood from the Netherlands, not only as his court officials but also as settlers, offering them subsidies and tax incentives, and throwing open his cities and the surrounding land to craftsmen and farmers. In this way, he not only began to build up the depleted population but also brought in specialists in all the skills he so desperately needed. Besides planning and construction, these included the agricultural techniques in which the Dutch were then the most advanced nation in the world: dairy farming, cattle breeding and vegetable growing.

Princess Louise herself grew the first potatoes ever seen in the city in her own garden. The new vegetable was received with great mistrust by the Berliners – indeed, it would be well over a hundred years before they finally took it into the heart of their cuisine, inventing ever more ingenious recipes around it. In a more decorative mood, Louise created a beautiful formal garden, the Lustgarten, outside the palace in the heart of Cölln, also in the Dutch style, with fountains, walks and geometric beds.

The settlers from Holland are remembered in various place and street names, most notably Oranienburg and Oranienstrasse. But they also left their mark in a far more practical and more visible way. Dutch engineers were responsible for one of Friedrich Wilhelm's most significant projects, the digging of a canal linking the Oder and the Spree. This created a continuous waterway stretching from Breslau and beyond right through to Hamburg, linking the North Sea and the Baltic for the first time. Berlin, of course, was at the heart of this waterway, well placed to become the hub of the entire communications system of northern Europe.

The Dutch were by no means the only racial group brought to Berlin by the Great Elector, and some of the others were to prove just as important. In 1671, when the emperor expelled the Jewish community from Vienna, Friedrich Wilhelm promptly offered 50 families refuge in his city on the Spree. Jewish fortunes in Berlin had ebbed and flowed over the centuries. As convenient scapegoats they had been blamed for every misfortune and disaster from the Black Death to so-called 'ritual murders'. The first 'court Jew', Michael the Financier, had been appointed in 1543, but 30 years later the Jews were accused of poisoning the elector. There were anti-Semitic riots, and the whole community had been expelled 'for all eternity'. Now, however, their talents – and their money – were needed again, for the Viennese Jews were not poor, penniless migrants but rich and successful merchants and financiers: the elector appointed three of them his official bankers.

Friedrich Wilhelm's attitude to religious differences was notably tolerant, largely thanks to the Dutch influence in his life – the Dutch had proclaimed freedom of conscience as early as 1579. Although he was himself a devout Calvinist, he welcomed both Catholic and Lutheran refugees from other parts of Germany, and allowed his subjects total freedom of worship – another important factor in the character of Berlin.

Again following the Dutch pattern, religious tolerance was extended to the Jews, who were not required to live in a ghetto but were allowed to buy houses or building plots wherever they chose, and to administer their own community affairs. Although they were barred from taking part in farming or handicrafts, and from trading in various commodities such as leather, timber and furs, they could still find more opportunities in Berlin than in most parts of Europe. The initial 50 families soon became 96, and more Jews kept slipping in to found a community that was to have a permanent effect on both the business and intellectual life of the city.

The elector's tolerance continued to provide bonuses for Berlin, as industrious Protestants imbued with the stern work ethic of Luther and Calvin fled from Catholic persecution in other parts of Germany and Europe and found refuge there. There were both Jewish and Protestant refugees from Poland. A hundred Calvinist Huguenots from France were followed by groups of tradesmen from northern Italy, both bringing with them new crafts and businesses to enrich the life of the city. The first Italian store, 'where, as is well-known, all sorts of fine goods and luxury foods are kept', could be found between a French bakery and a 'Quincailleries-Handlung', a French hardware store where one could buy 'fashionable trimmings, braid and similar knick-knacks'.

Fifteen years later, in 1685, Louis XIV of France withdrew freedom of worship from French Protestants. The Huguenots fled the country en masse. Many went to England, some to America, some to Holland. Fifteen thousand found refuge in the Mark Brandenburg, no fewer than 6,000 of them as a self-governing colony in Berlin. Each Huguenot family received a grant of land, which they were able to pass on to their descendants and for which they were required to pay only a nominal rent. They were also exempted from all other taxes for a period of 15 years, and were free to come and go as they pleased.

Six thousand Huguenots represented an enormous influx for a city of 20,000, and was a major new ingredient in the ethnic stew. Quite suddenly, more than one Berliner in every five was French. Excluding the army, the figure for civilians was almost one in three. With the Dutch, the Jews, the Poles and the Italians, plus large numbers of Swedish and Swiss soldiers, as much as a third of the city's entire population was non-German. With such a base, it is small wonder that Berliners always claim to be a different breed from the rest of Germany.

To cope with the flood of immigrants, Friedrich Wilhelm had started building a new suburb on spare land inside the new city walls, opposite Cölln on the south-western bank of the Spree, in 1662. He called it Friedrichswerder, 'Friedrich's development', and set it up as a third municipality, quite separate from the other two. Most of the French immigrants set up home there in a self-governing colony with its own schools, churches and customs, bringing a certain elegance, as well as their industry, to Berlin. Others were directed to an area north-west of the city, outside the wall and on the opposite bank of the river. It was a desolate, barren spot, which they called 'Terre Maudit', 'accursed land'. Over the years, the name was Germanicized into Moabit, the site of Berlin's main jail and, more fittingly, birthplace of the city's industrial revolution nearly 200 years later.

It is almost impossible to overestimate the effect the Huguenots had on Berlin, both in the short and the long term. Their influence spread swiftly into every facet of court and city life: the economy, administration and armed forces were affected as much as the arts and sciences, education and fashion. The old, handwritten roll of French refugees which can be seen today in the Huguenot museum in the French cathedral on the Gendarmenmarkt clearly shows the diversity which the settlers brought to Berlin. On the first page, for instance, are listed two Protestant ministers and their families, three gardeners and a merchant. On the following pages, hundreds of other names appear against literally dozens of trades and professions – the kind of skills Berlin desperately needed if it was ever to become a major city.

The Huguenots introduced no fewer than 46 new trades to the city, paving the way for many future industries, most notably jewellery manufacture and the production of silk, fine fabrics, and felt for hat making. They also revolutionized the city's cuisine, introducing such novelties as French white bread, asparagus, cauliflowers and artichokes, which the native Berliners embraced enthusiastically. Even more significantly, they are credited with introducing Weissbier, the highly individual Berlin brew made from wheat rather than barley.

For many years, Berliners of all classes were overwhelmed by a mania for everything French. The French language threatened to replace German for the upper and middle classes; it was spoken almost exclusively at court for the next 150 years. It has left its mark in the Berlin dialect – a Berliner's local environment is his *'Milljöh'*, or *milieu*, and a spicy meatball, for instance, is still known as a *Bulette*, from the French *boulette*. They can be seen today, piled high among the *Eisbein* and *Bratwurst* in the refrigerated counters of meat stalls in the Berlin markets. The size of a small fist, brown and a little flattened, they look like the droppings of some strange beast, but nevertheless taste delicious. Many Berliners still have Germanicized old French family names: Lothar de Maizière, the last prime minister of East Germany, is a typical example.

Friedrichswerder may have been the most fashionable area in the city, but it was not the grandest. In 1670, the Great Elector gave a parcel of land just outside the city walls as a wedding present to his second wife, Dorothea von Holstein – Louise of Orange had died in 1667. Dorothea was a formidable and rather sinister woman, according to her stepson, the future Elector Friedrich III, who was convinced she had tried to poison him. She was certainly an excellent businesswomen, dividing her land into building plots which she sold to noblemen for a handsome profit. To make the approach to her new town, Dorotheenstadt, more attractive to potential buyers, she had 1,000 lime trees planted four abreast along its southern boundary, to form a broad avenue outside the city gate on the road to Spandau – and so created the Under den Linden. Eighteen years later she created a further suburb on the other side of the Linden, which she named Friedrichstadt after her eldest son.

The new suburbs were well planned, spacious, airy, and modern. Those who lived there were not subject to many of the taxes, restrictions and impositions placed on those who lived in Berlin or Cölln. They were not liable, for example, to be called for compulsory labour on the Elector's building projects. The most notable of these was an immense 250-foot-wide defensive rampart around the old twin cities, which took 25 years to complete. It consisted of a deep moat up to 150 feet (46 metres) wide, encircling a new wall 30 feet (9 metres) high and 20 feet (6 metres) thick with 13 huge bastions and six gates, each with a Dutch-style drawbridge across the moat; part of its line can be traced today in Niederwallstrasse and Oberwallstrasse, running from Spittalmarkt up to the Linden, opposite the Neue Wache and the Zeughaus. Best of all, though, people living in the suburbs did not have to provide billets in their homes for the rough soldiery of Friedrich Wilhelm's new army. Within the twin cities, all new buildings had to have an attic or top storey specifically to accommodate soldiers.

The army was the single most important feature of Friedrich Wilhelm's plans for his territory, more important even than the development of trade and industry; indeed, one of his main reasons for encouraging trade and industry was to help pay for the army. His experience in the Thirty Years' War had taught him a bitter lesson, which he set down for his successors in his Political Testament, a remarkable exposition of *Realpolitik*, written in 1667. 'Alliances are well enough,' he wrote, 'but one's own forces are even better, since they are more to be relied upon. A ruler is of no consequence if he does not have adequate means and forces of his own; that alone has made me – I thank God for it – a force to be reckoned with.'

When Friedrich Wilhelm became elector, he inherited a force of 2,000 ill-trained and poorly equipped troops. Beginning by pressing into service all the Swedish deserters left behind by King Gustav Adolf, he steadily built up a professional standing army which by his death in 1688 numbered over 30,000 men. The Berlin garrison accounted for 20–25 per cent of the entire population of the city – a proportion that remained more or less constant until the middle of the nineteenth century.

The Great Elector would have been a hard act to follow at the best of times. An impressive figure, tall, heavily built, he looked every inch a man of power. Had everything gone according to plan, he would have been succeeded by his eldest son, Karl Emil, an equally formidable-looking fellow. But Karl died suddenly at the age of 19, while visiting Strasbourg and so into the Great Elector's shoes stepped the unlikely figure of his second son, Friedrich, whom the Berliners, with their talent for unkind and irreverent nicknames, christened 'schiefer Fritz', 'crooked Fritz'. A childhood accident had resulted in a permanently damaged spine, leaving him with a twisted body and an incipient hump, which in later life he tried to disguise by wearing unfashionably long wigs and ornate clothes.

There are some people who are innately ridiculous, whose tragedies turn to farce and whose great moments are always sabotaged. Friedrich was one of those. Not content with being a mere elector, he desperately longed to be a king. And not just any king, either, but Louis XIV of France, the Sun King himself. No pop star ever had such a loyal fan: Friedrich worshipped Louis and did everything in his power to imitate his idol. He rose when Louis did, spent his day as Louis did, had a mistress as Louis did (although he doesn't seem to have liked her very much) and only in the evenings, after a hard day trying to be Louis XIV, did he settle down with a few friends to smoke and drink beer, like any good Berliner. It was as though he believed that if he became the Sun King, his spine would straighten and his hump miraculously disappear.

Fritz's own grandson, Friedrich the Great, was merciless in describing his appearance and character when he came to write his *History of the House of Brandenburg*: 'He was small and deformed; his expression was haughty, his physiognomy was vulgar. His mind was like a mirror, which reflects each object. So those who had obtained a certain influence on him could excite or subdue his spirit at their pleasure. The praise given so copiously to Louis XIV impressed him, and he came to believe that if he elected himself king, he too would receive unfailing praise. In short, the Berlin court would ape the court of Versailles; everything was imitated: the ceremonials, the fine speeches, the measured steps, the precise words, the "grands mousquetaires", and so on. The generosity which he loved was wastefulness.'

Eventually, Friedrich got his chance to become a real king – though by a terrible irony he had to betray his hero to achieve his ambition. The German emperor of the time, Leopold I, desperately needed allies to thwart the expansionist plans of France. Above all, he needed troops, and Friedrich was able to offer him 8,000 fully trained and equipped men from the army that his father had so painstakingly built up. In return, Leopold agreed that he could become a King, provided his kingdom was outside the Holy Roman Empire, where the law allowed only the emperor himself to have royal status. As it happened, there was a precedent that challenged Hohenzollern pride and ambition – the elector of Saxony had just become King of Poland. Friedrich's Prussian dukedom was outside the empire – in fact, it had been officially part of Poland until the Great Elector obtained its independence in 1660, and some parts of Prussia were still under Polish rule. This raised another problem; clearly, Friedrich could not be king of half of Prussia. He found the solution by coming up with one of those brilliant, meaningless phrases so loved by the Hohenzollerns: he would be King *in*, not of, Prussia. It was fine distinction, but one that he felt certain would reassure both the emperor and the Saxon King of Poland.

In December 1700, the would-be sovereign gathered his entire court together and led them off to Königsberg in a royal progress so massive that 30,000 horses, more than one for every inhabitant of Berlin, had to be provided in relays along the way. On 18 January 1701, in a suitably grandiose ceremony, he placed a crown on his head with his own hands and proclaimed himself no longer the Elector Friedrich III, but Friedrich I, King in Prussia.

So Berlin became a royal residence, with Potsdam as its embryo Versailles. Friedrich and his second wife Sophia Charlotte had already embarked on a wildly ambitious building programme designed to make the city look the part, whatever it cost.

Sophia Charlotte, daughter of the elector of Hanover and sister of George I of Great Britain, had been brought up by an aunt at the French court, where women were expected to be both clever and pretty. Small and round, with bright blue eyes and coal-back hair, her striking appearance was matched by her intelligence. She was one of the most cultured and accomplished women of the age, and, inspired by the French example, she attempted to make Berlin a centre of culture to match Paris. She invited artists, philosophers and architects to the city, among them Gottfried Wilhelm Leibnitz, the first in a long and distinguished line of Berlin philosophers. Under her patronage, the sculptor Andreas Schlüter founded an academy of art in 1696, and Leibnitz an academy of science in 1700.

Schlüter, who came from Hamburg, was appointed court sculptor in 1694. His first task was to carve a set of figures and decorations for a new Long Bridge between Berlin and Cölln, which was then being built by Arnold Nering, the Dutch architect who had been brought to the city by the Great Elector. In 1695, Sophia Charlotte commissioned Schlüter to build a palace for her near the village of Lietzow, in the woods outside the city beyond Dorotheenstadt. The new palace, Schloss Lietzenburg, was a triumph of baroque delicacy, with its elegant dome and cupola and yellow stucco walls. Inevitably, yet another suburb grew around it: a new community of about a hundred houses engulfed Lietzow. Equally inevitably its name was changed to Charlottenburg after the queen's death in 1705, at the age of 36. Friedrich, however, continued extending the palace, as did Sophie's grandson, Friedrich II.

The Berliners, of course, had their own name for the place: they called it '*Lottchens Lustenburg*', 'Little Lottie's Fun Palace'. The queen may have thought she was creating her own Versailles, the 'court of the muses' where intellectuals and artists could congregate. Berliners saw it as a giant boudoir where she could sport with her lovers.

While the queen was engaged in creating a salon for intellectuals and artists, the king was concerned with sterner buildings: at the same time as his queen was commissioning her pleasure palace, he ordered Nering to design and construct an armoury for him on the Unter den Linden close to the royal palace. The Zeughaus, as this was named, was another superb example of Berlin baroque, whose outward appearance belied its military purpose of making and storing weapons. Schlüter was commissioned to provide sculptures both for the outside, which he decorated at roof level with carvings of armoured and helmeted figures, the trophies of war, and for the inner courtyard. Here, he chose to present the grimmer face of war, with a masterly series of 22 heads of dying warriors, their faces contorted in agony, one over every doorway and window. When Nering died a year after work began, Schlüter took his place, overseeing the design and construction of the whole building.

As a result of his success, Schlüter was asked to design an impressive new post office building. He was then given the task of redesigning and enlarging the royal palace, a conglomeration of different buildings that had grown up over the centuries on the site of Iron-tooth's Zwingburg. He approached the job with relish, bringing a unity of form to the higgledy-piggledy confusion and creating a building of considerable grandeur, if little grace. It was, in fact, quite the ugliest building in Berlin, and remained so even after Schlüter's best efforts.

With Friedrich's encouragement, Schlüter aimed to emulate the work of Sir Christopher Wren, who was in the process of trying to rebuild London to a great master plan after its destruction in the great fire of 1666. Sadly, like Wren, he was never to bring his plans to fruition. Unlike Wren, however, he failed because of his own shortcomings: he forgot that Berlin was built on sand and marsh, failed to strengthen the foundations sufficiently to bear his additions, and the palace almost collapsed. Schlüter was replaced as court architect, but kept his post as court sculptor. His enduring masterpiece, besides the dying warriors' heads in the Zeughaus, is an equestrian statue of the Great Elector which originally stood at the beginning of the Long Bridge, but which is now appropriately placed in front of Charlottenburg Palace.

Other architects, however, continued to erect new buildings in and around Berlin, both for the king and for his noblemen. Eosander von Göthe, the Swede who replaced Schlüter to complete the royal palace, built an elegant, almost frothy palace, aptly named Monbijou, for the king's mistress, Katharina von Kolbe, on Oranienstrasse, where Louise of Orange had grown Berlin's first potatoes. In Friedrichstadt meanwhile, a new city centre was taking shape as new streets were laid out: Friedrichstrasse, Charlottenstrasse, Wilhelmstrasse and Markgraffenstrasse were all named in 1706. Initially, the buildings were all private palaces and mansions. Later, they would house most of the great offices of state.

Like so much of his life, Friedrich's death was like a scene from a low farce, brought about by his determination to ensure the continuation of the Hohenzollern line. His only son, Friedrich Wilhelm, had married Sophia Dorothea, another Hanoverian princess, this time the cousin of King George I. By 1708, the couple had managed to produce only one child, which died within the year. Friedrich, therefore, became convinced that it was up to him to provide another male heir, in case anything should happen to Friedrich Wilhelm. He married for a third time, to yet another Sophia. Princess Sophia Louisa of Mecklenburg-Schwerin was deemed a suitable match. She was 24 years old, deeply religious, and, it later turned out, as crazy as a jaybird. By the time her mental condition was clear, Friedrich Wilhelm and his Sophia were producing babies with monotonous regularity – first Wilhelmina, then Fritz, the future Friedrich the Great. His grandfather doted on young Fritz, whose birth had finally removed all pressure from the unfortunate monarch. Poor Sophia Louisa could be safely consigned to be looked after in her apartment in the palace, while Friedrich could settle down to enjoy a pleasant old age.

Early one morning, however, Sophia Louisa escaped from her attendants and went to see her husband, dressed only in her shift. The king was asleep in bed, behind a glass door. Sophia Louisa walked right through the glass, which shattered around her. Friedrich awoke to the sight of a figure in white, covered with blood from a dozen different cuts. He must have thought she was the legendary White Lady of the Hohenzollerns, the ghost of one Countess Agnes von Orlamünde, who was said to appear when a member of the family was about to die. Friedrich had a heart attack. He did not recover, and died a few days later.

To pay for his wildly extravagant ambitions, Friedrich I had plunged the whole of Brandenburg-Prussia into debt and squeezed his subjects dry with ever-increasing taxes. The Berliners, raised in a spirit of Calvinist and Lutheran thrift, resented the royal ostentation, and were not sorry to see their first king depart in 1713. But in spite of his excesses, Crooked Fritz had in his own way carried the torch lit by his father. The Great Elector had brought Berlin-Cölln back from the brink of extinction, and given it new life. But it was his despised, crook-backed son who changed it from a scruffy small town in the back of beyond into a royal capital with pretensions to greater things. During his 25-year rule the population had grown from less than 20,000 to more than 60,000, despite another outbreak of plague in 1709. Although it still seemed unlikely ever to become a Weldtstadt, a 'world city', it was already well on the way to achieving the status of Grossstadt, 'big city'.

And when Friedrich's son, Friedrich Wilhelm I, succeeded to the throne, he inherited a unified city. For on 18 January 1709, Friedrich had decreed that at long last all five towns – Berlin, Cölln, Friedrichswerder, Dorotheenstadt and Friedrichstadt – would be combined into one city under the name Berlin.

CHAPTER 3

Sparta on the Spree

'UNDER FRIEDRICH WILHELM the state changed its character almost completely,' wrote his son, Friedrich II. 'Under Friedrich I, Berlin had become the Athens of the north; under Friedrich Wilhelm, it was its Sparta. The city became like an armoury. In Berlin powder mills were set up, in Spandau sabre factories, in Potsdam arms factories, and in Neustadt workshops for iron and leather working.'

Friedrich was almost as hard on his father as he had been on his grandfather. And he had good cause, for Friedrich Wilhelm had made life a misery not only for his people but also for him. Friedrich Wilhelm believed it was a child's duty to obey its parents without question. For years, he had been disgusted with his own parents' profligacy, but as a dutiful son had said nothing. When his father died, his last act of filial duty was to give him the lavish funeral he would have wanted. No expense was spared. But that was the last piece of generosity or extravagance he ever showed. Returning to the palace, he immediately discarded his fancy wig and fine clothes, rolled up his sleeves, and personally set about stripping every luxury from the building. He even banned carpets and upholstered furniture – bare wood suited his frugal nature better. Selecting a five-roomed apartment for himself and his family, he turned the remainder of the palace over to offices. Later, he moved out of Berlin altogether, taking his family to live in the country retreat built by his grandfather in Potsdam.

To Friedrich Wilhelm, the state was everything, and came before everything; the individual counted for nothing. In pursuing this philosophy and imposing it on his people, he achieved the dubious honour of creating the concept of the Fatherland, with unquestioning obedience as the highest virtue in its children. Other rulers in Germany were equally autocratic, but they regarded their principalities as their personal possessions to be dealt with as they pleased. He saw himself as the servant of the state, and demanded total submission to himself not as an individual but as the state's representative. Martin Luther had written that the authority of kings and princes was divinely ordained: as a devout Lutheran, Friedrich Wilhelm believed that anyone who questioned his authority was opposing the will of God and must be punished accordingly.

The army was always important to Berlin's rulers, but to Friedrich Wilhelm it was everything. He dreamed of making his state – now universally known as Prussia though it still contained only the eastern half of that province – a power in Europe. And since he believed his grandfather's dictum that a ruler is respected only for the military power he can command, he knew he would need an army that was superior to all others in numbers, skill, equipment and, above all, in discipline.

Building such an army would be expensive, however, and the state Friedrich Wilhelm had inherited was bankrupt. Other rulers might choose to finance their armies through foreign loans and mortgaging their possessions, but to him such an approach was unthinkable: he would be beholden to no man. Instead, he was determined to find the money from the resources of his own kingdom, through increased efficiency and ruthless economies.

The economies began at home, in the royal palace. The new king sold his father's jewels and wines, fine furniture and even his clothes. He had all the gold and silver plate, candlesticks and ornaments melted down. He reduced the palace staff from around 150 to twelve, and got rid of all the nobles and courtiers apart from four gentlemen-in-waiting. The artists, architects, musicians, dancing masters and philosophers recruited by his father were sent packing; Andreas Schlüter took himself off to Russia, to serve Tsar Peter the Great in the building of St Petersburg.

The sudden advent of austerity came as a great shock to those who lost comfortable sinecures and high salaries. But the Berlin wits had a lovely time. A few days after the new king had started clearing out his household, a large notice appeared overnight outside the main gate. 'This palace for sale, complete with the royal residence city of Berlin,' it proclaimed cheekily. And when formerly wealthy courtiers were forced to abandon their luxurious carriages and go about on foot, the Berliners claimed it was a miracle – 'The king has made the lame walk!' they cried.

Efficiency, frugality and hard work were Friedrich Wilhelm's orders of the day for the ordinary citizens, as well as for his courtiers and officials. To be idle was to be ungodly – even the market women were ordered to keep themselves busy between customers by knitting socks. Pastimes which the king considered 'godless, a nuisance or detrimental to Christianity', such as the theatre, were banned. Only 'pure, innocent things for honest entertainment' were allowed. All taverns were ordered to close by 9.00 pm.

During the times of the Great Elector and Friedrich I, Berlin's trade and industry had been geared to the court. Now, they were turned to supplying the army with all it needed in arms, equipment and clothing. Spurred on by Friedrich Wilhelm's determination that his state should be self-sufficient in all essentials, several industries, such as the state cloth mills in Berlin, were able to fulfil all domestic needs and start exporting their wares. The Industrial Revolution that was already under way in Britain would not reach Berlin for several decades, but the groundwork for the city's great manufacturing industries was laid by Friedrich Wilhelm.

Steadily, the debts shrank and the army grew. Most armies at that time were made up of foreign mercenaries, but this system had two disadvantages: the troops' loyalty was not always guaranteed, and recruiting in other countries was expensive. Friedrich Wilhelm decided that his army would include an unusually high proportion – over 50 per cent – of men from his own lands, forcibly conscripted for periods of 20 years, with death as the penalty for desertion. For years, no young male traveller in Prussia was safe from Friedrich Wilhelm's press gangs.

To the young men of Berlin, the prospect of military service was so grim that most of them fled as soon as conscription started. Since this age group included all the apprentices and newly qualified craftsmen, the city was soon at a standstill. To save the trades and industries on which his army depended, Friedrich Wilhelm had to exempt Berliners from conscription. Once again, the Berliners were able to regard themselves as a special breed, different from the rest of the Prussian population.

Friedrich Wilhelm liked to be known as 'the soldier king', but the Berliners, who knew a thing or two about soldiers, dubbed him, more accurately, 'the sergeant-major'. In their kinder moments they called him, as they would Hermann Göring two centuries later, 'Fatso' or 'Fatty', for the obvious reason. In fact, like some ogre out of a gothic fairy tale, Friedrich Wilhelm belongs more in the pages of the Brothers Grimm than in the history books. Short, bloated, purple-faced, he looked like a grotesque caricature of a caricature: at the time of his death he weighed nearly 280 pounds (127 kilograms) and had a waistline measuring 102 inches (2.6 metres). And his behaviour was as bizarre as his appearance.

In recent years, all this has been put down to the effects of porphyria, a group of hereditary metabolic disorders in which the body produces abnormal quantities of substances called porphyrins. Friedrich must have inherited the delinquent gene from a descendant of Mary Queen of Scots, who seems to have infected several of the royal houses of Europe. The symptoms include sensitivity to sunlight, sweating, rapid heart rate, acute abdominal pain, vomiting, constipation, dark purple-coloured urine, paralysis – or, as in the case of Friedrich Wilhelm, painful weakness – of the limbs, plus various disorders of the nervous system, including psychotic disorders.

By 1725, the disease had taken such a hold that he must have been in constant pain, which he attempted to alleviate by late-night smoking and drinking sessions with his cronies, the so-called *Tabakcollegium*. As it happens, that was the worst thing he could have done, since, as we now know, alcohol exacerbates the condition.

One of the unfortunates obliged to attend these interminable drinking sessions was the diminutive Baron Grundling, a learned bore employed by the king to read the news to him and his family. Grundling, who couldn't hold his liquor and passed out regularly, was the perfect butt for Friedrich Wilhelm's brutal practical jokes.

On one occasion, the king and his cronies lowered poor Grundling from one of the castle windows on a rope and used him, like a stone, to break the ice on the river. Another time, they actually set fire to him. As a final joke, when he died, the king had him buried with great pomp – in a wine barrel.

So outrageous did Friedrich Wilhelm's behaviour become that the French ambassador remarked: 'Thanks to his instability, the King of Prussia is neither useful to his friends nor dangerous to his enemies.' He was, however, extremely dangerous to his unfortunate family and subjects. His wife, Sophia Dorothea, the sister of George II of Great Britain, both loathed and feared him, his children learned to cower in his presence, and his son and heir, the future Friedrich the Great, suffered appalling physical and psychological damage at his hands.

His subjects learned to flee from him as, purple-faced and belli-cose, scorning any other dress but uniform, he stomped around the city on foot, bawling orders at them and personally beating anyone whose manner or actions displeased him. Most people naturally tried to keep out of his way, rushing indoors and closing their shutters as he approached. On one memorable occasion, a young Jew was not quick enough, and was caught by the king's escort as he tried to run away. When he explained that he had been afraid, the king was furious. 'Love me! Love me!' he bellowed as he thrashed the young man with his cane. 'You're supposed to love me, you scum, not be afraid of me!'

While other monarchs, once the demands of the succession had been attended to, turned to mistresses – which at least gave their wives some respite from the rigours of constant child-bearing – Friedrich Wilhelm was both too mean and too puritanical for such *gentillesse*. For him, the task of producing babies went on night and day. He fathered no fewer than 14 children, of whom ten survived, but it was his eldest son and daughter who were to bear the brunt of his attentions.

The king planned his eldest son's upbringing in the minutest detail. He directed when young Fritz should rise in the morning; in order that he should get used to the sound of gunfire he was woken by the discharge of a cannon firing a blank charge directly under his bedroom window. From then on, every moment of the boy's day was regimented, even down to how long he was to take to dress. By the age of five, he knew all 54 movements of the Prussian drill code.

At six, he was given command of his own company of child cadets. By the age of eight, he was expected to be familiar with every weapon of war.

The king also decreed the subjects his son should study. Latin was banned, on the grounds that southerners were degenerate. So, too, was history prior to the sixteenth century, unless it concerned the House of Hohenzollern. Mathematics and political economy were acceptable, since they might prove useful to a future general. The king's fury knew no bounds when he discovered that, behind his back, young Fritz had persuaded one of his tutors to teach him Latin and another how to play the flute.

Fritz aroused his father's temper in other ways, too. There were, for instance, the matters of his wanting to wear gloves while out hunting in mid-winter, and seeming to prefer to read a novel rather than stalk deer. But perhaps worst of all, he chose to eat with a three-pronged fork instead of the two-pronged variety which any right-thinking man would choose. Was the boy degenerate? 'What,' the king demanded when he was twelve, 'is going on in his little head? I know he does not think as I do.' No doubt there were some at court who thought this was no bad thing.

Undoubtedly what preserved young Fritz's sanity was the fact that his father, no matter what else he might be, was a hard-working, conscientious monarch. He travelled frequently, visiting every part of his domain, leaving Fritz to seek the company of his mother and sister, who were both sympathetic and cultured.

When he was 16, young Fritz accompanied his father to Dresden, on a state visit to the court of the Elector Augustus the Strong of Saxony, who was also King of Poland. Augustus, who kept a harem of about 50 women, including one of his own daughters, and had fathered some 354 illegitimate children, decided it was time the young prince was introduced to the joys of sex. Unfortunately, in the process, Fritz seems to have caught a venereal disease. To cure him, doctors performed an operation so drastic that it left him impotent.

By the beginning of 1730, Friedrich Wilhelm's brutality towards his son had reached fresh heights. He forced him to kiss his boots in public, and on one occasion dragged the 18-year-old prince round by his hair, while thrashing him with his cane. Later, he said contemptuously of his son: 'Had I been treated so by my father, I would have blown my brains out, but this fellow has no honour.'

Some of Friedrich Wilhelm's suspicions were well founded. Fritz formed what was almost certainly a homosexual relationship with Hans von Katte, a handsome guards captain a few years older than himself. While the king was away on one of his tours of inspection, the two of them planned to run away away together to France, and then to England. They were betrayed. Fritz was imprisoned in Küstrin fortress, on the Oder. Katte was court-martialled and sentenced to life imprisonment, but this did not satisfy the king, who imposed the death penalty instead. Katte was to be beheaded in front of the window of Fritz's cell. When Katte's father, a distinguished soldier, appealed for clemency, Friedrich Wilhelm sent him a short note. 'Your son is a scoundrel,' he wrote. 'So is mine – and so what can we poor fathers do?' Katte was executed. Fritz fainted before the blow was struck.

Deciding that what his son now needed was a wife, Friedrich Wilhelm looked around for the plainest, least intelligent girl he could find. He found Elisabeth Christine von Brunswick-Bevern. Fritz's mother summed her up as 'a proper goose . . . with a stupid laugh'; one of Fritz's sisters said that she stank. The marriage was not exactly unhappy – Fritz always treated his wife courteously – but it simply wasn't a true marriage. After the nuptial night it is doubtful if he ever touched her again, and once he became king, he saw her as rarely as possible. She was not allowed to come to his palace in Potsdam, but was confined to Berlin, where she occupied herself with good works and lived out Friedrich Wilhelm's vindictive little joke.

With Friedrich Wilhelm's obsession with enlarging his army, the Berlin garrison by 1735 had grown to 18,257, against a civilian population of some 60,000. Clearly, the city had to expand to house them all – at the time, the only troops who had their own accommodation were the cavalry, who lived in the stables with their horses. The first barracks for other soldiers and their families were not built until 1752–3, by Friedrich II in Kommandantenstrasse; until then they were billeted in private homes throughout the city. Like his father and grandfather, Friedrich Wilhelm boosted the growth of the city by encouraging immigration from other parts of Germany and the rest of Europe, attracting large numbers of Protestants from Salzburg and Bohemia, and further influxes from France, Holland and Switzerland.

'The king guaranteed tax exemption and rewards to all who settled in the cities of his lands,' wrote Friedrich II. 'In his residence he built up the whole of Friedrichstadt and filled the old city walls with houses. Every quarter of the city was given a police department. At the same time, hackney cabs were introduced. The city was cleared of idlers who scraped a living through persistent begging and found accommodation in public poor houses.'

Of course, building so many new houses – all of which had by law to have a top storey used for soldiers' quarters – was expensive, but the king had his own way of involving private enterprise. 'The fellow who is rich shall build!' he declared. He had 1,400 new plots marked out in Friedrichstadt alongside his father's original 1,000, then selected purchasers from the aristocracy and prosperous burghers. These lucky men were informed that the king had chosen them to receive their plots free of charge. He would even cover 10 per cent of their building costs. All they had to do was find the other 90 per cent. Naturally, no one was allowed to refuse the king's generosity, even though many of the plots turned out to be swampland.

As the new suburbs developed, the ramparts and moat of the Great Elector's city walls, on which so many Berliners had laboured for 25 years, became an irksome restriction to the expanding city. They also occupied a great deal of land, land that could be used for building. So, in 1734, Friedrich Wilhelm ordered them to be demolished, replacing them with a new wall, 20 feet (6 metres) high and eight and a half miles long (13.7 kilometres), further out and enclosing all the new suburbs as well as the old twin cities. It also enclosed large areas of agricultural land, most of it heavily cultivated market gardens, that would provide ample space, especially in the south-eastern districts, for all Berlin's building needs until halfway through the nineteenth century.

The new wall had three functions, one economic, one social, and the other military. Economically, it was a customs barrier, ensuring that taxes were collected on everything imported into the city through its fourteen new gates. Socially, it ensured that a check could be kept on all comings and goings, so that beggars and other undesirables could be kept out. Its military purpose – an uncanny precedent for the wall of the 1960s, which ironically would be built partly along the same line – was not to keep invaders out but to keep Friedrich Wilhelm's soldiers in. Conditions in the army were so harsh that there were at least two suicides in the Berlin garrison every week, and desertion was a constant problem.

Friedrich Wilhelm's obsession with the army had a great effect on shaping the future city centre. The Karree (later Pariserplatz) at the western end of the Linden, the Oktagon (later Leipzigerplatz) near the Potsdam gate, Wilhelmplatz, Dönhofferplatz – were all parade grounds. Outside the Brandenburg Gate, in the Tiergarten, he had a large number of trees felled to create a ten-hectare exercise place, which until 1850 was the scene of the grand annual review of Berlin regiments. The Berliners promptly christened this great expanse of sand 'the Sahara'. At the other end of the Linden, he tore out the exotic plants and fountains of his grandmother's Lustgarten to turn it, too, into a drill square. Friedrichstrasse was widened and extended to allow the guards regiments to march out to their principal exercise and parade ground at Tempelhof.

The whole idea of foot drill was an innovation, introduced to the modern world by Friedrich Wilhelm and his companion, Prince Leopold of Anhalt-Dessau. The two soldier princes had rediscovered the art of marching in step, which had been lost with the demise of the ancient Roman legions. They had perfected it on their crack regiment, the Life Guards, generally known as the 'Giants' Guard', since every man had to be at least 6 feet 3 inches (1.9 metres) tall. For the first time, units of men marching in step could be wheeled and turned to order, able to change position and fire volleys at high speed. Foot drill began as a form of practice for such manoeuvres, but soon developed into a means of instilling *Kadavergehorsam*, corpse-like blind obedience, turning men into perfectly disciplined automata. So, in the streets and squares of Berlin, the modern, well-drilled army was born.

'The most beautiful girl or woman in the world would be a matter of indifference to me,' Friedrich Wilhelm declared, 'but soldiers: they are my weakness!' His favourites were not just any old soldiers, but men tall enough for his Giants' Guard, his *lange Kerle*, 'long fellows'. So obsessed was he with acquiring men for the regiment that he sent press gangs all over Prussia, to take men by force. His agents did not confine their activities to their own country or even their own countrymen. One very tall Austrian diplomat was snatched while getting into a cab in Hanover – he had to be freed after a terrible furore. James Kirkman, an Irish giant, was kidnapped on the streets of London, an operation that cost the king £1,000 even then, and which resulted in the Prussian ambassador's being banned from Great Britain.

Foreign governments knew of Friedrich Wilhelm's weakness, and took advantage of it. It was common knowledge in the courts of Europe that it was possible to buy the King of Prussia, not with territory or trade, but with the gift of a few freaks. Peter the Great of Russia, and Augustus the Strong of Saxony and Poland periodically sent him batches of of very tall men in order to retain his political allegiance. Even the British government was not above sending him 15 Irish giants when they wanted something from him.

Friedrich Wilhelm was constantly on the lookout for taller and taller men. Some of his guards were over 8 feet (2.4 metres) tall in their stockinged feet – and their distinctive, pointed helmets, shaped like a bishop's mitre, added at least an extra foot (30 centimetres) to their height. At one point, he even tried breeding his own giants, forcing very tall men to marry very tall women in the hope that their children would be even taller than their parents. Nature, however, refused to co-operate in this precursor of the Nazi *Lebensborn* programme, and the various unions produced their fair share of normal-sized offspring.

The giants were, of course, generally freaks, suffering from an excess of growth hormone due to over-active pituitary glands. They tended to be slow, simple-minded, physically fragile, and in some cases actually deformed. They were useless as soldiers; they could not possibly have survived the rigours of combat. Fortunately, there was never any likelihood that they would have to, since Friedrich Wilhelm regarded them as far too valuable to risk in a real fight.

Most of the men found life in the guards utterly intolerable. Discipline was barbaric: men were regularly flogged into submission. As a result, mutinies were frequent, and from time to time the men tried to burn down Potsdam. When that failed, suicide or self-mutilation often seemed the only way out: once a man was in the guards he was there for life, or until the king decided to dispense with his services. Despite the horrendous punishments meted out to anyone who attempted to escape – a man spared death by hanging could have his nose or ears sliced off, or be incarcerated for life in Spandau fortress – there were 250 desertions a year.

Many of the officers were as tall as their men, and also found themselves trapped in a military madhouse. Baron Bielfeld described an evening spent at the colonel's house: there were no women present, and after a drunken dinner, the officers danced with each other until, overcome by 'repeated bumpers of champagne', they collapsed.

For all his faults, Friedrich Wilhelm made a vital contribution to the development of Berlin. Through the Prussian virtues of thrift and good management, at his death he left his once bankrupt state with a war chest of six million thalers, equivalent to one and a half years' revenue. He also left many social benefits, not least the introduction of universal education in the city, and the establishment of the Charité hospital and medical school in 1720. But the cost was high, as his son noted: 'It was unfortunate that during all this valuable innovation, the Academy of Science, the liberal arts and trade were allowed to fall into complete decay. The Academy of Arts folded. Stonemasons appeared as sculptors and bricklayers as architects.'

When in 1740, Friedrich Wilhelm at last 'had the decency to die' – though not without having a furious argument with the doctors at his deathbed – the Berliners rejoiced, looking forward to a new and enlightened era under his popular heir, the sensitive and cultured Crown Prince Friedrich, 'Young Fritz'. 'Science and art have mounted the throne,' proclaimed Voltaire.

CHAPTER 4

'The monstrous piece of clockwork'

T HE NEW KING was a man of rare talents, combining the best qualities of his father, grandfather and great-grandfather. The title bestowed on him by history, Friedrich the Great, was well-deserved: he was a great military leader, a superb administrator, a lover of the arts, and a seeker after glory. Alongside his aim of making Berlin the spiritual centre of Europe, however, he nursed a dangerous dream: he believed it was his manifest destiny to transform Prussia into a great power, and he wasted no time in setting about it.

As well as an overflowing treasury, Friedrich had inherited an army of 80,000 men, superbly trained and equipped, but never tested in battle – his father had been too mean to risk wasting his precious guardsmen and grenadiers in petty wars. Within six months of coming to the throne, Friedrich marched them south-east to seize Silesia, a province as big as the original Mark Brandenburg, then owned by the mighty Austria. It was Prussia's first direct challenge to the supremacy of Austria and the old empire, an ominous portent of things to come.

Silesia was a wealthy province, rich in minerals and agriculture. Annexing it into the kingdom of Prussia increased Berlin's importance by extending the city's hinterland, and providing a vital source of raw materials and fuel for its future industries. But above all, Silesia provided that most vital commodity, people, adding perhaps the most dominant ingredient to the modern population's unique mix. It has long been a standing joke that every true Berliner is a Silesian. Ask any Berliner where his or her family comes from, and there is a good chance that the answer, accompanied by a broad grin, will be: 'Silesia – of course!'

The Silesians are themselves a strange racial mixture, half German, half Slav, as different from the Prussians as the Scots are from the English – one more reason why Berlin came to regard itself as a singular city. As it happened, the Scots also played a part in seasoning Berlin's ethnic stew: five years after Friedrich came to the throne, the city welcomed a strong contingent of Jacobites from Scotland, fleeing the wrath of the English after the failure of their attempt to put Charles Edward Stuart, 'the Young Pretender', on the throne in London. Even today, many generations later, there are many genuine Berliners with names like Angus MacLean.

Friedrich regarded building, not soldiers, as his recreation, his 'dolls', as he put it. Once he discovered that his father's precious Giants' Guards cost the state 250,000 thalers a year in upkeep, to say nothing of the enormous costs of recruitment, the 'long fellows' were doomed. For the same money, he could raise 16 battalions of infantry, soldiers a thousand times more effective in real warfare than the towering, simple-minded guardsmen. The regiment was disbanded. Most of the men were simply turned loose and told to find their own way home. Those with any intelligence or talents were found jobs or transferred to other units. The Irishman, James Kirkman, for example, who was highly intelligent, became a valued palace servant for the rest of his life.

Throughout the 46 years of his reign, Friedrich continued to build up the suburbs inside his father's new customs wall, increasing the number of dwelling houses in the city from 4,500 in 1740 to 6,644 by his death. By 1750, the population – including over 26,000 military personnel – had passed the 100,000 mark, to qualify Berlin as a *Grossstadt*. By the time he died, 36 years later, it was half as much again, at over 150,000.

During that time, Berlin blossomed as never before. For years, while sweating under the strictness of his father's regime, Friedrich had dreamed and planned, preparing for the day when he would take over. With his friend Georg Wenzeslaus von Knobelsdorff, who at the age of 30 had resigned his commission in the army to devote himself to painting and architecture, he had drawn up ambitious plans for new streets, squares and buildings in a distinctively Prussian style, rejecting the rococo niceties of Schlüter and Nering in favour of a neoclassical form harking back to the great days of Rome. He had barely ascended the throne before work started on the new centre of his city, the *Forum Fridericianum*, on marshy land at the start of Unter den Linden where the old moat and ramparts had just been filled in and levelled.

Significantly, Friedrich's first building was the opera house, which he intended to be the finest in the world. In itself, this was a significant departure from tradition: it was the first court theatre to be built outside a royal palace. Knobelsdorff's design for the exterior was influenced by Palladio, with a classical pillared portico bearing the inscription in gold: *Fridericus Rex Apollini et Musis*, 'To Apollo and the Muses from King Friedrich.' In contrast, the interior was a triumph of delicate ornament and decoration, a balanced combination of severity and gaiety that was to become known as 'Frederician Rococo'.

The opera house cost the enormous sum of a million thalers. The first sod was turned in July 1741, and the opening was only eighteen months later, on 7 December 1742, with the first performance of the opera *Cleopatra e Cesare* by Friedrich's director of court music, Carl Heinrich Graun, to mark the king's triumphant return from his Silesian campaign. It was a bitterly cold day of driving snow and howling wind. The exterior of the house was still under scaffolding, the ceiling of the auditorium was shrouded in sheets, and there were only bare wooden benches for seats. But the production was splendid, and it was followed by a glittering investiture ceremony and a masked ball that continued right through the night.

The opera house cost 400,000 thalers a year to run, and admission was free – for those whose social position was high enough to allow them to attend. Most Berliners were barred. They were not even permitted to stand at the back of the stalls; opera was obviously considered as beyond their comprehension.

A little later, a fine royal library was built facing the opera house – the Berliners promptly named it '*die Kommode*', 'the dresser', because of its shape and curved front. And to complete Opernplatz, Friedrich ordered the building of a Catholic cathedral, St Hedwig's, placed diagonally to the square between the opera house and the library. Built to a design by Friedrich himself, based on the Pantheon in Rome, with a great copper cupola, the new cathedral was a shrewd move by Friedrich, intended to please his new Silesian subjects – Hedwig was their patron saint, the wife of Duke Henry of Silesia in the early thirteenth century. The building was funded by contributions from Catholics both inside and outside Prussia, and from a state lottery which the king introduced.

Although he was himself an atheist, Friedrich also built a new cathedral as the chief church of Prussian Protestantism, on the Lustgarten, alongside the old royal palace, demolishing the decaying old mediaeval cathedral, the former church of the old Dominican convent which had been dissolved in 1536. The old cathedral had been on the other side of the palace square. Friedrich deliberately moved its site to switch the emphasis away from the old cities of Berlin and Cölln, redirecting it towards the newer baroque developments of Friedrichswerder, Dorotheenstadt and Friedrichstadt. The new building, completed in 1750, was topped with the inevitable dome, which the Berliners promptly christened 'old Fritz's teacup'.

Friedrich had originally planned to move the royal palace, too, replacing it with a new building facing Opernplatz across the Linden, to complete his Forum Fridericianum. But he lost interest in the project, and his brother, Prince Heinrich, took over the site and built a grand palace for himself, instead.

To improve the rest of the Linden, Friedrich had 48 older houses demolished and replaced with 33 more impressive structures to accommodate state offices. The bureaucrats who filled them were a different breed from those employed by earlier rulers: to remove any danger of his civil servants thinking for themselves, Friedrich employed aristocrats in place of the middle classes who had been his father's officials, and filled the lower positions with army pensioners – former sergeants, corporals and privates. He personally made all the decisions, no matter how small. All his officials had to do was make sure they were carried out, to the letter.

On the Gendarmenmarkt, the bustling chief marketplace of Fried-richstadt, the stables and guardhouse of the king's French cavalry unit, the *gens d'armes*, were replaced by the Schauspielhaus, a large new playhouse which was originally known as the French Comedy Theatre, then as the German National Theatre, and finally as the Royal National Theatre. The new theatre was built between two Protestant churches facing each other across the square, one French Calvinist, the other German Lutheran, to each of which Friedrich added an impressive classical portico and a domed tower. In a typical Berlin disaster, the new tower on the German church collapsed in 1781: like Schlüter's additions to the palace, its foundations proved inadequate.

For himself, Friedrich had Knobelsdorff add a new east wing to his grandmother's palace at Charlottenburg. But he preferred to live and work in Potsdam. While he was still crown prince, his father had posted him to a regiment at Neuruppin, some 40 miles north of Berlin. He had bought and refurbished a tumbledown mediaeval castle at nearby Rheinsberg, where he set up his own little court and surrounded himself with men of wit and culture. There he had spent some of the happiest years of his life. Now that he was king, he decided to recreate the idyll of Rheinsberg in Potsdam, this time not in a copy of a mediaeval castle, but in a new palace built in French rococo style.

Knobelsdorff found an ideal setting for such a palace, on top of a steep hill looking out over the town of Potsdam and the river Havel. Friedrich knew exactly what he wanted, and had no compunction about imposing his own ideas on the architect. Before building began, he had the hill terraced and planted vines on each of the six levels. The vines were soon abandoned, to be replaced with glass-houses on each vertical wall, in which fruit and flowers could be grown almost all the year round.

For the palace itself, Friedrich wanted a single-storey building with a central dome. Knobelsdorff proposed raising the palace slightly, with steps leading down to the terrace, pointing out that otherwise it would scarcely be visible from the bottom of the hill. Friedrich rejected his advice. He insisted on being able to walk straight out of the dining-room windows on to the terrace, as if he were stepping out into his garden.

Today, as one climbs the six flights of 24 broad steps from the foot of the hill, it is clear that Knobelsdorff was right. The palace does not dominate its surroundings, but peeps over the brow of the hill, like a cautious soldier peering over a parapet. In fact, that is part of its charm: it is a remarkably unassuming palace. But standing on the top terrace, where Friedrich himself would have stood, and looking out across the great fountain at the foot of the hill and down the long straight avenue to Potsdam, one is aware that this is one of the great vistas of Europe. It is the view *from* the palace, not the view *of* the palace that is important.

Friedrich called his new palace Sans Souci, 'without care'. He surrounded it by a gracious new residential town reminiscent of Bath in England. The French name and style were appropriate, for Friedrich spoke and wrote almost entirely in that language: it was said that he spoke German 'like a coachman'. In Sans Souci he wrote histories and poetry, practised the flute, attended to correspondence, and oversaw every tiny detail of the administration of his kingdom, rising at 3.00 am to make enough time. In the evenings he listened to music or opera, and indulged in barbed intellectual conversation round his dinner table – where the company was exclusively male, for he was a lifelong misogynist. The only woman ever invited to these intellectual *Tabakcollegia*, as his father and grandfather would have described them, was his favourite sister, Wilhelmina.

Friedrich liked to think of himself as 'the philosopher king', but there was nothing romantic about his philosophy. He was a product of the age of reason: cool, calculating and hard-edged in all his thinking. He liked philosophers, provided they knew their place. One of his closest intellectual companions for some time was the French radical thinker and writer Voltaire, whose biting wit matched his own cynical approach to life. For four years, from 1749, Voltaire lived at Sans Souci – Friedrich gave him a lodge at the foot of the hill – but eventually he overstepped the mark, and had to go, never to return. Another Frenchman, the astronomer and mathematician Pierre de Maupertius, proved more amenable, if less exciting.

Friedrich demonstrated his commitment to enlightenment almost immediately he came to the throne, by abolishing judicial torture and instituting freedom of the press. Berlin was even then a city with a passion for newspapers, its first having been established as early as 1617. The new king permitted the Berlin publishers Haude and Spener to print a new gazette, without censorship. 'Muzzled gazettes,' he said, 'make dull reading.' But Friedrich's idea of freedom from censorship extended only to local news not foreign – he had no intention of allowing local hacks to interfere with his foreign policy.

As a man of culture, Friedrich encouraged the arts and restored the academies of art and science. But he despised almost everything German, particularly in art, drama and literature, hating the plays of Lessing, Goethe and that 'Germanic writer', William Shakespeare, whom Lessing introduced to the Berlin theatre. Only in music was he prepared to consider the work of German composers and musicians – Johann Sebastian Bach visited him in Potsdam and Bach's son, Carl Philipp, became Friedrich's *Kapellmeister*.

Friedrich was never a patron of the arts – he told Mirabeau that he believed they flourished best when left alone – but he did at least create a climate in which they could thrive. He allowed his subjects considerable freedom to follow their own tastes, refusing to impose his own upon them. Fortunately, there were three remarkable private citizens in Berlin – the writer Gotthold Lessing, publisher and bookseller Friedrich Nicolai and self-taught philosopher Moses Mendelssohn – who between them established the beginnings of Berlin's future role as a centre of German theatre, scientific thought and literature.

Typically, neither Lessing nor Mendelssohn was a Berliner by birth. Mendelssohn entered Berlin for the first time at the age of 14, in 1743, through one of the two city gates, Prenzlau and Halle, which Jews were allowed to use. There were then 333 Jewish families, 1,945 people in all, living in the city. Mendelssohn made his fortune as a silk manufacturer and his reputation as a philosopher. Influenced by Leibnitz and Plato, he was a syncretist rather than an original thinker, combining Platonism, with its concern with the nature of goodness, truth and beauty, with the Judaic belief in God. He was the model for the hero of Lessing's play, *Nathan the Wise*, which was written as a plea for religious tolerance.

Lessing and Mendelssohn, who are said to have met over a game of chess, had both arrived in Berlin as penniless teenagers. Lessing had been so poor and down at heel that he had only been allowed in on condition that he report to the gate every Friday, although he was guaranteed by his cousin, the editor of one of the city's two newspapers. He started out as a journalist, but his work soon broadened into books and plays, and when Voltaire came to stay at Sans Souci, Lessing became his secretary and interpreter.

From the very beginning of his reign, Friedrich had made it clear that he was intent on overturning the status quo of European politics. In 1756, having digested Silesia, he invaded Saxony and Bohemia. Austria, still smarting from its earlier losses, joined forces with Saxony, and with France, Sweden and Russia, to destroy the upstart kingdom in what has become known as the Seven Years' War. Friedrich chose to call it the second of his Silesian wars – 183 years later, Adolf Hitler echoed his hero by calling the invasion of Poland his 'Silesian war'.

Friedrich's scattered territories were now spread from Frisia on the North Sea (acquired as recently as 1744) to East Prussia on the Baltic, and from north to south they stretched for virtually the whole length of the Oder, from Stettin down to the borders of Hungary. Encircled on three sides by his enemies, and with only Great Britain and Hanover as allies, his kingdom appeared to be indefensible. But the Prussian war machine proved to be virtually invincible. By the time Peter the Great made a separate peace in 1762, there could be no doubt that Prussia had to be recognized as a great power. It had in fact become the principal military power in continental Europe, having crushed not only Russia but also both Austria and France, who conceded defeat in 1763.

While Friedrich was winning his battles far away, Berlin was left to fend for itself, its garrison reduced to invalids and pensioners. Twice, the city was almost lost. In 1757 the Austrian General Hadik mounted a surprise attack, besieged Berlin and extracted a ransom of 200,000 thalers. Hadik's forces were not strong enough to occupy the city, but three years later, in 1760, a Russian army marched in from the east and took possession. As usual, the Berliners opened their gates and welcomed the invaders hospitably; from the ordinary citizen's point of view there could not have been a great deal of difference between an army of occupation and a regular garrison of 26,000 troops. Perhaps the greatest difference was that the invaders demanded a ransom of four million thalers, a sum that left both the mayor and the military commander of Berlin paralysed with shock. It was left to a Polish-born businessman, Johann Ernst Gotzkowsky, to negotiate a reduction to one and a half million. The Russians left hurriedly when they heard that Friedrich was approaching with a relief army – they had no wish to fight such a military paragon.

The peace treaty of 1763 confirmed Friedrich's possession of Silesia, and nine years later he expanded his kingdom again, adding West Prussia when he joined Russia and Austria in carving up Poland. In contrast to its original position as an eastern outpost of empire, Berlin now found itself nearer to the western boundaries of the lands of which it was the capital.

The years immediately following the end of the Seven Years' War brought hard times to Berlin again, exacerbated by a near-famine that finally persuaded the Berliners to start eating the previously despised potatoes, which Friedrich handed out to them freely. But the momentum of growth could not be halted for long, particularly now that Berlin was the capital of a major power.

Friedrich embarked on a massive new construction programme to repair the war damage, and resumed his plans for the city's aggrand-izement. He founded a Prussian state bank with his own money, to reduce Berlin's dependence on other cities like Hamburg. He built up other industries such as printing, metalworking and textiles, especially silk and velvet, which were his own personal favourites. In partnership with Johann Gotzkowsky, he set up a state porcelain factory on Leipzigerstrasse, which used the state sceptre as its trademark. While the older-established manufacturers of Meissen and Sèvres smothered their wares with ornate decoration, Royal Berlin porcelain, with good Prussian restraint, specialized in white. State monopolies and protectionism ensured their success: the king not only forbade the import of competitive goods but even refused to allow their transit through his lands. One of the measures he introduced to help the sales of his porcelain was to oblige all Jewish brides to buy dinnerware from the royal factory.

Soon, there were 15,000 workers employed in the woollen indus-try and 5,000 in silk processing, while the Royal Warehouse be-came the largest cloth mill in Germany, with 5,000 employees. At the same time, a new government department was set up in Berlin to develop the mining and working of coal, iron and lead in Silesia.

As aristocrats and merchants regained their prosperity, they began building themselves new palaces in and around Berlin, several of which survive today. One of the most beautiful is the Ephraim Palace, a town mansion built by the court jeweller and banker Veitel Ephraim, its ornate façade laced with delicate gilded ironwork, which has been faithfully reconstructed on the corner of Mühlendamm and Poststrasse. But by far the grandest was Prince Ferdinand's Bellevue Palace, outside the city walls in the Tiergarten, the former royal hunting reserve which Friedrich's architect friend Knobelsdorff had laid out as a formal public park early in his reign. The palace, which is today the official residence of the German president, attracted wealthy Berliners to build their own grand houses on the edge of the Tiergarten, creating an imposing new residential district.

With the coming of peace, it might have been expected that the army would be reduced to its earlier size again. But Friedrich knew only too well that his power came solely from its strength. He decided to maintain it at 150,000 men, well over one in 25 of the entire population of Prussia. The French historian Count Mirabeau had a valid point when he said Prussia was not so much a state with an army, as an army with a state.

Friedrich did, however, make a certain number of changes in the army's organization. The most far-reaching was getting rid of all middle-class officers – in future, only aristocrats would hold commissions. Since most Prussian aristocrats were Junkers, the old feudal landowners, this fuelled the notorious arrogance of the officer corps, traces of which lingered in the German army as late as 1945. A perfect illustration of the Prussian regard for officers came when one of Friedrich's cabinet councillors, Count Schwerin, complained that a young ensign had appropriated his place at an official dinner in Berlin. The king rebuked Schwerin, telling him he should know that any Prussian officer, even an ensign, outranked any councillor, even one who was a count. Schwerin promptly resigned his position and enlisted in the army as an ensign.

Maintaining the army at such a high level was, of course, extremely expensive. So, too, was the reconstruction of the battered state and its buildings. To pay for it all, Friedrich imposed ever higher taxes and excise duties. The state monopolies in tobacco, coffee and salt, were three of his biggest milch cows – he raised both the prices and the duty. Illicit coffee drinkers were denounced to the authorities by official 'coffee sniffers'. Citizens were obliged to buy large quantities of salt, and every household had to keep a 'salt book', to show that it had bought the required amount. Searching desperately for ways of using the salt, Berliners created several culinary innovations that have become staples of Berlin cuisine: the pickled gherkin, sauerkraut, and *Kassler Rippchen* – smoked pork chops cured in a salt solution to a recipe created by a butcher named Kassler – are just three examples.

Friedrich took a cynical attitude to the Berliners' reputation for disrespectful talk and subversive humour. 'They can *say* what they like, as long as they let me *do* what I like,' he declared. And he was not averse to bolstering his reputation as '*Alte Fritz*', 'Old Fritz'. Once, riding through the city, he spotted a crowd laughing at a placard on a rooftop. On discovering that it was a cartoon of himself with a large coffee-grinder between his knees – a satirical protest at the tax on coffee – he ordered it to be hung lower, 'so that the people should see it properly'. The delighted crowd cheered him as he rode away. As he grew older, he became increasingly eccentric, going about in stained and patched old clothes, receiving the worship of war veterans and citizens with his customary scepticism: 'They would cheer just the same for an old monkey in a uniform,' he observed.

Behind the crusty façade, however, Friedrich was every inch the typical Hohenzollern despot. One of his less happy bequests to Berlin was his creation of the secret state police, with agents infiltrated into the underworld and keeping a close eye on the supposedly free press. Gotthold Lessing, for one, found it all too much, and left the city. He described the atmosphere in Friedrich's later years, in a letter to a friend: 'How can one be healthy in Berlin? Everything one sees there makes one's gorge rise. Don't talk to me about your "Berlin freedoms" to think and to write. It boils down quite simply to the freedom to make as many sottish remarks about religion as one likes. But let someone get up in Berlin to defend the rights of the subject and attack exploitation and despotism, as happens daily in France or in Denmark, and you'll soon see which country in Europe today is the most abjectly enslaved.'

No matter how many 'free' newspapers or books were published, no matter how many operas or plays performed, or fine new buildings erected, Berlin remained a city dominated above all else by the military. In 1778, while Friedrich was creating the Alexanderplatz, his last great building project in Berlin, Prussia and Austria were again at each other's throats in the mercifully bloodless war of the Bavarian succession. Goethe, who was then the chief minister of Weimar, where literature was considered more important than fighting, visited Berlin at that time and recorded his impressions in a letter to his friend Frau von Stein. He wrote of 'the splendour of the royal city, its life and order and abundance, which would be nothing without the tens of thousands of human beings ready to be sacrificed. Men, horses, wagons, guns, ammunition: the streets are full of them. If only I could adequately describe the monstrous piece of clockwork spread out here before one's eyes! From the movements of the puppets one infers the existence of hidden wheels and in particular the ancient, mighty wheel with F.R. on it that is responsible for the movement of all the others.'

By his ruthless and aggressive use of his 'monstrous piece of clockwork', Friedrich had brought glory and power to Prussia, and had set Berlin firmly on the road to becoming a great world city. When he died, according to his niece, Princess Luise, the court, and no doubt the aristocracy in general, 'dissolved in tears'. But the ordinary Berliners celebrated, just as they had when death freed them from the Soldier King's oppression 46 years earlier.

CHAPTER 5

'The king has lost a battle'

FRIEDRICH THE GREAT had made Prussia a European power and set Berlin on the way to becoming a world city. But his successors almost threw away everything he had achieved. His nephew, Friedrich Wilhelm II, who came to the throne in 1786, was lazy, superstitious and licentious. He was almost unique among the Hohenzollerns in being both approachable and fond of women. Unfortunately, he was too fond of them, devoting every night to debauchery with his many mistresses. After enduring 75 years of high-minded Puritanism, the court eagerly followed his example. Soon, the whole of Potsdam was said to be one huge bordello.

Because Friedrich the Great had always insisted on controlling every detail of their administration – not even the most junior clerk or postman could be employed without his approval – the two main engines of the state, the civil service and the army, had come to depend entirely on the personal direction of the king. Deprived of this, and with no one else capable of taking any decision, they soon began to ossify. For a while, the illusion of power continued. There was even further territorial expansion when Friedrich Wilhelm shared what was left of Poland with Russia and Austria in a second partition in 1793. But the Poles have always been difficult to govern and the new lands only brought more problems.

In spite of – perhaps because of – the royal apathy, the city itself continued to grow. Indeed, as far as Berliners were concerned, the new reign began well: Friedrich Wilhelm II abandoned the state monopolies on coffee and tobacco and continued to beautify the city. In 1792, the court gardener, Sello, began a partial redesign of the Tiergarten, replacing the earlier formal gardens with more natural landscaping in the English style, turning it into the country park we know today. The road through the park to Charlottenburg was upgraded to a high road in 1798–9. The only other road leading into and out of the city to be paved was that to Potsdam; all the others were still nothing more than sandy tracks.

Between the southern edge of the Tiergarten and the Potsdam road, a new residential district, known as Friedrich's Vorstadt, became the most sought-after quarter for wealthy burghers. The district later became known simply as Tiergarten, and its main street as Tiergartenstrasse. By 1800, eighteen 'country' residences had been built along it, among numerous summer houses rented from the market gardeners who still grew their produce there.

The quarter boasted eight restaurants or inns, but the most popular spot for excursions from the city was the Zirkel, on the other side of the Charlottenburg road, in the northern part of the Tiergarten. In 1745, two Huguenots had been given permission to put up two refreshment tents near the bank of the Spree, where the modern Congress Hall now stands – the Berliners' 'Pregnant Oyster', whose sweeping roof provides an architectural reference to an open tent. From 1767 onwards, the tents had been replaced by wooden and brick buildings which could stay open all year round, and in due course, other bars, restaurants and coffee houses opened up, to cater for all tastes and pockets. In winter, people gathered there to skate on the frozen river Spree. Despite the more solid new structures, the track along which they stood was still known as 'In den Zelten', 'In the tents', a name it retains today.

The first postal service was set up in 1800 by the tradesmen's guilds, with eight deliveries a day in summer and six in winter. There were no pillar boxes, but mail was collected by messengers

walking through the streets four times a day, announcing themselves with handbells. It cost six pfennigs to send a letter by local
mail, and four pfennigs to receive one. Non-local and foreign
deliveries, of course, cost considerably more: a letter to Moscow,
for instance, cost 250 pfennigs. Maybe because of the mail service,
houses in Berlin were numbered for the first time, and street signs
were erected at corners, all in gold letters on a blue background.

The first regular street lighting was introduced in 1803, with oil
lamps on all the main thoroughfares, tended by a company of 60
disabled military pensioners, led by a sergeant-major and five sergeants. To save money, the oil was carefully measured so that the
lamps would go out in the middle of the night. The light they gave was
pretty dim, and even on moonlit nights, pedestrians were still advised
to carry their own lanterns, to avoid falling into the deep gutters and
filthy potholes. Most streets were still unpaved. In the wet, they were
ankle-deep in mud. When it was dry, the sandy soil made so much dust
on the Linden, for instance, that it had to be sprayed almost continuously, at first with hoses, later with water carts.

In the end, the only thing of any lasting value left to Berlin by
Friedrich Wilhelm II was yet another new city wall, completed in
1802 after 15 years' work, under the direction of an architect from
Breslau, Karl Gotthard Langhans. The number of gates was increased to 14, most of them flanked by massive but simple columns,
with the name of the gate and the date of its completion inscribed in
gold. A few were more elaborate: the Rosenthal and Potsdam gates
were lavishly ornamented; the Oranienburg was built like a Roman
triumphal arch, crowned with an obelisk; the Hamburg was decorated with two pyramids. But the grandest by far was the enlarged
gateway completed in 1791 at the western end of the Linden.

The new Brandenburg Gate, topped with the Quadriga, Gottfried
Schadow's magnificent copper sculpture of a four-horse chariot
driven by the goddess of victory, was built to commemorate Friedrich
the Great's military triumphs. Less than a year after it was finished,
however, the legend of Prussian invincibility established by Friedrich
was shattered by a humiliating defeat at Valmy, when his nephew
foolishly joined Austria in trying to suppress the French revolution.

Prussia's decline continued during the reign of Friedrich Wilhelm
III, certainly a more worthy man than his father, but later described

by Friedrich Engels as 'one of the greatest blockheads ever to reign on a throne'. Instead of learning the lessons of Valmy and trying to revitalize the army, he opted for neutrality and appeasement. For eleven years he stood back as Napoleon crushed Prussia's Austrian rivals and their allies in battle after battle.

Life in Berlin, meanwhile, continued on three quite separate levels. The court, led by Friedrich Wilhelm's beautiful and popular young queen, Luise, was less dissolute than before but equally addicted to frivolity. The workers struggled along as they always had – even in 1780, one Berliner in every ten had been registered for poor relief, and the situation had deteriorated steadily ever since. But for the middle classes, things were changing fast. Although they were still barred from the administration and the army, they began at last to develop an intellectual and cultural life of their own, largely through the influence of the 4,000-strong Jewish community.

The Jews, with their long tradition of scholarship and learning, had always been more cosmopolitan in their interests and connections than most other Berliners. They visited and corresponded with friends and relatives scattered throughout Europe, bringing to Berlin the latest ideas from other, less remote, cities. They encouraged medical science by financing the building of a fine new hospital in Oranienburgerstrasse near the Spandau Gate, 'four storeys high and twenty windows wide', and played an important part in the development of higher education.

Three Jewish women, Henriette Hertz, Rahel Levin, and Moses Mendelssohn's daughter Dorothea Veit, established the city's first salons, where for the first time intellectuals from all sections of Berlin society could mix and talk freely together. It was to Rahel Levin's house in Jägerstrasse that Heinrich von Kleist, the greatest Prussian writer of all, came on his return to Berlin in 1810. Rahel Levin was then a handsome, witty woman of 37 who did not always find it easy to get on with people. When she and Kleist failed to hit it off – possibly because of his growing anti-Semitism – he turned to Henrietta Vogel, the hostess of another Berlin salon. Kleist's friends, the writers Clemens von Brentano and Achim von Arnim, the leaders of the romantic movement in Germany, adorned many of the salons.

It was in these salons, under the influence of French revolutionary ideals, that Berlin's tradition of liberalism was born. Despite the dreadful carnage that had been unleashed by the Revolution, most middle- and lower-class Berliners were sympathetic at least to its ideals. In the political and military struggles that were raging through Europe, they supported the French, particularly where they were fighting the Austrians and the Russians. The Junkers, the Prussian aristocrats and landowners who held all the high positions at court and in the army, preferred imperial Russia as an ally. The friendship between the two courts left its mark on Berlin: to celebrate the state visit of Tsar Alexander I in October 1805, the cattle and wool market in front of the Königs Gate, where the roads from Frankfurt-an-der-Oder, Landsberg, Prenzlau and Bernau converged, was renamed Alexanderplatz.

The Junkers were determined that the upstart Napoleon be taught a lesson, and the dangerous egalitarian nonsense of republicanism be crushed. Blinded by arrogance, and oblivious to the fact that it had been allowed to run down for three decades under Friedrich the Great's successors, the Junkers went on boasting about the 'invincible' Prussian army. When Napoleon, who had inflicted shattering defeats on the Austrians at Ulm and Austerlitz in 1805, dissolved the Holy Roman Empire in 1806 and replaced it with a confederation of German states under his tutelage, they persuaded the king to send an ultimatum, demanding that the French emperor withdraw all his forces from southern Germany. Napoleon, at the head of an all-conquering army of 220,000 troops, treated the ultimatum with contempt. A collision was inevitable.

On the morning of 17 October 1806, placards ordered by the military governor, Count von der Schulenburg, suddenly appeared on all the street corners of Berlin. 'The king has lost a battle,' they announced, truthfully but inadequately. 'The first duty of all citizens is to stay calm. I make this appeal to the inhabitants of Berlin. The king and his brother are alive.' Schulenburg's appeal for calm was ruined by his own panic: he immediately packed his bags and left, taking with him what remained of the city's garrison, and leaving Berlin wide open for Napoleon. It did not take the Berliners long to realize that the king had lost far more than a battle at Jena-Auerstedt – he had lost everything.

Incredibly, Schulenburg's placards were the first the Berliners had officially heard of any war with France. When the troops of the garrison had marched out of the city in August and September, Berliners had been told they were going on large-scale manoeuvres.

And when the king and the court had scuttled out of Berlin in closed carriages on 20 September, they had been told nothing at all. So it was small wonder that when Napoleon rode in triumph through the Brandenburg Gate on 27 October, in 'the most beautiful weather in the world', the Berliners greeted him not as a conqueror but as a liberator, cheering him with cries of 'Vive l'Empereur!'

At first, it seemed they were right. That same evening, while men of his Imperial Guard bivouacked around camp fires in the Lustgarten, Napoleon took up residence in the palace and sent for the civil governor and members of the city council. He proceeded to dismiss the governor, Prince Hatzfeld, the son-in-law of Schulenburg, and ordered the councillors to assemble 2,000 well-to-do burghers, who were to elect a new 60-member general city council, and a seven-man executive committee. The burghers met in the Petrikirche in the evening of 29 October. It was the first time since Friedrich Iron-tooth crushed the *Unwillen* in 1448 that Berliners had been able to elect their own council.

On the whole, the French troops behaved well – in many ways, they were preferable to the normal garrison troops, being less brutalized. The Berliners had been amazed at the relaxed way they slouched into the city, their hats and uniforms worn as the fancy took them. And wonder of wonders, some had even been smoking pipes as they marched – the Berliners themselves were forbidden by law from smoking in the streets. But the honeymoon was short-lived. They watched with increasing bitterness as Napoleon's generals and officials set about stripping their city of its treasures. Any lingering support for the French disappeared when they took Schadow's Quadriga from the top of the Brandenburg Gate and hauled it off to the Louvre in Paris.

The cost of defeat was devastating: the peace treaties imposed huge financial penalties and virtually dismantled the Prussian state. The rift between king and people became wider than ever as Friedrich Wilhelm submitted to becoming a vassal of the French. But the occupation proved to be a turning point in the development of Berlin itself, and indeed of Germany as a whole.

The revolutionary ideals of liberty, equality and fraternity failed to take hold in a city that had known none of them since the arrival of the Hohenzollerns four centuries earlier. But another of the French emperor's gifts to Europe, the modern concept of the nation state, was seized on by minds seeking an escape from the humiliation of defeat. For the first time, men and women began talking seriously about German nationalism, of drawing together into one German nation all the individual princedoms that had spent a thousand years squabbling and fighting each other. And for the first time, Berlin was at the centre of events.

Nationalism became the great topic in the salons of Rahel Levin, Henriette Herz, Dorothea Veit and others. A rash of patriotic new journals appeared, with names like *The Fatherland* and *The New Firebrand*. But the man who really lit the fire was a philosopher, a small, untidy sparrow of a man called Johann Gottlieb Fichte. Fichte, who had sat at the feet of the great Immanuel Kant in Königsberg, was a refugee from the ancient university of Jena. Befriended by Rahel Levin, he settled in Berlin and gave a series of public lectures in Prince Heinrich's old palace on the Linden. Under the heading 'Speeches to the German Nation', these were disguised as lectures on philosophy. In fact, they were a highly inflammatory call to arms.

Fichte would never have been allowed to speak so freely under a Prussian king, but the revolutionary French officers attended his lectures and led the applause. They admired his rhetoric, seeing him only as an academic. They failed to realize either the weight attached to professors in Germany, or the explosive nature of what he was saying. In fact, although expressed more elegantly, Fichte's message to the German people was almost exactly the same as Hitler's during another time of humiliation in the 1920s. And like Hitler's it spread rapidly.

The king, during all this, was moving himself and his court further and further from the action, ending up in Memel, on the border of Lithuania, just about as far from Berlin as he could get. He was so demoralized by then that he even agreed to delegate responsibility to a chancellor. The first two holders of this office, Baron Karl vom und zum Stein and his successor Prince August von Hardenberg, happily were not Junkers but 'foreigners', and both were very much in tune with Fichte's ideas. Stein began making reforms, consolidated by Hardenberg, designed to encourage a national revival in Prussia that would eventually drive out the French.

It was typically Prussian that Stein's reforms, all of which covered areas that had long been taken for granted in other parts of Europe, were not demanded by the people, but paternalistically imposed on them from above. They included liberating the serfs (more than four and a half centuries after serfdom had died a natural death in England, for example), and enfranchising the middle classes – only 7 per cent of the population were actually given the right to a fairly meaningless vote, but for Prussia and Berlin even this was a giant step forward. They did away with restrictions based on class in employment, trades and commerce, partially emancipated the Jews, and gave Prussian towns and cities local self-government. Berlin, as the capital, was given a special position with its own city president and a new council made up entirely of burghers.

Stein only lasted a year in office; Napoleon became suspicious of him and he had to flee for his life, eventually finding safety in Russia. But in that short time he achieved more than any German politician ever had.

Among Stein's most important achievements was a wholesale reform of education at all levels. This culminated in the founding of the city's first university, brought about by the man he wisely appointed minister of education, Baron Wilhelm von Humboldt, a distinguished scholar and a member of an old Berlin family with an estate at Tegel. After Napoleon's destruction of Prussia, only two of its former five universities remained, Königsberg and Frankfurt-an-der-Oder, each with about 300 students. Displaced scholars found their way to Berlin, where Humboldt set up a high school for them attached to the Academy of Science. On 16 August 1809, the king was persuaded to agree to this becoming a university, based in Prince Heinrich's old palace on the Linden. It opened on 15 October 1810, and was inevitably named Friedrich-Wilhelms University (in 1945, the Soviet occupiers would make one of their few happy alterations to Berlin by renaming it the Humboldt University).

The timing of the new university's birth could hardly have been better. With Fichte as rector, and two of Europe's most distinguished scholars, Humboldt and his brother Alexander, as its sponsors, it attracted a formidable array of academic talent. Berlin was instantly established as Germany's intellectual powerhouse, a position it was never to relinquish.

The new patriotism expressed itself in many ways. Intellectuals trumpeted the achievements of Germans like Luther or Bach or

Dürer. Others, like the Brothers Grimm, drew attention to the common heritage of German culture by collecting traditional tales or folk songs. Romantic nationalists looked back through distinctly rose-tinted glasses to the achievements of the Teutonic knights, and called for a resurgence of their crusading spirit, and of the discipline and order they had imposed through a strictly regulated society.

Although most nationalists were liberals, the movement embraced all shades of political opinion. The extreme right was represented by the Germanic Christian Association, formed in 1811 by a group of reactionary writers, aristocrats and officers who were not only anti-French but also anti-liberal, anti-revolutionary and anti-Semitic. They thought Stein's reforms were undermining Prussia, turning it into a 'new-fangled Jew state'. They promoted an 'organic theory of the state', with an inbuilt caste system, publishing their ideas in a new and short-lived newspaper, *Die Berliner Abendblätter* (*The Berlin Evening Pages*).

The *Abendblätter* was the precursor of the modern tabloid newspaper. It was cheap, costing only eight pfennigs a copy, or 13 groschen for a three-month subscription, and consisted of only four pages. The editor and chief contributor, though he was never named, was the poet and dramatist Heinrich von Kleist. Kleist, born into one of the oldest Junker families, was a Protestant and a radical nationalist: 'Kill him!' he wrote of the French invader. 'History will not ask you the reason why.' The last, and best of his plays, *The Prince of Homburg*, ended with the clarion call: 'Death to all enemies of Brandenburg!'

The newspaper's editorial approach bore out Kleist's 'adversarial' principle, in which opposing views might be argued – but not at length. Ever conscious of the few pages at his disposal, Kleist wielded a brutal editorial blue pencil. He slashed one story from 28 pages to two and a half, and so savaged a piece by his friend Brentano that relations between the two men were never the same again. Kleist attacked anyone and everyone in the paper, including the director of the National Theatre, August Wilhelm Iffland, a well-known homosexual who did not appreciate the little jokes made about him. Not surprisingly, Iffland retaliated by refusing to stage any of Kleist's plays, dealing a financial body blow to the writer, who was always short of money.

The *Abendblätter* was an overnight success. Guards had to be posted when the sales office behind St Hedwig's cathedral was besieged with would-be readers, and after ten days the paper was forced to move to larger offices at 25 Jägerstrasse. Even so, the publisher, Julius Edouard Hitzig, complained of losing money: under pressure from all sides, *Die Berliner Abendblätter* ceased publication on 31 March 1811.

Eight months after the paper closed, Kleist and his friend, the hostess Henriette Vogel, went to stay at the Neu Krug inn at the lakeside resort of Wannsee. Henriette Vogel was suffering from an incurable cancer of the uterus, Kleist from despair. On the afternoon of 21 November, on the banks of the Wannsee, Kleist shot first Henriette and then himself. He was 34 years old. His grave can be found nearby, in a quiet spot in the woods, overlooking the lake.

When Kleist died, the students and youths of Berlin were flocking to follow Friedrich Ludwig Jahn, a teacher at the prestigious Graue Kloster high school, who was known as the '*Turnvater*', the founder of modern gymnastics. Jahn's nationalism embraced a new 'volkische' ideology, glorifying strength and racial purity. He denounced all forms of physical or mental softness, which included drinking alcohol or coffee, smoking tobacco and eating sweets, as un-Germanic. He also, incidentally, led the fight to get rid of French words and expressions, opening an institute dedicated to the purification of the German language.

Jahn set up a *Turnplatz*, an open-air gymnasium, alongside the army rifle range at Hasenheide, near Tempelhof, a woodland area that had been enclosed by the Great Elector in 1678 for the breeding of hares. The location near the army training and parade grounds was chosen deliberately: Jahn saw his exercises – including marching to and from the Turnplatz via the Halle gate – not as mere sport but as a form of military drill. He wanted his young men to become 'valiant by training with weapons, agile by playing new war games, alert, armed and prepared, courageous in battle through love for the Fatherland'.

The Hasenheide, and the pretty village of Tempelhof, were popular excursion spots, with several inns and refreshment tents nearby. Soon, watching the young men at their exercises became a popular diversion for less militant Berliners. Jahn was horrified, and moved his training ground deeper into the woods.

The army itself, meanwhile, was being reborn under the guidance of a new breed of military thinkers, men with names that have since become legendary: Scharnhorst, Gneisenau, Boyen and Clausewitz.

They were widely travelled and highly intelligent, in striking contrast to old-style Junkers like Marshal Blücher, who regarded education as 'bad for the character'. They opened up the officer corps to the middle classes, and prepared to deal with Napoleon by studying his own methods.

The king had returned to Berlin at the end of 1809, to be greeted with a sullen silence. He remained completely out of touch with popular feeling. Two years later, Berliners were disgusted when he gave in to Napoleon's demands for an alliance against Russia, allowing the *Grande Armée* to cross Prussia on its way to attack Moscow. They were even more furious when they learned that Friedrich Wilhelm had agreed to provide not only supplies and recruiting facilities for the French, but also an auxiliary corps of 20,000 men.

The terms of the king's agreement with Napoleon were so humiliating that many senior officers, Gneisenau, Boyen and Clausewitz among them, refused to have anything to do with it and left for England or Russia. Several senior government officials followed suit. Berlin police president Gruner went to Prague where he became the chief agent of the Russians, setting up a secret intelligence organization against the French.

In March 1812, the French occupied Berlin again. But this time they were not welcomed by the Berliners. The parade for Napoleon's birthday was stoned by a mob that had to be driven back with bayonets. Volunteers flocked to form a secret army 9,000 strong to prepare for the day when they would rise against their French oppressors. Ludwig Jahn's gymnasts and the students and faculty of the new university quickly became the focal points for resistance groups. They regularly attacked and wounded French sentries, and sabotaged supplies passing along the city's waterways and canals.

The king, of course, took no part in the resistance. Even when Napoleon retreated in disarray from Moscow, and his beaten troops began staggering back through Berlin, Friedrich Wilhelm still could not summon up the courage to act. Instead, he abandoned his capital again and fled with his court, this time to Breslau. It was General Hans Yorck von Wartenburg, commanding the Prussian auxiliary corps with the *Grand Armée*, who finally took charge of events. Tearing up the king's agreements with Napoleon, he threw in his lot with the Russians, opened the frontiers to the Tsar's armies, and joined them as they pursued their fleeing enemy.

For the second time in just over half a century the Russians entered Berlin. An advance guard of 300 Cossacks rode into Alexanderplatz and took the surrender of 10,000 Napoleonic troops, many of whom were not French but Italians, Swiss, and above all Rhineland Germans. The Berliners welcomed the first Cossacks, but they were not too sure what to expect when the main Russian army arrived a week later and took over the whole city. Were they to be liberated from Napoleon, only to find themselves under the knout of the Tsar? After another week of confusion the uncertainty was resolved when General Yorck's Prussian troops arrived, and greeted their former Russian enemies as brothers-in-arms.

For the ordinary Berliners, however, Yorck's presence raised yet another doubt. He was an old, hard-line Prussian Junker, who would undoubtedly want to do away with the reforms introduced by Stein and Hardenberg. Fortunately, Baron vom Stein was among the first to return from Russia, sent by the Tsar as administrator. Without waiting for the king's approval, he convened the first Prussian parliament, which immediately authorized the formation of a citizens' militia.

It was Stein himself, as the Tsar's representative, who presented the king with a document calling his people to arms against Napoleon. 'Sign, or abdicate!' he told him. And the king, 'white as a sheet and trembling', signed. The 'king's' message reached Berlin from Breslau the day after Yorck's arrival. Headed '*An Mein Volk*', 'To My People', and signed 'Your Friedrich Wilhelm', it created a sensation. Never before had a Prussian ruler appealed directly to his subjects, or even acknowledged them in his plans. Never before had a Prussian army called for volunteers. The tidal wave of patriotic fervour it released was unlike anything seen in Berlin since the citizens had risen against Iron-tooth nearly 400 years before.

In the space of a few days, no fewer than 6,500 Berliners rushed to join the new *Landwehr*, some 4.5 per cent of the city's entire civilian population. The rest of Prussia's five million people could only muster about 3,500. Berlin's volunteers came from all sections of society. The small Jewish community provided 450 – at least half of all its eligible young men. Friedrich Jahn formed his gymnasts into a company of the Lützow Freikorps. Professors stood alongside students; artists, writers and philosophers alongside merchants and craftsmen; aristocrats alongside apprentices. Many of them brought their own horses and weapons, including antique arms and armour dating from as far back as the crusades.

In the great surge of popular feeling, there was no need for taxes to be imposed to pay for the war of liberation. Public collections in churches plus donations from private and municipal funds raised nearly two million thalers. The business community raised a loan of 1.2 million thalers. The women of Berlin played their part by contributing 'gold for iron' – 160,000 gold rings, earrings, necklaces and other jewellery poured into the treasury. Some women took a more direct role: several are known to have put on male clothes to fight alongside their men.

The younger, fitter men, aged between 17 and 40, marched off with the army. Virtually every remaining man and boy turned out to form a *Landsturm*, a last-ditch 'home guard' to protect their city. Fichte appeared, looking more like a diminutive pirate than a distinguished philosopher, with two pistols stuck in a belt so broad it could have been a breastplate, and a huge cutlass dragging on the ground behind him. The sculptor Schadow led a crowd of artists. Iffland appeared at the head of a stage contingent, wearing the stage armour and shield of Joan of Arc. Fortunately, they were never called on to fight.

On 23 August, at Grossbeeren, a mere twelve miles from Berlin, a 70,000-strong French army was met by a combined force of Swedish, Russian and Prussian troops, including the volunteers of the *Landswehr*. The gunfire could be heard clearly in the city, as the allies smashed Napoleon's troops. On 6 September, at Dennewitz, the Prussian army again demonstrated its new-found strength as Generals Bülow, Tauentzien and Borstell, together with their Swedish allies, destroyed another 70,000-strong French army heading for Berlin under Marshal Ney. And finally, on 21 October, the city went wild when it received news of the great allied victory in the Battle of the Nations at Leipzig. Berlin was safe. It would not have to face another foreign army for 132 years.

The Prussian army entered Paris in the spring of 1814, and reclaimed the plundered treasures from Berlin, including the Quadriga, which was carried back in triumph on six great wagons each drawn by 32 horses. It was carefully restored, but on the king's orders the young architect Karl Friedrich Schinkel replaced the helmet, armour and shield carried by the goddess with a staff crowned with the Prussian eagle above a wreath of oak leaves surrounding an iron cross – Friedrich Wilhelm had introduced this new military decoration, designed by Schinkel, the year before.

The Quadriga was replaced on the Brandenburg Gate in time for the victory celebrations, when the king led a great military parade through the gate and up the Linden, and the whole city was described as 'a sea of light'. In honour of the victories, the square in front of the gate, previously called the Karree, was renamed Pariserplatz, and the Oktagon, by the Potsdam gate, became Leipzigerplatz.

CHAPTER 6

The Biedermeier Years

SADLY FOR THE CITIZENS of Berlin, everything they had fought for was ignored at the Congress of Vienna in 1815. A new confederation of states was set up with the aim not of uniting Germany but of 'maintaining external and internal security and the independence and integrity of the individual states'. The German people had achieved liberation from French tyranny, but there was to be no escape from the tyranny of their own rulers – the princes were interested only in preserving their individual sovereignty. And while most Berliners dreamed of Prussia being absorbed into Germany, their king was only interested in Germany being absorbed into Prussia.

In fact, the Vienna settlement turned out to be a significant step towards the realizing of Friedrich Wilhelm's dream. Most of the troublesome Polish lands were taken away from Prussia and given to the Tsar and, as compensation, Prussia was given huge new territories, including Westphalia, Pomerania, parts of Saxony, and – most valuable of all – the Rhineland. At one stroke, the population of the kingdom of Prussia more than doubled, to ten million. Suddenly, Berlin was the capital of a state that stretched from France to Russia and included ancient and formerly rival cities such as Cologne, Aachen, Mainz, Trier, and Saarbrücken in the west, as well as those in the east and north, such as Breslau, Danzig, Königsberg and Memel.

At first sight, the new lands in the west seemed to threaten even more problems for Friedrich Wilhelm than the Poles had done in the east. The Rhineland contained more than three million freemen, mostly Catholics, tainted with French ideas about democracy. They were a soft people living in a soft country, knowing nothing of the harsh realities of life on the northern plains. What no one realized at the time was that Prussia's new territory included both the Saar and the Ruhr Basin, with their enormous deposits of coal and iron.

The dream of a united Germany was not dead, though it would have to wait for another day, another year. Two Prussian statesmen were far-sighted enough to realize that the dream could only be turned into reality if the right preparations were made. In 1818, Friedrich von Motz and Karl Maassen set about establishing a customs union, a *Zollverein*, allowing free passage of goods between all 39 German states, with a single currency to remove the stumbling block of varying exchange rates. Motz and Maassen reasoned that once the states' economic interests were integrated, their political interests would also converge. The way would then be clear for political union. And since Prussia had the most powerful economy, it followed that Prussia would also dominate the political scene.

In the euphoria of victory, Friedrich Wilhelm had promised his people a written constitution. It was, of course, a barefaced bribe to smooth over his shameful derelictions during the Napoleonic Wars. But once he was safely back in power, his promises were withdrawn, together with many of the reforms that had already been granted. The king and the Junkers were terrified that what had happened in Paris in 1789 might be repeated in Berlin. So, instead of the new age of enlightenment they had hoped for, the Berliners found themselves entering a new era of repression and fear. The once free city became the centre of a police state.

In the university, student societies were closed down and the secret police monitored all lectures, imprisoning students and professors alike in their determination to root out anything and anyone they might regard as subversive. Even eminent theologians were interrogated and their sermons examined for seditious content. Secret police agents and informers, the predecessors of Hitler's Gestapo and the communist Stasi, haunted Berlin's taverns and salons. Although Beethoven had dedicated his ninth symphony to Friedrich Wilhelm, his opera *Fidelio*, with its theme of liberation from unjust oppression, was banned from the Berlin stage for 22 years. The press was ruthlessly censored and controlled. Many books were banned – the first to go was the printed version of Fichte's famous 'Speeches to the German Nation'.

Fichte himself had died in 1814; if he had still been alive, he would surely have been sent to the scaffold. His place at the university had been taken by Georg Friedrich Hegel, another of the northern philosophers who glorified the all-powerful state. Through his use of dialectics, Hegel 'proved' that Prussia's absolute monarchy was the divinely ordained embodiment of justice and order.

The application of divine justice and order did not stop at artists, writers and academics. Friedrich Jahn and many of his followers were arrested on suspicion of plotting to set up a pan-German republic. Their open-air gymnasium was closed down, and for the next two decades, all forms of athletic training were forbidden, as breeding grounds for revolution. Jahn was held without trial for six years, and although a high court judge – the writer E.T.A. Hoffmann – found him innocent, he still served two more years in jail before being released on condition that he did not stay in Berlin or any other town that had a university or a high school. He lived under police supervision for another 16 years.

No one was above suspicion. Senior ministers and officials had their correspondence opened and read in Berlin's 'black chamber', by censors searching for any hint of dissent or sedition. The king's paranoia even extended to his minister for war, Hermann von Boyen, and to the chief of the general staff and several other generals, who were dismissed because they had been involved with the commission to reform the army.

The volunteer *Landswehr* was allowed to wither away, but the regular army was strengthened still further as an instrument of repression. Everyone was made constantly aware of the presence in the city of a garrison of some 25,000 troops, few of them Berliners, each one of whom had been made to swear an oath of personal loyalty to the king.

Faced with what had clearly become a hopeless struggle against an absolute authority, the former leaders of the reform movement gave up the fight. Wilhelm von Humboldt resigned from public life in protest. So, too, did Baron vom Stein, though his erstwhile colleague, Hardenberg, chose to stay on, becoming steadily more and more reactionary. As for the majority of Berliners, they did what they had always done and, apart from two or three brief outbursts, would continue to do right up to 1990: they found ways of getting on with their lives by working hard, playing hard, grumbling loudly and joking quietly.

One of the less happy results of the war with France was the number of soldiers left crippled. The Invalidenhaus built by Friedrich the Great to house wounded veterans was crowded out. Many were reduced to begging on the streets. One of them became particularly well-known as an authentic Berlin character, his story passing into Berlin folklore as a prime example of the perpetual conflict between the army and ordinary Berliners.

Fritz Werkmann had lost both legs at the battle of Leipzig. He had been decorated with the Iron Cross and given permission by the king to earn a living playing a barrel organ in the streets of Berlin. Tottering unsteadily about the Linden, the Gendarmenmarkt and Friedrichstrasse on two short wooden stumps, his medal on his chest, he enlivened the scene with spirited, if ironic, renderings of popular airs. 'I am a Prussian: do you recognize my colours?' was a particular favourite with civilians – but not with army officers, who were not amused by the sardonic edge he brought to a patriotic military song.

They were even more enraged by Werkmann's own ditty, telling his personal story with black Berlin irony. In loose translation from Berlinisch, it goes something like this:

> In the war that has just ended
> Both my legs were shaved away,
> But my manly chest was garnished
> By my king by way of pay.
>
> And he said, 'My dearest Fritze,
> So that you may live at ease,

We will grant a further favour:
Crank an organ in the streets.'

So through the king's great mercy
I make a penny for a song,
Oh, it is too short for living,
And for dying it's too long.

Therefore this old freedom fighter
Lives today to do his thing,
Standing proudly to attention,
Calling: 'Three cheers for our king!'

To the army officers, Werkmann's songs were a slur on the holy dignity of the uniform. They protested to the king, and Werkmann's performing licence was withdrawn. Faced with the prospect of starving to death, he tried to commit suicide. Fortunately, he failed. The Berliners, outraged at the treatment he had received, raised a fund for him. With the money they collected, they set him up for life as a publican in a popular cellar bar on Artilleriestrasse.

Incredibly, despite all the harsh repression carried out in his name, Friedrich Wilhelm III remained one of the most popular of all the rulers of Prussia. With characteristic perversity, the Berliners admired him for his personal fairness and kindness, but perhaps most of all for his marriages, first to the popular Queen Luise, and later a morganatic love match with the Countess Auguste von Harrach, a beautiful young woman 30 years his junior, who they said looked after him 'like a true burgher's wife'. There was genuine sorrow in Berlin when he died in 1840.

Herr Biedermeier never existed. He was a mythical creation, a humorous pseudonym used by several Berlin poets in the early years of the nineteenth century. The name is a combination of *bieder*, a derogatory word for bourgeois, and Meier, the German equivalent of Jones or Brown, put together to represent a cosy respectability. The period between 1815 and 1848 became known as 'the Biedermeier years', or 'the quiet years'. By Prussian standards nothing much happened: there were no wars, no revolutions, only a steadily increasing prosperity.

But during those years, Berlin became completely schizophrenic, split between Prussian militarism and a new intellectual fervour centred around the university. The army, with Karl von Clausewitz as head of the war college, was as important as ever to the Hohenzollerns and the aristocracy. But the city was also attracting some of the finest civilian minds of the age.

For the city of Berlin itself, one man stood out during the Biedermeier years: Karl Friedrich Schinkel transformed the appearance of the city, creating the very 'look' of Berlin with a series of buildings that dictated its unique visual style. A small man with short, curly hair and the kind of face found on ancient Greek statues of boxers, Schinkel was the son of a Brandenburg stonemason, born at Neuruppin, 40 miles north of Berlin, in 1781. The family moved to Berlin in 1794, and the young Karl was educated at the Graue Kloster high school. He trained as a pupil of Friedrich Gilly, a brilliant young architect who died at the tragically early age of 28, working on the reconstruction of a village that had been destroyed by fire. In 1803, he went to Italy, to study classical architecture at first hand, but when he returned, in the middle of the Napoleonic occupation, there was little scope for new building, so he turned his attention to painting and designing stage sets.

His talent as a draughtsman was soon noticed. In 1807, he turned down the professorship of geometry and perspective at the Prussian Academy. On 19 May 1810, he became a civil servant, when Wilhelm von Humboldt selected him to be a senior assessor with the Royal Building Authority. After five years, he was appointed royal building master, and presented with an unrivalled opportunity to establish himself as a major architect.

In spite of the fact that he had had precious little to do with it, the defeat of the French had gone to Friedrich Wilhelm III's head, and he conceived the idea of turning the Unter den Linden into a great Via Triumphalis, where future Prussian victories could be celebrated in style. Schinkel accepted the challenge eagerly. He started the first major building, the Neue Wache, the New Guardhouse, between the university and the armoury, in 1817. It was completed a year later. Built to accommodate the palace guard, it is a remarkably effective building, dignified, solid, yet on a human scale, based on the plan of a Roman fort. Since 1919, it has served as a national war memorial – both the Nazis and the communists used the building as a focus for goose-stepping military displays and wreath-layings.

The Neue Wache was quickly followed by the impressive new Schauspielhaus on the Gendarmenmarkt, started in 1818 to replace the Royal National Theatre, which had burnt down the year before. Suddenly, Schinkel's work seemed to be everywhere. His new Schlossbrücke, the bridge across the river outside the old royal palace, was a work of art, with its cast-iron railings and eight white marble statues depicting the life of a Greek warrior. And in 1822, at the other end of the Lustgarten, he started building his greatest masterpiece, what is now known as the Old Museum, with its massive colonnade of 16 Ionic columns. It was built to house all Prussia's art treasures, including those just returned from Paris. Many critics today regard Schinkel's Old Museum as the starting point for the modern movement in architecture, its abstract simplicity directly influencing twentieth-century modernists like Walter Gropius and Ludwig Miës van der Rohe. In front of the museum, Schinkel restored the Lustgarten, replacing the Soldier King's drill square with an elegant formal garden that survived until Hitler turned it back into a parade ground in 1935.

In and around the city, Schinkel's many other buildings included several churches, a number of private houses, and two additions to Charlottenburg palace: a mausoleum for Queen Luise, the wife of Friedrich Wilhelm III, and a charming summer house, the Neue Pavillon, for the king. Standing at the end of the Knobelsdorff wing of the palace, in a corner of the grounds next to the road bridge over the Spree, it is said to be based on the Villa Reale Chiatamone near Naples, where the king had enjoyed a pleasant stay in 1822. It is a delightful little place, a simple cube on two floors, with a fireplace in the corner of every room and lovely views over the river and the palace gardens. It is one of those apparently effortless pieces of architecture, where everything fits seamlessly into place like a Mozart sonata.

A little further from the city centre, Schinkel redesigned Kleinglie-nicke palace on the banks of the Wansee near Glienicke bridge, and rebuilt Tegel palace, for Wilhelm von Humboldt, who wanted to house his collection of classical sculptures. Both were in his familiar classical style. But he deserted classicism for the gothic when design-ing the Prussian national war memorial, a 65-foot-high (20-metre) concoction in carved stone and wrought iron that is like an amalgam of London's Charing Cross and Albert Memorial, on a hill in open countryside outside the Halle gate. The hill – at 217 feet the highest point in the entire region – soon became known as Kreuzberg, 'Cross Hill'. Little more than 50 years later, it would be at the centre of the city's most densely populated district.

In 1826, Schinkel was invited to accompany his friend Peter Wilhelm Beuth, head of the technical trade delegation, on a trip to France, England and Scotland. Britain was at that time the world's pre-eminent industrial nation, and ambitious countries like Prussia were desperate to acquire British technological know-how, so the trip involved a degree of what we would now describe as industrial espionage. Schinkel's own beautifully illustrated notebooks are full of detailed drawings of Manchester and Glasgow gasworks, huge brick factories, shipyards, and the iron construction of London's Tobacco and East India Docks.

Schinkel was not concerned with tasteful views of the Tower of London or baronial castles in Scotland. What clearly fascinated him was the use of brick in British industrial buildings. This inspired the Bauakademie (Building Academy), erected between the Werderschemarkt and the Spree from 1831 to 1836, another of his acknowledged masterpieces. Schinkel used red brick, with terracotta decoration over doorways and windows, to create the austere yet subtle lines of classical architecture. It was an astonishingly modern design, which would not have looked out of place if it had been built at any time from the 1920s until the present day. As principal of the academy, an offshoot of the Academy of Arts, founded by Friedrich Wilhelm III in 1799, Schinkel taught generations of architects and designers to continue his line.

One name which keeps cropping up in Schinkel's career, particularly at times when he was working for Crown Prince Wilhelm, later to become Friedrich Wilhelm IV, is that of Peter Josef Lenné, the greatest German landscape designer of the period. Of Huguenot descent, Lenné was appointed to supervise the gardens of Potsdam in 1816, his first commission being to create the Neuer Garten. Schinkel's first commission there came five years later. Between them, Schinkel and Lenné transformed the sandy wasteland of the 'Isle of Potsdam' into a paradise of Roman villas set in gardens of delight.

Like many nineteenth-century men, Schinkel's energy at times seems almost demonic: one wonders how he ever found time to sleep or to have any home life. He was much more than an architect: he was also a painter, a sculptor, a designer of ceramics and furniture – his cast-iron chairs and tables look remarkably modern even today – and a stage designer. In the theatre, he was particularly associated with the Staatsoper and the National Theatre, though not until after 1814, when August Iffland died. The man who had refused to produce Kleist's plays had also refused to employ Schinkel, because of his 'modernism'. The new director, Duke Karl von Bühl, immediately invited Schinkel to design an opera, and over the next 14 years he created more than a hundred sets. His designs for *The Magic Flute* were said to have still been in use up to the First World War.

While Schinkel was transforming the face of Berlin, the city's cultural character was being redefined by other artists, writers, musicians and theatrical performers. Divorced from the king and his court, they were able at last to shape the city's cultural life as it pleased them. And it pleased them to follow their own, German line, in opposition to the tastes of the king. While the king favoured Italian opera, for instance, and specifically the work of Gasparo Spontini, a Neapolitan whom he brought from Paris to be his director of music, the Berliners wanted only German music.

Spontini's first performances were disasters, savaged by the reviewers and derided by the public. But Carl Maria von Weber, who had written *Songs of Liberty* for the volunteers of 1813, enjoyed an enormous triumph with his new and intensely German opera, *Der Freischütz*. It opened Schinkel's rebuilt Royal National Theatre on 18 June 1821, the anniversary of the battle of Belle-Alliance (otherwise known as Waterloo) when Napoleon had been beaten for the final time by Marshal Blücher and his Prussians (with a little help from an Anglo-Irish general called Wellington).

The artists, musicians and writers came from all levels of society. The sculptor Schadow, who was responsible for the Quadriga and who dominated the city's artistic life as director of the academy until his death in 1850, was the son of a poor tailor. Karl Friedrich Zelter, who headed both the choral society known as the Sing-Akademie and the Institute of Church Music, was a master builder by trade. Both Zelter and Schadow were renowned throughout their lives for their earthy Berlin humour and rough manners.

Goethe, visiting the city from the more genteel surroundings of Weimar, greatly admired Zelter, managing to see the real man beneath the gruff manner. 'At first meeting,' he wrote, 'he seems harsh, perhaps even coarse. But this is merely superficial. I know almost no one who is at the same time so *gentle* as Zelter. And don't forget, he's lived in Berlin for more than half a century. I see in everything that this is a city filled with such an impertinent species of mankind that one doesn't get far using delicacy with them; to keep one's head above water in Berlin one has to be somewhat coarse oneself.'

Even on his deathbed, Zelter stayed down-to-earth. His last words, to the doctor who was mopping his brow, were typical of his life. 'Don't just wipe that off as though it's nothing, Doctor,' he said. 'That's something people like you won't see every day – honest bricklayer's sweat.'

Zelter had a special building erected for the Sing-Akademie in 1827, on a street off the Linden called Am Festungsgraben, 'On the Fortress Moat', where the Great Elector's original fortifications had been filled in, partly with the remains of the Royal National Theatre which had burned down in 1817. It was Berlin's first purpose-built concert hall, originally designed by Schinkel – who was an honorary member of the society – but actually built to a modified plan by one of the great man's pupils, Karl Theodor Ottmer. The beautiful building still stands, restored in 1952 as a theatre named after the Russian writer Maxim Gorky.

Cultural leaders from other parts of the social scale included E.T.A. Hoffmann, famous for his tales but also an accomplished composer, who was, as we have seen, a high court judge. Bettina von Arnim, who succeeded Rahel Levin as the leading salon hostess, and who also wrote two controversial books drawing attention to the plight of the city's poor, was an aristocrat. And the musical prodigy Felix Mendelssohn-Bartholdy was a Jew, a grandson of the famous Moses.

Mendelssohn was actually born in Hamburg, but grew up in Berlin. At the age of eleven, he joined the Sing-Akademie, where Zelter encouraged and promoted his prodigious talent. Together with Zelter, Mendelssohn was responsible for the renaissance of the music of J.S. Bach when, at the age of 20, he conducted a performance in the Sing-Akademie of the *St Matthew Passion* on 11 March 1829, the first time it had been performed since the composer's death. When Zelter died, Mendelssohn desperately wanted to be appointed his successor as director of the Sing-

Akademie, but with typical Berlinisch cussedness the choir chose a musical nonentity, Karl Friedrich Rungenhagen, opting for safety rather than the dangerous inspiration of genius. 'Berlin is the sourest apple one can bite,' the slighted young composer commented.

Mendelssohn was not the only Berlin composer to be cold-shouldered by the city at that time. Another was Giacomo Meyerbeer – he was born Jakob Liebmann Beer – the son of another distinguished Berlin Jewish family. Meyerbeer was another of Zelter's pupils and protégés, but he had to travel abroad to achieve recognition, notably in Paris and London. Unlike Mendelssohn, however, he was eventually accepted by his native city, being appointed musical director of the royal opera in 1842, when Spontini died.

Berlin never had a pictorial tradition like Munich or Dresden. Great painters never settled in the city. The Prussian court was unsympathetic to the arts, particularly painting unless it depicted battles or military parades, and the city itself was still too provincial to attract artists like Caspar David Friedrich, the German romantic landscape painter, who worked in Dresden. But in the days of Schinkel – himself no mean painter, of course – there was a local artist who is well worth mentioning. Eduard Gärtner painted lifelike street scenes and striking panoramas of the city, often consisting of two panels to be hung across the corner of a room, so that the viewer might more easily 'read' the roofscape – for that is essentially what they are.

Two of Gärner's panoramas, a matching pair showing views in two directions from the same church rooftop, now hang in an upstairs room in Schinkel's Pavillon at Charlottenburg. Although they show panoramic views of the early nineteenth-century city, they are by no means just architectural, but are peopled with ordinary Berliners, getting on with their lives in beautifully observed detail. In the foreground of one scene, for example, a father is chasing his wayward little son, who has climbed across the roof of the church in pursuit of a toy.

As well as the lively figures, immaculate technique and perfect perspective, what is particularly impressive about Gärtner's pictures is the light: he has managed to catch that blue, diamond-sharp, hard-edged Berlin light, almost East Anglian in its quality, the product of flat landscapes, vast skies, and the persistent glimmer of water. He has also, one feels, caught the flavour of Berlin in those pre-industrial years, bringing it vividly to life.

Although Berlin was still firmly in the grip of the iron hand of censorship, cultural activity, particularly in the theatre, was more broadly based than ever before. And even though its citizens were denied any involvement in politics, that did not stop them talking or arguing, in the new cafés or *konditoreien* which had recently become an essential part of city life.

There had been taverns, coffee houses, beer gardens and restaurants in and around the city for some years. An English pastry-cook called Grey opened a restaurant and coffee house complete with billiard tables in 1735 in the Drewitz house on Breitestrasse, where he provided lunches and special dinners, with fine wines, and catered for weddings. A former royal cook named Gebhart is recorded as moving in 1771 from the restaurant '9 Churfürsten' in Scharrenstrasse to the 'Weisser Schwan' in Jüdenstrasse, where his pâtés were highly prized delicacies. But establishments like these, or the inns and taverns in the Tiergarten quarter and nearby country villages which were increasingly popular for outings and excursions, were never seen as places for daily social intercourse.

In 1820, however, a new type of establishment, a combination of coffee house and sweet shop, opened in the very heart of the city on the corner of Friedrichstrasse and the Linden. The Café Kranzler revolutionized society life in Berlin. It was such an instant success that it was immediately followed by several similar cafés and konditoreien, all founded and run by confectioners and pastry-cooks from Switzerland. By the mid-Thirties there were over a hundred in the city. As well as becoming social centres, the new cafés were also a valuable source of information and ideas. Many of them provided newspapers not only from Berlin but also uncensored journals from the rest of Germany and beyond, including Paris, Rome, Amsterdam, Stockholm and London.

Each of the principal cafés quickly became the meeting place for a particular group: the Kranzler itself was the haunt of lieutenants of the guard, young aristocrats and foreign diplomats; D'Heureuse, in Breitenstrasse, was home-from-home for the liberal property-owning bourgeoisie; Courtin, near to the bourse and post office, was naturally frequented by bankers and businessmen; Josty, on

Potsdamerplatz, catered for military pensioners complaining about the ways of the young; Spargnapani, at 50 Unter den Linden, provided small, individual tables where civil servants could talk discreetly; Stehely, in Jägerstrasse off the Gendarmenmarkt, was the centre of the literary and artistic intelligentsia, who argued in the 'Red Parlour' at the back of the main café before finishing off the evening in the older wine and beer cellar of Lutter and Wegener nearby, the Lutter Keller, where editors, lecturers and students (including the young Karl Marx and Friedrich Engels) debated the long-promised constitution.

The Berlin café soon became a lasting institution. And, possibly because of the hopelessness of the political situation at the time of its birth, so did the habit of much talk and little action.

CHAPTER 7

'The old, sacred loyalty'

THE INDUSTRIAL REVOLUTION that had been in full flower in Great Britain since 1750 had been slow to take root in continental Europe, and Berlin seemed an unlikely seedbed. At the end of the Napoleonic Wars in 1815, there was still not a single steam engine in the whole of Berlin, nor indeed in the whole of Prussia. Apart from the state porcelain factory, and the long-established gold and silver workshops, the most important parts of Berlin's industry were there primarily to serve the army: the textile mills and garment business, by far and away the city's biggest employers with over 28,000 workers, existed mainly to provide uniforms; the budding chemical industry was based on the production of dyes for these uniforms, and on explosives; the Royal Iron Foundry was established in 1805 to make cannon and shot – though it also, incidentally, produced 5,041 Iron Cross medals between 1812 and 1815.

Prussia was already second only to Britain as a European industrial power, but the gap between them was so wide that almost

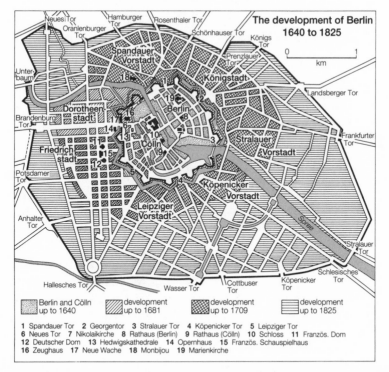

The development of Berlin 1640 to 1825

Berlin and Cölln up to 1640 — development up to 1681 — development up to 1709 — development up to 1825

1 Spandauer Tor 2 Georgentor 3 Stralauer Tor 4 Köpenicker Tor 5 Leipziger Tor
6 Neues Tor 7 Nikolaikirche 8 Rathaus (Berlin) 9 Rathaus (Cölln) 10 Schloss 11 Franzős. Dom
12 Deutscher Dom 13 Hedwigskathedrale 14 Opernhaus 15 Franzős. Schauspielhaus
16 Zeughaus 17 Neue Wache 18 Monbijou 19 Marienkirche

every advance in Berlin's manufacturing capabilities relied on British technology. As early as 1795, British spinning frames and weaving looms, followed later by fabric printing machines, were imported to revolutionize the manufacture of textiles. The mass production of earthenware and pottery was made possible by equipment brought in from Staffordshire. Berlin's first gas lighting was installed in 1816 by a British company, the Imperial Continental Gas Association of London, which went on to build the city's first gasworks to the east of the Halle Gate, under an exclusive 21-year licence. Ten years later, the company lit the first gas lamps on the Linden – despite the loud protests of many Berliners, who feared that leakage from the gas pipes would poison the roots of their precious trees.

It was an Englishman named Watson who in 1832 introduced a mechanical telegraph system that transmitted messages from Berlin to the furthest reaches of the Prussian kingdom in the Rhineland via a series of six-armed mechanical semaphore signals, mounted on rooftops and church steeples at intervals of several miles. Passed by skilled operators with powerful telescopes, a message of 30 characters could be received in Cologne no more than one and a half hours after leaving the roof of the telegraph office in Dorotheen-strasse.

Yet another English concern gave the city piped drinking water, filtered and purified from the Spree. It also introduced the first water closets, despite the fact that the city had no sewerage system until 1873, only open gullies running down the streets and empty-ing into the river. These were supplemented by night-soil women, known as 'Nachtemmas' (night Emmas), who collected household ordure at 11.00 pm every night and carried it to the river in covered pails – Eimer in German, hence the nickname. Inevitably, typhoid and cholera were a constant threat. There were serious cholera epidemics in 1831 – Hegel was one of the victims – and again in 1866.

But by far the greatest contribution made by British engineers to Berlin's industrial development was the introduction of steam power, both to factories and for transportation. The first steamships oper-ating on the Spree and Havel rivers were built by the English firm of Humphreys and Biram in 1816. By 1844, they had supplied seven steamships and ten steam tugs, to supplement the 580 horse-drawn or sailing vessels that carried freight and passengers along Berlin's crowded rivers and canals. The British-built ships operated a thrice-weekly passenger service to Hamburg, reducing the journey to between 24 and 30 hours. Another British firm, Braithwaites of London, supplied the Berlin police department with two steam-powered fire-fighting ships – eminently practical in a city with so many waterways.

The government in Berlin, well aware of the technological gap between Prussia and Britain, took steps to close it. A Ministry of Trade and Industry was set up in 1818, followed by the Society for the Advancement of Industry in Prussia. A state technical college was opened in 1821, and the first industrial exhibitions were staged in 1822 and 1827. The ministry sent officials – such as Schinkel – as well as engineers abroad, especially to Britain, to obtain informa-tion and machine drawings, to buy specific machines, to recruit skilled labour, and even to persuade British manufacturers to defect and set up plants in Berlin.

The first steam locomotive on the continent was built in Berlin by two technical officials who had just returned from Britain. Con-structed for a coal mine at Gleiwitz in Silesia, it was completed in

July 1816. Thousands of Berliners paid four silver groschen each to view this mechanical wonder. Running on toothed wheels driven by external push-rods, it was designed to haul a load of 2.5 tons at a speed of 45 metres a minute. Unfortunately, when it was delivered to Gleiwitz it failed miserably. So, too, did a second locomotive, intended to work in the Saar, and two steam engines for a Berlin wool spinner, which broke down irreparably after only ten minutes. Clearly, observation, no matter how detailed, was no substitute for practical experience.

It was two more Englishmen, the brothers John and Charles James Cockerill, who succeeded in bringing steam power to Berlin's mills and factories. First, they set up their own steam-powered wool spinning mill, then they established an engineering works and began building and installing stationary engines and other modern machinery throughout the city. Of the 30 steam engines operating in Berlin in 1830, at least 15 were theirs, including two in the royal paper mill on the Spree, which soon grew to become the third largest mill on the continent, working on a new 'endless paper' process. When the patent expired in 1833, three private mills were opened, marking the start of Berlin's position as one of Europe's major centres of papermaking.

It was the railways, however, that brought the most sensational changes to Berlin. Already the focal point of waterway transportation in northern Germany, in the mid-nineteenth century the city quickly established itself as the heart of the growing rail network for the whole country, no mean feat for a city so far from the geographical centre.

Berlin celebrated the opening of its first public railway on 29 October 1838, with suitable pride. Lenné was commissioned to landscape the 18 miles of its route between Berlin and Potsdam, and leading architects were given the task of designing and building its stations. But its six locomotives were all built by George and Robert Stephenson in Newcastle, England, as were all the rails, points, switches and signals. Only the coaches – two state cars for the royal family, five first class, nine second class, and 28 third, plus baggage and livestock wagons – were built in Berlin. As the line was extended, a further seven locomotives were imported, five from Britain, two from America. Already, however, there were Berliners who were resolved to change all that. Even as the first rails were being laid, the right man stepped on-stage from the wings.

August Borsig was a carpenter from Breslau, who came to study at the Berlin Trade Institute. After graduating, he worked for a British-trained engineer, Franz Anton Egells, who had opened first an engineering works and then an iron foundry, close to the Royal Iron Foundry outside the Oranienburg gate. The young Borsig soon mastered the business and became manager of the Egells foundry. In 1837, at the age of 33, he left to start up on his own on a site alongside the city wall next door to Egells. He was determined to break the British domination of heavy engineering.

Borsig's first locomotive entered service on the Berlin–Juterborg line in July 1841, knocking ten minutes off the journey time of his British rivals. Within the next twelve months, three new rail lines were opened from Berlin. All used Borsig locomotives and equipment. By 1847, he was celebrating the completion of his hundredth locomotive.

By 1850, there were more than 3,400 miles of track radiating in all directions from Berlin; it was possible to travel by train all the way to Paris. Borsig's production had outstripped even the biggest of his competitors in Britain. His order book was full, his factory was already working at maximum capacity, and he had bought land some two and a half miles further west in Moabit, just across the Spree from the Tiergarten, to build a vast new establishment.

Other engineers rushed to set up their foundries and factories in the new industrial district outside the Oranienburg gate. Where before there had been only cemeteries and the Fusilier Guards' barracks, more than 4,000 workers hammered and slaved over red-hot metal, day and night. The Berliners called the area *Feuerland*, 'Fireland'.

By 1844, Berlin's manufacturers had sufficient confidence to mount a great exhibition of industry for the whole of the German customs union. No fewer than 700 exhibitors came from the city itself, reflecting the diversity of its manufacturers, particularly in the growing machine-tool industry. Three years later, the foundations were laid for the electrical industry that was to become such an important element of Berlin's manufacturing base, when a young artillery lieutenant named Werner Siemens set up in business in the back court of a house in Schönebergerstrasse with a mechanic called Johann Georg Halske. They set out to build their own version of the electric telegraph, invented ten years earlier by the American,

Samuel Morse. Watson's English semaphore signals were soon forgotten.

Siemens was another graduate of the Berlin technical college, who had then gained experience in Britain, together with his brother Wilhelm. Wilhelm stayed in England, starting up his own electrical engineering company; amongst other things he built some of Britain's first trams and designed the first ship for laying underwater cables. Werner Siemens's own first patent, in the same year as he started his business in Berlin, was for underwater cable transmission. The two brothers amalgamated their businesses in 1867, but continued to work in both countries – Werner was later ennobled by the Kaiser, while Wilhelm was knighted by Queen Victoria.

As industry expanded, Berlin continued to suck in people from the countryside in ever-increasing numbers. The city's population grew by 100,000 in the 20 years following 1815, but the next 100,000 came in only ten years, bringing the population in 1845 to 400,000 and making Berlin the fourth-largest city in Europe, topped only by London, Paris and St Petersburg. Almost overnight, it seemed, the city had become the most important centre of heavy industry on the continent.

Berlin's mushroom growth inevitably brought as much misery as prosperity. There were immense problems in housing the huge influx of people. Bettina von Arnim, the society hostess, who had gallantly organized medical services for the poor during the cholera epidemic of 1831, visited the slums that were growing up around the factories, and was so shocked by what she saw that she wrote a book about it, heading it 'This Book Belongs to the King' in the hope of stirring the royal conscience. She reported that factory workers were living in dirty, damp accommodation, often 20 people to a room, six or seven to a bed. But the king was unmoved. Friedrich Wilhelm IV persisted in regarding his subjects as the happy peasants in some imaginary operetta.

Because he had seemed cultured, even civilized, while crown prince, many people had expected him to institute a period of liberal reform when he became king. But this was not to be, for there were other voices speaking to the king. Among them was the voice of God, for Friedrich Wilhelm, like a good Hohenzollern, firmly believed that he was king by divine ordination. 'I know I hold my crown from God alone,' he declared at his accession. He once remarked to a startled official that there were things 'one only knows as a king which I did not even know as a crown prince and have only learned as a king'. Unfortunately, the Lord was destined to play an increasingly important role as the king's personal adviser during the rest of his reign.

As for the happy peasants, nothing was done for them for many years, and then it would be the industrialists themselves who would take the lead. Meanwhile, if their living conditions were bad, their working conditions were often worse. The early success of industrialists like Borsig depended as much on the sweat of men, women and children working from 12 to 19 hours a day, six days a week, as it did on the use of new machines and engineering brilliance. In the textile industry, children as young as five or six years old were used to crawl through the confined spaces beneath looms and frames.

In savage contrast to the Berlin of Schinkel and the Café Kranzler, a contemporary chronicler described the population as including: '10,000 prostitutes, 12,000 criminals, 12,000 barge people, 18,000 serving maids, 20,000 weavers who cannot make ends meet through their work, 6,000 receivers of alms, 6,000 poor invalids, 3–4,000 beggars, 2,000 prisoners in jails, 2,000 illegitimate children, 2,000 children in care, 1,500 orphans.'

Surprisingly, there was little unrest during the 'Biedermeier years'. Perhaps the workers were simply too exhausted. They may also have been too scared. In 1830, following the July Revolution in Paris, the excitement in Berlin's cafés and taverns spread to the workers. Many of them joined students, middle-class intellectuals and artists in street demonstrations that became known as the 'Tailors' Revolution', since most of them were garment and textile workers protesting, not against the reactionary regime, but against their starvation wages. The government reacted – or over-reacted – by sending in 14,000 troops armed with guns, bayonets and sabres, to clear the streets.

Five years later, what the Berliners sardonically dubbed the 'Fireworks Revolution' was sparked off by the arrest of a few youngsters letting off firecrackers, as they always did on the king's birthday. The revolt was hardly a battle for freedom, more a reaction to what Berliners saw as an attempt to deprive them of one of their traditional pleasures. But three days of rioting left 100 wounded, two of whom later died. When the city's first strikes took place in 1844, by garment workers seeking better wages, they were put down again by armed police.

In 1847 and 1848, however, Berlin was caught up in the revolutionary bushfire that swept through the whole of Europe. It was a time of great political turmoil, characterized, though not sparked by, the publication of the Communist Manifesto by a young graduate of Berlin university, Karl Marx. Marx's doctrine, developed during long, beery arguments in Berlin taverns and cafés, followed Hegel's Prussian philosophy with its emphasis on the supremacy of the state over the individual, but in mirror image. 'I stood Hegel on his head,' Marx wrote, 'and put him the right way up.'

The revolution erupted in Paris in February 1848 and spread rapidly into southern Germany. In March it arrived in Berlin like a spark falling into an open tinder box. 1847 had been a year of great unrest in the city. The workers had been hit by a slump in the textile industry that brought mass unemployment and reduced wages. At the same time, they were faced with rocketing food prices caused by the failure of the corn harvest and a serious outbreak of potato blight. Desperation and the threat of starvation produced a series of food riots. Meanwhile, the Berlin middle classes, better informed than ever before about the political situation in the rest of Europe thanks to the newspapers in their cafés, were demanding a constitution and more involvement in government.

Friedrich Wilhelm IV should have been prepared. But like all the Hohenzollerns, he was totally incapable of divorcing himself from his romantic notions of the essential rightness of absolute monarchy: 'I am moved to declare solemnly,' he wrote, 'that no power on earth will ever succeed in prevailing upon me to transform the natural relationship between prince and people . . . into a constitutional one. Never will I permit a written sheet of paper to come between our God in heaven and this land . . . to rule us with its paragraphs and supplement the old sacred loyalty.'

Convinced that his subjects loved him, he was taken completely by surprise when they took to the streets in March 1848. Clashes soon developed between demonstrators and the troops in their new spiked helmets, the *Pickelhauben*. But there were no serious incidents.

On Saturday, 18 March, a great crowd gathered around the refreshment rooms on In den Zelten. After listening to a number of speeches, they marched from the Tiergarten into the city, assembling in front of the royal palace in good Prussian order, to present their demands to the king. The workers wanted bread and jobs, the right to form trade unions, and free education. The middle classes wanted guaranteed freedom of the press, the withdrawal of all troops from the city, their replacement with an armed citizens' militia, the immediate summoning of the state assembly, a constitution, a customs union extended to all German states, and the adoption of the banned black, red and gold flag for the whole of Germany.

A delegation was sent to meet the king, who received them courteously. Later, waving cheerfully to the crowd, he appeared on the balcony alongside the mayor, who announced the result of the talks: freedom of the press at once, with the other reforms to follow.

The crowd went wild with delight. But one reform had been conspicuously absent from the king's list: there was no mention of withdrawing the troops. Having apparently achieved so much, the Berliners saw no reason why they should not win this concession, too. A chant began to build up: '*Militär raus aus der Stadt! Wir bleiben hier am Ort, bis die Soldaten fort!*' – 'Troops out, out of the city! We stay here, till the soldiers clear!' Nervous troops of the palace guard began moving to clear the square. The crowd roared its disapproval. Suddenly, no one knows from where or why, two shots rang out. The crowd panicked. In a flash, the orderly, good-humoured gathering became a revolutionary mob. The cry turned to: 'Treachery! To arms! To the barricades!' The troops charged. People poured out of the square, fleeing across the Schlossbrücke to turn the city centre into a battlefield.

'Screams of fury and vengeance rose along Königstrasse, then through the whole city,' wrote an eye-witness. 'Paving stones were torn up, arms stores plundered, cleavers and axes fetched. In no time, twelve barricades appeared on Königstrasse, made from cabs, omnibuses, woolsacks, beams – big, efficient, well-made barricades. House by house, roofs were dismantled. On their dizzy edges stood men with tiles in their hands, waiting for the soldiers . . .

Friedrich Wilhelm, the Great Elector, was the founder of modern Berlin. He is seen here welcoming Huguenot refugees to the city in 1685. The French Protestant immigrants were to leave an indelible mark on the city *(AKG)*

Prospect oder Weg, gegen dem Thier-Garden vor Berlin

The peaceful face of seventeenth-century Berlin: the Unter den Linden and the Tiergarten *(LBS)*

Below: The Leipzig Gate, one of the fourteen entrances to Cölln and Berlin through the customs wall *(LBS)*

Bottom left: Elector Friedrich III, an ardent admirer of the French 'Sun King' Louis XIV, crowned himself King Friedrich I in – not 'of' – Prussia, in the city of Königsberg in 1701 *(AKG)*

Bottom right: Friedrich Wilhelm I, the so-called 'Soldier King', suffered from porphyria – hence the wheelchair and bandaged legs. When his son, the future Friedrich the Great, attempted to escape to England with his intimate friend, the handsome guards captain Hans von Katte, Friedrich Wilhelm had Katte executed. This fanciful picture purports to show the eventual reconciliation of father and son *(AKG)*

Left: Adolph Menzel's famous etching shows the more familiar aspect of Friedrich the Great's character, as 'Alte Fritz' *(AKG)*

Far left: Johann Gottfried Schadow, architect and sculptor, depicted here at the age of eighty, designed the Quadriga, the four-horse chariot carrying Nike, the Goddess of Victory, which tops the Brandenburg Gate (AKG)

Above: the first triumphal entry through the new gate, however, was made by Napoleon in 1806. At first, Berliners enthusiastically greeted the French as liberators – but had second thoughts when they looted the city's treasures, including Schadow's Quadriga *(LBS)*

Left: The prophet armed: Johann Gottlieb Fichte, the great philosopher and first rector of Berlin University, was ready to do his duty with the Landsturm, Berlin's 'Home Guard' *(AKG)*

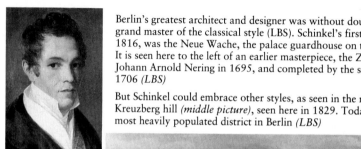

Berlin's greatest architect and designer was without doubt Karl Friederich Schinkel, grand master of the classical style (LBS). Schinkel's first major building, completed in 1816, was the Neue Wache, the palace guardhouse on the Unter den Linden *(below)*. It is seen here to the left of an earlier masterpiece, the Zeughaus, or Arsenal, begun by Johann Arnold Nering in 1695, and completed by the sculptor Andreas Schlüter in 1706 *(LBS)*

But Schinkel could embrace other styles, as seen in the national war memorial on the Kreuzberg hill *(middle picture)*, seen here in 1829. Today, this is the centre of the most heavily populated district in Berlin *(LBS)*

Even after improvements made by Schlüter in 1698, the city Schloss, the old royal palace, was always regarded by Berliners as the ugliest building in the city. Badly damaged in the second world war, it was demolished by the East German government in 1950 *(LBS)*

Right: Following the revolution, police president Carl Ludwig von Hinkeldey reorganised Berlin's police, fire and refuse services along military lines, and incidentally introduced far reaching social measures *(LBS)*

Above: By 1860, Berlin had become the greatest centre of heavy industry in continental Europe, led by the Borsig works in Chausseestrasse, Moabit *(AKG)*

Right: Berlin's impressive central Jewish synagogue on Oranienburgerstrasse was completed in 1866. Although Berlin had a higher proportion of Jews than any other German city, including Vienna, anti-Semitism was never a serious problem until the Nazis, who burnt down this synagogue in 1938. It was rebuilt, more splendid than ever, in 1992 *(AKG)*

By 1872, evening concerts in Kroll's establishment in the Tiergarten were a central part of the Berlin social scene *(AKG)*

Below: the marriage of Crown Prince Friedrich and Vicky, eldest daughter of Queen Victoria, was a love match. But she disliked Berlin and found the old Schloss, their first home, hideously uncomfortable. Both were implacably opposed to Bismarck *(AKG)*

Above: The architect of the Second Reich, Otto von Bismarck (right), made his master, Wilhelm I, its first Kaiser. The two men enjoyed a stormy relationship for twenty-six years *(AKG)*

Inset: When Friedrich died in 1888 after only ninety-nine days on the throne, he was succeeded by his son, Wilhelm II, usually known as 'the All Highest' *(AKG)*

29 Jahre 1888.

Above: In 1901, Wilhelm I created the Siegesallee, the Victory Walk, 'where even the bird-shit is made of marble'. He commanded his favourite sculptor, Rheinhold Begas, to carve thirty-two statues glorifying his Hohenzollern ancestors *(LBS)*

Berliners at play: officers and gentlemen take their wives for an outing on the Spree in one of the new pedalos, while a working-class group from Neukölln share the simple pleasures of life in their 'Ost-Elbien' garden colony *(LBS)*

Above: Berliners at work: the production hall of the huge AEG electrical engineering works epitomised Berlin's industrial might at the turn of the century *(AKG)*

The elevated S-Bahn revolutionized transport in Berlin. At Dennewitzstrasse, the line even ran through the middle of a building. This photograph was taken in 1905 – but the line and the building are both still there *(LBS)*

Between four and five o'clock, the first shots crackled over König-strasse from the Kurfürstenbrücke.'

The fighting continued for 16 hours on some 200 barricades throughout the city. Men, women and children, rich and poor, fought alongside each other against the army, with tiles, bricks, chimney pots, stones, and assorted improvised weapons, though they had some guns and even a few cannon taken from the armoury. They even poured boiling water from the rooftops on to the troops below. Street fighting did not figure in the army training manuals, and it was not long before the morale of the soldiers broke and they retreated to the safety of their barracks.

Meanwhile, back at the palace, Friedrich Wilhelm had ordered his generals to use the cavalry to put an end to 'that scandalous business out there'. The queen and his brother, Crown Prince Wilhelm, demanded firm action. The army commander General von Gerlach declared himself delighted at the prospect and eager to attack the enemy – nothing more clearly demonstrates the narrowness of the Prussian military mind and the contempt the court felt for Berliners than the fact that they should be regarded, like the Austrians, the French or the Russians, as 'the enemy'. But fortunately, before there was more bloodshed, the king's re-solve faltered. He dithered, lost his nerve, then did what his ances-tors had always done when faced with a difficult situation: he changed sides.

In his new role as the people's friend, the king announced that he would withdraw the guards to Potsdam, and grant all their other demands. What was more, he would appear on his balcony again, to receive the homage of 'his beloved Berliners'. At that, the revolu-tionaries promptly laid down their arms and left the barricades. Next day, they flocked to the palace, carrying the bodies of 183 of those who had been killed. The king, decked out with black, red and gold ribbons, paid his respects to the dead. On 21 March, accompanied by his princes and ministers behind the flag of a united Germany, he led the survivors in a procession through the streets of the city to the university, where he made a suitably vague speech, full of high-flown phrases but in fact promising nothing.

The long years of subjugation had left an indelible mark on the Berliners. Friedrich Wilhelm represented lawful authority, and as such they automatically respected him. They were even prepared to love him, simply because he asked them to, reserving their rage for his brother, Crown Prince Wilhelm, who had commanded the troops during the battle. The king had Wilhelm – dubbed 'the Cartridge Prince' by the Berliners for ordering the soldiers to open fire on the people – smuggled out of the city to the old fortress at Spandau. When he was discovered there, he was moved to a folly built for one of Friedrich Wilhelm II's mistresses in the form of a ruined castle on Pfauen Insel, the largest of the islands on the Havel.

To escape from Berlin, Wilhelm had to ask his son, Friedrich, to bring scissors and help him cut off his imposing beard. Clean-shaven and unrecognizable without his whiskers, he was smuggled ignominiously out of the city and the country, to find refuge with Queen Victoria and Prince Albert in London. He never forgave the revolutionaries of Berlin for what he saw as forcing him to shame himself in front of a foreign court. Whether he would actually have come to any harm had the citizens got hold of him is hard to say. Their attack on his town palace was halted simply by two words chalked on it by students: 'National Eigenthum', 'national property'.

But the revolutionaries were not all so law-abiding. With the army out of the way, there were constant disturbances and looting became commonplace. Hundreds of middle-class men volunteered to form an armed auxiliary police force, the *Burgerwehr*, providing day and night patrols throughout the city. But as the alarm horns called them from their beds virtually every night, the volunteers soon began to lose interest. More and more men dropped out, discipline suffered, and lawlessness increased steadily.

The new state assembly met in the Royal National Theatre in May after Prussia's first democratic elections. It spent the next six months arguing about a constitution, the debates becoming more and more stormy against a background of increasing unemployment and hardship. As the assembly moved radically to the left, the revolutionary coalition of workers and bourgeoisie began to split. Bourgeois fears of a socialist uprising were aggravated when a mob seized the weapons from the armoury on 14 June.

The storming of the armoury was final proof that the Burgerwehr was quite incapable of maintaining security in the city. The government decided it had to set up a powerful full-time police force. Typically, the revolutionaries sought the king's permission first, and only when he had given it did they announce the formation of a *Schutzmannschaft*, a new civil constabulary along the lines of the London 'bobbies' created by Sir Robert Peel 20 years earlier. The first 1,000 men signed up on 22 July, starting their duties on the streets of Berlin next day. Like their English counterparts, they wore top hats and short frock coats, though unlike the London force they were armed with swords.

Despite the carefully non-military uniforms, the general population regarded the new constabulary with great suspicion – the Burgerwehr, too, had worn top hats, but they had not hesitated to fire on mobs of workers to restore order. To assuage their mistrust, the newly appointed Police President von Bardeleben issued a public statement of policy that was unprecedented in Berlin:

> The constabulary shall seek to carry out its tasks through remonstration, admonition, solicitation, and above all in an amicable manner. They will conscientiously avoid not only any intrusion into the freedom of the people, but also all needless disturbances and interferences in public activities. The constabulary may only proceed to the application of enforcing discipline when amicable means have proved themselves unsuccessful or inadequate.

The king watched and waited from the safety of Potsdam, biding his time while his aristocratic supporters played the two revolutionary factions off against each other. Bourgeois alarm at 'the spectre of communism', which Marx and Engels claimed was haunting Europe, was raised when the first German Workers Congress met in Berlin in August. In September, encouraged by successful counter-revolutions in Paris and Vienna, Friedrich Wilhelm sent his troops back into the city under Count Friedrich Wrangel. There were no protests from the citizens, most of whom were fast losing patience with the bickering and indecision of their delegates.

On 10 November, Wrangel decided it was time to put an end to the charade. Surrounding the theatre with armed troops, he called for a chair and sat himself down in the middle of the square with all the studied arrogance of a true Junker. An officer of the militia appeared, warning the general that he and his men were prepared to defend the freedom of the people and the safety of the National Assembly. 'We shall yield only to superior force!' he declared.

Wrangel did not move, but replied in broad Berlin dialect: 'Tell your militia that force is ready for 'em.' He took out his watch, and announced that the assembly and the militia had 15 minutes to disperse. Both left quietly. The revolution was over, defeated by 'the old sacred loyalty'.

Wrangel immediately declared martial law, forbidding all meetings or political activity. On 12 November, he took direct control of the constabulary, reimposing strict censorship and surveillance through the minister of the interior, Ferdinand von Westphalen, the brother-in-law of Karl Marx. On 5 December, the king imposed his own constitution, designed to thwart any future efforts at democracy. There was to be a two-chamber assembly. The upper would be a house of lords, the Herrenhaus. The lower chamber was to be elected by a general franchise, but it would have no power. Its 'decisions' would be little more than recommendations, which the king could accept or reject as he pleased.

The first elections resulted in landslide victories for the democratic left in all nine electoral districts of the capital. The legend of 'Red Berlin' was born. The king was not pleased. His mouthpiece, the twice-daily *Neue Preussische Zeitung*, fulminated against 'rotten Berlin', whose people had elected as their representatives 'men who had insulted the king in his own house'. But worse was to follow: the first thing the new House of Representatives did was to declare the state of emergency in the city illegal, and call for its removal. The king removed the House of Representatives instead.

Shortly afterwards, he announced new elections under a revised system. The secret ballot was abolished, and voters were divided into three classes, depending on how much tax they paid: the few rich aristocrats in the first class, together with well-to-do property owners in the second, were guaranteed always to outweigh the majority votes of the third class, the general run of taxpayers. But whatever happened, the king would always have the last word.

The same three-class voting system was imposed on Berlin, for the election of the city council. The right to vote was granted only to those with an annual income of more than 1,200 marks, which effectively disenfranchised the vast majority of Berliners. To give even more protection to the interests of the aristocrats and large taxpayers, there was a new ruling that at least half its members must own property in the city. And to make sure that the council behaved itself, its officials were closely supervised by the state government. Both the imposed constitution and the three-class voting system were to remain in force in Prussia and in Berlin until 9 November 1918.

CHAPTER 8

Blood and Iron

*I*N APRIL 1849, a delegation arrived in Berlin from the 'German National Assembly' in St Paul's church, Frankfurt. They had come to offer the imperial crown of a united Germany to Friedrich Wilhelm IV. The Berliners, who had fought on the streets for a united Germany only a year earlier, should have been delighted. Instead, they just sat back and grinned. They couldn't take the delegation seriously – its members were all frock-coated Herr Biedermeiers, with not a single uniform among them; they even rode to the palace in hired cabs. 'What, *they're* going to make our king a Kaiser?' scoffed the errand boys on the Linden. The king was even more dismissive. In typical Hohenzollern fashion, he declared that it was a violation of divine right for commoners to offer him a crown; he could only consider such a proposal from his fellow princes.

And so, the delegation returned to Frankfurt, and the rest of Germany returned to the Austrian-dominated confederation of south German states set up in 1815. The question of a unified Germany did not arise again for another 20 years. Politically, Prussia was not yet strong enough to take the lead; the army was at one of the low points in its perpetual cycle of reform and decay; and Berlin, for all its size, was still too much of a parvenu among German cities to be considered as the national capital.

Once again, the Berliners turned their backs on their rulers, and got on with the serious business of making a living, which for the next 20 years they did very successfully. In spite of the setbacks to political union, economic unity was already becoming a reality through the Prussian-dominated Zollverein, and there was significant progress towards a single German currency.

With the whole of Germany as its effective home market, Berlin's industrial production and foreign trade both doubled in the 1850s. More than 1,000 new factories opened in the city, along with dozens of new banks, a new stock exchange, more railways, three more urban canals and a large inland harbour. The existing canals, most notably the Landwehr canal which left the Spree at Treptow in the east and ran right across the city to rejoin it near Charlottenburg Palace, were widened and enlarged, and beautified with trees planted along the banks.

Berlin was already the leading industrial city in continental Europe. Surprisingly, it was also the leader in protecting its workers against exploitation by employers. New regulations far ahead of those in any other industrialized nation laid down a standard minimum wage, forbade payment in overpriced goods in lieu of money, banned the employment of children under twelve in factories, and appointed inspectors to supervise working conditions.

True to Prussian form, of course, these social advances were not won by workers' action. Like every regulation in Prussia, they were imposed from above, without consultation, this time by the prime minister, Otto von Manteuffel. Of course, Manteuffel, who governed without the encumbrance of a parliament, was not entirely guided by humanitarian motives. His new regulations were partly intended to combat socialism by keeping the workers happy, but more importantly to clip the wings of the king's real enemies, the progressive and liberal-minded industrialists.

There was a similar lack of altruism behind other new regulations to improve living conditions in Berlin. These were imposed, again without pressure or agitation, by one of the city's most remarkable officials, Karl Ludwig von Hinckeldey. In 1849, immediately after the abortive revolution, Hinckeldey was appointed president of police, the most important position in the city. As well as being responsible for law and order, he had a wide range of other powers,

including censorship, issuing passports, and licensing and controlling all businesses. He also had the authority – which he often made
use of – to overrule the city council if he believed they were not
fulfilling their duties.

Hinckeldey began by reorganizing the constabulary into a military-
style force – the top hats and frock coats were replaced with spiked
helmets and blue tunics – and thus tightening the grip of the
Prussian police state. His intentions were as illiberal as any Prussian
autocrat's, but in the course of improving security, he found himself
turning into a reformer.

As Berlin grew ever more crowded, the danger of fire became one
of the most serious threats to safety and public order. To deal with
it, Hinckeldey established the city's first professional fire department, as part of the police, again along military lines. He also
instituted the first regular refuse service. In previous times Berliners
had simply carted their household waste outside the walls, and
dumped it along the sides of the unmade roads, where the stench
became a permanent feature of the approaches to the city. But as
the city grew, this had become more difficult, and people had taken
to piling it in their streets and courtyards, where it had become a
serious fire hazard. Hinckeldey organized a collection service to
remove it.

Since his firemen could not do their job without water, Hinckeldey
had pipes laid and fire hydrants installed in all the streets. To pay
for this, he demanded one million thalers from city funds, giving the
council three days to think about it. When he had not heard from
them, he simply went ahead and gave the contract for a waterworks
to a British company. With the mains in place, there was soon a
demand for piped water for households, too, and supplies were
even laid on in the back courtyards of slum tenements. Next came
public bath houses, an indoor swimming pool and a public steam
laundry.

Hinckeldey also introduced the first building regulations to impose some sort of control over Berlin's notorious '*Mietskasernen*',
the 'rental barracks' that were already becoming a feature of the
poorer new districts in the north and east of the city. These huge
tenement buildings, up to 400 metres square, came about almost by
accident. The city plan for new districts was based on main boulevards at least 30 metres wide, linked by 26-metre-wide cross streets.
As in Haussmann's Paris, these broad thoroughfares were intended

to make the building of barricades more difficult and to provide a clear field of fire for troops, in case of insurrection. The original plan was for the blocks between the boulevards to be subdivided by a network of smaller streets, on which houses and apartments would be built. But as the price of building land rocketed, it became too costly to waste on unproductive side streets. The Mietskasernen were thrown up as fast as possible, each covering all four sides of an entire city block in an unbroken hollow square.

The interior of each block was filled in with a honeycomb of more apartments built in a series of square courts or wells, stretching back as many as six deep, with a single access from the street through a dark tunnel of archways. Each block housed hundreds of families, with shared kitchens and no drainage, perfect incubators for disease: it is no wonder typhus, tuberculosis, bronchitis and malaria were endemic, with the threat of cholera always looming in the background. In many of the inner courts, small workshops and factories were crammed in alongside the communal earth privies, adding to the noise and dirt. The earth privies have long since gone, but the small back court factory still remains a feature of Berlin today. Some of the city's most successful businesses – the giant Siemens electrical company is one example – started life that way.

Hinckeldey's regulations still allowed an extremely high density of building: like his water supply and refuse collection service, they were less concerned with health or safety than with limiting the danger of these valuable properties being destroyed by fire. He restricted the height of the buildings to five storeys (the highest any firemen's ladder could then reach) and laid down that courtyards had to be at least 5.3 metres square (the minimum turning circle for a Berlin fire engine).

But it was not the police reforms, the fire service, or even the municipal refuse collection that was to be Hinckeldey's most visible memorial. That was the cylindrical poster pillar, which may still be seen on any Berlin street. Having been outraged by the fly-posting of unauthorized bills on walls and windows during the unrest in 1848, Hinckeldey hit on the idea of the pillar as a means of control. He approached a printer called Ernst Litfass, and in 1854 offered him a contract to instal 150 pillars, in exchange for the sole right to print and display posters in the city for the next 15 years. All other bill-sticking was strictly banned. In fact, Litfass and his heirs –

Litfass himself died in 1874, having made a huge fortune – held the monopoly until 1880, when it was taken over by the city authorities themselves. Sadly, perhaps, Hinckeldey's role remains anonymous. To this day, the displays are known in Berlin as Litfass columns, though in the early days the Berliners, typically, christened them *'dicke Damen,* 'fat ladies'.

With such promising beginnings, who knows where Hinckeldey's sincere efforts at police repression might eventually have led him? Unfortunately, after only eight years in office, he was killed in a duel with another Junker officer who objected to his closing down an aristocratic gaming club in 1856.

Theodor Fontane recalled the senseless tragedy of Hinckeldey's death a few years later in one of his novels, using it to point up the rigid code by which the Prussian nobility lived and died: 'Apparently one of his non-military counsellors who was unusually close to him had done everything he could to dissuade him, pointing out that all duels were absurd and criminal, especially one undertaken in these circumstances. But on this occasion Hinckeldey suddenly got on his high horse and, playing on his position as a nobleman, answered him sharply and arrogantly: "Nörner, you don't understand these things." And a hour later he was dead. Why? Because of some fantasy, a nobleman's folly that was stronger than reason, stronger even than the law which it was his duty to protect and uphold . . . our background does determine our actions. The man who obeys this rule may perish, but at least he dies more honourably than the man who defies it.'

In the five years after the failed revolution of 1848, well over a million despairing Germans emigrated to America. The exodus reduced the populations of many towns and cities, but despite the appalling living and working conditions, people continued to flock into Berlin in their tens of thousands. By the end of the decade, the city was bursting at the seams with almost half a million inhabitants, and the Prussian authorities decided it was time to enlarge its boundaries again.

In 1860, the city walls were finally pulled down for the last time. Only the Brandenburg Gate remained as a physical reminder; the other old gates became little more than names on the map. The following year, in spite of opposition from the city council, the workers' districts of Gesundbrunnen, Wedding and Moabit to the north and north-west, and the more affluent suburbs of Tempelhof and Schöneberg to the south and south-west beyond the Landwehr canal, were incorporated into the city, which was then divided into 16 districts.

To house the enlarged city administration, a new building was started that same year opposite Schinkel's post office and close to the old Molkenmarkt, on Königstrasse, where the revolutionaries of 1848 had built their strongest barricades. In mock Italian renaissance style, with a 245-foot (75-metre) tower and three courtyards, all in bright red brick and terracotta, it quickly became known as the Red Town Hall. Later, the name became an apt tag politically as well as architecturally.

In January 1858, Victoria, the eldest and favourite daughter of Queen Victoria of Great Britain, married Prince Friedrich Wilhelm, eldest son of Wilhelm the 'Cartridge Prince'. The marriage was a genuine love-match between Vicky, the 17-year-old Princess Royal, and her gentle, 26-year-old Fritz. But it was a match that had been carefully arranged by the British queen and the Prussian crown prince. Wilhelm saw it as a way of counterbalancing the alliance between Britain and his traditional enemy France, who had fought side by side against Russia in the Crimean war three years before. Victoria saw it as a way of introducing British ways and values to Prussia, to lead it out of the dark ages of absolutism and into the light of a constitutional monarchy. But merging fire and water into a single element would have been simpler than creating a genuine alliance between a liberal democracy built around the freedom of the individual, and an autocracy that glorified militarism and total obedience.

Vicky soon came to loathe Berlin. Her state entry into the city after her marriage in England was distinctly uncomfortable. The weather was icy, yet the princess and her ladies-in-waiting were obliged to change into evening gowns at Potsdam, and then ride through the streets of Berlin in open carriages with no wraps to keep them warm. It was a bad start, but things were to get worse.

The newly-weds' first home in the city was an apartment in the old royal palace, which had grown piecemeal around Friedrich Iron-tooth's 'Coercion Castle' since the fifteenth century. According to Vicky, it still boasted the original plumbing. 'I spent the first year without WC, baths or water,' she wrote later. Indeed, on the rare occasions when the king himself wanted to take a bath, a tub would be brought in from the Hotel du Rome, and water to fill it carried through the palace by squads of soldiers. To her husband, a professional soldier who had become a lieutenant in the guards at the age of ten, scrubbing himself down from a bowl of cold water was the most natural thing in the world. To poor Vicky, brought up in an altogether softer environment, it was a torture not to be endured. But when she asked for hot water, the Prussian court was horrified at her lack of respect for its traditions: her request was seen as an affront to the royal dignity.

The palace was cold and dark, the rooms were immense, the furniture creaked and groaned in the wind which, on a winter's night, shrilled through ill-fitting doors and windows. And it had ghosts. In addition to the white lady who had frightened Friedrich I to death, Vicky's bedroom was right next to the room where Friedrich Wilhelm III had died, and which had been left untouched for decades out of respect for his memory. She had to pass through it every time she went to her dressing room or boudoir, and she was convinced it was haunted.

There were no cupboards for Vicky's clothes, which had to remain in boxes. In one big empty room she found the corpses of thousands of bats. And there were bugs everywhere. The servants were dishonest, impertinent and dirty: when she ordered them to burn the infested beds, they simply ignored her. As for Berlin itself, she considered it was 'an awful hole. No drainage, fearful pavements, awful smells.'

After a year of this torment, and the even greater torment of constant exposure to the undisguised hostility of the rest of the court, Vicky and Friedrich were able to move into their own home in the small palace at Babelsberg, on the lake near Potsdam. This was another of Schinkel's creations, with grounds designed by Lenné and Prince Hermann von Pückler-Muskau, the other great Berlin landscape gardener of the period. Queen Victoria, who visited her daughter at every opportunity, was enchanted by the little palace, which she described as 'a Gothic bijou'. But Vicky's father, Prince Albert, was more aware of the importance of show in German court circles. He suggested that the young couple move into Friedrich the Great's enormous Neue Palais in Potsdam, neglected and decaying, but suitably grand, and the king gave his permission.

Their new homes gave Vicky and her husband some relief from the rigid narrowness of the Prussian court, which came as such a shock to the young princess after the educated, liberal and loving royal family in which she had been brought up. It also helped to cushion them slightly from the intrigues, suspicions and spying of the political establishment, which regarded Vicky as a dangerous British agent sent to undermine their way of life. In marked contrast, the ordinary Berliners took Vicky to their hearts from the first, won over by her charm, intelligence and honest simplicity.

Like the soldiers he commanded, the general population had a high regard for Prince Friedrich. They believed that, unlike most Hohenzollerns, he had their best interests at heart, and they looked forward with high hopes to the time when he came to the throne. For once, their trust was not misplaced: for a man with his background, Friedrich was surprisingly liberal and open-minded, always at odds with his militarist father, who ruled as regent from 1859, when Friedrich Wilhelm IV was declared insane.

In his later years, Friedrich Wilhelm's behaviour had become increasingly bizarre. Since the uprising in Berlin, he had avoided the city, choosing to live at Sans Souci and keeping the Havel, like a *cordon sanitaire*, between himself and his happy but clearly ungrateful peasants. He liked to walk on his own at night in the gardens of the palace, but since he was short-sighted, he was always stumbling and falling over, walking into trees or, worse still, into the muskets of his own sentries. In the darkness, the men often failed to recognize him, and as his memory was failing he could never remember the password. This gave rise to several embarrassing incidents – on one occasion in the middle of winter he was kept prisoner for over an hour by a sentry, until the sergeant of the guard arrived with the relief. In 1857, he suffered a stroke and was diagnosed as incurably insane. He died in 1862, to be succeeded by his brother, as Wilhelm I.

Wilhelm I's reign began promisingly, with the election of a new parliament and an amnesty for political offenders. Even the 43-year-old Karl Marx felt it safe enough to return from his exile in

London. He stayed in Berlin for a while with the founder of the German socialist party and trade union movement, Ferdinand Lassalle. It was not the king but his liberal ministers who refused to allow Marx to reclaim his Prussian citizenship.

But the illusion of political emancipation was predictably short-lived. Wilhelm was still the Cartridge Prince, who had returned from his exile in England in 1848 to take charge of the Prussian army again. He had marched two corps south to Baden the following year to crush the last spark of revolution in Germany, avenging his past humiliation by hanging most of the officers of the radical army.

Wilhelm was determined to establish Prussia once and for all as the undisputed leader of the German states. This would involve deposing Austria, almost certainly by force. The Prussian army, though, was in no state to fight. Wilhelm's unstable brother had allowed it to decay once more; a partial mobilization in 1859 to counter the threat of an attack by France had been a disorganized and hopeless failure. Wilhelm single-mindedly set about restoring the army to its former glories. He began by proposing to increase the annual intake of conscripts from 40,000 to 63,000, and doubling the time spent in the reserve from two to four years. This would mean creating 39 new infantry regiments and ten cavalry regiments, almost doubling the size of the army.

To pay for all this, Wilhelm and his war minister, Count Albrecht von Roon, drew up a military budget that would account for well over 90 per cent of all national expenditure. The elected representatives in parliament rejected it. Instead, they proposed cutting the period of conscription from three years to two. Wilhelm, like the true Hohenzollern he was, dissolved parliament and dismissed all those ministers who opposed him. 'We are,' he explained to his brother-in-law in an access of righteous indignation, 'actively and resolutely opposing democracy.'

The constitutional crisis that followed threatened to be even worse than the 1848 attempt at revolution. At its peak, the king even drew up the documents for his abdication in favour of his son. But even as the liberals rejoiced at the prospect of being ruled by their first progressive monarch, the opportunity was thrown away by Friedrich himself. Despite his disagreements with his father, the crown prince was a Hohenzollern, drilled from birth in filial obedience. He pleaded with Wilhelm to stay on, reminding him of the dangers of a Prussian king allowing himself to be driven from the throne by mere politicians. Wilhelm listened, and stayed. In fact, although he was already 64, he stayed for another 26 momentous years.

Vicky, who was away from Berlin with her mother at Coburg, had tried to persuade Friedrich to accept the throne. 'I see no way out,' she wrote, 'and consider you should make this sacrifice for the country. If you do not accept, I believe that you will regret it one day.' That day came sooner than she expected. In a last, desperate move to resolve the crisis, Wilhelm was persuaded by von Roon to appoint as premier and foreign minister the man Friedrich and Vicky feared most, a man he had himself described in 1848 as a dangerous 'red reactionary, smelling of blood': the 48-year-old Otto von Bismarck-Schönhausen. Bismarck was a traditional Junker, and proud of it. He claimed that he had learned his rough, tough style of diplomacy in the horse fairs of his native Pomerania. He was a big character, larger than life in every respect, emotional, fiery-tempered and arrogant, totally ruthless and utterly insubordinate. As a young man, he had survived only one stormy year of military service. He had then taken a civil service post, which he left after four unsatisfactory years because he 'could not put up with superiors'. He preferred, he said, 'to make his own music'.

Physically, Bismarck cut an imposing figure. He was over 6 feet (1.83 metres) tall, with broad shoulders, a powerful chest and, until he developed a paunch in later life, a surprisingly narrow waist. He was bald on top well before he reached 50, but still grew bushy hair on the rest of his head, to match his dense eyebrows and heavy, walrus moustache. His bulbous eyes always seemed to stare arrogantly out at the world he dominated. But his hands and feet were small, even delicate, and his voice was surprisingly thin and reedy, a high tenor rather than the basso profundo that might have been expected from such a massive frame.

As a young man, Bismarck was a brilliant all-round sportsman, complete with a duelling scar caused by an opponent's sword breaking – the only time he was touched in 25 fights during his year at Göttingen University. He rode, swam, shot and gambled as well as any man in Germany, and ate and drank considerably more. All his life he consumed heroic meals, swilled down with enormous quantities of beer and brandy, and suffered from chronic indigestion as a result. He smoked 14 cigars a day, and said he hoped to finish 5,000 bottles of champagne before he died. He was also a great womanizer, leaving a trail of passionate affairs and scandals in his wake, even after his marriage in 1847.

For all his hearty physical energy, Bismarck was by no means the typical thick-skulled Junker he liked to play. He had a brilliant mind, spoke fluent French, English and Russian, and had an unrivalled grasp of political reality. He had entered public life in 1847, as a member of the right-wing Junker party in parliament, where he had declared: 'Only two things matter for Prussia: avoiding an alliance with democracy and securing equality with Austria.'

When he was appointed Prussian representative to the confederation diet in Frankfurt, he became infamous for his aggressive bad manners in pursuing Prussian interests to the exclusion of everything else. The king obviously appreciated and shared his brutal approach: after eight years of unremitting hostility to Austria in the diet, Bismarck was sent briefly as ambassador to Vienna. From there he moved on in the same role to St Petersburg. In the summer of 1862, he was transferred to Paris, but had only been there a few months when the call came to return to Berlin.

Bismarck's first speech to the Prussian parliament as prime minister set out his views with unnerving clarity, views that Adolf Hitler was to echo 70 years later. 'The great questions of the day will be settled not by speeches and majority votes – that was the mistake of 1848–49,' he declared, 'but by blood and iron.' With conscious irony, he held up an olive leaf as he spoke, but soon made it clear that he would have no hesitation in using the sword and the gun to settle any problems.

Bismarck solved the problem of the military budget by simply withdrawing the bill, saying he would finance the army reforms by direct taxation. And when the liberals proposed that the people should refuse to pay their taxes, Bismarck echoed General Wrangel by replying that he had 200,000 soldiers ready to persuade them. For the next four years the taxes were collected and the army was reorganized and re-equipped, with total disregard for parliament. Its first test came within a year, when Bismarck formed a temporary alliance with Austria to prise the duchies of Schleswig and Holstein away from Denmark. It was not only the restored army that had proved itself: for organizing the defeat of the Danes, Bismarck was ennobled as a count.

Bismarck set a peerless example for all future dictators – and for Adolf Hitler in particular – showing how to exploit events in the rest of Europe by seizing every opportunity, however fortuitous. He was utterly unscrupulous in playing his opponents off against each other. He used propaganda equally ruthlessly, manipulating truth to suit his purposes, even doctoring telegrams and messages received. He reintroduced press censorship, more savagely than ever, closing down any newspaper that published reports that he considered were 'endangering the public welfare'. He banned the newly emerging socialist parties. He used secret police spies to infiltrate every stratum of society. He deliberately created grievances and 'provocations' as excuses to attack other countries. He regarded the Poles as troublemakers who should be exterminated. And he invented the notion of 'the Second Reich', to replace the Holy Roman Empire that had been dissolved by Napoleon. He saw a renewed German empire as the only way to unite the different German 'tribes', as he called them.

Bismarck disliked Berlin intensely, and never bought a home there. When a friend asked him why he never wore his spectacles when walking in the city as he did in the country, he replied that there was nothing there worth looking at. He hated the Berliners for their cheek, their irreverence, and for their sardonic wit. Berliners, he told his biographer, 'must always be in opposition and have their own ideas . . . They have their virtues – many and estimable ones – they fight well, but they would not consider themselves to be as clever as they ought to be unless they knew everything better than the government.' But above all, Bismarck hated the Berliners for their liberal or left-wing sympathies.

At first, most Berliners disliked Bismarck in return, until he won them round with an amazing display of personal courage. In May 1866, as he walked down the Linden after an audience with the king, a would-be assassin fired three pistol shots into his broad back at point-blank range. Fortuitously – or so it seemed – the pistol was so defective that none of the bullets managed to pierce his thick overcoat, or the silk-lined, padded vest he happened to be wearing. Bismarck turned, grabbed the young man by the wrist, and handed him over to a squad of guards who were marching past, before walking on, unaided, to his office.

The Berliners had always appreciated insouciance like that – even General Wrangel had become something of a folk hero after his performance outside the National Theatre. As word spread of Bismarck's coolness, a great crowd assembled in the Wilhelmstrasse to cheer their new hero. Any doubts about the genuineness of the attempt were quashed when the young man somehow managed to get hold of a razor in his cell, and cut his own throat. That, at least, was how his death was presented. In any case, he was no longer around to answer awkward questions.

The Berliners continued to cheer when Bismarck provoked a war with Austria only a few days later, over the fate of Schleswig and Holstein. And they cheered even louder when the army he had made them pay for finally ended Austria's predominance with a devastating victory over the combined armies of Austria and the lesser German states. This time, Bismarck's reward was promotion from lowly lieutenant – the rank he had reached before quitting the army as a young rebel – to major-general. The promotion was particularly important in one respect: it meant he could discard his civilian frock coat in favour of a uniform. For the rest of his life he wore only a general's Prussian blue tunic, breeches and thigh boots, with the spiked Pickelhauber helmet or a soft, peaked cap.

The Berliners cheered again four years later, when Bismarck picked a fight with the hated French and inflicted a humiliating defeat on Napoleon III's armies. At last, Prussia was in a position to absorb the remaining German states into its own new empire, which was technically a fairly loose federation of equal and consenting German states, excluding Austria. On 18 January 1871, against the background noise of Prussian guns bombarding Paris, Bismarck proclaimed Wilhelm I as German Kaiser or Emperor, not in Berlin but in Louis XIV's Hall of Mirrors in the palace of Versailles – how Friedrich I would have approved! Germany was finally united, but in true Prussian fashion, it was once again a benefit imposed on the people from above. Significantly, the constitution of the new Reich contained no bill of human rights.

Ten days later, Paris capitulated. An armistice was signed and for the second time in under 60 years, Prussian troops marched victoriously through the Arc de Triomphe and down the Champs Elysées. Now, no one could question Prussian economic, military or political supremacy, not just in Germany but in the whole of continental Europe. As his reward, Bismarck was raised to the rank of prince. He was also presented with the estate of Friedrichsruh, near Hamburg, and with the Grand Cross of the Hohenzollern

Order set in diamonds. His reaction to this was typical: 'I'd rather have had a horse or a good barrel of Rhenish wine,' he declared.

CHAPTER 9

'The fig leaf of absolutism'

BERLIN WAS AN IMPERIAL city at last, the seat of government not only for Prussia, but for the whole of Germany. So it was to Berlin that the staggering sum of five billion gold francs extracted from the French as 'war reparations' was paid. So, too, were the revenues from the provinces of Alsace and Lorraine, taken back from France, which had annexed them in 1648 and 1766 respectively.

The sudden influx of so much money, coupled with the ending of all remaining tariff barriers between the states of the new Reich, was momentous. Berlin became one huge gambling casino as new companies mushroomed and stock speculation became the order of the day. Whole industries moved there lock, stock and barrel. The new capital city quickly took over from Frankfurt-am-Main as Germany's financial capital, too. New banks appeared overnight like a sudden rash, while older institutions from western Germany or, like the Dresdner Bank, from Saxony, transferred their headquarters there.

These were Berlin's *Gründerjahre*, the boom years. And as in any boom town, there was a demand for more of life's luxuries and pleasures. Smart shops filled their windows with fine clothes and jewellery. New dance palaces sprang up; the finest was the Orpheum in Alte Jakobstrasse, with its profusion of gilt and velvet. 'Feasting restaurants' along the Linden were packed every night.

Less extravagant citizens found entertainment in music-halls and popular theatres, such as Mutter Gräbert in Weinbergsplatz, where they consumed great quantities of sandwiches, generally with ham and that peculiarly Berlin delicacy 'Schmaltz', salted lard or pork dripping. At the Konzerthaus Bilse in Leipzigerstrasse, one could eat ham sandwiches and put away gallons of beer while listening to the Leonora overture or Mendelssohn's wedding march – an apt favourite, for Bilse was known as 'the biggest and most reliable matrimonial bureau in Berlin'. And further down the scale, there were the beloved local pubs and bars, the *Weissbierstuben* and *Kneipen*, where so many Berliners sharpened their wit in jocular banter. Not surprisingly, the brewers could hardly keep up with the demand; the Schultheiss brewery was soon claiming to be the biggest in the whole of Germany.

Another popular source of entertainment for Berliners, the zoo in the south-western corner of the Tiergarten, was caught up in the general mood of growth. When it was founded in 1844 by the zoologist Martin Lichtenstein, the Berlin zoo had been the first in Germany. The gardens had been laid out by Lenné, and the first animals came from the royal menagerie on the Pfauen Insel, as a personal gift from the king. The zoo had remained a modest establishment, offering free entrance to its 84-acre (34-hectare) grounds. But in 1869 a new director had been appointed, and as the boom years took off, he eagerly set about expanding it, building elaborate new animal houses and enlarging the collection, determined to make the Berlin zoo one of the world's greatest.

It was a heady, hysterical time. Property speculation became a fever. Land prices and house rents soared. Demand for accommodation in the new middle-class apartment houses shooting up around and to the west of the Tiergarten was so great that people scrambled to pay advance rent for buildings that were not even completed. The farmers of Schöneberg became millionaires overnight by selling their potato fields to the developers, whose plans were so ambitious they would have provided a city big enough for nine million inhabitants.

But among the city's 850,000 population, over 50,000 were made homeless in the first six months of 1871 because they could no longer pay their rents. The city's refuges and dosshouses became so crowded they had to be shut down. One of the results was the unique custom of *Schlafburschen*, 'sleep-ins': either out of compassion or because they needed the extra money to help pay the rent, families with an apartment would let some homeless wretch spend his nights in a corner for a few marks. The practice continued in Berlin for several decades. Other families solved their accommodation problem by sharing their apartments on a shift basis: one family worked during the night, the other during the day, taking turn and turn about in the same beds.

Those with an apartment to share were the lucky ones. Outside the city gates thousands bedded down in old, upturned boats, under railway arches, in board shacks, in holes in the ground. Several families were even found sleeping under the locomotive turntable in the rail marshalling yards. When firemen were sent in to break up and clear the shanty towns, in the interests of public safety, there was trouble. During two days of rioting in July 1872, 159 people were cut down by police sabres; 37 of the wounded survivors were arrested and sentenced to long terms of imprisonment when they recovered.

The bubble burst in 1873 in a stock market crash that left thousands penniless. Many building developments were abandoned or delayed – the construction of Kaiserallee, for instance (today's Bundesallee, just south of the zoo), was held up for 25 years. But some people, as always, benefited from the crash. Among them was the British Foreign Office, which took advantage of the property slump to pay an absurdly low price for a brand-new mansion, number 70 Wilhelmstrasse, to house the embassy. Conveniently close to the German Foreign Office, which occupied numbers 74–76, it was a fine building, with a wide and dignified frontage on to the Wilhelmstrasse and a large rear garden. It had just been completed for the railway magnate Bethel Henry Strousberg, who had gone spectacularly bankrupt.

Almost inevitably, there were many who blamed Berlin's Jews for the crash, since they were so prominent in banking and finance. A new political party, the Christian Socialist Workers Party, was formed on an anti-Semitic platform by a rabble-rousing Protestant minister named Adolf Stöcker. The son of a former army sergeant who ended up as warden of a prison, Stöcker also happened to be the court chaplain, so his was a voice that one could not dismiss. His creed was simple, and had an eerily prophetic ring to it, declaring that liberalism, the stock market, usury, and all forms of economic speculation, not to mention socialism, were Jewish inventions and therefore of the devil.

Stöcker was not alone: some distinguished figures, such as Heinrich von Treitschke, professor of history at Berlin University and editor of the Prussian Year Book, shared his views. Treitschke argued that the problem would only cease to exist if Jews could become assimilated into real German life, becoming true Germans. Moses Mendelssohn had advocated precisely this, many years before, but Treitschke declared that such assimilation was impossible for 'Asiatics'. Stöcker was ahead of his time – when he stood for election in Berlin, he received a mere 380 votes.

Gradually, Berlin regained its confidence. Financial stability was restored as the empire adopted the gold standard and established a single coinage and currency. More and more imperial institutions were set up, all with their headquarters in the city, including the new Reichsbank. More solid industries began to take root alongside existing giants like Borsig and Siemens, firms such as the German Edison Company founded in 1883 by Emil Rathenau, which after four years merged with others into AEG, the German General Electric Company, to become one of Europe's most important manufacturers.

The pharmaceutical industry, drawing on the work of scientists at the university, emerged from private laboratories and apothecaries' shops to assume a dominant position in Germany. The massive Schering concern, for example, began as a small shop, the Grüne Apotheke, started by Ernst Schering in 1852; it became a world-class business with the development and production of drugs including chloroform and cocaine, and synthetics which removed the need for expensive imports of raw materials.

Alongside pharmaceuticals, the budding chemical industry, which for so long had been tied to the military, grew rapidly to become another of the enduring mainstays of the Berlin economy. Again, the industry's expansion was based on the development by Berlin scientists of synthetic substances: in this case the most important were aniline dyes. The company formed to manufacture them was called Aktiengesellschaft für Anilinfabrikation – AGFA for short.

AGFA was one of six companies which later merged into the famous trust, I.G. Farben, to monopolize the German dye industry. Trusts and cartels formed the backbone of German industry in almost every sphere, controlling the market, fixing their own prices and profit levels. In 1875, there had been some eight cartels in the new German Reich. Ten years later there were 90. By 1905 there were 366, and the number was rising ever more rapidly. By the end of the First World War the number had risen to over 3,000.

Unlike other countries, where such restraint of trade was either illegal or at least frowned upon, Germany actively encouraged cartels and gave them legal protection. It was an approach that was typical of Prussia, with its long traditions of state interference and control. Both government and people saw cartels as a rational way of eliminating wasteful competition, and imposing order on the distasteful chaos of the free market. Kaisers and governments liked them because their very size enhanced German prestige. Capitalists liked them because of the huge profits they could make. Even German socialists liked them, seeing them as examples of the benefits of economic planning. And so they flourished.

A large proportion of the dyes produced by AGFA were used in the city itself. In the early years of the nineteenth century, the textile mills had begun moving out of Berlin to cheaper towns like Cottbus, further up the Spree some 70 miles to the south-east, and Brandenburg, on the Havel about 40 miles south-west. But the cloth they wove came right back to the city, to be made up in the sweat shops which had sprung up everywhere. There, life was hard: the life expectancy of women workers was 26. If they survived to the age of 30, they were old women. But it was thanks to them that Berlin became the centre of the garment industry for the whole of the new German empire, and its undisputed fashion capital.

Berlin had become a large and complex city, advancing rapidly towards the twentieth century. Yet, thanks partly to Bismarck, all effective power was still held by the Kaiser and his Prussian court –

a mere 1,000 persons in a population fast approaching two million. Although many of the daughters of bourgeois millionaires were marrying into the aristocracy, Berlin's neo-feudal society was as rigidly structured as ever; there were no fewer than 50 officially recognized gradations on the social scale, and the uniform still reigned supreme. Politically, the city was still in the dark ages. Even wreaths commemorating the 'March dead' of the 1848 rising were censored by a police official waiting at the cemetery gates with a pair of scissors to snip offending words from the ribbons.

The city was allowed to become a separate administrative district in 1881, but it was not granted autonomy. Its mayor still had to be personally confirmed by the Prussian king, who was now, of course, the German Kaiser. Although it had become the imperial capital of the Second Reich, state and national governments both interfered in its affairs. In the end Berlin was still subject to the autocratic whim of one man.

In the new constitution for the Reich, Bismarck had taken care to make sure that it was impossible for Prussia to be outvoted in the upper house, the Bundesrat, whose members were not elected but appointed by the rulers of their states. The Reichstag, which was elected by universal male suffrage, was little more than a talking shop. Bismarck saw it as a safety valve for the lower orders, though in fact no fewer than 147 of its 357 deputies were from aristocratic families. It was as powerless as the Prussian lower house, for which the old three-class franchise remained unchanged; the labour leader Wilhelm Liebknecht dubbed it 'the fig leaf of absolutism'.

The various ministries that had to be created to cope with the ever-increasing complexities of running the empire were treated as departments of the chancellery. Bismarck would not allow their state secretaries to become responsible ministers, but treated them like chief clerks, answerable to him. He, of course, was not answerable to the Reichstag or the Bundesrat, but directly and only to the Kaiser, who had appointed him. And since he bullied the Kaiser mercilessly, Bismarck was absolute ruler of Germany in all but name.

The personal relationship between Bismarck and Kaiser Wilhelm I was always stormy. Both men were emotional and highly excitable, shouting and throwing things at each other during arguments. On one famous occasion, Bismarck left in such a temper that he tore the handle off the door. But the chancellor always got his way

111

in the end. And if the Reichstag became troublesome, as it did in 1878 when it refused to approve strict new censorship controls and threw out his bill to ban the infant socialist parties, he simply asked the Kaiser to dissolve it.

Setting another precedent that would be repeated in future years, Bismarck publicly (and entirely falsely) blamed the socialists for two assassination attempts on the emperor that year, and the liberals for failing to protect him. He then called new national elections. Berlin, as always, voted overwhelmingly for the left, but the rest of the country returned a right-wing majority that was happy to carry out Bismarck's wishes. Knowing that if they refused he would simply dissolve the Reichstag again, they passed his anti-socialist bill, banning all socialist associations, meetings and publications. The police were given sweeping new powers and went to work with gusto. Thousands of Berlin's social democrat supporters were seized and imprisoned or deported without trial, often without being given any chance to provide for their families.

Having, as he thought, destroyed the socialist and liberal parties, Bismarck tried to keep the workers quiet by stealing his opponents' clothes, creating a social welfare system unprecedented in any other country of the world. The most striking of his innovations – once again imposed on the people from above – were free medical treatment, death benefits, guaranteed old-age pensions, and injury and sickness insurance. As always, there was a military element involved; among the reasons behind the welfare provisions were complaints from the army that a growing number of conscripts, especially from industrial areas, were unfit for military service.

The workers, of course, were not fooled. Both socialists and liberals saw Bismarck's paternalistic measures as simply another step in strengthening the power of the state. In fact, Bismarck's actions achieved the otherwise impossible task of uniting the forces of the left, bringing together all the factions that normally spent most of their energies bickering and fighting with each other.

To counter this potentially dangerous situation, Bismarck tightened his authoritarian rule. In particular, he imposed even stricter censorship on newspapers. Some brave souls, however, continued the fight for freedom. They were led by Berlin's latest press magnate, Leopold Ullstein, a Jewish merchant who bought two newspapers, including the *Berliner Zeitung* in 1877, to found what was to become the biggest publishing company in Europe. Ullstein, who introduced political cartoons into German newspapers for the first time, announced his policy line in a memorable editorial: 'The *Berliner Zeitung* calls for constitutional government – no chancellor absolutism! It demands that the German people be set free and that they should no longer be treated like a conquered nation!'

Ullstein editors, like their colleagues on other papers, were constantly being brought to trial for reporting the truth as they saw it. On one occasion, no fewer than nine Berlin editors were tried simultaneously and sent to prison for telling how police had beaten up unemployed workers with rubber hoses. Soldiers in the guards regiments were forbidden from reading liberal newspapers, particularly the *Berliner Zeitung*.

In November 1881, Jules Laforgue, a young French poet whose work was later to inspire T.S. Eliot and Ezra Pound, moved into the Prinzessin Palais – what is now the Opern Palais – opposite the armoury on the Linden. He was employed to read French and Belgian newspapers and magazines to the 70-year-old Empress Augusta, selecting and censoring the news so that the old lady's ears should be preserved from scandal or liberal ideas. The 21-year-old Frenchman had a good, if quirky, eye for the passing scene, and has left us a sharp picture of Berlin life in the early 1880s.

Laforgue noticed odd things that less talented writers might have missed, such as the absence of babies in the street – there were no perambulators; the fact that Berlin nursemaids were not young and pretty, as they were in Paris, but old and 'downright grotesque'; the number of small carts pulled by large dogs, and the fact that all Berlin's dogs had to wear muzzles. One thing he couldn't miss, of course, was the ubiquitous presence of the army, and the way anyone in uniform automatically had precedence over any civilian. He saw a porter carrying a tower of boxes on his head forced to step off the pavement to make way for an army sergeant. He missed the kind of street activities he was so familiar with in Paris: there were no knife grinders, no itinerant glaziers, no men offering to recane chairs, no street cries. And in summer, there was an extreme parsimony with water: there were no watercarts sprinkling the streets, so the dust got into everything. He did, however, notice that there was a singular lack of graffiti on Berlin's walls.

Berlin working girls, Laforgue complained, were less attractive than their Parisian counterparts – their figures were good, but they had red noses, thick ankles and huge feet. In fact, he seemed rather obsessed by German feet, which he said were the size, shape and colour of giant black puddings.

As a good Frenchman, Laforgue was appalled by Berlin restaurants and couldn't find a good word to say about them. He noted that whenever a Berliner entered a restaurant, whether he was an army officer or a civilian, he immediately produced two small brushes from his pockets and brushed his hair, letting loose hairs and dandruff fall where they might. And table manners were frightful: people shovelled food into their mouths with their knives – it was a wonder they didn't cut their lips – and only used forks for pâtés and mustard. They smoked everywhere and at every time, scattering ash freely on the baskets of bread rolls and toothpicks. He preferred eating out at night, he said, because then at least he couldn't see the stains on the waiters' jackets. And he could never get used to waiters leaving dirty plates on the tables until they had taken a new customer's order.

Laforgue was also shocked by the Berlin habit of serving food anywhere and everywhere. In theatres, apart from the two royal theatres, and café concerts, there were always running buffets, where one could enjoy little slices of bread laden with caviare or smoked tongue or lobster or Gruyère cheese or whatever. At a Berlin Philharmonic concert, one could drink beer and be offered such delicacies as partridge fricassee. Even in the National Gallery, there were posters hanging alongside pictures, advertising what the café or restaurant was serving that day.

Although Laforgue was amazed at the number of shops in Berlin, particularly along Leipzigerstrasse and Friedrichstrasse, he was not impressed by their window displays, which could never compare with those in his native Paris. Windows were crammed with goods, he commented, with everything piled higgledy-piggledy and little effort to achieve an attractive display. He considered that only Berlin florists showed any sense of style or imagination, though they all tended to have the same centre-piece, a huge lyre of flowers. But in Laforgue's eyes the most extraordinary displays of all were in shops selling coffins. In wealthy districts like Charlottenburg, there were expensive metal caskets and catafalques draped in crepe, along with ornate cremation urns. In working-class areas like

Wedding, the coffins were piled up on the pavements outside the shops, with signs advertising: 'Huge Range of Coffins at Factory Prices.'

Although intellectuals and artists came low in the pecking order at court (none ranked higher than forty-seventh in the 50 recognized social grades) one man somehow managed to overcome the Prussian prejudice. The painter Adolf Menzel was a most unlikely figure, a true original who became a Berlin institution in his own right. Almost a dwarf (Laforgue, who met him at a court gala, described him as being 'knee-high to a cuirassier's boot'), Menzel was born in Breslau, the son of a lithographer, and came to Berlin at the age of 15 in 1830. His big chance came nine years later, when he produced no fewer than 400 illustrations for a book on the works of Friedrich the Great. These established his reputation not only in Berlin but also abroad: Degas later much admired his skill. At about the same time, he first saw some paintings by John Constable and became fascinated by the fluidity of his technique. Largely self-taught, and under the influence of the English master, Menzel became an impressionist almost by accident, 25 years before Manet, Monet and the other French painters began forming their new school. As early as the 1840s, he was producing works of astonishing modernity: interiors, landscapes and even portraits. Some of his grittily realistic early pictures show Berlin's industries in all their dirt and grime. And his 'Houses in the Snow', a cityscape often reproduced in art books, is by any standards a *tour de force* for the time in which it was painted.

As he grew older, however, Menzel, like a reformed rake, seemed to forget the paintings of his youth. When a Jewish collector showed him some paintings which he had bought in Paris, including works by Manet, Monet and Degas, he was appalled. 'Have you really paid money for this trash?' he demanded. Whether through ambition or a fascination with things Prussian or simply because he wished to enlarge his range, he turned his attention more and more to 'official' subjects, painting grand historical scenes and pieces of Friedrichian myth. 'The Flute Concerto', another much reproduced Menzel painting, shows Friedrich the Great playing the flute, accompanied by a small group of musicians, in the candle-lit music room at Sans Souci.

Not surprisingly, such paintings established Menzel's reputation at court. Soon, no official court function was complete without the presence of the tiny painter. He was seen everywhere, bedizened with orders and decorations, glittering like a Christmas tree, busily dashing hither and yon to greet anyone with an impressive title. He was rewarded for his efforts by being appointed professor at the Prussian Academy of Art, and finally honoured with the title 'Excellenz'. When he died at the age of 90, in 1905, he was given a state funeral, and the Kaiser walked in procession behind his bier. It was a scene Menzel himself would have loved to have painted.

1888 was 'three-Kaiser year' in Berlin. For a long time, it had seemed that old Wilhelm I was immortal: he just went on and on. Meanwhile, Crown Prince Friedrich had developed a worrying throat problem, which proved to be a growth on the larynx. His doctors decided to burn it away, using a red-hot platinum wire. Every day, they inserted the glowing wire into his larynx and burned away a little more, ignoring the fact that they were unable to give their patient an adequate local anaesthetic. Friedrich suffered two months of agony, before they reported that the growth had gone, and that it had not been cancerous. A month later, it was back, and there could be no doubt that it was a cancer after all.

In March, in the midst of this anguish, came the news that Wilhelm I had died at last, at the age of 91. But it was all too late: Friedrich III was a dying man himself when he ascended the throne, and altogether too ill to push through any of the liberal policies with which he and his wife had dreamed of transforming Germany. Indeed, he could barely get through the few official functions he was forced to attend. Desperately, Vicky tried to keep him alive. However much she may have loved him – and there is no doubt that theirs was a true love-match – she could see their chances of wielding real political power together ebbing away with her husband's life. Right up to the end, she insisted that Friedrich was 'merely ill', and not dying from cancer.

Standing ready in the wings was their son, who became Wilhelm II on his father's death, and who longed to be another soldier king. His first act was entirely in character: while his father's body was still warm, he had his palace surrounded by a regiment of hussars carrying rifles, imprisoning his mother while his agents searched

Friedrich's rooms. They were hunting for state documents and evidence of liberal plots. They found none. Vicky had wisely taken the precaution of having her husband's private papers shipped to England in the British diplomatic bag a few days earlier – a move that did nothing to lessen Wilhelm's hatred and distrust of her and his dead father.

Wilhelm II, the last of the Hohenzollern dynasty, was a cripple both physically and psychologically. He had almost died during a difficult birth, a breech presentation in which the child had to be dragged manually into the world. In the process, he was badly mauled. His neck was injured, tilting his head to the left and severely damaging the nerves controlling his left arm. The arm and hand were paralysed and useless, their growth stunted. His left ear was also damaged, causing not only deafness but also, as he grew older, an impaired sense of balance – a serious handicap which, for example, made it almost impossible for him to mount a horse without immediately falling off again on the other side.

As he grew up, his mother, who herself had nearly died giving birth to him, found it more and more difficult to come to terms with his injuries. She agreed to a series of brutal measures to deal with them. The young prince put up manfully with the barbarism inflicted on him by his doctors and tutors throughout his childhood. He eventually succeeded in overcoming most of his handicaps, including the worst, his inability to sit a horse, and learned to conceal the rest. Emotionally rejected by both parents, he in turn blamed them, particularly his mother, for all that happened to him.

Seeking the affection he so desperately needed, Wilhelm worshipped his grandfather, who took care to see that he was imbued with the traditional Hohenzollern arrogance. But his deepest love was reserved for his maternal grandmother, Queen Victoria, whom he visited often. In his youth, therefore, he was torn between the opposing royal traditions of Prussian absolutism and English liberalism. But it was clear which he would choose to follow.

For all his problems, it would be a mistake to assume that Wilhelm had an entirely unhappy childhood, that he was a shy, withdrawn child, hating his parents. Poultney Bigelow, the son of a US diplomat, formed a quite different picture of the future Kaiser. Bigelow played with Wilhelm as a boy at the Neue Palais, which Princess Vicky thought the finest place to bring up children after Osborne, where she had spent her happiest years. 'The New Palace as a playground for us boys was unequalled,' wrote Bigelow, 'at least on rainy days. There was an immense attic running the whole length of the palace roof, and here . . . we kicked a football about until the broken panes of glass attracted Dr Hinzpeter's attention.' Hinzpeter was the prince's tutor, a stern disciplinarian, but clearly he was not constantly on the scene. Potsdam, recalled Bigelow, was 'a wilderness of palaces, barracks, fountains, temples, esplanades', an ideal adventure playground for boys. He remembered, too, nursery teas – 'milk and nursery cake and stewed fruit' – with Wilhelm and his brothers and sisters and their parents. What went wrong with Wilhelm, suggested Bigelow, was that the Prussian military got hold of him and moulded him in their image.

Although he had a quick brain, and spent a few months each at the universities of Bonn and Berlin, the most important part of Wilhelm's education came when he joined the first regiment of the guards in Potsdam. In fact, he learned very little about real soldiering, or about military science. What he did learn was the '*Potsdamer Ton*', the peculiar accent and tone of voice of the elite officer corps, a loud, grating, high-pitched nasal bark, in which grammar and vowel sounds were mangled together in an exaggerated version of the Brandenburg-Berlin accent. Liberally spattered with coarse epithets, it marked its users unmistakably as men accustomed to command. In a modified version, it spread throughout the rest of the German army, and into the civil service, the police, even into schools, to become the hallmark of the ruling classes, and of all who aspired to authority.

On his accession, the new Kaiser expected above all things to be obeyed without question. He made this plain to new guards recruits at their swearing-in ceremony: 'You have surrendered yourselves body and soul to me,' he barked. 'There is only one enemy for you, and that is my enemy. The socialist unrest of today could lead to my giving you an order to shoot down your own relatives, brothers – yes, even your parents, may God prevent it! – but, even then, you must obey my command without hesitation!'

Such a man, determined to rule his people himself, was clearly incompatible with Bismarck. One of them had to go, and there could be no doubt which it would be. Wilhelm's opportunity came in 1890, when Bismarck tried to revive an old Prussian cabinet order of 1852, under which ministers were only allowed to communicate with the king through the chancellor. Wilhelm, understandably, objected to such a blatant restriction of his personal authority. After almost 30 years in the saddle, the old chancellor was forced to resign. He left Berlin on 29 March 1890 from the Lehrter railway station, seen off with what he himself described as 'a first-class funeral'. A squadron of hussars lined the platform, a military band played, and ministers, ambassadors, generals and thousands of admirers cheered and sang *Die Wacht am Rhein* (*The Watch on the Rhine*) as the train steamed out.

In Bismarck's place, Wilhelm appointed General Count Leo von Caprivi. It was an astute choice. Bismarck had recommended Caprivi for the post of minister-president, believing him to be a strong man who would stand no nonsense from liberals and socialists and the like; as a general he commanded automatic authority; and as an army officer, he would be obliged to carry out his supreme commander's orders without question.

Caprivi, with his ramrod-straight back, ruddy face and moustache like a pair of white buffalo horns, lasted four years in the post. Surprisingly, he did have ideas and policies of his own. He started by dealing successfully with the liberals and socialists through conciliation rather than confrontation. He introduced a progressive income tax for the first time, and extended the social welfare system with new acts that banned Sunday work and the employment of children under 13, limited women's working hours to eleven a day and youths under 16 to ten, and set up industrial arbitration courts with representatives from both employers and workers.

Then, declaring 'Germany must either export people or goods', he set out to increase trade and reduce the flow of emigrants by lowering international tariff barriers. Berlin's manufacturers and merchants naturally welcomed these measures, which helped to establish Germany as the leading industrial nation in Europe by 1900. But the aristocracy, whose income as landowners was damaged by imports of cheap grain, mounted a vicious campaign against Caprivi, which the Kaiser was eventually forced to heed. In an interview lasting precisely one minute, Wilhelm told him: 'My nerves cannot stand it any longer. I must dismiss you.'

Caprivi was followed by a 75-year-old nonentity from Bavaria, Prince Chodwig zu Hohenloe Schillingfürst, a frail, bent old man who had neither a mind nor money of his own and was therefore entirely dependent upon the Kaiser. It took him six years of inactivity and two serious heart attacks within a month before he could summon up the courage to beg permission to resign. During that time the government was calamitously run by bureaucrats and officials. The worst of them all was probably the permanent head of the political department in the foreign ministry, Baron Friedrich von Holstein, a vindictive and pathologically suspicious figure with hard, mistrustful eyes above a white spade beard, who shut himself in his room in the Wilhelmstrasse and refused to speak to anyone, even the Kaiser himself. Some officials called him 'the grey eminence'; others knew him as 'the monster in the labyrinth'. Until 1906, when he finally fell foul of the sort of conspiracy he had always feared, Holstein's dicta on foreign policy were treated as holy writ. The results were catastrophic for Germany's international relations.

Holstein's blunders were compounded by Prince Bernhard von Bülow, an archetypical aristocrat with an unrivalled gift for sycophancy. When he was appointed state secretary for foreign affairs in 1897, he gave his impressions of the Kaiser to his mentor, Prince Philip von Eulenburg, who was Wilhelm's closest friend: 'He is so distinguished! Of all the great kings and princes, he is by far the most significant Hohenzollern who has ever lived. He combines in a manner such as I have never known before, geniality, the truest and most profound geniality, with the clearest good sense. He possesses an imagination that raises me on eagle's wings above all the pettiness and thereby gives me the clearest appreciation of what is possible and realizable. And, added to that, what energy! What a memory! What swiftness and certainty of viewpoint! Today at the privy council I was simply overwhelmed!'

Bülow, not surprisingly, was Wilhelm's favourite chancellor, his Bismarck, as he called him. Replacing Hohenloe in 1900, Bülow remained in office for nine fateful years, feeding the Kaiser's insatiable hunger for glory. Encouraged by such advisers, Wilhelm ineptly tried to emulate his more successful Hohenzollern ancestors, whose aggression had marched Prussia from sandy backwater to major world power. His imperialist ambitions made Berlin the focus of the world's fear and distrust. Its name became a byword for bombast and unbridled militarism.

CHAPTER 10

'Even the bird shit is made out of marble'

EMIL RATHENAU, THE FOUNDER of AEG, was a Jew, like many of the new breed of entrepreneurs who flourished in the new business climate of the time. In 1871 there had been 47,489 Jews living in Berlin, many of them the descendants of the original families imported by the Great Elector 200 years before. Between 1871 and 1910, however, the Jewish population increased nearly fourfold, raising it to nearly 10 per cent of the population of the city. For generations, Jews had played an important role in the intellectual, cultural and economic life of the city. Now, they were a significant part of the city's ethnic mix, too.

Yet Berlin was never a Jewish city in the sense that Vienna was. Where almost everyone was an incomer, what did it matter if a person was Jewish? The important thing was that he or she was a Berliner. Indeed, one of the great complaints of orthodox Jews was that their fellow Jewish citizens kept marrying out of the faith. Soon, some of them complained, there would be no genuine Jews left in the city.

The Jews who came to Berlin were only part of the great flow of incomers. Freedom of movement within the new Reich diverted yet more Germans from other parts of the country who would otherwise have emigrated to America: moving to Berlin was as good as moving to New York or Chicago, and a great deal simpler. Before the end of the Seventies, the population passed the million mark, of whom some 70,000 had no permanent homes but only lodgings by the night. Yet still the immigrants flooded in. By 1900 the city itself had nearly two million inhabitants, with another 750,000 in the immediate suburbs.

With typically black pride the Berliners boasted of having the worst industrial slums in all Europe. The Mietskasernen marched steadily outwards from the central districts, though some of the larger and more enlightened industrialists, led by Siemens and Borsig, began moving their factories out into greenfield sites to the north of the city – where land was cheaper – and building model suburbs around them for their employees.

Many university professors and high-ranking bureaucrats still lived in villas or apartment houses in 'Der alte Westen', the old west end around the Tiergarten. A few of the more old-fashioned millionaires also stayed on in the quarter, happy to cling to the gentler, less frantic atmosphere of the Biedermeier years. But the majority of the middle classes hurried to settle in the new western and southwestern districts which were then engulfing the old villages of Charlottenburg, Wilmersdorf and Schöneberg. The richest and most successful of them took apartments in the new buildings lining the old Kurfürstendamm, which until 1890 was still an open road where army officers exercised their horses each morning between the Tiergarten and the Grunewald.

Bismarck had declared that Berlin ought to have an avenue like the Champs Elysées, connecting the Tiergarten with the Grunewald, just as the centre of Paris was joined to the Bois de Boulogne. He and his contemporaries seem to have overlooked the fact that Berlin already had its own grand avenue in the Unter den Linden, which could hold its own with any foreign thoroughfare, and which, along with the Wilhelmstrasse, managed to keep its restrained Prussian dignity. The Kurfürstendamm never achieved the scale of the Champs Elysées. It was only half the width and lacked the grand vistas of the Place de la Concorde and the Etoile. And the mock gothic Kaiser Wilhelm Memorial Church, built in 1891 as a focal point for the city's new west end, could hardly compare with the Arc de Triomphe. Its ruins at the start of the Kurfürstendamm have been a landmark since the end of the Second World War – one of the few buildings in Berlin that were actually improved by the bombing.

In spite of its shortcomings, the Ku'damm developed its own individual style and elegance. But by the end of the century it was already being overtaken as Berlin's most fashionable address: wealthy aristocrats and bourgeoisie alike were building their villas in and around the Grunewald forest and on the shores of the Wansee and the Havel.

Official Berlin, of course, more than kept pace with the private sector, giving the city dozens of new landmarks, all of which fitted the Berliners' favourite word at that time: 'kolossal!'. The first of the new era, appropriately enough, was a 'kolossal' victory column, the Siegessäule, clearly based on the July monument in Paris's Place de la Bastille, which was erected in Königplatz to celebrate the defeat of France. (Hitler later had it moved to the Grosse Stern in the Tiergarten, where it still stands today.) The irreverent Berliners, of course, invented their own names for the column: the 'Siegesspargel' (victory asparagus), or the 'Siegesschornstein' (victory chimney), while the winged goddess became 'Siegestante' (victory auntie), 'the most respectable woman in Berlin, because she has no lovers'.

Behind the Siegessäule in Königplatz, an even more colossal headquarters was built for the enlarged general staff of the army, one of many new government departments and ministries needed by the new Reich, though for his own official residence the chancellor took over the old palace of the Schulenburg family next door to the new foreign office in Wilhelmstrasse.

Other new public buildings included an impressive stone-faced general post office on the corner of Mauerstrasse and Leipzigerstrasse, countless barracks for the ever-increasing garrison, an officer cadet establishment at Lichterfelde, and, more ominously, a big modern prison complex at Plötzensee. The purpose of the Plötze, as it soon became known, was made quite clear: it was built, Wilhelm II declared, as a precaution 'in case the city of Berlin should ever break down and rise once more in impudent intemperance against its sovereign'. As though to prove how little had changed, it was to become Hitler's main execution centre for those who plotted against him during the Second World War.

But the most notable of all the new buildings was the Reichstag, erected on Königplatz, near the new general staff building and the Siegessäule. It was a monumental stone edifice, its roof-line abundant with statuary, a heavy square turret at each corner, a neo-baroque squared dome at its centre, and an imposing pediment supported by six Corinthian columns framing the entrance. Neither Bismarck nor Wilhelm I was particularly keen on the idea of a special building for the Reichstag; they were quite happy for the deputies to go on meeting in the old state porcelain factory, and the foundation stone was not even laid until 1884. In fact, Bismarck would have liked to move the Reichstag out of Berlin altogether, to Potsdam, where it might be less dominated by the Berlin representatives who were naturally always present.

The third-biggest building in Berlin, after the Reichstag and the rambling old royal palace, was a new police headquarters, built at a cost of 5.5 million marks. It opened on 1 October 1889 on the Alexanderplatz, a more convenient site than the old HQ at number 1 Molkenmarkt, which had housed the police since 1849. The hard core of the city's criminals lived around the Alex, and it was handy for the workers' districts in the east and north-east, where civil disturbances were most likely. With a street frontage of 540 yards (494 metres) and a usable floor area of 114,000 square feet (10,590 square metres), it was big enough to serve the Berlin police's needs right through to May 1945. Until then, every Berliner who needed a permit for just about anything, from a passport to a trading licence, had to visit the vast, four-storey brick building that dominated the Alexanderplatz.

The Reichstag building was finished five years later, the same year that work started on a new Protestant cathedral, the Dom, in place of Friedrich the Great's building on the Lustgarten. The new Dom was another heavy, neo-baroque building topped by a bigger and more ornate dome than 'old Fritz's teacup', which it replaced. In 1898, work started on the Kaiser Friedrich Museum – which was to sport yet another, slightly less ornate, dome – on 'Museum Island', the northern tip of Cölln island. Now renamed the Bode Museum, after Wilhelm von Bode, director-general of the royal museums from 1906 until 1920, who was largely responsible for its creation, it was a model of what a good museum should be, particularly in lighting and layout.

The mad Friedrich Wilhelm IV had designated the marshy wedge of land behind Schinkel's original museum building as the site for 'a sanctuary of art and learning', and the classical New Museum and the National Gallery had already been completed there. Friedrich Wilhelm's scheme was finally completed with the construction of the splendid Pergamon Museum between 1912 and 1930, by which time this small area of Berlin housed an unparalleled accumulation of treasures, enhancing the city's claim to be the Athens of the north, as well as its Sparta.

The passion for museums, and for archeology, ethnography and art, which swept Berlin in the last quarter of the nineteenth century was part of the rush for world status, and the quest for colonies. It was in part an expression of Germany's need for a capital that could compete with the older imperial centres of London and Paris. But it was also the result of the labours of a number of remarkable German archaeologists working in the Middle East, particularly in Egypt, Mesopotamia, Assyria and Greece, often alongside military missions gathering intelligence.

The best-known of them all was Heinrich Schliemann, who first located the ruins of Troy in 1871, and two years later uncovered the fabulous treasure of King Priam: 'Gold beakers weighing pounds, huge silver jugs, golden diadems, bracelets, necklaces made from thousands of small plates joined together,' he wrote excitedly. He photographed his Greek wife, Sophia, as a Trojan princess wearing the incredible jewellery, then sent the whole treasure to Berlin, 'to be kept safely together in perpetuity'. But Schliemann's treasures from ancient Troy were only a small part of the incredible range of antiquities and great works of art that found their way to the Berlin museums at the end of the nineteenth century and in the early years of the twentieth. They include enormous pieces of architecture like the Ishtar gate from Babylon and the amazing Pergamon altar, small individual items like the famous painted bust of the Egyptian Queen Nefertiti, and superb paintings including the powerful *Man in a Golden Helmet*, attributed to Rembrandt.

The great expansion of Berlin's museums and treasures had been masterminded by Crown Prince Friedrich until he ascended the throne in 1888: he had been given the task by his father, no doubt at Bismarck's suggestion, to keep him occupied and out of mischief.

Although Wilhelm's motives may have been cynical, the appointment of Friedrich was an inspiration. It provided the ideal outlet for his tastes and energies, and – equally important – for those of Princess Vicky, who was thus able to follow the example of her father, Prince Albert, in Britain. Friedrich may not have had the chance to establish his more liberal ideas as Kaiser, but at least in the superb museums of Berlin, he was able to leave an appropriate legacy to the city and the nation. It was largely as a result of his patronage and direction that Berlin was able to take its place as one of the world's great centres for the study of archeology and ancient history.

Most of Berlin's new buildings towards the end of the nineteenth century, whether rental barracks, expensive apartments, luxury villas, or public institutions, showed a significant change of style from previous times. The old Berlin of Langhans, Schlüter and Schinkel had been provincial but handsome. The new metropolis that swarmed around its remains was worldly but ugly. Traditional Prussian restraint was replaced by a brash exuberance that was deliberately ostentatious; critics called it 'Reich braggadocio'. Most of its new public buildings were bombastic and overblown. Its stuccoed apartment blocks were badly proportioned and festooned with heavy-handed decoration, every doorway and balcony supported by muscular caryatids or straining Atlases. In the leafy suburbs around the Grunewald, many of the rich men's villas were mock baronial, mock renaissance, or imitation mediaeval.

The age of architectural kitsch had arrived in Berlin. It reached its epitome with the new Siegesallee, the Victory Way, in the Tiergarten. Conceived by Wilhelm II on his thirty-sixth birthday in January 1895 and completed in 1901, this was a promenade flanked by 32 marble statues of incredible banality, representing a selection of Wilhelm's Hohenzollern ancestors, carved by his favourite sculptor, Rheinhold Begas. Berliners, naturally, were not over-impressed; with their usual perverse pride they claimed Begas as the worst sculptor in the world. The artist Max Liebermann blamed the Kaiser for forcing him to wear dark glasses for the rest of his life, so that he would not have to see it. A typical Berlin cartoon of the time shows an out-of-town couple regarding the statues with awe. 'My, how beautiful everything is here!' the man declares. 'Even the bird shit is made of marble!'

But for all their lack of taste, the buildings and monuments of the Wilhelmine era still evoke the energy and confidence of the new imperial city. And to be fair, they were very much of their time, and had many admirers. In 1860, an American visitor, Henry Adams, had described the city as 'a poor, keen-witted provincial town, simple, dirty, uncivilized, and in most respects disgusting'. But a little over 30 years later, Mark Twain saw something very different.

'It is a new city,' Twain wrote, 'the newest I have ever seen. Chicago would seem venerable beside it . . . The next factor that strikes one is the spaciousness, the roominess of the city. There is no other city, in any country, whose streets are so generally wide . . . Only parts of Chicago are stately and beautiful, whereas all of Berlin is stately and substantial, and it is not merely in parts but uniformly beautiful.'

One man who did not share Twain's enthusiasm was Wilhelm II, who spent as little time in the city as possible. He averaged about 200 days a year travelling abroad and to various parts of the Reich in his luxurious special train. The Berliners, ready as always with a nickname, called him 'the Reise-Kaiser', 'the travelling Kaiser'. Wilhelm was highly amused, but kept right on moving. He was in Trondheim in Norway in 1892 when Caprivi tried to persuade him to sanction a world's fair in Berlin four years later, to mark the twenty-fifth anniversary of the Second Reich. He dismissed the idea with total disdain.

'The glory of the Parisians robs the Berliners of their sleep. Berlin is a great city, a world city (perhaps?), consequently it has to have an exhibition,' he wrote sarcastically. But, he went on, Berlin was not Paris: 'Paris is the great whorehouse of the world; therein lies its attraction independent of any exhibition. There is nothing in Berlin that can captivate the foreigner, except a few museums, castles, and soldiers. After six days, red book in hand, he has seen everything, and he departs *relieved*, feeling that he has done his duty. The Berliner does not see these things clearly, and he would be very upset if he were told about them.'

The Berlin world's fair never took place. An exhibition was held in Teltow in 1896, and was highly successful, but although it was on a grand scale it remained an industrial trade fair. Nevertheless, it did demonstrate to the world what Germany had achieved in such a short time, and it did undoubtedly establish Berlin as the world city its people so desperately wanted it to be.

Transport and public services in Twain's newest of cities grew as quickly as the suburbs. At the time of unification, Berlin had 36 horse-drawn bus lines, 2,200 hackney cabs, and a partially completed elevated ring railway connecting the various main-line rail terminals, much of it built along the line of the last city walls and moat. But the city still had no sewerage system: that was not started until 1873. The telephone arrived in 1881, starting with 200 subscribers, along with the world's first electric street cars, designed and built by Siemens. The first lines of the Stadtbahn, the elevated metropolitan railway, opened the following year. The first public power station went into operation in 1885, and electrification of the mass transit system began in the Nineties. In 1902, Berlin opened its first underground railway line, 39 years after London but two years ahead of New York City.

Berlin came into its own in the last quarter of the nineteenth century. And Berliners, too, blossomed in the luxury of open spaces, clean water, and functioning water closets. They learned how to enjoy themselves in a truly metropolitan style. They strolled in the Tiergarten, took family picnics in the Grunewald, or by the lakeside at Wannsee, Tegel or the Müggelsee, caught *Kanalforellen*, 'canal trout' in the newly opened Teltow Canal, and generally took advantage of the Berliner Luft, the Berlin air which Berliners have always believed to have special qualities. In the evenings, they thronged to the many new theatres, or to the city's two permanent circuses, or to concerts by a new orchestra founded in 1882 by a group of breakaway musicians from the Konzerthaus Bilse on Leipzigerstrasse, that famous provider of ham sandwiches, beer and marriage partners. Herr Bilse was a former military band director, and no doubt continued to treat his musicians as a military bandmaster would. Eventually, it became too much for some of them, who left and set up on their own. They called their new ensemble the Berlin Philharmonic Orchestra.

If the weather was fine, the Berliners joined the *Bummel*, the leisurely promenade along the Linden or the Ku'damm, window shopping, watching other promenaders, taking a little refreshment in one of the many pavement cafés. Before 1870, there had been only a very limited number of good restaurants in Berlin itself, as opposed to cafés, Kneipes and Weinstuben. Most of them were situated along the Linden or in the banking quarter around Behren-strasse and Französischestrasse, old and expensive establishments such as Dressel, Hiller and Borchardt (which, incidentally, re-opened on its old site in 1992). Increased general prosperity created new markets, however, and restaurateurs with an eye to more popular tastes soon began setting up shop.

The most prominent was a Jewish entrepreneur called Kempinski, who built a splendid new restaurant on Leipzigerstrasse, one of the main shopping streets and convenient for the newspaper district, the opera and the theatres. It aimed to attract professionals, shop-pers and visitors, providing a wide range of excellent food at modest prices: half a dozen oysters cost 75 pfennigs, the same price as a glass of German sparkling wine, for example. The shrewd Kempinski decorated the walls of his dining rooms with tiles from the Kaiser's own factory. He was rewarded by the presence of the Kaiser himself at the gala opening. Kempinski's was off to a flying start from which it never looked back until the Nazis expropriated the business. The family spent the war years in London, but re-turned to Berlin after 1945, and opened a new restaurant and luxury hotel on the Kurfürstendamm in 1952.

Rivalling Kempinski's for the popular trade was the Aschinger chain of Bierstuben. Aschinger soon had 40 outlets throughout Berlin, famous for simple food at low prices – a sandwich cost ten pfennigs, and hot dishes 30. But their most popular innovation was providing unlimited free bread rolls for anyone who bought a beer.

Aristocrats had always enjoyed travelling abroad, and continued to do so. Gradually, the better-off middle classes began to follow suit, though many still clung to the old custom of renting holiday cottages in the countryside of the Mark Brandenburg, or on its many lakes and rivers. Poorer people were, of course, more re-stricted in their leisure time, but many ordinary Berliners were able to enjoy a pleasure unknown to most city dwellers in other coun-tries. For evenings, weekends and holiday times, they had their 'Schrebergärten', thousands of small private gardens, each with its own little summerhouse, clustered in colonies on the outskirts of the city. With the true Berliners' passion for organization, they formed clubs and societies, with embroidered banners and enam-elled badges. They built children's playgrounds. They held sports days and festivals and excursions. They formed bands for making music. They published their own newspapers and magazines. They created their own well-ordered little communities.

Londoners have their allotments, of course, but they are poor, utilitarian things by comparison, simple plots intended for growing vegetables and perhaps a few flowers. The Berlin colonies, on the other hand, are bucolic retreats intended for the good of their owners' souls. Named after Dr Daniel Schreber, who began the movement in Berlin in the 1860s, the idea soon spread throughout the rest of the Reich. The Schrebergärten or *Laubenkolonien* (summerhouse colonies) flourish today in every city and large town in Germany, but nowhere has their development been brought to such a fine art as in the dozens of colonies in and around Berlin.

Berlin in the nineteenth century was a city without a Dickens or a Balzac or a Perez Galdos to do it justice, to record its changes and its people and its sheer vibrancy. In truth, German literature at that time was hardly geared to the real world, rather than the world of poetic and romantic fantasy, but even so, few of its great names gravitated to Berlin. The city did not exert the spell that Paris did over French writers, or London over the English. But there was one man who did manage to catch the flavour of Berlin life: an elderly, unsuccessful ex-apothecary turned novelist, Theodore Fontane, who knew Berlin and dealt with her as she really was.

Fontane, uniquely in German literature, wrote about women, Berlin women, with vast affection and rare understanding. Indeed, 12 of his 14 novels have a woman as the principal character. Coming from a Huguenot family and thinking of himself as half-French, he found his inspiration in French literature. He was born in Neuruppin in 1819, the son of an apothecary who was also a gambling man. As a result, the family was forced to move frequently from town to town, leaving behind a trail of unpaid bills. The young Fontane qualified as an apothecary at trade school in Berlin, but he was never cut out for business. He married a Huguenot girl, who spent the rest of her life complaining of his failure as a breadwinner, as a father, and as just about anything else she could think of.

Fontane's first efforts at writing consisted of patriotic verse inspired by Scottish Border ballads, which proved mildly popular but didn't bring in much money. They were, however, good enough to bring him some newspaper work, and eventually he got a job as a correspondent based in England – largely to get as far away as possible from his wife, who bullied him mercilessly. He was never what we would today regard as a foreign correspondent, but merely a stringer who happened to live in London for several years. He never took to Britain or the British, longing for Berlin all the time he was away, though he wrote two modestly successful travel books, one on London, the other on Scotland. When he returned home, he found a job on the right-wing newspaper, *Die Kreuzzeitung*, and began writing five volumes of topography, describing his explorations of the Mark Brandenburg, which even in their day were regarded as boring.

Fontane covered each of Bismarck's three wars as a correspondent, and produced a book about each, though it would be hard to imagine anyone less fitted to write about war. In the course of the Franco-Prussian war in 1870, he succeeded in getting lost behind the French lines, where he was promptly arrested as a spy. He told his captors that he had gone to visit Domrémy, the village where Joan of Arc came from. His story was so far-fetched it had to be true, and it must be said that even to the most suspicious Frenchman he could hardly have seemed the stuff that spies were made of. They still wanted to shoot him, however, and only after his friends in Berlin had interceded on his behalf did the French minister of justice order his release.

Back in Berlin, his friends found him a safer job as one of the secretaries to the Academy of Arts, but after three months he resigned, or was asked to leave, it is not quite clear which. By then he was almost 60, but he wrote to his publisher: 'I am only beginning. There is nothing behind me; everything is before me.' And for once in his life, he was proved right. During the next 20 years he wrote his 14 novels, three books of short stories, two volumes of autobiography, and innumerable letters to an astonishing range of people.

Fontane was not a natural novelist. His books, even his masterpiece, *Effi Briest*, lack suspense or any strong storyline – indeed, for much of the time he simply retold the same story. But he wrote with grace, acuity and unassuming humour, and remains a unique voice in European, and particularly German, literature, a sane, sympathetic man, concerned with the social conditions of his day. He has been described, with some justification, as 'the sociologist of the human heart'. Certainly, he captured the life of a large section of Berlin society in the late nineteenth century with great accuracy.

Most of Fontane's books concern adultery and misalliances between the different classes. His women are uniformly strong, stoical and sensible, his men weak, cowardly and emotionally retarded, unable to face the consequences of their liaisons. Grand passions rarely exist in Fontane's world. His subjects are martial boredom, casual sexual attraction, and the waste of human decency.

In lesser hands, the stories could easily have become mawkish. What saves them is Fontane's cool tone and sinewy style, and above all his understanding of the characters. There are no villains here: no one sets out to be deliberately cruel. As the heroine of one of his novels, Lene Nimptsch, says: 'It was nobody's fault. Nothing can be changed, not even the fact that nothing can be changed.'

Lene Nimptsch appears in one of Fontane's most charming and most typically Berlin novels, *Irrungen, Wirrungen*, which has twice been translated into English, once under the title *A Suitable Match*. She lives in a tiny house 'on a large market garden at the intersection of the Kufürstendamm and Kurfürstenstrasse, diagonally opposite the Zoo'. Lene becomes the lover of Baron Botho von Rienäcker, a lieutenant in the imperial cuirassiers, but both are aware that their relationship is doomed: marriage is not possible because they belong to different social classes.

At one point, Botho, out riding in the woods, comes upon a cross marking the spot where the former police president, Ludwig von Hinkeldey, met his death in a duel. 'What is this monument trying to tell me?' he asks himself, and answers: 'One thing at least, that our background does determine our actions. The man who obeys this rule may perish, but at least he dies more honourably than the man who defies it.'

When Botho finds himself in the same situation as Mr Micawber – annual income in his case 9,000, expenditure 12,000; result misery – the only solution is marriage. A suitable match is found. She is the daughter of a Prussian Junker and comes with a more than adequate dowry. Käthe Sellenthin is a pretty bubblehead and chatterbox, with the most irritating laugh in literature and all the sensitivity of a suet pudding, totally the wrong woman for Botho.

Lene, meanwhile, has acquired another suitor, Gideon Franke, a 50-year-old factory supervisor with religious leanings: a serious man. One day, he turns up at Botho's apartment, and explains that

Lene has told him everything about their relationship and has insisted that he check up. Soon after, Käthe sees a marriage notice in the paper: Gideon Franke and Magdalene Nimptsch have married that day. She is amused by the names – Gideon and Nimptsch: what absurd names! 'Whatever have you got against Gideon, Käthe?' asks Botho. 'Gideon's better than Botho.'

Fontane makes it clear that Botho has lost a jewel and knows it. But what is so delightful about the book is Fontane's mastery of dialogue, character, and Berlin background. Dörr, the market gardener, and his wife, friends of Lene and her mother, are Berlinisch to their fingertips. He grows asparagus, as well as marjoram and other herbs used by sausage makers, but above all he grows leeks. A true Berliner, he insists, 'needs only three things in life: a glass of Berlin beer, a schnapps, and leeks. Nobody's ever gone short on leeks.'

The Kaiser was never a great reader; he never expressed an opinion about books or showed much interest in their authors. But he more than made up for this where writers for the theatre were concerned. Wilhelm II regarded the stage as 'one of my weapons with which to fight materialism and the un-German type of art'. His favourite dramatist was Ernst von Wildenbruch, an illegitimate sprig of the Hohenzollern family, who wrote turgid historical dramas and pageants. These were so appalling that students of the university once gathered in the Royal National Theatre to boo his *Henry II* off the stage, but then kept quiet because Wilhelm and the Kaiserin were in the royal box.

Wilhelm reserved his hatred for the work of Gerhart Hauptmann, Germany's leading exponent of social realism and naturalism. One of Hauptmann's plays, *The Rats*, showed Berlin slum life in all its horror. The court and the upper reaches of Berlin society were duly shocked by the play, but of course did nothing about the slums. But the play of Hauptmann's that caused the greatest furore was *Die Weber* (The Weavers), which depicted a rising in 1844 by starving Silesian textile workers. When it opened in 1892, Wilhelm made his displeasure known, and the police moved in, bringing a record number of prosecutions. Hauptmann was arrested and charged with fomenting revolution and with being an *Umsturzdichter*, a poet of subversion. To get around the ban, the Deutsches Theater formed itself into a members' club, so that performances were technically private.

Hauptmann and his producer, Otto Brahm, changed the face of drama in Berlin, bringing it into the modern world. But when a literary jury awarded the dramatist the annual Schiller prize, worth 6,000 marks and a gold medal, the Kaiser stepped in and quashed their decision, handing the prize to Wildenbruch instead. The young woman painter, Käthe Kollwitz, who had been awarded a gold medal for her illustrations to the published version of *Die Weber*, was also regarded as subversive, and deprived of her prize.

The Kaiser had no qualms about interfering in the world of art. 'Art that transgresses the laws and parameters which I lay down ceases to be art,' he declared. 'The misused word "liberty" leads to licence and presumption. If art is to fulfil its proper role, it must affect people deeply – but it must be uplifting and not degrading.' When the Association of Berlin Artists invited the Norwegian expressionist painter Edvard Munch to exhibit his work in Berlin in 1892, Wilhelm was apoplectic. The critics followed his line, and the show closed after two days. Out of the turmoil, however, sprang the Berlin *Sezession* movement, led by Max Liebermann, the now little regarded Walter Lestikow, and Lovis Corinth, who later turned to expressionism himself after a stroke affected his hand so that he could no longer manage the delicate brushwork required for the impressionist style. Other members of the group included such artists as Frank Skarbina, Lesser Uri, and Käthe Kollwitz.

The *Sezessionists* staged an exhibition in a salon on the Ku'damm that May. It, too, caused a furore, again led by the Kaiser, who described it as 'the art of the gutter'. Army officers wishing to visit it were ordered to wear plain clothes, lest it should seem that the army approved of such decadent, un-Prussian art. But the exhibition attracted foreign buyers, and Liebermann in particular found his work in demand in London and Paris.

Nothing, of course, succeeds like success, and Liebermann was fast becoming a celebrity: he was already beginning to overtake the aging Menzel as Berlin's premier artist. The son of a highly successful businessman with a grand house in Pariserplatz immediately alongside the Brandenburg Gate, he had studied in Paris and ingested French impressionism at an early age: Manet and Monet were his masters. Unlike Menzel, Liebermann did not do 'official' subjects, but painted ordinary people in ordinary surroundings.

Also unlike Menzel, he was that rare creature a Berliner born and bred. Although Jewish, like so many Berlin Jews of that period he thought of himself as a Berliner first and a Jew a long way second. Eventually, he even managed to overcome the appalling handicap, at least in the eyes of the Berlin art establishment, not of being a Jew, but of being an impressionist.

In the fullness of time, Liebermann became the president of the Academy. But it is clear from his later self-portraits that success did not change him; he remained the same sharp-tongued, curmudgeonly character he had always been. He stares disapprovingly out from the canvas like some Prussian general who is wondering whether to have a bunch of inept recruits shot or merely flogged to within an inch of their lives. Moustached, balding, with the sort of lived-in face that could sour canned milk, Liebermann is still clearly his own man. Never one to suffer fools gladly, his attitude to his art and his admirers is summed up perfectly by the way he once dealt with a gushing female who wittered on about how marvellous it must be to be a painter, able to go to his studio and just paint and paint when the inspiration moved him. 'Are you mad?' snarled Liebermann. 'I shut up shop at five, like everyone else.'

CHAPTER 11

'I am the sole arbiter'

BERLIN APPROACHED the twentieth century as a full-blown metropolis, totally unlike any other city in Germany. One mark of its metropolitan status was the wealth of spanking new hotels that opened up after unification, mostly around the Linden and Friedrichstrasse. The grandest of them were very grand indeed, and could stand comparison with any in Europe. Leading the way, in 1875, was the Kaiserhof, situated on the Wilhelmplatz, immediately opposite the chancellery. It opened for business on 1 October, caught fire and burned down ten days later, and was immediately rebuilt to an even higher degree of splendour. Old Kaiser Wilhelm I was so impressed by its furnishings and fittings that he declared: 'I have nothing like this in my own home!' Fifty years later, Adolf Hitler made it his home and headquarters in Berlin in the period before he achieved power. After he had moved into the chancellery, he still visited the Kaiserhof regularly for afternoon tea.

But the Kaiserhof was soon eclipsed by an even more luxurious establishment with that extra touch of magic that placed it immediately in the exclusive ranks of the world's greatest. Lorenz Adlon had the dream of creating a hotel that would rank alongside the

Savoy in London, the Crillon and the Ritz in Paris, the Excelsior in Rome. He even had the perfect address for it: Number 1, Unter den Linden, on the corner of Pariserplatz and Wilhelmstrasse, next door to the British embassy. The only snag was that the site was occupied by a town house built by Schinkel for Count Redern. The current Count Redern, a compulsive gambler, was in serious financial trouble, having lost his entire family fortune during one week of gaming with King Edward VII of Great Britain. He was desperate to sell. But the property was entailed, and therefore could not be disposed of. In any case, the very idea of demolishing a house by Schinkel was sacrilege.

However, Adlon had a powerful patron. Kaiser Wilhelm II, recognizing the added prestige Adlon's hotel would bring to Berlin, took a personal interest in the plan, overruled all the legal difficulties, and dismissed the objections of the Office for the Preservation of Architectural Treasures. But the site of the Redern Palace was not really large enough for the hotel, so Wilhelm made a personal request to the British ambassador, Sir Frank Lascelles – a request, of course, which no diplomat could refuse – to sell part of the new embassy's large garden to Adlon, to increase the size of the plot. The result for the embassy, as a future ambassador, Sir Nevile Henderson, complained, was 'a catastrophe . . . shut off on the south from the sunlight by the great edifice of the Adlon and sullied by the smoke from the hotel's vast kitchen chimney, the house was always dark and always dirty'. To Wilhelm, this must have been a source of added satisfaction, a subtle way of literally rubbing Britain's nose in the dirt.

Wilhelm even helped to arrange the enormous finance required for the hotel. Costs soared to an unheard-of 20 million marks, but with the Kaiser backing the project, no one dared call a halt. The results were everything Adlon and the Kaiser could have hoped for. Nothing was spared to ensure that the Adlon Hotel was the very last word in taste, elegance and luxury. The Kaiser was so impressed that he made a habit of accommodating all his important guests there, rather than in the shabby discomfort of the royal palace.

The Adlon Hotel became and remained a Berlin landmark, until the final few days of the Second World War. The very last of the grand hotels still operating, it was eventually put out of action at the beginning of May 1945 by a combination of British and American bombs and Russian shells.

Five years after the opening of the Adlon, the Ritz-Carlton company built a hotel designed to compete with it, the Esplanade, on Bellevuestrasse and Potsdamerplatz. By the outbreak of the First World War, Berlin had no fewer than twelve hotels of international standing. And during the first decade of the new century, new cafés and restaurants seemed to open every day in the west end. The population, swelled by diplomats and traders and foreign travellers – there was a community of several thousand Americans, for example, well before the turn of the century – was increasingly cosmopolitan and sophisticated. And the pace of life, the *Berliner Tempo* of which its citizens were so proud, was increasingly hectic.

The new century brought a great change in German political ambitions. To the Kaiser and his officials it was no longer enough for Germany to be recognized as a major European power. Now they must establish the Second Reich as a world power, on a par with Britain, France and Russia. The first steps had already been taken in 1884–5, under Bismarck. In a sudden rush for colonies, Germany had acquired South West Africa, German East Africa, Togoland and the Cameroons.

In 1897, the Germans had seized the Shantung peninsula in China and established a naval base at Tsingtao. The following year, they tried to elbow aside the Spanish in the Pacific, demanding a naval base in Baja California, Mexico, and attempting to occupy the Philippines. When the United States stood in the way of both moves, Germany bought the Caroline and Mariana islands, and a year later acquired part of Samoa. These German possessions were never more than an illusion of empire, a desperate attempt to keep up with the neighbours, Britain and France. For Berlin, of course, they brought more ministries, more civil servants, and more of the trappings of imperial administration.

As a major industrial nation, it was right and proper that Germany should take her place among the world powers. But it was a bad time to begin jostling for position: the existing powers – Britain, France, Austria-Hungary, Russia, the waning crescent of the Ottoman empire and the rising sun of Japan – were involved in a frenetic game of brinkmanship, in which partnerships and alliances shifted with bewildering rapidity. Germany approached this volatile situation with an explosive mixture of paranoia, envy and deep insecurity masked by bombast.

For the first dozen years of the new century, Germany lurched from one international crisis to another. The situation was not helped by Wilhelm II, who boasted that he had never read the German constitution, still saw himself as an absolute monarch by the grace of God, and interfered in foreign affairs at every opportunity. 'I am the sole arbiter and master of German foreign policy, and the Government and country *must* follow me,' he wrote to Edward VII in December 1901, concluding, with his usual tact: 'May your Government never forget this . . .' Berliners, with their usual irreverence, said he approached every problem with an open mouth.

When the so-called 'Boxer rebellion' erupted in Beijing in 1900, Wilhelm organized the international military expedition to restore order. For some time, he had been loudly warning the world of 'the yellow peril'. Now, he urged his soldiers to make the name German as feared in China as the Huns had been in Europe centuries before. Later, without consulting one of them, he announced that he was taking the world's 300 million Muslims under his protection.

But perhaps Wilhelm's most serious error of judgement was the way in which he outraged British public opinion by his support for President Kruger in what was to become the Boer War. After one Boer victory, he sent a message of sympathy to his uncle, the newly crowned Edward VII, urging him to accept defeat with the same sporting spirit as he had the loss of the recent cricket Test Match against the Australians. Edward was not amused. He reminded Wilhelm that the war was not a game: the future of the British empire was at risk.

The future of Anglo-German relations, however, was at risk from something far more serious than ill-judged remarks about cricket. No one in the whole of Germany was more in love with Britain than the half-British Kaiser – and nobody in Germany was more insanely jealous of Britain's position. The two feelings fused in what was the maddest and most grandiose of all his fantasies. During his many visits to his grandmother and relatives across the Channel, he had seen that Britain's power depended upon the Royal Navy, the greatest fleet ever seen on the high seas. It therefore followed that if Germany was to become greater than Britain, then Germany must have a greater navy than Britain's. So, in June 1897, Wilhelm

appointed 48-year-old Rear Admiral Alfred Tirpitz State Secretary
for the Navy, with a brief to build warships. Tirpitz, a massive
figure with high, domed head and fiercely forked beard, began by
demanding the money to build no fewer than 17 battleships in
seven years. Six months later, after a noisy propaganda campaign,
the number was increased to 36.

For Britain, the new German navy was both a challenge and a threat.
The challenge created a massive race to build more and bigger battleships. The threat alienated Britain, destroying any hopes of an alliance
and driving her into the arms of France and Russia, Germany's
enemies. Wilhelm got his fleet, though it was never a match for the
Royal Navy. But the price was to prove very high.

As the Kaiser stumbled from one *faux pas* to another, more and
more people began expressing their discontent. But, like good Berliners, they complained in private, and did nothing. Max Weber,
the country's leading professor of economics, wrote to his friend
Friedrich Naumann, editor of the political journal *Hilfe*: 'The degree of contempt which we as a nation now encounter abroad (in
Italy, America, everywhere) – and rightly, which is what matters –
because we suffer *that* regime of *that* man, has by now become a
factor of first-class "world political" importance for us. Anyone
who reads the foreign press for a few months must notice this. We
are being "isolated" because that man rules us in that way and
because we *allow him to do so and make excuses . . .*'

Intellectuals and social democrats might complain about the Kaiser
and the German caste system which he headed, but in pre-First-
World-War Berlin, caste still ruled supreme. The old three-class
electoral system remained virtually unchallenged, but the pinnacle
of social ambition was occupied by the reserve officer corps. Its
snob appeal sprang from the fact that in the old Prussian army only
aristocrats had been allowed to hold commissions. So, becoming an
officer of the reserve, preferably in an elite regiment, allowed a
middle-class man to enjoy the pretension of nobility, and provided
a key to social advancement.

The reserve played an important role in establishing the spirit of
militarism in the bourgeoisie, a class that had traditionally been
anti-war. At the beginning of the twentieth century, its gung-ho
attitudes were reinforced by various extreme right-wing leagues

and associations, the most important of which were the Pan German League and the Navy League.

The cult of the officer corps and the importance of the uniform remained undiminished right up to the First World War. In 1913, US Ambassador James Gerard suffered an incident curiously reminiscent of Count Schwerin's experience with Friedrich the Great and the young ensign who usurped his place at a banquet. While enjoying a day at the races, Gerard found that an officer and his wife had taken over his box while he and his brother-in-law were out looking at the horses in the paddock. 'I called the attention of one of the ushers to this,' he recounted later, 'but the usher said he did not dare ask a Prussian officer to leave, and it was only after sending for the head usher and showing him my Jockey Club membership and my pass as an ambassador that I was able to secure possession of my own box.'

Dramatic – and hilarious – proof that a Prussian officer could get away with anything in Berlin had been provided in October 1906, by an itinerant cobbler named Wilhelm Voigt. Voigt had spent half his 60 years in jail for various petty offences, including forgery and deception, and was down on his luck. Later, he claimed the only thing he wanted was a passport, so that he could emigrate. With no papers, no money, and a long criminal record, this seemed impossible. But Voigt had a brilliantly simple idea. With his last few marks, he bought a complete captain's uniform from a second-hand clothing shop, put it on and stepped boldly out. Judging by police photographs, it is hard to imagine anyone looking less like a Prussian officer, but the uniform obviously worked its magic.

On the street in central Berlin, Voigt stopped a passing detachment of some ten soldiers and ordered them to accompany him by train to the south-eastern suburb of Köpenick. There, he and his men occupied the town hall. Claiming that he was under orders to clear up certain irregularities, he arrested the mayor and his clerk, but for some reason released the police chief, who pleaded that he needed a bath. Unfortunately, the police chief was the only person with the authority to issue a passport, so Voigt decided to seize the municipal funds instead, taking some 4,000 marks in cash but ignoring negotiable securities worth two million. Returning to Berlin, he dismissed the soldiers, and disappeared with the money. Throughout the whole episode, no one had dreamed of questioning him or his orders: he was wearing a captain's uniform, and that was enough.

Voigt might well have got away with his exploit, but he couldn't resist boasting about it to a former prison friend, who denounced him to the police. He was sentenced to four years' detention, 'for wrecking the entire administrative machinery of the city'. The Berliners, naturally, found the whole thing vastly entertaining. So, more surprisingly, did the Kaiser, who ordered Voigt's release, saying that the episode proved 'how fabulously the people had learned to toe the line!'

1907 was Kaiser Wilhelm's *annus horribilis*. The year began with the first voyage in full service of the new British super battleship HMS *Dreadnought*, which instantly made every other warship obsolete, including all those being built for the Imperial German Navy. Worse followed later in the year, when the British joined Russia and France to form the Triple Entente, in opposition to the Triple Alliance of Germany, Austria and Italy. In Berlin this raised the spectre of encirclement, and stepped up the arms race. Meanwhile, trouble was boiling up in the Balkans, where Serbs, Croats and Bosnians were causing problems not only for Austria and Italy, but also for another German ally, Turkey.

At home, the Reichstag was proving difficult again. First, it rejected a bill to make the Colonial Department a Reich ministry, then it went on to refuse money for putting down guerrilla activity in South West Africa. At this point, in a typically Bismarckian move, Bülow abruptly dissolved the Reichstag, provoking another constitutional crisis. But for Wilhelm, this was completely overshadowed by a scandal that exposed the moral corruption of his court circle, and, what was even worse, impugned the sacred honour of the army. His closest friend and confidant for over 20 years, Prince Philip von Eulenberg, was publicly accused of homosexuality, along with Count Kuno von Moltke, the military commander of Berlin, and three of the Kaiser's military aides-de-camp. And, horror of horrors, the allegations included 'disgusting orgies' with men of the elite guards regiments. Encouraged by Wilhelm, Moltke sued the editor who had published the accusation. But Eulenberg refused to do so, returned his Order of the Black Eagle, and resigned from the diplomatic service.

When Moltke's case opened in October, Wilhelm took to his bed for two days. Due to make an official visit to England on 11

November, he decided he could not face his British relatives. On 31 October, he told Bülow that he was not fit to travel. He had had a fainting fit, he said, and had fallen off a sofa. 'My head hit the ground so hard that my wife was alarmed by the noise and came rushing to me, terrified,' he told the chancellor. He told Edward VII a different story, saying he was suffering from 'bronchitis and acute cough . . . a virulent attack of influenza'. His protestations were totally undermined, however, when the British ambassador in Berlin passed the 'seriously ill' Kaiser in the Tiergarten that very morning, 'galloping along with a group of his aides, in very good spirits'.

Bülow persuaded Wilhelm to make a miraculous recovery, and to go to Britain as planned. After the official part of the visit was finished, he decided to stay on for a short holiday, renting a mock Gothic castle at Highcliffe, on the south coast near Bournemouth. During his stay, he talked at some length to the owner of the house, Colonel Edward Montague Stuart-Wortley. Nearly a year later, Stuart-Wortley wrote an article for the *Daily Telegraph*, setting down all that the Kaiser had said. He submitted the text to Wilhelm in Berlin, who for once acted with due propriety and passed it to his chancellor for clearance. Bülow was preoccupied with the international crisis caused by events in Bosnia-Herzegovina, which Austria had just annexed. Faced with the threat of a major war, he did not pay much attention to the article, but passed it on to the Foreign Office. The Foreign Office officials assumed that Bülow approved of the article. They checked it for accuracy, and passed it back. It was published on 29 October 1908, and a furore instantly broke out on both sides of the Channel.

Wilhelm's comments on Anglo-German relations, faithfully reported by Stuart-Wortley, managed to offend just about everybody. In the article, he complained that the English were mad not to appreciate his friendship. The hostile 'distortions and misinterpretations' of the British press, he said, hampered his efforts to promote friendship, which was already difficult enough since the majority of Germans disliked the English. He claimed that during the Boer War Russia and France had tried to persuade him to join with them in a Continental coalition that would 'humiliate England to the dust'. He had, of course, refused, and had written to his grandmother, Queen Victoria, telling her about it. He had also, he claimed, personally worked out a plan of campaign for the British in South

Africa, which 'as a matter of curious coincidence . . . ran very much on the same lines as that which was actually adopted by Lord Roberts'. As for the German Navy, it was not being built up against England. In fact, 'it may even be that England herself will be glad that Germany has a fleet . . .' And so it continued, with indiscretion piled on indiscretion.

The storm that broke in the Reichstag and in the press was unprecedented in Prussia. For the first time ever, there was loud and public criticism of the Kaiser and his 'personal government'. Bülow, who was not known as 'the eel' for nothing, managed to evade responsibility, shifting all the blame on to the Kaiser and the unfortunate official in the Foreign Office who had failed to spot the dangers.

For a few days, it seemed that the moment had at last arrived for genuine reform, and for the establishment of democratic government. But yet again, the people's representatives could not agree among themselves. In the end, Bülow forced Wilhelm to give a promise, in writing, that he would respect the constitution, and the Reichstag settled for that.

Wilhelm was shattered by the experience. At the peak of the crisis he even offered to abdicate, though of course he forgot all about this as soon as everything had blown over. He never forgave Bülow, and determined to take his revenge. He did not have to wait long. The following year, the chancellor failed to get the Reichstag to approve the finance bill needed to pay the heavy costs of the navy and the colonies. The social democrats were opposed to any increase in indirect taxes, and the conservatives and centre parties refused to accept the new idea of death duties. Bülow played his usual card by offering his resignation. To his horror, Wilhelm immediately accepted it.

Inviting himself to dinner with the Bülows the night the resignation was made public, Wilhelm told Princess von Bülow that 'those fellows' in the Reichstag had overthrown her husband, 'because they didn't think he showed enough zeal defending his imperial master'. When she asked what her husband should have done, he replied: 'He ought to have declared in the Reichstag: "I won't have any more of this insolent speech about the Kaiser. How dare you speak like this? Quick march! Get out!" '

As Bülow's replacement, Wilhelm chose Theobald von Bethmann Hollweg, the vice chancellor and secretary of the interior, a personal friend who would do exactly what his imperial master wanted, thus giving Wilhelm more direct, personal control over the government than before.

When Bülow warned that his successor, while excellent on domestic matters, knew nothing about foreign affairs, Wilhelm replied with some relish: 'You leave foreign policy to me. You've managed to teach me something, you know.' With equal relish, he concluded: 'Just wait till that great tall fellow stands up in the Reichstag and glares at all the "honourable" members. Why, he'll scare them to death. They'll run off and hide in their mouseholes.' In the event, the members may not have run away, but they did nothing to oppose the appointment of a man who was so obviously the Kaiser's puppet. The spirit of imperial autocracy remained unbroken.

CHAPTER 12

'It needs only a spark'

ERLIN HAD GROWN at an almost unbelievable rate during the nineteenth century. But during the first few years of the twentieth it positively exploded. Between 1900 and 1914, the population doubled yet again, rising from two million to almost four million, the equivalent of nearly 400 new inhabitants every single day. Suddenly, Berlin was the sixth-biggest city in the entire world.

Such rapid growth inevitably brought stresses and strains, and political unrest. During the first dozen years of the new century, Berliners staged a stream of increasingly powerful demonstrations. They called for the end of the three-class voting system, they protested against militarism and preparations for war, they demanded equality for women. At the same time, strikes over wages and working conditions became more frequent – one of the most notable was by 14–16-year-old boys working in haulage and transport for a miserly 3.90 marks a week, which brought the entire city to a standstill. The police banned all open-air public meetings and demonstrations, but the workers got round this by organizing picnics and outings to parks and lakes. When they were all there, banners and platforms suddenly appeared, and the picnics 'spontaneously' turned into political rallies before the police could move in.

By 1911, clashes with the police were becoming more and more violent. During one battle, two workers were killed and 150 injured. When a worker called Paule Singer was killed by police on 31 January 1911, more than a million mourners turned out for his funeral. They formed a dense and continuous line from his house in Brückenallee (today's Bartningallee), near Bellevue S-Bahn station, to the Socialist Cemetery in Friedrichsfelde more than seven miles away.

Even when they were enjoying themselves in the forests and on lake shores, Berliners were not free from the heavy hand of authority. Swimming in the lakes around Berlin was forbidden by law. But swimming was one of the Berliners' favourite occupations, so every summer hundreds of police were deployed in an effort to stop umpteen thousand 'free bathers' splashing in the Grunewald lakes, and the Wannsee and the Müggelsee, often in the nude. Watchtowers which in any other country would have been used by lifesavers were manned by security police armed with loud whistles. Most keen swimmers evaded them by simply swimming away into the middle of the lake.

Eventually, the authorities conceded defeat: official public bathing establishments were opened on the Wannsee in 1907 and, in the east, on the Müggelsee in 1912. Over the succeeding years, both were developed as lidos, with sandy beaches, promenades, and all the facilities normally associated with life at the seaside. The Wannsee beach is 1,275 metres long and 80 metres deep, with space for 50,000 bathers, the biggest inland beach in Europe. The slightly smaller Müggelsee lido can accommodate 20,000.

A major addition to recreational facilities in the city itself came at the beginning of 1911, when the Sportpalast opened at 72 Potsdamerstrasse. Originally billed as 'the biggest ice palace in the world', it started well but was soon in financial trouble. Its manager, struggling against bankruptcy, had the idea of staging six-day cycle races. They were a sensational success, and have remained a distinctive feature of Berlin life ever since, reaching their peak of popularity in the Twenties and early Thirties.

In the west, the vast new Deutschlandhalle opened at the end of the Ku'damm near Halensee, specializing in staging patriotic festivals; the hall was rebuilt for the 1936 Olympics, on the same site, and is still the city's premier exhibition centre. A little further out, on the shores of the Halensee itself, an Anglo-American consortium built Luna Park, a great fairground modelled on New York's Coney Island, near the restaurants, cafés and taverns which entrepreneurs like Kempinski and Aschinger had already established in this popular leisure area. A few hundred yards away, another, more significant, leisure complex was being laid out in the northern tip of the Grunewald. Recognizing Berlin's status as a world city, the International Olympic Committee had chosen it as the venue for the games due to take place in 1916, and a new stadium was being built to house the athletic competitions.

Always ready to welcome any new sensation, the Berliners were enthralled in 1911 by the arrival over the city of one of Graf Zeppelin's great new airships. At night, as the Zeppelin hovered over the city, powerful searchlights projected advertisements for cigarettes and bicycles on to its sides. As the very latest thing, flying became an obsession, with thousands of well-to-do Berliners lining up for short joyrides from the city's first airfields at Johannisthal and Tempelhof.

On the ground, meanwhile, the city was experiencing its first real traffic problems, as the motor vehicle started making its impact. One-way streets were introduced in the old city centre, and the first traffic cops appeared at the busiest junctions, equipped with loud whistles, to control both vehicles and pedestrians.

During the early years of the twentieth century, working-class Berlin at last found its own true chronicler. What Fontane had done in his novels for the genteel bourgeoisie, Heinrich Zille – 'Pinsel Heinrich', 'Paintbrush Henry', as the Berliners called him – did for the lower orders through cartoons, drawings and photographs. Inevitably, he was born somewhere else – in Radeburg, a small town in Saxony, just north of Dresden, on 10 January 1858, the son of a watchmaker and goldsmith who moved the family to Berlin nine years later, to escape his creditors and make a fresh start.

The fresh start, however, was a difficult one, for this was the time when Bismarck's wars were turning Berlin into a boom town for the fortunate, and a poverty trap for the unfortunate. The Zille family was just one of the thousands flooding into the city, and they were lucky to find an unfurnished cellar to live in. They managed to scrape by only with Zille's mother working from home and the young Zille himself bringing in a few pfennigs running errands and doing odd jobs. The experience of those years gave Zille more than an affinity with Berlin's poor – he was one of them, and never forgot it or them, no matter how successful he became in later years.

When he left school at 14, Zille's parents wanted him to work for a local butcher – no doubt thinking that in that way at least they would never go short of meat. But he had already discovered a love of drawing, and obtained an apprenticeship to a lithographer, to be trained as a commercial artist. He attended Professor Hosemann's art classes at the Academy twice a week, later moving on to Professor Domsche's life classes. It was Hosemann who advised him to give up copying Roman plaster casts and take his pad and pencil out on to the streets of Berlin, possibly the best piece of advice he was ever given. The streets of Berlin, and the back courts of the Mietskasernen, received him like an old friend.

At the end of his five-year apprenticeship, Zille found a job as an artist and photographer with a photographic company where he stayed for the next 30 years, apart from his two years' compulsory military service, which he hated. In 1883, he married the 18-year-old Hulda Friescke, who bore him three children. They set up home in a basement room in the workers' district of Rummelsburg, in the east of the city, and over the next few years, moved house twice, still in Rummelsburg. When the photographic company moved to Charlottenburg, however, Zille and his family moved with them, settling into a modest corner apartment on the fourth floor of a pleasant building on Sophie-Charlotten-Strasse, where they stayed for the rest of his life. But although he was living in a comfortable, bourgeois district, Zille's heart remained with the workers in the north and east of the city. In his free time, he still travelled to the mean streets and the seething back courts of the Mietskasernen, sketching and observing the people and their life.

It was not until around the turn of the century, when he was already over 40, that Zille really found his personal style, to suit his 'Milljöh' (milieu), as he called it. One of the first cartoons revealing this mature style is an aquatint entitled 'The Kaiser's Birthday', dated 1899. It shows a drunken Prussian soldier, Pickelhaube awry, holding up a wall under a street lamp: a kind of male Lili Marlene 40 years before her time, a typically humorous antidote to the glorification of the military. In 1901, some of his drawings were exhibited in a small gallery in Kantstrasse, and before long his work was in demand, though many respectable Berliners were shocked as much by his savage social criticism as by his earthy humour and racy subjects.

But art remained a sideline, still little more than a hobby for Zille, until he lost his job with the photographic company in 1907, and turned to full-time freelance work. His cartoons began to appear regularly in the satirical magazine *Simplizissimus*, in *Die lustiger Blätter*, and in *Die Jugend*. Other commissions started to come his way: he designed posters, sheet-music covers, advertisements, he illustrated books, anything to earn a living. During the First World War, many of his anti-war cartoons and more explicit satirical and sexual drawings were banned: some of his cartoons during and immediately after the war, showing legless ex-soldiers begging in the street, are as brutal as anything George Grosz ever drew.

Zille is to Berlin what Daumier and Steinlem were to Paris: the recorders of certain aspects of the city they loved and understood only too well. But in Zille's case there is also more than a touch of Donald McGill, the English king of the comic picture postcard. Zille's work features on many of the postcards sold today in stationers and souvenir shops all over Berlin. Most of his cartoons are of women and kids. They have all the best jokes, and the butt of their humour is usually men. There is no condescension about Zille. He genuinely liked women – something unusual in a male cartoonist – and he loved their bodies, particularly their bottoms, 'those friendly, ever-smiling double faces', in the words of a poem he once illustrated. His is a world of broad-beamed, large-breasted, often pregnant working-class Berlinerin, surrounded by their snot-nosed kids. Chamber pots, kids peeing in the streets, kids spitting blood because of TB, kids twisted with rickets like wind-blasted saplings, these are his subjects.

Zille caught the bleak, ferocious humour of his Milljöh with cartoons like one entitled 'Mother Earth', in which a group of neighbours, mostly women with hordes of kids, stand watching as a father wheels away a small coffin on an old baby carriage. Two older children walk in front, one carrying a wreath. The mother, pregnant, a toddler at her feet, leans out of the entrance to their basement and yells after him: 'Don't get drunk! And bring the coffin back. The Müllers need it for tomorrow morning.'

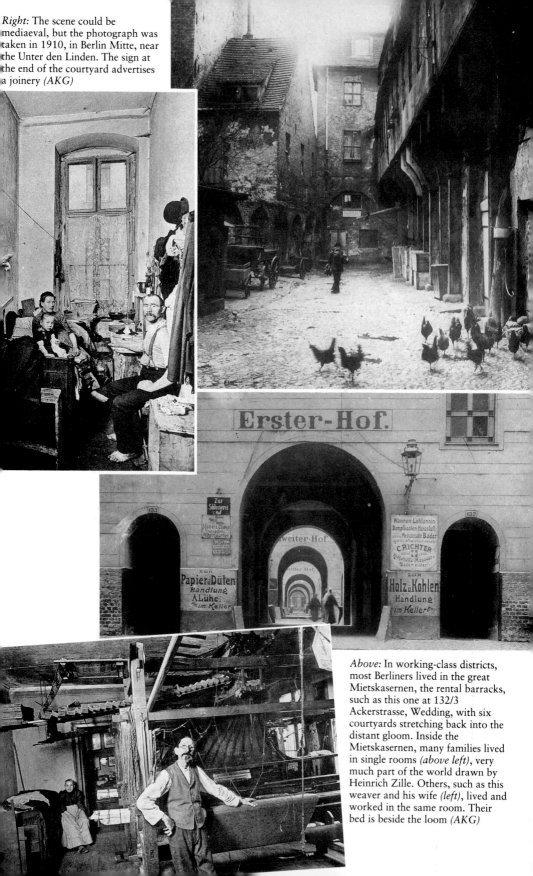

Right: The scene could be mediaeval, but the photograph was taken in 1910, in Berlin Mitte, near the Unter den Linden. The sign at the end of the courtyard advertises a joinery *(AKG)*

Above: In working-class districts, most Berliners lived in the great Mietskasernen, the rental barracks, such as this one at 132/3 Ackerstrasse, Wedding, with six courtyards stretching back into the distant gloom. Inside the Mietskasernen, many families lived in single rooms *(above left)*, very much part of the world drawn by Heinrich Zille. Others, such as this weaver and his wife *(left)*, lived and worked in the same room. Their bed is beside the loom *(AKG)*

More fortunate Berliners could sample the luxury of fashionable department stores such as Wertheim's on Leipzigerstrasse, designed by Alfred Messel and completed in 1906 (AKG)

But the Hotel Adlon – address 1, Unter den Linden and built under the auspices of the Kaiser himself – was where the very grand and the very rich dallied. Like the old Schloss, the Adlon was badly damaged in the second world war, and pulled down by the East German government (AKG)

Everyone, however, could enjoy the 'Berlin Bummel', the leisurely promenade down the Linden (AKG)

Left: August 1914. In the beginning, Berliners welcomed the first world war, and marched happily with their loved ones to the station, where volunteers *(below left)* set out euphorically 'to thrash the French' *(AKG)*

Below: To raise money for the war effort, a giant statue of the army commander-in-chief was erected in front of the Siegesssäule on Königplatz, in October 1915. People paid 1, 5, or 100 marks for an iron, silver, or golden nail, which they then hammered into the 'Wooden Hindenburg' *(LBS)*

Below left: The Kapp Putsch of 1920 was defeated by the Berliners' favourite weapon – the general strike. Freikorps units, here seen outside the Dom, patrolled largely empty streets *(LBS)*

The golden twenties began miserably for many in Berlin, such a limbless ex-servicemen reduced to begging; and homeless women force to seek refuge in overcrowded shelters, like this one in Prenzlauerberg *(AKG,*

Below: The social scen was recorded with varying degrees of comment by the leadin Berlin artists of the da *(left to right)* the fashionable but sardon Max Liebermann, seen here in a self-portrait; the humorous Heinric Zille, some of whose sharply observed drawings decorate this book; and the savage satire of Georg Grosz, whose work reflected his Marxist beliefs *(AKG, LBS, AKG)*

Lakeside lidos, like the swimming enclosure at Wannsee, the biggest inland beach in Europe with space for 50,000 bathers (LBS)

Two actresses above all others epitomized the Berlin stage and screen in the twenties: Lotte Lenya *(far left)*, seen here in the film of *The Threepenny Opera*, and Marlene Dietrich *(Ullstein)*

Right: The young Joseph Goebbels, seen here in 1931, was almost single-handedly responsible for the rise in strength of the Nazi Party in Berlin *(AKG)*

The most spectacular of all the victory parades through the Brandenburg Gate was staged by Goebbels on 30 January 1933, to celebrate Hitler's coming to power *(Ullstein)*

Exactly one month after the great parade, the Nazis staged a second great spectacle alongside the Brandenburg Gate – the burning of the Reichstag *(AKG)*

The aged Hindenburg still lent a spurious respectability to Hitler. On May Day 1933 they rode together to the Rally of German Youth *(AKG)*

Below left: Berlin's finest hour came in 1936, with the Olympic Games *(AKG)*

Below: Even as war approached, the Cafe Kranzler on the Kurfürstendamm retained its elegance – free of Jews and other 'undesirables' *(LBS)*

BERLIN · 1936
OLYMPISCHE SPIELE
1·16. AUG.

As yet physically untouched by the second world war, Berlin gave a rapturous reception to troops returning victorious from France in July 1940 *(AKG)*

Four years later, as Allied bombers inflicted harsh punishment on the city, Berliners had to pick their way through streets reduced to rubble *(AKG)*

With the Kaiser gone and the explosion of artistic freedom in the Twenties, Zille was accepted as an establishment figure: in 1921 he was given an exhibition in the National Gallery, and in 1924 he was elected a member of the Academy of Arts. When the Märkisches Museum mounted an exhibition of his work to mark his seventieth birthday, the crowds of visitors broke all records. His characters were so well known and his broad Berlinisch humour so popular that he was even taken up by the movies: he wrote scripts for a host of comedy shorts and some full-length features, but none of these has survived.

Zille died of a massive cerebral haemorrhage in 1929. He is buried in the Südwest cemetery in Stahnsdorf, just beyond the eastern boundary of the city. There is now a statue of him on the Alexanderplatz, where he stands, cast in bronze, sketch pad and pencil in hand, while a bowler-hatted shoemaker's apprentice, looking as though he had just stepped out of *The Threepenny Opera*, peers over his shoulder to see what he is doing. But his real memorial lies in his work, still to be found on teatowels and souvenir mugs and countless postcards, as well as in the Berlin Museum or the privately owned Zille Museum, devoted to his life and work, under the arches of Friedrichstrasse station.

Another true Berlin artist of the period, who attacked the same social evils as Zille, but with less humour and greater intensity, was the painter and sculptor Käthe Kollwitz, a prominent member of the Sezession movement. Kollwitz came from Königsberg in East Prussia to study art in Berlin, where she met and married a medical student, to become a doctor's wife in working-class Prenzlauerberg. Taking the poor of Prenzlauerberg as her subjects, she soon made a name for herself with her sculptures, powerful charcoal drawings and woodcuts of staring, hollow-eyed women and children.

Kollwitz had two sons, the younger of whom, 18-year-old Peter, was killed in Flanders only a few weeks after the start of the First World War. Previously a socialist and feminist, she became a passionate pacifist as a result. Unlike her friend Zille, she survived well into the Nazi era. They loathed her work, of course, as much as her politics, and when they came to power banned any exhibition of her work and dismissed her from her teaching post at the Academy.

For over 50 years, Kollwitz's home was at 25 Weissenburgerstrasse, right in the centre of Prenzlauerberg. In 1943, it was
destroyed by a British bomb, and she was forced to leave Berlin and
settle in the countryside near Dresden, where she died just before
the end of the war. Today, Weissenburgerstrasse has been renamed
Kollwitzstrasse, and a copy of her 1935 sculpture *The Mother* sits
in Kollwitzplatz. But her museum is at 24 Fasanenstrasse, just off
the Ku'damm – a smart, fashionable address that could be a million
miles from her Milljöh.

In spite of – or perhaps because of – the international tensions, the
theatre in all its forms flourished in Berlin as never before during
the early years of the new century. There were at least 33 theatres
in the city, and most of them were packed every night. Hauptmann
was still writing his social dramas – to the Kaiser's disgust he was
awarded the Nobel prize for literature in 1912 – and Wildenbruch
was still churning out his turgid historical epics, but there was also
plenty of lighter fare, with comic plays, musical comedies and
operettas everywhere. Cabaret had arrived in the city around the
turn of the century, and writers, composers and performers were
already developing the sharp individual style that has signified
Berlin ever since. Glamorous large-scale revue followed in 1906,
with the opening of the Berliner Folies Bergère, and this, too, was
quickly absorbed and adapted to become a permanent feature of
the Berlin scene, with beautiful dancers, frothy costumes and glittering sets.

For theatre as spectacle, one man rocketed to world stardom in
Berlin during the years before the First World War. The Austrian
Max Reinhardt, born Max Goldmann in Baden, near Vienna in
1873, started his stage life in Berlin as a not very good actor with
Otto Brahm's company at the Deutsches Theater, the home of
modern naturalism, where Hauptmann's plays alternated with those
of other serious writers like Ibsen. In 1901, he discovered a talent
for production when he started one of Berlin's first cabarets, Schall
und Rauch (Sound and Smoke). Two years later, he was running
the Neues Theater, and two years after that took over the Deutsches
Theater from Brahm. In the years that followed, he turned it into
the leading house in Germany with a succession of dazzling productions covering a truly amazing range, from Sophocles and Shake-

speare to Lessing, Ibsen and Strindberg. He dreamed of providing theatre for the masses, and bought the Grosses Schauspielhaus circus building, which he converted into a vast arena stage. In marked contrast, he built the small, intimate Kammerspiele along-side the main house of the Deutsches Theater to cater for the intellectual audience. Reinhardt was a wizard, capable of creating magic in the theatre, and it was largely due to him that Berlin in those heady pre-war days could claim to have become the theatrical capital not just of Germany, but of the world.

In serious music, too, Berlin was suddenly at the centre of world culture. The Berlin Philharmonic went from strength to strength. Under the direction of Arthur Nikisch, who had been wooed to the city from Leipzig in 1895, it was already regarded as probably the best orchestra in the world. Spurred on by the Philharmonic's success, the previously moribund Royal Orchestra – the Staats Oper orchestra – had found fresh life under the Austrian Felix von Weingartner, and was soon competing vigorously for supremacy.

Between them, the two orchestras, to say nothing of the Sing-Akademie and other choirs and musicians, provided Berlin music-lovers with a permanent feast of the highest possible standard. The American *Musical Courier* described Nikisch and Weingartner as 'the world's two greatest conductors', and as such they acted as magnets for the most celebrated artists and composers: Enrico Caruso, for example, returned annually for sell-out concerts. When Weingartner moved back to his native Austria in 1908, to replace Gustav Mahler as director of the Vienna Court Opera, his place was taken by Richard Strauss.

The city had almost an embarrassment of riches in the field of opera, too. In 1896, to compete with the old Staats Oper and to provide a venue for visiting companies, the administration of the Royal National Theatre had bought the Kroll Oper and set about enlarging it as the 'Neuen Königlichen Operntheater'. The old theatre had been built in 1851 on the western edge of the dusty 'Sahara' parade ground outside the Brandenburg Gate, on the site of a restaurant and entertainment establishment owned by Joseph Kroll. The 'Sahara' had since become Königsplatz, and the theatre now found itself opposite the Reichstag and the Siegessäule. In 1913, at the personal insistence of the Kaiser, the old building, was demolished, and work started on a new, much grander edifice. Meanwhile, in 1905 a producer called Hans Gregor had started an independent company which he named the Komische Oper. Based in a theatre at the Weidendammer bridge, the Komische Oper was devoted to the ideal of introducing realistic acting and production into opera performances, a worthy aim which it has pursued ever since. And finally, to complete the amazing depth of operatic production in Berlin, a fourth major opera house opened in 1912, the Deutsche Oper on Bismarkstrasse, built on the initiative of wealthy citizens of Charlottenburg, which was still an independent municipality.

Amid all the high culture, the German military was growing increasingly arrogant and powerful, and was determined to flex its muscles before long. The officer corps dreamed of glorious battles and quick victories; Berliners dreamed of other things, like music and beer and food and sex. Berlin's eternal dichotomy has never been more clearly marked than it was during those years. As the century entered its second decade, the divisions continued to widen; so, too, did the divisions within Europe. Bethmann Hollweg's period in office was probably the most turbulent of any Reich chancellor until that time, even including Bismarck, as the whole of Europe began to slide out of control towards world war.

Along the way, there was a series of smaller, but still vicious, conflicts. In 1911, Italy and Turkey went to war over Tripoli in North Africa. That same year, Germany and France came close to war over France's claim to a protectorate over Morocco, when Tirpitz and the new foreign secretary, Alfred von Kiderlen-Waechter, a belligerent diplomat in the Bismarck-Holstein mould, bullied the Kaiser into agreeing to send warships to the south Moroccan port of Agadir. Kiderlen made things worse by demanding the whole of the French Congo as compensation for the supposed loss of German interests in Morocco. Britain joined France in warning Germany that any interference with their interests would mean war. The Agadir crisis was resolved, Germany trading recognition of a French protectorate in return for 275,000 square miles (712,000 square kilometres) of the Congo, but it was a close-run thing.

In 1912, Serbia went to war with Turkey, to wrest control of the remains of the Ottoman empire in the Balkans. Austria was alarmed; if the Serbs could seize parts of the Ottoman empire, they could well do the same to Slav provinces of the Austro-Hungarian empire, such as Bosnia, Herzegovina and Croatia. Wilhelm pledged German support for Austria, rallying eagerly to the ancient cause of Teuton versus Slav. With the Russians standing behind their fellow Slavs, and allied to France and Britain, the threat of a general conflagration was enormous. But the Austrians were not yet ready for war, and again the danger passed.

Wilhelm and his chief of staff, Count Helmuth von Moltke, were bitterly disappointed. Wilhelm had been incensed when the British had again warned that they would not stand aside, and had been eager to seize the chance of teaching them a lesson: since the Agadir incident, German propaganda had turned Britain into public enemy number one. At a meeting of the Crown Council on 8 December 1912, the Kaiser and his advisers decided that the time was not quite ripe for starting a major war. It would be better to wait until work on widening the Kiel Canal was complete, so that the new German battleships could move safely and quickly between the Baltic and the North Sea. The canal was expected to be ready in 1914. Until then, preparations for war would continue.

In 1913, Berlin celebrated the twenty-fifth anniversary of Wilhelm's accession to the throne. For the Berliners it was a good excuse for making merry, though for some there was an irksome restriction: the Kaiser specifically forbade officers in uniform from dancing the tango, which was then all the rage in the city's night clubs and cabarets. He regarded it as immoral. But the festivities were overshadowed by another war in the Balkans, with Serbs and Bulgarians fighting over Macedonia. Bethmann and Moltke urged caution on the Austrians, but once again Wilhelm offered his unconditional support, encouraging Austria to send an ultimatum demanding the immediate withdrawal of Serbian troops from the newly independent Albania. 'Now or never,' he exclaimed. 'Some time or other, peace and order will have to be restored down there.' The Serbs backed down, and yet another crisis passed.

Wilhelm was by no means alone in his enthusiasm for war. Whipped by the censored press into a state of righteous indignation at all the supposed slights and insults heaped upon Germany by Britain and her partners, the German people were by now baying for satisfaction. Even though they were still overwhelmingly for the left, with a staggering 75 per cent of their vote going to the social democrats, the Berliners were no exception. For the moment, the anti-imperialist demonstrations were forgotten. Since 1912, in fact, the whole country had followed Berlin's example and returned the social democrats as the biggest single party in the Reichstag, but even this traditionally anti-militarist, anti-war party was now happily voting in favour of increased military budgets.

The great literary success of 1913 in Berlin was a book called *Vom heutigen Kriege* (Today's Wars), by General Bernhardi, in which he argued that war was a biological necessity, and a convenient way of getting rid of the weak. His views were widely accepted, not just by lunatic extremists but by otherwise responsible academics, journalists and politicians. When Colonel Edward M. House, the close friend and personal adviser of President Wilson of the United States, visited Berlin in the summer of that year, he was appalled by the bellicose chauvinism he encountered, particularly among the military. But, as he reported to the president, Berlin was not alone. 'The whole of Europe is charged with electricity,' he wrote. 'Everyone's nerves are tense. It needs only a spark to set the whole thing off.'

The spark was not long in coming. Ironically, German relations with Britain were actually improving. But this was more than offset by a catastrophic deterioration of relations with Russsia. Offended by the sending of a German military mission to help Turkey reform her armies, which had been badly battered by the Serbs, the Russians began a massive rearmament programme, specifically aimed at Germany. Wilhelm retaliated by declaring: 'Russo-Prussian relations are dead once and for all. We have become enemies.'

Convinced that they were encircled by a band of steel, Germans everywhere prepared for the inevitable battle. For Berlin, it was like a return to the early days when Albrecht the Bear and his warrior knights rode out to crush the barbarians from the east.

On 28 June 1914, the heir to the Austro-Hungarian throne, Archduke Franz-Ferdinand, was assassinated by a Serb-trained terrorist in the Bosnian capital, Sarajevo. Wilhelm pledged total German support and urged Austria to go to war with Serbia. Bethmann and his foreign secretary, Gottlieb von Jagow, did the same, believing that any conflict could be localized – surely, they argued, the Russian Tsar would not act in support of regicides? Wilhelm decided there was no reason to postpone his annual holiday cruise, and set sail in the royal yacht for the Norwegian fiords. For almost a month, the Austrians dithered while the diplomatic world became a maelstrom. The Kaiser returned from his cruise on 28 July and, characteristically, changed his mind about the need for war. But by then it was too late to stop it. Austria had at last summoned up the courage to declare war on Serbia, and next day Austrian guns began bombarding Belgrade.

CHAPTER 13

Dancing with Death

A T 5 . 0 0 P M O N F R I D A Y , 31 July 1914, Lieutenant
von Viehbahn of the Kaiser Alexander Grenadier Guards,
immaculate in Prussian blue uniform with red and gold
facings and spiked helmet, took up a position in front of the statue
of Friedrich the Great on the Linden. After a roll of drums from
four drummers, he read out a proclamation from General von
Kessel, military commander of the Mark Brandenburg. With immediate effect, it said, Kessel was taking 'complete power' in the city.
All officials would take their orders directly and only from him. All
civil rights were suspended. Civilians were barred from buying or
carrying arms. All houses were liable to be searched at any time. All
strangers who had no good reason to be in the city were given
24 hours to leave.

Only the foreigners complained. Berliners took the imposition of
martial law for granted. They all knew war was imminent, and
almost all of them welcomed it, having been conditioned to believe
right, as well as God, was on their side. Naturally, the Kaiser and
his military chiefs had not informed the people what was going on.
They had even carefully avoided any consultation with either the
Bundesrat or the Reichstag. And indeed why should they have

consulted anyone, when the Kaiser could still declare: 'I, heaven's chosen instrument, am responsible for my actions to God and myself alone.'

The following day, Germany declared war on Russia, which had already mobilized 1,200,000 men. Berlin erupted in a frenzy of patriotic fervour. 'Crowds of people everywhere,' the actress Tilla Durieux noted in her diary, 'and soldiers marching out of the city, showered with blossoms as they went. Every face looks happy: we've got war! Bands in the cafés and restaurants play *Hail to You in the Battle for Victory* and *The Watch on the Rhine* non-stop, and everybody has to listen to them standing up. One's food gets cold, one's beer gets warm: no matter – we've got war! Lines of people form, offering their motor cars for service . . . Soldiers at the railway stations are offered mountains of buttered sandwiches, sausages, and chocolate. There's a super abundance of everything: of people, of food, and of enthusiasm!'

Everyone knew the war would be over by Christmas, or at the very latest in six months, after which the victorious troops would be parading through the Brandenburg Gate again. The euphoria did not last. Christmas came and went, and the reality of modern warfare became more dreadful with every passing day. By the following spring, more than a quarter of the social democrats in the Reichstag were refusing to vote for renewal of war credits, and in June more than 1,000 members of the party signed an open letter denouncing the war. In marked contrast to democratic France and Britain, where any public dissent was quickly suppressed, anti-war sentiment grew quite openly in Berlin. There was even an anti-war motion in the Prussian parliament in June 1916, demanding among other things 'that the German government, before all other governments, should take the first step and should relinquish their plans of conquest, thus paving the way for peace'.

As the war dragged on and casualties mounted, life on the home front deteriorated alarmingly. Although the city was not damaged physically, hardly a family was left untouched by the appalling losses at the front as Berlin took its share of Germany's 1,750,000 dead. After more than 40 years of peace and steadily growing prosperity, Berliners suddenly had to accustom themselves to hardship. Meat, potatoes, sugar and soap were rationed. Coal grew increasingly scarce. Milk was restricted to children under six and sick people with a doctor's certificate. In the summer of 1915, some

500 Berlin housewives staged a protest in front of the Reichstag. They wanted their men back, they were unhappy about the high food prices – and what was more, the whipped cream, their beloved *Schlagsahne*, was nothing like it had been before the war.

In October 1916, the 27-year-old Adolf Hitler paid his first visit to the city, from a nearby hospital at Beelitz, where he was recovering from a leg wound. He was deeply distressed by 'the dire misery everywhere' caused by hunger, and was angered by 'those few wretched scoundrels agitating for peace'. But things were to get much worse: by 1917, the Allied blockade and the failure of the harvest reduced food supplies to near starvation levels. Even potatoes were virtually unobtainable: the Berliners called it 'the turnip winter'.

The Berliners' resistance to the policies of their leaders was strengthened by three important events in 1917 and early 1918. First, the almost bloodless Russian revolution in March 1917, with the abdication of the Tsar, gave them hope. Some 200,000 workers downed tools in Berlin and Leipzig, demanding democracy in Germany and immediate peace negotiations. The strike was put down by the army, but anti-war sentiment continued to grow. Then, in January 1918, President Wilson's announcement of his Fourteen Points for peace appeared to offer grounds for a just and honourable settlement. This was in marked contrast to the peace terms being forced on Russia by the German High Command, which were so harsh that they underlined the brutal stupidity of the German leaders, and the need to get rid of them.

Munitions workers in Berlin led a nationwide strike for peace and democratic government, just at the moment when Quarter Master General Erich von Ludendorff was preparing for his last great thrust against France. Again, the strike was put down with force. But Ludendorff's spring offensive failed. A fresh American army entered the field on the western front, and as Germany's allies Bulgaria, Austria and Turkey crumbled in the east, he faced complete military defeat in the field, and a political revolution at home.

In a typically Prussian move, Ludendorff forestalled the revolution by staging one of his own. Relinquishing the powers held since 1916 by himself and the commander-in-chief, Field Marshal Paul von Hindenburg, he set up a constitutional government under Prince Max of Baden, answerable not to the Kaiser but to the

Reichstag. Yet again, change had been imposed on the people from above. And yet again, the change was made to suit their rulers, for Ludendorff and Hindenburg knew that their only hope of hanging on to power was to hold on to the army: they had to make peace with the Allies before the army disintegrated. But they also knew the Allies would never negotiate with a military dictatorship. And so, on 29 September 1918, Berlin, together with the rest of Germany, finally achieved the prize its citizens had sought for 700 years, not won as a result of insurrection but granted as a favour by a military autocracy.

Peace came six weeks later, with the armistice on 11 November. But even before it was signed, the seeds of future cataclysm had been sown. When negotiations began, Ludendorff issued a proclamation to the German army, claiming that the enemy was demanding unconditional surrender, which was 'unacceptable to us soldiers'. Incensed by this unauthorized interference, Prince Max demanded the general's resignation, and Ludendorff was forced to spend the last month of the war skulking in a Berlin pension before fleeing to Sweden disguised behind dark glasses and a false beard. And so the legend was born of Germany's brave soldiers, undefeated by the enemy but betrayed and stabbed in the back by their own politicians.

In the meantime, a genuine revolution had begun, not in Berlin for once, but in the unlikely setting of the great naval base at Kiel. The crews of two battleships had mutinied at the end of October, followed by the rest of the base, and within a few days the entire fleet was in the hands of the rebels. The revolt spread to Hamburg, then to Munich, and finally arrived in Berlin on 8 November, when hundreds of thousands took to the streets, waving red flags, overturning vehicles, ransacking and destroying government offices, tearing the badges of rank from army officers and in a few instances killing them. Crack military regiments sent in to crush the uprising joined it instead. Guards on barracks and public buildings refused to fire on the people.

General Wilhelm Gröner, who had taken over from Ludendorff, warned Prince Max that the army could not hold out more than another day on the western front. At the same time, the social democrats threatened to withdraw from the government unless both the Kaiser and the crown prince abdicated immediately. Prince Max telephoned Wilhelm, who was still lording it over his generals at his supreme headquarters in the Belgian resort of Spa. 'Your abdication has become necessary to save Germany from civil war,' he told him. 'The troops are not to be depended upon. This is the last possible moment. Unless the abdication takes place today, I can do no more.'

The Kaiser, as usual, refused to face reality. He could not believe that his soldiers would ever renege on their vows to him, and threatened to lead his army back to Germany, to reconquer his own country by force. He blamed Prince Max for the crisis. 'You sent out the armistice offer,' he barked. 'You will have to accept the consequences.' And then he put down the phone and went to bed.

Back in Berlin, the left-wing parties called a general strike, to begin next day at 9.00 am, unless the Kaiser had by then agreed to go. When there had been no word from him by that time, the social democrat government resigned. Prince Max had been trying to reach the Kaiser since first light, but had been unsuccessful: Wilhelm's villa in Spa had two telephones, but his aides had deliberately taken one of them off the hook, and kept the other busy, so that no one could get through. In desperation as the mobs gathered on the streets of the capital, chanting and waving red flags, Prince Max took matters into his own hands and simply declared that the Kaiser had abdicated.

Unaware of the declaration, Wilhelm was still arguing with his generals, and preparing himself to lead his army back home to quell the rebels. Gröner had to tell him: 'Your Majesty, you no longer have an army.' But he refused to believe it. Even when regimental commanders confirmed that officers and men wanted peace, he put off taking the decision. The crown prince supported him in true Hohenzollern style: 'After a good lunch and a good cigar, things will look better,' he told his father.

After lunch, however, things looked worse than ever. News of Prince Max's declaration arrived, provoking Wilhelm into a paroxysm of rage. 'Treason, gentlemen!' he screamed. 'Bare-faced, outrageous treason!' But eventually, even he had to accept that his life was in danger from his own troops. After a long and bitter argument, his generals persuaded him to take the royal train across the border into nearby Holland, and beg Queen Wilhelmina for asylum.

With the Kaiser toppled from the imperial throne, all the other royal rulers of the individual states of the Reich were also deposed. Prince Max handed over the chancellorship to the leader of the social democrats, Friedrich Ebert, who was furious when his deputy, Philipp Scheidemann, speaking from a window of the Reichstag to a great crowd of Berliners, proclaimed a republic. Although he was a socialist, Ebert had already agreed to a period of regency, to be followed by a fully constitutional monarchy. In fact, Scheidemann had little alternative, for he knew that the leader of the left-wing socialists, Karl Liebknecht, was about to declare a soviet socialist republic from the balcony of the royal palace, which a Berlin shopkeeper named Schlesinger had draped with a red blanket.

The German left had splintered into rival factions during the later stages of the war, and there were now three socialist parties in Berlin, all fighting each other as much as the common enemy. As confusion threatened to become anarchy, only one thing was certain: the rule of the Hohenzollerns was finally at an end.

For the next three months, Berliners lived in a world where sporadic street fighting, mostly between Ebert's moderate socialists and the supporters of Liebknecht's far left Spartakus League, was regarded by most of the people as merely an inconvenient intrusion into the normal life of the city. Most of the public services continued to run smoothly. The telephones kept working. The luxury hotels functioned as usual. Bars, theatres and cabarets were still packed every night, with performers and customers alike ignoring the occasional bullet flying through the windows. Dance halls were still officially closed under wartime regulations, but their place was taken by hundreds of clandestine night clubs. Trams kept to their timetables, carrying more passengers than usual, since it was announced that all the warring parties had agreed not to shoot at them. When a Spartakist machine-gun nest on top of the Brandenburg Gate disrupted traffic crossing the Linden on Friedrichstrasse, regular periods of ceasefire were agreed, controlled by signal flags, to keep it moving.

Count Harry Kessler, an ardent socialite and patron of the arts, considered that all this proved that Berlin had come of age as a world city. He noted in his diary that its metropolitan character was now 'so basic that even a revolution affecting world history, such as this one . . . was little more than a minor disturbance in the to-and-fro of Berlin, as if an elephant were to receive a cut from a penknife. It shakes itself, but proceeds as if nothing had happened.'

Kessler also recorded that 'throughout the blood-letting, hurdy-gurdies played in the Friedrichstrasse, while street vendors sold indoor fireworks, gingerbread, and silver tinsel. Jewellers' shops in Unter den Linden remained unconcernedly open, their windows brightly lit and glittering. In the Leipzigerstrasse, the usual Christmas crowds thronged the big stores. In thousands of homes the Christmas tree was lit and the children played around it with their presents ... In the imperial stables lay the dead, and the wounds freshly inflicted on the palace and on Germany gaped into the Christmas night.'

Like any good petit bourgeois (he had been a saddler before entering politics) Chancellor Ebert was mainly concerned with law and order. To warn of the dangers of chaos and destruction, he turned to the Litfass poster columns, plastering them with notices. Typically, he used a line from a poem by Walter Mehring: '*Berlin, dein Tanzer ist der Tod.*' 'Berlin, your dancing partner is death.'

But even Ebert knew better than to rely on posters alone. Admitting that he 'hated revolution like sin', he had already done a secret deal with General Gröner. He had in effect placed his government at the disposal of the army, promising to maintain the Prussian military tradition in return for protection. And when Hindenburg's front-line troops marched smartly back into the city, garlanded and cheered by a huge crowd, he greeted them at the Brandenburg Gate as though they were conquering heroes. 'As you return undefeated from the field of battle, I salute you!' he told them, deliberately reinforcing the legend of the army's invincibility and the 'stab in the back' that had betrayed them.

As the Spartakists moved ever further left, changing their name at the end of December to the Communist Party of Germany, the KPD, so they became more and more violent. The fighting escalated, with revolutionary sailors forming the core of the communist forces. Ebert called in loyal troops of the regular army, and then instructed his war minister, Gustav Noske, to form irregular volunteer companies, the Freikorps, from outside Berlin. Between them, they smashed the revolutionaries. Liebknecht and his fellow communist leader, Rosa Luxemburg, were arrested and murdered in cold blood by Freikorps officers. Liebknecht's body was dumped in the Neue See, the lake in the middle of the Tiergarten about 150 metres to the north of the Landwehr canal. During the political and gang violence that was to continue for another 15 years, the canal was a convenient and popular depository for unwanted corpses. Rosa Luxemburg's floated to the surface six months after her murder.

The martyred couple were still able to arouse strong passions nearly 70 years later. It was not until 1986, and then after much acrimonious debate, that the West Berlin authorities agreed to erect memorial plaques to them. And then they placed them where they were virtually impossible to find. Luxemburg's is hidden underneath the Lichtensteinbrücke where it crosses the canal. Liebknecht's is tucked away somewhere on the bank of the lake.

By mid-January, the revolution appeared to be over. The first elections for a new national assembly were held on 19 January 1919, with a universal franchise for all adults over the age of 20, both men and women, voting on a proportional representation basis. The result was an overwhelming success for Ebert and his social democrats (SPD), who received 38 per cent of the total votes, giving them 163 of the 421 seats in the Reichstag. The Catholic Centre Party came second with 89, then the Liberal Democratic Party with 74. The more extreme parties were marginalized: on the right, the Nationalist Party won only 42 seats, and the independent socialist USPD only 22. The communists boycotted the whole affair, pinning their hopes on gaining power through the workers' and soldiers' soviets. Of the 35 women elected, nearly half were for the SPD. In Berlin, the voters in the north and east of the city voted solidly for the SPD, with a smaller vote for the USPD. The middle-class west and south favoured the liberal democrats. The Catholics and conservatives came nowhere.

Ebert was elected as the republic's first president, with Scheidemann as chancellor. With Berlin still in crisis, they chose to convene the new assembly in Weimar, the town of Goethe and Schiller 150 miles south-west of the capital, where the soldiers of the Freikorps and the army could protect them more easily until it was safe to return to the Reichstag. They met to decide on a new constitution in the opera house where Franz Liszt had conducted the first performance of Wagner's *Lohengrin*. With elements borrowed from the United States, Britain, France and Switzerland, the result was a document that looked good on paper but which in fact was fatally flawed, leaving in place all the social, economic, and above all military forces of the Hohenzollern empire. The Kaiser himself had gone, but the legacy of absolute rule remained. The president was to be the supreme commander of the army, he could appoint officials, and – most dangerously – he could suspend civil liberties and rule directly 'if public order and safety were endangered'.

While they were debating, trouble flared again in Berlin. In early March, the Spartakists tried to seize power. Noske declared a state of emergency in the city, and assumed dictatorial powers. By then, Freikorps numbers had been swollen by thousands of new recruits, and they attacked the revolutionaries in the fiercest fighting that Berlin had yet seen. Both sides used artillery and mortars. The Freikorps even brought in aircraft. Noske ordered that anyone seen with a weapon in his hand should be shot immediately, and his orders were carried out with enthusiastic brutality. By the time order was restored, the 'white terror' of the Freikorps had claimed at least 1,200 victims.

A year later, the Freikorps turned against the government. They believed it had betrayed Germany by accepting the punitive terms of the Versailles Treaty, the *Diktat* or 'slave treaty' as they called it. At Versailles, France had gained her revenge for the five billion gold francs she had had to pay to Berlin after the Franco-Prussian war in 1871 by insisting Germany pay massive punitive reparations to her and the other Allies. Germany had also been forced to hand back the fruits of Bismarck's wars: Alsace-Lorraine was returned to France, and northern Schleswig to Denmark. She had been stripped of her colonies, and of her share of the 1815 carve-up of Poland. She had been ordered to withdraw all military forces from her own territory west of the Rhine, which was occupied by the French army. She had lost Wilhelm's navy: most of the grand fleet already lay at the bottom of the sea in the British anchorage of Scapa Flow in the Orkneys, scuttled by its own captains. She was forbidden to build new warships. But to the Prussian militarists, who still insisted they had not been defeated on the battlefield, the bitterest pill of all was that the army was to be partially disarmed and restricted to 100,000 men. It was not even to be called the army, but the Reichswehr, the Imperial Defence Force.

The final straw came when the government ordered the Freikorps to be disbanded, as part of the reduction of the army. On 13 March 1920, its crack Erhardt Brigade marched on Berlin in perfect parade-ground order, flying the black, white and red colours of the old Reich, gleaming steel helmets adorned with one of the Freikorps' favourite emblems, the swastika. Their aim was to overthrow the

government and replace it with a new administration led by Gustav
Kapp, New York-born founder of the extreme right-wing Fatherland Party, under the patronage of General Ludendorff.

As the brigade approached, Ebert and his ministers wisely decamped to Dresden, and then to Stuttgart, leaving the city open.
General von Seeckt, the new commander-in-chief of the regular
army, had declined Ebert's plea for military support with the cool
reply: 'Troops do not fire on troops . . . When *Reichswehr* fires on
Reichswehr, then all comradeship within the officer corps will have
vanished.'

Although he could not count on the army, Ebert found he could
count on the Berliners. Deprived of guns and bullets, he turned
instead to the traditional socialist weapon. As he fled the city, he
issued a proclamation to the press, calling for a general strike. The
Berliners responded immediately, bringing the city to a complete
standstill. Nothing worked, nothing moved. There was no water,
no gas, no electricity, no services of any sort. There were no
newspapers, no hotels, no shops. Civil servants stayed away from
their offices. The shut-down was total. After six days, the putsch
collapsed, Kapp fled to Sweden, and the men of the Freikorps
marched out of the city again, still in parade-ground order.

The new decade had started as it was to end, with confusion,
violence and political instability. The sudden end of Hohenzollern
rule meant there had been no period of transition from an ancient
regime to a modern democracy, and this lack of preparation led to
a succession of weak governments plagued by insurrections and
assassinations.

Traditionally, Prussian rulers had always been maintained in
power by the army. But the Reichswehr, though now only 100,000
strong, had withdrawn into itself, becoming more than ever a state
within a state. It could no longer be relied upon to support any
government it disapproved of. So, the political parties formed their
own private armies, uniformed and equipped like regular troops:
the Stalhelm on the right, the social democrat Reichsbanner, the
communist Rotfrontkampferbund and, initially much smaller than
the others, the Nazi Sturmabteilung, or SA.

To some people, these paramilitary organizations were a direct
replacement for the disbanded Freikorps. But for most of their

members they were a sort of unofficial reserve for the regular army, a way of cocking a snook at the Versailles restrictions, of staying in training for the day of reckoning. And, of course, they could wear a uniform. For the first six years, they dressed up, held their parades and marched to military bands with banners flying, content for the most part to play at soldiers.

CHAPTER 14

Babylon-on-the-Spree

1919 SAW THE START of another stream of incomers into Berlin. This time they were White Russians, fleeing from the civil war in the wake of the bolshevik revolution. When the White Russian army was defeated, the stream became a flood. Over a million Russians left their native land, and many settled, temporarily at least, in Berlin. Indeed, thousands who had gone on to Paris returned to Berlin when, in 1921, prices in France rose sharply, while Germany was still a cheap place to live. Berlin was also, of course, nearer to Mother Russia.

No one knows exactly how many Russians settled in Berlin, but it was probably about 50,000. According to the writer Ilya Ehrenberg, who arrived in the city towards the end of 1921 and took lodgings in Pragerplatz, then a modestly smart area of Wilmersdorf, Russian could be heard everywhere, and there were dozens of Russian restaurants, 'with balalaikas, and zurnas, with gypsies, pancakes, shashlyks and, naturally, the inevitable heartbreak'.

Ehrenberg set out to explore his quarter and discovered that all was not as it seemed. The mark was falling, and shopkeepers adjusted their prices daily. Anyone with hard currency could – and some did – buy up the Ku'damm, where nothing was as it seemed.

Outfitters now sold pink and blue dickeys, because whole shirts were too expensive for ordinary folk. The sweet cakes at Café Josty on Potsdamerplatz were made from frost-bitten potatoes, the so-called 'Mocha' was a wishy-washy imitation, and cigars labelled 'Havana' or 'Brazilian' were made out of dried cabbage leaves, steeped in nicotine.

Even the famous Berlin night spots weren't always what they appeared to be. Ehrenberg and a friend were approached one evening by a man who offered to take them to an interesting new club. The two Russians agreed, and followed the man down the U-Bahn. They travelled out into the suburbs, then walked miles through dark streets and finally found themselves in a respectable flat, with family portraits of officers in uniform and a painting of a sunset hanging on the walls. The visitors were given 'champagne' – lemonade laced with spirits. Then the host's two daughters appeared, naked, and began to dance, while their mother studied the two Russians, wondering whether they would be tempted by her daughters, and whether they would pay in hard currency, such as dollars. 'Is this life?' sighed the respectable mama. 'It's the end of the world . . .'

The mother was echoing a popular song of the day, 'Tomorrow's the end of the world.' But of course it wasn't, and in Berlin at least catastrophe wore a respectable face. Even those damaged by the war camouflaged themselves discreetly before they roamed the streets. 'The artificial limbs of war cripples did not creak,' wrote Ehrenberg, 'empty sleeves were pinned up with safety pins. Men whose faces had been scorched by flame-throwers wore large black spectacles.'

By no means all of the Russians who flocked to Berlin were fugitives from the bolshevik regime. Stanislavski brought his Moscow Arts Theatre company on an official tour. Sergei Eisenstein, the film director, came to the UFA studios at Babelsberg to study the latest developments in film technique, so that Soviet cinema would not lag behind the capitalist world. Others, however, like the painter Wassily Kandinsky, the pianist Vladimir Horowitz and the cellist Gregor Piatigorski, were true refugees: Piatigorski was so poor he had to sleep on a bench in the Tiergarten, with his instrument tucked underneath the seat.

It has been said that at that time almost every Russian writer of note either visited Berlin or was living there. They included such names as Sergei Essenin, who came with his wife, the dancer Isadora Duncan, Gorky, Mayakovsky, Pasternak, and the 21-year-old Vladimir Nabokov, the future author of *Lolita*.

The Nabokovs arrived in 1920: V.D. Nabokov, the novelist's father, who was a magazine editor and a politician, Elena, his mother, brothers Sergei and Kirill, sisters Elena and Olga, and their grandmother Maria. They all moved into a flat at 1 Egerstrasse, off the Hohenzollerndamm, which reverberated to the noise of trams but was less than half a mile from the peace of the Grunewald. Almost immediately, Nabokov senior and two friends began negotiations with the Ullstein press to set up the city's first Russian publishing house, Slovo, which was to publish Vladimir's first novel, *Mary (Mashen'ka)*. The next venture was a Russian-language newspaper, also printed by Ullstein, with V.D. Nabokov as editor. The first issue of *Rul'* (*The Rudder*), hit the streets at 4.00 pm on 15 November 1920. It became the city's principal Russian newspaper, and surprisingly earned Ullstein much valuable foreign currency: wherever in the world Russian refugees settled, the first thing they did was order their copy of *Rul'* from Ullstein in Berlin.

Russian Berlin has been aptly described as 'a cultural supernova'. More books and periodicals were published in the three years up to 1924 than most countries publish in a decade. There were three daily and five weekly newspapers; no fewer than 17 new Russian-language publishing houses opened in one year, bringing the total by 1924 to an incredible 86. There was also at least one exclusively Russian theatre. Some of the publishing houses were financed by Moscow, because at that time the bolsheviks still hoped to persuade intellectuals to return home: some did, many of them to die later in Stalin's gulags.

For a while, the boundaries between the émigrés and Soviet Russian writers seemed blurred in Berlin, as they congregated in the same publishing offices and literary cafés, most notably the Café Leon in Nollendorfplatz. This created a dangerous kind of no-man's-land, where intrigue and murder flourished. There were many Soviet agents in Berlin, and many émigrés who would have rendered their grandmothers down for glue if the price was right. And of course there were fanatics of every hue, ready to kill those who opposed their beliefs.

V.D. Nabokov belonged to the right wing of the Kadet Party, the constitutional democrats who were against any compromise with

Lenin or the Russian left. Leading the other faction in the Russian diaspora was Paul Milyukov, former foreign minister and now editor of the Paris-based *Poslednie Novosty*, a Russian magazine similar to *Rul'*. Milyukov believed there were socialists in Russia who did not want to follow Lenin's path, and with whom it was possible to deal. In spite of their differences, Nabokov invited Milyukov to Berlin to speak about his recent trip to the United States. The subject of his talk was to be 'America and the restoration of Russia', which has an eerily familiar ring to it today. About 1,500 Russians turned up at the Philharmonie to listen. At about 10.00 pm, a fanatical tsarist from Munich, Peter Shabelsky-Bork, rose from his seat, marched to the platform and started shooting at Milyukov. Nabokov leapt to tackle the would-be assassin, but a second gunman fired several shots at him as he wrestled with Shabelsky-Bork, hitting him twice in the spine and once through the heart and lung. Milyukov was saved, but Nabokov died almost instantly.

1922 was to be a prime year for political assassinations in Berlin, with home-grown as well as émigré politicians facing the threat of gun and bomb. The most famous victim was the social democrat foreign minister of the new Germany, Walther Rathenau, son of the founder of AEG, the giant electrical combine. On the morning of 24 June, Rathenau left his house in Königsallee, in the Grunewald, for his office in Wilhelmstrasse. Although the police had recently warned that they could not guarantee his safety if he persisted in such foolishness, he was driven as usual by his chauffeur in his open car. His assassins were waiting for him, in their own car. They were five young men, all from good families: naval Lieutenant Erwin Kern and Hermann Fischer, both aged 25, two 20-year-old cadets, Ernst von Salomon and Ernst-Werner Techow, the son of a Berlin magistrate, and 17-year-old Hans Stubenrach, the son of a general. As Rathenau's chauffeur slowed down to cross tram tracks by Erdenerstrasse, they drew alongside. Kern pulled out a gun, rested the butt in his armpit, and opened fire. Five bullets struck Rathenau, smashing his jaw and entering his spine. As the murder car accelerated away, Hermann Fischer tossed a hand grenade into Rathenau's car, to make sure of the kill.

Techow, the driver, was soon captured by the police, having been given away by his uncle. Salomon and Stubenrach were also quickly rounded up. After a nationwide hunt, Kern and Fischer were cornered in the uninhabited Seeleck Castle, 150 miles south of Berlin, where they shot it out with the police. Kern was killed by a bullet in the head, whereupon Fischer shot himself. Both were given military funerals, with full honours.

At their trial, the three captured killers produced a bizarre reason for the murder. According to Techow, Kern had been convinced that Rathenau was a 'veiled' bolshevik, and one of the 300 Elders of Zion seeking to impose Jewish domination on the world. These ideas arose from his study of *The Protocols of the Elders of Zion*, a fake book concocted in about 1895, apparently by the tsarist Russian secret police, intended to discredit the Jews with scurrilous tales of bloodthirsty practices and deep conspiracies. It aroused little interest in Russia, but sold 100,000 copies when translated and published in Germany, and was taken up by Henry Ford, who distributed it in the USA.

The public's reaction to the Rathenau assassination was astonishing. While his body lay in state in the Reichstag, where President Ebert read the oration and an orchestra played Siegfried's funeral music, the labour unions decreed a national day of mourning. Despite the fact that he was an industrial aristocrat, an arch-capitalist, and a rather cold and aloof personality, an estimated one million people marched through the streets of Berlin to protest the murder.

But many Berliners saw the murder as part of a right-wing plot to eliminate any leadership but that of the right, leaving the left leaderless. With Rosa Luxemburg and Karl Liebknecht liquidated two years before, now Rathenau, and later that year Hugo Haase, leader of the Independent Socialist Party, who was gunned down on the steps of the Reichstag, such a fear was clearly not unfounded. That same year, too, the prime minister of Bavaria, Kurt Eisner, was shot on the streets of Munich, and Matthias Erzberger, finance minister and signatory of the 1918 armistice, was murdered while walking in the Black Forest.

During the four years from 1918 to 1922, there were 376 political murders in Germany: 354 by right-wing groups, 22 by the left. Ten of the left-wing assassins were executed, and seven received long prison sentences. But 326 of the right-wing killers went either uncaught or unpunished. Those who were caught received an average sentence of four months; for the left-wing murderers, on the other hand, the average sentence was 15 years. In the Rathenau case, Techow was sentenced to 15 years imprisonment, which was commuted to seven, of which he served only four. Salomon served five years. Had they been left-wingers, they would undoubtedly have been executed.

The popular image of Berlin's 'Golden Twenties' is so well-known that it almost needs no description. The Berlin of Bertolt Brecht and George Grosz, of Josephine Baker and Christopher Isherwood's Sally Bowles, has been enshrined in countless books, plays, films, musicals: a wild city of sexual licence and perversion, of alcohol and cocaine, Babylon-on-the-Spree. The image has become a cliché, but like most clichés it is largely true. Released from the oppressive rule of the Kaisers, deprived of its social standards and restraints, eager to drown the memory of the horrors of the great war, many of the survivors plunged blindly into a frantic quest for pleasure.

Inevitably, there was no shortage of people willing to supply them: whores, criminals and drug dealers multiplied. When he first came to Berlin, the future playwright and screenwriter Carl Zuckmayer was broke and ready to take any job he could find. One was as a hustler for night clubs. Part of his job was selling cocaine on the street, though the substance he was selling turned out not to be cocaine at all, but a mixture of powdered aspirin and cooking salt. Fortunately, a friendly Polish street-walker, whose beat was in Tauenzienstrasse near the Ka-De-We store, warned him of the dangers and managed to sell his 'cocaine' for him.

Cocaine – the real thing – was the drug of choice for anyone in Berlin who could afford it. There was no shortage of the stuff: it was available from the hostesses in almost every night club, or from peddlers on even the most fashionable streets. Some doctors regularly prescribed cocaine and morphine as painkillers, with the result that morphine was almost as widely used as cocaine. The Nazi leader Hermann Göring became a morphine addict after being wounded in the hip during Hitler's attempted putsch in Munich in 1923. The wound became infected and filled with pus. To kill the pain, his doctors gave him massive doses of morphine, and in a short time he was hopelessly addicted.

Supplies and suppliers of drugs, like most crime in Berlin during the Twenties, were controlled by the so-called Ringvereine, or sporting clubs. These organizations, mostly based in the poorer sectors of the city, went by resounding but innocuous-sounding names like *Immertreu* ('For ever true'), *Hand in Hand*, *Felsenfest* ('Firm as a Rock'), *Deutsche Kraft* ('German Strength'), or *Glaube, Liebe, Hoffnung* ('Faith, Love, Hope'). Some chose more racy titles, like *Nordpiraten* ('Northern Pirates') or *Apachenblut* ('Apache Blood'). Each club had its own embroidered silk banner, and its flowery motto – 'One hand washes the other', for instance, or 'What God permits us, must be allowed us'. Members wore special rings and enamelled badges of membership and rank, obeyed strict rules, and paid regular subscriptions which were faithfully entered in their membership books. Meetings were conducted with solemn formality, with the leaders dressed in top hats, cutaway coats and silk sashes.

Although they had been in existence since the Nineties, the Ringvereine reached their peak between 1920 and 1932, by which time there were 62 clubs in Berlin, each controlling its own *Kiez* or neighbourhood with absolute authority. For the sporting clubs were the Berlin version of the Mafia, running all the rackets, organizing crime, and imposing their protection on businesses large and small, from amusement halls and Kneipen in Prenzlauerberg to chic jewellers on the Ku'damm.

The Ringvereine had started life in 1891, with official encouragement, as the Reichsverein ehemaliger Strafgefangener, the Imperial Society for Former Prisoners, aimed at the rehabilitation of released convicts. It was not long before the former prisoners took over from the do-gooders, recognizing the society as a wonderful umbrella for their activities. By 1895, the first contacts had been made with the Cosa Nostra in America. Three years later, the organization had split into five criminal societies, linked in what they called the *Grossen Ring*, or the *Deutscher Ring*, with branches throughout northern Germany. But Berlin remained at the centre, and individual clubs proliferated within the Berlin Ring.

Membership of a Ring club was a carefully guarded privilege: candidates had to be over 21 and have served a minimum of two years in prison. They also had to provide the finest character references, including at least two guarantors from within the club itself, before they were allowed to take the oath and pay the stiff entrance fee. Ring brothers rejoicing in names like 'Muscles Adolf', 'Coke Gustav', 'Climbing Maxie' and 'Canal Fritze' (bodies were always being fished out of the Landwehr canal in those days) enjoyed hero status in districts like Wedding, Rixdorf and Kreuzberg, and the *Zylinderleute* ('top hats') were feared and respected everywhere.

The 'brotherhood' imposed its own discipline on members. They were expected to submit themselves to the authority of their club *Führer* without question, even being prepared to go to jail for another brother if he ordered them to. Those foolish enough to transgress the code faced fines, savage beatings, expulsion – a serious matter, since it deprived a criminal of permission to work – and ultimately the death penalty. But the brothers stood solidly together against all outsiders; woe betide anyone who raised a hand against one of them. Any brother in trouble was provided with the best legal help, and the benefit of as much pressure as could be brought on the police, the court, and of course on witnesses. If this failed to keep him out of jail, he and his family would be looked after while he was inside. His rent would be paid and pocket money and parcels of food and goodies provided for wife and children. Wives or girl friends of prisoners were out of bounds to all other brothers, on pain of immediate expulsion.

Funerals were always special occasions, conducted with the maximum show. When a brother died, his club would always take care of everything. Section 17 of the rule book of Immertreu read: 'The club holds it as an honourable obligation to bury each member as the honour and dignity of Immertreu demands.' And it demanded a great deal. All the other members were required to turn out as mourners, wearing top hats and frock coats, to walk behind the coffin in what sometimes seemed endless processions. A male voice choir from the club would sing at the graveside, songs such as 'I had a comrade' and – with no trace of irony – 'Loyalty and honesty for ever'.

The Ringvereine had the police in their pockets, and received donations from officials in the police president's office, high government officials, businessmen and industrialists. Celebrities from the worlds of sport, show business and the press, even Germany's biggest star of stage and screen Gustav Gründgens, were honorary members. Two annual events held by the Ringvereine, the foundation ball and the spring ball, were among the highlights of the social year in Berlin, particularly among the prosperous bourgeoisie. The ten biggest clubs took it in turn to organize these affairs, where the highest standards of dress, language and behaviour were demanded. No smutty jokes or personal abuse were allowed, even though the ladies accompanying the brothers usually went by names like 'Droschkengaul' (Taxi-Nag) or 'Rohrfeger' (Besom).

Throughout the madcap years of the Twenties, the Ringvereine flourished, almost as a law unto themselves. But at the beginning of 1929, they finally went too far when members of Immertreu, led by Muscles Adolf, went to avenge the stabbing of a Ring member by a carpenter. The carpenter's friends foolishly laid an ambush, and attacked them with billiard cues, axes and clubs in a bar called the Dixi in Breslauerstrasse. A brother managed to get to the phone and raised the 'Ringalarm'. Within minutes, more than 100 members of Immertreu and the Nordpiraten arrived, and laid into the carpenters with pistols, black jacks, clubs and daggers. The landlord of the Dixi later said he counted over 100 pistol shots. The battle raged for half an hour, during which time the original culprit had his skull smashed. The police, naturally, kept out of the way until it was all over. When they finally turned up, all the brothers had vanished, taking their wounded with them.

After such a public display, the authorities found it hard to keep quiet, and had to move against the Ringvereine. Police squads poured out of their headquarters at the Alex, and set about rounding up the two gangs who had been involved in the fracas. The trial opened on 4 February. The small courtroom at Moabit was packed to overflowing every day with sympathizers. The press had a field day, and for the first time the respectable population of Berlin began to learn what had been going on in their city for so long. But even though the prosecution painted lurid pictures of the activities of the Ringvereine, it had great difficulty producing any tangible evidence. Nobody had seen anything. Nobody had been harmed. Nobody had ever been intimidated, or subjected to extortion. The silence was said to have cost the clubs an average of 30 marks a witness, and it was clearly money well spent. Muscles Adolf was sentenced to ten months for breach of the peace. Ring cashier Lass got five months. Everyone else was acquitted.

The high days of the Ringvereine were over, however. The police president issued an edict banning them, and they were forced to go deeper underground as survival became a battle of wits between police and criminals. The most celebrated incident in the police campaign came with the rounding up of a Ringverein that had established an apparently impregnable summer headquarters in an inn called the Grosse Zug (the Big Swig), on an island in the Dahme in the south-east corner of Berlin. The island could only be reached by boat, and the brothers, claiming to be a water sports club, had bought control of all the boats and ferries in the area. For once, however, the police outsmarted them. They formed a society of their own, a Singverein, or singing club, and wrote to the Grosse Zug booking the inn for their annual outing, and promising to give a concert there. They arrived on a chartered steamer, and came ashore – in plain clothes, of course – to be greeted warmly by the brothers who had assembled to enjoy the music. The 'choir' lined up, and went into their first number, an old Berlin favourite called 'Who Owns You, Beautiful Forest?' The gangsters were still applauding when the singing policemen whipped out their revolvers and arrested them all, marching them on to the waiting steamer to be ferried back to the Alexanderplatz.

The end of the Ringvereine came with the Nazis. Hitler's ban on 1 January 1934 proved more effective than the former police president's, being unhindered by such niceties as evidence. The remaining Zylinderleute were among the first inmates of the new concentration camps, and many brothers died there, including Muscles Adolf.

The high life of fashionable Berlin was enjoyed by only a minority of Berliners, of course. While the few thousand better-off citizens roared their way round the west end or Friedrichstrasse or Pariserplatz, for the vast majority the city centre was the far less glamorous Alexanderplatz, to the north-east of the royal palace. Many never got beyond their own local centres in the poorer districts like Wedding, Kreuzberg or Neukölln.

For most Berliners, the Twenties were a time of constant uncertainty, hardship, and misery. Shopkeepers, small businessmen, pensioners, all those relying on savings, middle-class families and workers alike, were ruined by the hyperinflation of 1923. It was without question the single most important event of the entire decade: if they couldn't rely on money, was there anything that could be relied on? The collapse of the currency was largely responsible for the collapse of moral standards, totally undermining the foundations of German society, and paving the way for the unprincipled extremism that was to follow.

The great inflation was caused by a combination of factors, not least a cynical attempt by the government and big business to clear Germany's gigantic war debts and the Allies' punitive reparations demands by devaluing the mark. Once the process had begun, it quickly got completely out of hand. The traditional pre-war rate of 4.20 marks to the US dollar had slipped to 75 by 1921 – bad, but not disastrous. By the summer of 1922 it had reached 400, and panic began to set in, which aggravated the problem. By January 1923 it was down to 7,000. When the French lost their patience, and seized the industries of the Ruhr, the helter-skelter really began. By mid-summer the figures had reached astronomical proportions: tens of thousands became hundreds of thousands, then millions, then hundreds of millions, then billions, and eventually trillions of marks to the dollar. And still the government kept printing more money, even though it cost more to print even the biggest note than it was worth. They even commandeered Ullstein's high-speed newspaper presses in an effort to keep pace with demand.

It became the custom in Berlin to pay wages every day at noon, and every day at noon the city would come to a standstill as workers dashed from their offices into the nearest shops, carrying sacks and baskets of worthless paper money, trying to buy anything that was on offer before the money became even more worthless. Barter was the order of the day, and the strongest currency of all was food.

At the height of all this, no one in Berlin paid much attention to a farcical coup attempt in far-off Munich. There had been several far more serious threats in various parts of the country since the war. This was just a hiccup, a minor south German politician called Adolf Hitler playing at soldiers with an insignificant private army. The only important thing was that the real army had stood firm against it, even though General Ludendorff was involved.

What was infinitely more important at that moment in November was that a brilliant young financier named Hjalmar Schacht, called in by the desperate Finance Ministry, set about the inflation with utterly ruthless determination, and by the end of the year he had stabilized the mark at the old rate of 4.20 to the dollar. The crisis was over, but the damage to the German psyche was permanent. Of course, there were many who had profited by the inflation; sharks and racketeers will always make the most of such confusion, and the really big industrialists ended up even bigger and richer than before. Foreigners poured into Berlin in their thousands, to take advantage of the power of foreign currency at a time when $50 would buy a whole row of elegant houses in one of the city's best districts. But the vast majority of the population suffered a trauma which would take years to overcome.

A typical example of the hardship caused by the inflation was the experience of Christabel Bielenberg's gardener, Herr Neisse, who had scrimped and sacrificed for years to scrape together enough to marry his sweetheart, Hilde, and to buy a tiny plot of land. Everything had vanished overnight. 'The inflation, you see, Frau Doctor; suddenly we had nothing. With my savings I was able to buy just one cup and saucer which I gave to Hilde instead of her marriage lines. Funny, wasn't it, that I should be so keen on the saucer?' When Herr Neisse spoke of those times, Mrs Bielenberg recalls, 'his voice shook with emotion, and the usual concise movements of his hands became nervous and erratic. The loss of his little bank account had not only shattered whatever faith he might have had in constitution or government, but also struck at the root of his very being, his self-respect, and his right to be respected. The saucer, perhaps there was something respectable about a saucer . . .'

Large-scale loans from Germany's former enemies, the Americans and the British, helped the prospects of recovery. They were worth billions of dollars, way in excess of the reparations that were still being collected. Soon, the Twenties became literally golden in the financial sense. Germany was paying the highest rates of interest for short-term loans, so foreign bankers were queuing up to lend money – money for anything, it didn't matter what. The country, and that meant Berlin in particular, was riding the crest of the Wall Street wave, borrowing money to expand industries and to invest in public works, borrowing money even to speculate on Wall Street itself. Borrowing, borrowing, and why not? It was boom time, everyone had gone a little mad – surely it was never going to end?

In December of 1925, following the death of Friedrich Ebert, a new president was elected: the old warhorse and national hero, Field Marshal Paul von Hindenburg, a reassuring link with better, more certain times, the soldier who had been defeated only by the stab in the back from the enemies within.

CHAPTER 15

The Golden Twenties

T HE DECADE BETWEEN 1920 and 1930 has been immortalized in Berlin legend as 'the Golden Twenties', and in many respects, they really were golden years for the city. Released from the Hohenzollern straitjacket, the arts flourished as never before or since, as writers, painters, musicians, actors, directors, flocked to find freedom there. Under the Kaisers, the arts had had to conform to royal taste. Fifteen years later, Adolf Hitler would reimpose exactly the same artistic limitations, with more ferocious penalties for those who dared to transgress. In the years between, however, anything went, and Berlin became, briefly, the centre of all that was modern and unconventional in art.

Leading the way was the Dada movement – Dada is a French word meaning a child's hobbyhorse. The name was adopted by a group of young writers and artists in Zurich in 1915. The whole point of Dada was that there was no point: 'Dada has no meaning,' one of the founders, Tristan Tzara, declared in a manifesto, before going on to insist that he was against manifestos in any case. Needless to say, the movement spawned manifestos by the hundred. On one level, Dada was a revolt against official art, official taste: '*Kultur*'. It was for the unconscious, for improvisation, for total freedom of expression, for bad taste. On another level it was a scream of rage by the young against the old establishment which had permitted the senseless butchery of the First World War.

In Berlin, Dadaism found fertile soil. The Dadaists put down roots at the Romanische Café, just opposite the Kaiser Wilhelm Memorial Church. It was a great barn of a place where everyone in the Berlin art world congregated – writers, actors, musicians, painters – it was the centre of everything. George Grosz, who was both Dadaist and Marxist, used to parade around in cowboy clothes, often carrying a large placard proclaiming 'Dada über Alles'.

Born in Berlin, but raised elsewhere and trained in Dresden, Grosz was a savage caricaturist of post-Wilhelmine Germany. His work depicted a kind of dance of death, with obscenely bloated capitalists, sabre-scarred Prussian officers, avaricious whores, and the poor and desperate and damaged as his corps de ballet. He was probably the most talented of the group that, for a time, included Hans Arp, Tristan Tzara, who soon left for Paris, and the Herzfelde brothers, of whom Hans became better known under the name of John Heartfield, one of the great pioneers of photomontage. Like expressionism, Dada extended beyond painting, into literature, film, the theatre, and even night clubs, where Walter Mehring, one of the founder members of Dadaism in Berlin, mounted his 'Political Cabaret'.

The theatre, both serious and frivolous, flourished with some 35 theatres packing in capacity audiences. The splendour of Max Reinhardt's productions competed with glamorous nude revues and the frothy musical comedies of Bernhard Rose. Bertolt Brecht scored his greatest success in 1928 with *The Threepenny Opera*, that acerbic updating of John Gay's eighteenth-century London underworld into an accurate portrayal of the world of the Berlin Ringvereine. Movie theatres, too, sprang up everywhere, ranging from hundreds of local *'Flohkinos'*, 'flea-pits', to the Ufa Palast am Zoo, a true movie palace, all dark brown velvet and deep-pile carpets, where silent pictures were accompanied by a 45-piece orchestra conducted by Nico Dostal. Performances were not continuous; at the giant Kinos there were only two shows a day, with one on Sundays.

The great era of German film, beginning with *The Cabinet of Dr Caligari* in 1919, and running right through the decade until *The Blue Angel* in 1930, was dominated by the UFA studios in Babelsberg, on the south-western edge of Berlin. Some of the UFA directors, like Fritz Lang, F.W. Murnau and Ernst Lubitsch went on to distinguished careers in Hollywood. In 1935, Lubitsch even became production chief of Paramount, a real case of a Berlin boy making good. Some of the actors, too, found careers on the other side of the Atlantic. Walter Slezak and Peter Lorre, to name but two, joined that repertory company of superb character actors that was one of the strengths of Hollywood until the decline of the major studios. And, as everyone knows, the star of UFA's *The Blue Angel*, the one and only Marlene Dietrich, went on to become a Hollywood legend in her own right.

Babelsberg also provided an opportunity to make a little money now and again for a lot of people living on the edge in Berlin. Vladimir Nabokov, who was frequently hard up, sometimes found work as a film extra, on one celebrated occasion in 1925 earning the princely sum of $10 for a day's work.

Musically, there can be no doubt that the Twenties were a golden era for Berlin. The young Erich Kleiber directed the State Opera, Bruno Walter the Deutsche Oper, and Otto Klemperer the Kroll. The Berlin Philharmonic Orchestra was directed by Wilhelm Furtwängler, who had taken over in 1922, on the death of Artur Nikisch. The city's many active composers were led by Arnold Schönberg, who succeeded Feruccio Busoni as professor of composition at the Academy of Art in 1925, making Berlin the world capital of modern music. His most important pupil was Alban Berg, whose *Wozzeck* caused a sensation when it opened at the State Opera in December of that year. And the number of world-class solo performers living and working in the city was almost endless: Busoni himself, Rudolf Serkin, Adolf Busch, Artur Schnabel, Claudio Arrau, Wilhelm Backhaus, Vladimir Horowitz – even the child prodigy, Yehudi Menuhin.

A less accomplished but highly enthusiastic violinist, who often joined some of his illustrious musical friends like Rudolf Serkin in private performances was Albert Einstein, who was then working alongside other great names such as Max Planck at the Kaiser

Wilhelm Institute in Dahlem, maintaining Berlin's tradition of scientific and academic research.

Under the leadership of Walter Gropius and his associates and students at the Bauhaus school of arts and crafts, Berlin was also at the forefront of the modern movements in architecture and industrial design. Although the Bauhaus itself was then situated in Weimar, Gropius and other architects and designers such as Ludwig Miës van der Rohe and Eric Mendelsohn had their studios in Berlin, and it was there that they carried out most of their work.

During the 20 years between the wars, the population of Berlin grew by only 300,000, a small increase by Berlin standards. But as more and more people sought to escape from the overcrowding and squalor of the Mietskasernen, the city experienced yet another building boom.

In 1920, the new state parliament had approved the incorporation of the city and its suburbs into the Greater Berlin we know

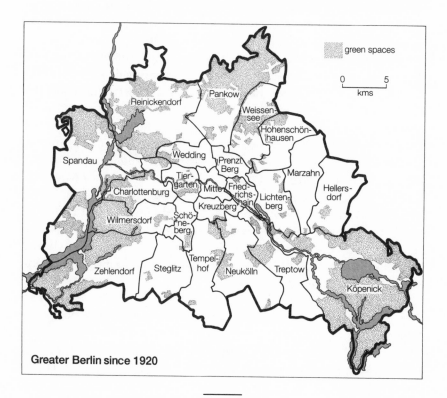

Greater Berlin since 1920

today. The independent boroughs of Charlottenburg, Köpenick, Lichtenberg, Neukölln, Pankow, Schöneberg, Spandau, and Wilmersdorf, together with 59 rural communities and 27 rural estates, were joined with the existing six Berlin boroughs (Mitte, Prenzlauerberg, Friedrichshain, Kreuzberg, Tiergarten and Wedding), to form a unified city of over four million inhabitants. The new city was divided into 20 districts, each with its own mayor and local council, overseen by a governing mayor and city council in the Red Town Hall. It covered the vast area of 878 square kilometres (339 square miles) – the whole of the industrial Ruhr valley would fit comfortably inside its borders. Over 350 square kilometres (135 square miles) were, as they still are, taken up with forests, lakes, rivers and parks.

In the new districts, the young architects designed and built fine modern housing developments, mostly through public-utility enterprises. Boldly and imaginatively planned, these included large estates of clean, low-rise, houses and flats, set amid gardens, lawns and parks, which still look modern today. The 135,000 new homes built during the decade gave a whole new look to the suburbs surrounding the old city: clean-cut, simple, restrained. And this new socially conscious style even extended to some industrial complexes, in particular the giant electrical works at Siemensstadt.

The wealthier citizens, meanwhile, commissioned the same men to design new single homes for them in the leafy surroundings of the Grunewald, resulting in many remarkable examples of modern domestic architecture. And in the public sphere, the overblown style of the Wilhelmine era was replaced with simple clean lines in buildings such as the new broadcasting centre and Tempelhof airport, and the glass and steel office buildings and stores of Miës van der Rohe and Eric Mendelsohn. In 1931–2, Mendelsohn transformed Potsdamerplatz by replacing the old Grand Hotel Bellevue, which had gone bankrupt, with a revolutionary new ten-storey building. Mendelsohn's Columbushaus, a totally functional design with glass walls around a steel frame, was as influential as Schinkel's Old Museum had been 100 years before, its streamlined horizontal lines creating a new standard for the whole world. The first major tenant, suitably international, was the F.W. Woolworth company.

Just around the corner in Leipzigerstrasse, Kempinski's opened a new super establishment in 1928, under the title 'Haus Vaterland'.

Its architectural style was more traditional than Mendelsohn's, a mixture of the cosy and the pretentious; its main external feature was a circular, stone-faced tower, topped with a glass, iron-framed dome. Claiming to be the biggest restaurant in the world, with room for 3,000 diners, it was like the Lyons Corner Houses in London on an even grander scale. It was a mammoth undertaking combining several restaurants, transforming what had been a boring collection of Wilhelmine halls and cafés into a fantasy world including a Turkish café, a Spanish bodega with romanesque vaulting, a rustic Hungarian village inn, the Puszta Czarda, and the Grinziger Heuriger, a café with a wine garden and a backdrop of the Vienna Woods. Through a window in the Löwenbrau Bavarian beer hall, the sun could be seen rising on the Zugspitze. On the Rheinterrasse Café an artificial storm raged every hour on the hour. Lastly, there was a Wild West bar with the waiters dressed in cowboy clothes and the hat-check girls incongruously as geishas.

Nearby was an even more impressive palace to consumerism, the Wertheim department store. With its huge, glass-roofed central hall, Wertheim was a magnificent example of north European monumental building, decorated with Nordic sculpture and striking stone carvings. When it was built a few years before, it had revolutionized Berlin store design by introducing plate glass display windows to the city.

On a gloomy day at the beginning of November 1926, a small, slim young man with a pronounced limp stepped off a train from Munich at Friedrichstrasse station. He carried one suitcase, a small sum of money, and a letter signed by Adolf Hitler appointing him 'Gauleiter of Greater Berlin, with full powers'. The young man was a 28-year-old Rhinelander, a failed writer with a doctorate in literature from Heidelberg University. He had been a Marxist before joining the fledgling Nazi Party in 1924. His name was Joseph Goebbels.

The grand title of Gauleiter (district leader) was almost farcical, for the Nazis were by far the smallest political party in Berlin, with well under 1,000 members. At the local elections just a year before, they had managed to notch up just 137 votes in their strongest district, Spandau, as against 604,696 for the social democrats, the SPD, and 347,381 for the communists. The party headquarters was 'a kind of dirty cellar, we called it the opium den' in a back court at 109 Potsdamerstrasse. The windowless room was thick with cigar and cigarette smoke.

Goebbels started reorganizing and invigorating the party at once. He found smarter premises at 44 Lützowstrasse, purged the membership of those whose commitment was less than total, and began forging the remainder into a hard fighting unit as he launched a vigorous recruiting campaign. Although he was not a Berliner, he sized up the city with cool and devastating accuracy. 'The pitilessness of this town has found expression in its people,' he wrote in his diary. 'The motto here in Berlin is: "Eat up, bird, or starve!" and anyone who has not learned how to use his elbows will go down.'

Realizing that his only hope of winning political power was not with reasoned argument, but with clubs and bricks and broken bottles on the streets, Goebbels deliberately provoked bloody confrontation with the communists. He set the brown-shirted stormtroopers of the SA to fight pitched battles with the communist Red Banner Fighters, and to roam the fashionable streets of the west end beating up 'bold, presumptuous and arrogant' Jews.

Goebbels's particular genius, of course, was as a propagandist, and he was soon putting it to work. 'Berlin needs sensation like a fish needs water,' he wrote in his diary. 'This city lives on it, and any political propaganda that does not take this into account is bound to fail.' Whatever happened, the Nazis had to be headline news. 'Let them curse us, libel us, fight us and beat us up,' he cried, 'but let them talk about us!'

To ensure that the party got headlines, and the sort of headlines he wanted, he started his own newspaper, *Der Angriff* (The Attack), in July 1927, first as a weekly, later as an evening daily. Convinced that martyrs make the best headlines of all, he celebrated every wounded SA man in its pages, and made as much as he could of every bruise and every stab wound. When there were no wounded martyrs, he created them, swathing healthy men in blood-stained bandages. And when an SA man was killed, of course, his propaganda machine went into top gear.

Goebbels's greatest coup came when a young SA agitator called Horst Wessel was shot by a communist pimp at the beginning of 1930. Wessel took six weeks to die, during which time Goebbels publicized every aspect of his condition, turning the young thug into 'a socialist Christ who had chosen to live amongst those who scorned and spat upon him'. The funeral was spectacular. The communists obliged by covering the cemetery walls with crude graffiti and even stoning the mourners at the graveside. The bloody brawl that followed was a gift to the young Gauleiter.

There was one final bonus from the death of Horst Wessel. He had submitted to *Der Angriff* a lyric to be sung to a melody from a communist song book, which itself had been adapted from a Salvation Army hymn. The main refrain ran:

> *Die Fahne Hoch! Die Reihe dicht geschlossen!*
> *SA marschiert mit ruhig festem Schritt.*
>
> The flags held high! The ranks closed tight together!
> The SA march with firm and steady tread.

Goebbels published it, and turned it into a party anthem. Three years later, to the disgust of all non-Nazis, it was to become a German national hymn.

When the Nazis won ten seats in the Reichstag on 20 May 1928, Goebbels was given one of them. It brought him a salary of 750 marks a month, immunity from prosecution, and greater political prominence. His star was rising fast, as fast as the party he represented. But neither he nor the party was ever able to win over Red Berlin. The city as a whole remained hostile territory. The Nazi party returned the hostility. Its attitude, and that of Hitler, who hated the place and never owned a home there, was summed up by the party newspaper, the *Völkischer Beobachter*, which was, of course, based in the Bavarian capital, Munich. In July 1928 it denounced the northern city as 'a melting pot of everything that is evil – prostitutes, drinking houses, cinemas, Marxism, Jews, strippers, negroes dancing, and all the vile offshoots of so-called "modern art"'. The Berliners, naturally, took the description as a compliment.

For 24-year-old Dennis Sefton Delmer, the latest Berlin correspondent for Lord Beaverbrook's *Daily Express*, the city had everything a journalist could ask for: 'sex, murder, political intrigue, money, mystery and bloodshed. Particularly bloodshed.' With the Nazis and communists fighting for possession of the streets, when the news desk in London phoned looking for an action story –

'Could you let us have a riot?' – Delmer was usually able to oblige. Riots and scuffles were an everyday experience.

At the same time, Delmer was enjoying the social whirl of Berlin parties and balls. In the circles in which he moved there was no sign of any slackening in the frenetic gaiety of free-spending Berlin. After some grand party at the house of Karl von Siemens, head of the electrical engineering firm, or at the house of the financier Hans von Lustig, no one ever thought of going home to bed – they went on to a club where they could carry on dancing until well after dawn. Ciro's or Quartier Latin were the two most fashionable spots. Or perhaps they might go to the six-day cycle races at the Sportpalast, where some of the cyclists, like the Italian Alfredo Dinale, were treated like film stars and ardently pursued by voracious young Berlinerin from good families.

Delmer's own special delight was to visit the Luna, a swimming bath with a huge wave machine, on Friday mornings. Fridays were reserved for the Berlin nudist club. Large ladies, he said, lay 'on gleaming tiles, like flounders on a fishmonger's slab, their arms and legs stretched wide apart, allowing the waves to give them a water massage. "Swoosh" and the wave swept bosoms back over their shoulders, "Swoosh" and returning, it washed them down to somewhere near their navels. On the side of the pool, shaven headed Herren, unclothed but for spectacles or monocles, were going through all the rigorous protocol of the Potsdam introduction ceremonial, bowing, kissing hands, and even trying to click their naked heels.'

Even the nudist clubs, however, were divided along political lines. On the one hand, the nationalist right, on the other, the republican left. At Motzensee, outside Berlin, Dr Fuchs ran his right-wing nudist camp, while Adolf Koch ran his physical culture and eurhythmics school on clear socialist lines within the city. Once, when Delmer was entertaining the visiting Mayor Cermak of Chicago, he took him to a display of calisthenics at Adolf Koch's club, given by a good-looking crowd of young nudists. Mayor Cermak was impressed. He leaned over to Delmer and observed: 'In Chicago, you couldn't get a show as good as this for a thousand bucks!'

At the end of October 1929, the fragile German economy was shattered again by the world crisis following the Wall Street crash.

After only a brief period of hope, Germany was once again on the way to becoming a nation of beggars, as business after business folded and unemployment mounted.

Into this gloomy scene, another Englishman, Christopher Isherwood, arrived in Berlin for a stay that would provide the material for the books that were to make him famous: *Goodbye to Berlin* and *Mr Norris Changes Trains*. Isherwood had first visited the city eight months earlier, in March 1929. He was 24 years old, had been educated at a public school and Oxford, and was very young for his age. His aim in going to Berlin, he wrote many years later in his autobiographical *Christopher and his Kind*, was 'to unchain his desires and hurl reason and sanity into prison'. Berlin in the 1920s seemed the perfect place to do it. To Isherwood, 'Berlin meant Boys.' His first visit only lasted a week or ten days, but it was long enough for him to have found a boy bar called The Cosy Corner, at 7 Zossnerstrasse, in Kreuzberg.

Returning for a longer stay in November, he found himself a room in In den Zelten, in an apartment owned by a sister of Dr Magnus Hirschfeld, whose Institut für Sexual-Wissenschaft (Institute for Sexual Science) stood next door. Hirschfeld, a homosexual himself, was a leading expert on homosexuality, which he described as 'the third sex'. He devoted much of his time to campaigning vigorously against paragraph 173 in the German Criminal Code, which forbade homosexual acts between men, though not between women.

Every Christmas one of the dance halls in In den Zelten organized a fancy dress ball for homosexuals. Naturally, many of the guests wore drag. One of the regulars had inherited a vast range of fabulous ball gowns, and wore a different one each year: he liked his friends and lovers to rip them off his body until, like Cinderella, he had only a few tattered rags left in which to get home. The guest of honour at the particular ball that Isherwood attended was the German film star, Conrad Veidt.

When Isherwood met the boy he called Otto Nowak in *Goodbye to Berlin*, he went to stay with him and his family, in order to save money. They lived in a slum tenement at 4 Simeonstrasse, near the Halle Gate in Kreuzberg (Isherwood gave the name of the street as Wassertorstrasse, which was in fact a continuation of Simeonstrasse, because he thought it sounded more romantic). It was a revelation to the young Englishman, with his respectable middle-class background. Lavatories were in short supply – there was one to every four flats in the Nowak's building, and theirs was one floor down – so if he needed to relieve himself in the night he either had to make his way downstairs in the dark or use the communal bucket by the stove, surrounded by the family in various stages of sleep. For washing, there was only the kitchen sink between six people; anyone who wanted a bath had to go to the nearest public bath-house.

In the human warrens of the Mietskasernen there was no such thing as privacy. There wasn't much light, either, especially in the deep wells of the courtyards. Anyone living on the ground floor at the back was in permanent gloom. But there was always plenty of noise, the courts acting like sound amplifiers. 'Somewhere on the other side of the court,' Isherwood recalled, 'a baby began to scream, a window was slammed to, something very heavy, deep in the innermost recesses of the building thudded dully against a wall. It was alien and mysterious and uncanny, like sleeping out in the jungle.'

Isherwood did not last long in the Nowaks' Mietskaserne. In December he moved from working-class to middle-class Berlin, to a room in a flat at 17 Nollendorfstrasse, just south of Nollendorf-platz. It was a slightly run-down district, even so. 'From my window, the deep solemn massive street. Cellar-shops where the lamps burn all day, under the shadow of top-heavy balconied façades, dirty plaster frontages embossed with scroll-work and heraldic devices. The whole district is like this: street leading into street of houses like monumental safes crammed with the tarnished valu-ables and second-hand furniture of a bankrupt middle class.'

The apartment belonged to Fräulein Meta Thurgau, whom he immortalized as Fräulein Schroeder in his books, a shapeless, in-quisitive, alert lady with fluid political convictions. In the Novem-ber 1932 Reichstag elections, for example, encouraged by the left-wing Isherwood, she voted communist; a year later, with Hitler in power, she was heard referring fondly to 'der Führer'. Like most Berliners, he said, she remained 'a muddled victim of her rulers – guilty only by association with them – no more and no less of a Nazi than a communist'.

Isherwood's most famous character, Sally Bowles, was based on Jean Ross, an English would-be singer-actress. At one stage she managed to get herself a walk-on part in Max Reinhardt's celebrated production of Offenbach's *Tales of Hoffmann*. She was one of the pairs of lovers carried on in litters during the course of the ball at the Venetian palazzo of the courtesan, Giullietta. Jean boasted that she had sex on stage with her partner, in full view of the audience, at every single performance. Isherwood attended a couple of shows armed with binoculars, but was never able to verify her claim.

While Isherwood was soaking up the atmosphere of *Cabaret*, Sefton Delmer was making the acquaintance of Captain Ernst Röhm, the new chief of staff of the SA, a man worth cultivating for any shrewd journalist. A fat, stocky little man, Röhm had been a brave front-line soldier in the great war, and had been wounded in action three times, which had left him with severe facial injuries. More importantly, he had known Hitler since the earliest days of his political career: indeed, he was the only one of the Nazi inner circle who was not under Hitler's spell, and who was more than capable of standing up to him. He was also one of the few men Hitler addressed with the familiar 'du'.

Röhm had been a captain in the Reichswehr, stationed in Munich, at the time of the 1923 putsch attempt. He had access to a secret cache of arms, with which he proposed to overthrow the left-wing government of Bavaria. After Hitler and his friends had bungled the putsch, Röhm lost both his job and the arms, and ended up as a military adviser in Bolivia. In 1930, Hitler brought him back from South America to take charge of the SA. Röhm transformed it from a rag-tag mob into a brutally efficient private army. He imposed military-style discipline, and set up a general staff and an officers' training school. During the first nine months under his command, its numbers grew from 70,000 to 170,000, making it almost twice as big as the Reichswehr. At such a size, it was virtually invulnerable.

Though normally based in Munich, Röhm made occasional trips to Berlin. One of the first was to 'cleanse' the Berlin SA of 'rowdy, undisciplined elements' after a mutiny. He did so, using as a weapon his right-hand man, Edmund Heinnes, a killer who enjoyed his work. Heinnes was said to have murdered 18 'traitors'. Röhm invited Delmer along to witness the result. Three thousand five hundred stormtroopers were paraded at the Sportpalast for Röhm's inspection. Most of them wore civilian clothes – they couldn't afford the brown shirt and breeches of the SA uniform. They looked like whipped dogs: any thought of further mutiny had clearly vanished. Whatever Heinnes and his henchmen had threatened them with, it was as nothing compared with the reality that faced them on the streets. Four and a half million Germans were now unemployed, and if nothing else, being in the SA at least guaranteed them food and housing, even if it was in one of the SA's dreadful basement barracks.

At the end of the parade, Röhm made a rabble-rousing speech which ended on a note of ominous caution. 'No one can teach me anything about making a revolution,' he told them. 'And if there is any barricade storming to be done, I shall be the one to lead you. But I am not calling you out now, to be shot down by the police of the Republic. For I know that victory is close at hand.'

Röhm found Delmer a useful contact and a congenial drinking companion. One day, he turned up at Delmer's office and suggested they go out on a pub crawl: 'We'll have some dinner first and then we'll go on a Bummel and you can show me some of the Berlin night life.' They dined at Peltzer's, a restaurant in Wilhelmstrasse much patronized by embassy staff, and then went on to the Eldorado, a dance bar where the hostesses were boys in drag. Delmer was surprised when one of them, 'a huge creature with a very prominent Adam's apple and a distinctly blue chin under the layer of powder', sat down and began chatting with Röhm about a party they had attended several nights before. Usually open and unashamed about his sexual preferences, Röhm was indignant when Delmer remarked that no female tart would ever approach a client and talk about their night together in front of a stranger. 'I am not his client. I am his commanding officer,' Röhm replied seriously. 'He is one of my stormtroopers.'

As the depression deepened, with the economy plunging and unemployment soaring, the fragile German democracy began to crumble. In March 1930, the social democrat government collapsed, and authority was exercised more and more by presidential decree. Since the aged Hindenburg was growing increasingly senile, this left real power in the hands of the close circle that surrounded him, notably his son, Oskar, and the head of administration at the War

Office, General Kurt von Schleicher. They appointed the head of the minority Catholic Centre Party, Heinrich Brüning, as chancellor, but Brüning's government also collapsed within a short time. Unabashed, Hindenburg and his aides called a general election.

Astonishingly, the vote for Hitler's National Socialist Workers' Party in Germany as a whole rocketed from the 800,000 it had received in the 1928 election to almost 6,500,000, raising its number of seats from 13 to 107 and making it the second strongest party in the Reichstag. From the first day, 13 October 1930, the Nazis showed how they meant to continue. Political demonstrations of any sort had always been forbidden in the area immediately outside the Reichstag building but the Nazi supporters ignored the ban, crowding around in their thousands, chanting slogans and singing marching songs.

The wearing of party uniforms and insignia had been banned in Berlin earlier that year by the Prussian state government. The stormtroopers had promptly switched to wearing plain white shirts, wrapping the brown rubber rings from bottle tops round one button as a badge. But the new Reichstag deputies were immune from prosecution once they were inside the building, so they carried their brown uniforms in with them and changed in the washrooms. They took their seats in the chamber as a solid mass of uniforms and swastika armbands, shouting down their opponents, disrupting the proceedings with threats of violence and loud singing. At the end of the session, they trooped out and led their followers on a march through the Potsdamerplatz to Leipzigerstrasse, where they smashed the windows of Jewish-owned department stores and beat up any Jews they encountered.

The next three years brought increasing political chaos. By late 1931, unemployment nationwide had topped five million, and there was nothing to stop it rising still higher. By the end of 1932, Berlin alone had 636,000 officially registered unemployed, almost as many as the figure for the whole of Germany at the beginning of 1929. Thousands queued at charity soup kitchens, while all over the city thousands of apartments were left empty as people were driven to seek ever cheaper accommodation, or left Berlin altogether.

The more recent immigrants were among the first to suffer. In severe financial straits, the Nabokovs – Vladimir, his wife Vera and small son Dmitri – were forced to move out of the two comfortable rooms they rented in the vast and gloomy apartment of General von Bardelen in Luitpoldstrasse, which bisects Martin-Luther-Strasse in Schöneberg. They moved into a single room in a crowded apartment at 29 Westfälischestrasse, where it was noisy and difficult for Nabokov to write. To make a little extra cash, he gave readings of his work in a friend's apartment.

Russian Berlin was beginning to die as a result of the depression. Russian cafés were closing, Russian concerts played to dwindling audiences, and *Rul'*, the paper founded by Nabokov's father, ceased publication. More and more Russians left Berlin, mostly for France or the USA; a few even returned to the Soviet Union. In December, a Russian student shot himself in the Tiergarten, an incident that may have inspired Yasha Chernyshevski's suicide in Nabokov's great Berlin novel, *The Gift (Dar)*. But in real life, it barely rated a newspaper paragraph; in Berlin suicide was known as 'the émigré crime'.

Somehow, Berlin theatre, particularly the opera, still flourished, thanks largely to a government subsidy of 2.5 million marks a year. The hits of the 1931–2 season were the operettas *Das Weisse Rössl* (*White Horse Inn*), Offenbach's *Die Schöne Helena*, which was playing at the Theater am Kurfürstendamm, and *Viktoria und Ihr Hussar*, with music by the Viennese composer Paul Abrahams. Modern serious operas were represented by Weinberger's *Schwanda* and Berg's *Wozzeck*. And in the grand Kinos, *Der Kongress Tanzt* (*Congress Dances*) was proving a success.

But on the streets outside, there was mounting violence as the Nazi stormtroopers clashed with socialists and communists. In just six weeks before new elections in July 1932, there were 461 pitched battles in the streets of Prussia, most of them in Berlin, where Röhm had appointed a dissolute young nobleman, Count Wolf von Helldorf as SA commander. Over 200 people were killed, mostly Nazis and communists, and hundreds more, seriously wounded.

The university was closed because the students were out of control. The Prussian state parliament, where the Nazis had won a sweeping majority in elections that April, was suspended, and Prussia was ruled by presidential decree. Finally, martial law was declared in Berlin itself, under the Reichswehr regional commander,

General Gerd von Rundstedt. Newspapers were ordered to cease publication. Soon, the cells of Plötzensee prison were filled to overflowing. Scientists, artists, writers, musicians read the writing on the wall and began moving to other countries. The Golden Twenties were dead and buried.

Faced with an undeclared civil war, and the threat of a return to the anarchy of ten years earlier, the voters of Germany turned to those who offered extreme solutions to their extreme problems. On 20 July 1932, Hitler challenged for the presidency and achieved 13,418,547 votes in the second ballot against Hindenburg's 19,359,983; eleven days later, in new national elections, the Nazis became easily the biggest single party in the Reichstag, with 230 seats. Only Berlin stood out, as always, against the general flow: almost three out of four Berliners voted against Hitler and the Nazis.

For six months, the old field marshal and the general who was the power behind the throne held out against offering the chancellorship to the former corporal. They dissolved the Reichstag again and called more elections. When these produced a similar result to the last, they put an aristocratic nonentity, Franz von Papen, into the role, hoping they could work him like a puppet. When this failed, Schleicher took office himself, reviving memories of the old military autocracy, and even prepared a military coup with the other Reichswehr generals. But eventually, on 30 January 1933, the pressure became too great to resist any further, and Adolf Hitler, the Austrian from Munich who had only taken German citizenship for his presidential campaign the year before, was appointed chancellor.

CHAPTER 16

River of Fire

HITLER'S APPOINTMENT as chancellor was announced at noon on Monday, 30 January 1933. At once, Nazi supporters poured on to the streets of Berlin, while their opponents retired to their homes for safety. Every SS and SA man in the city put on his uniform and turned out to do his duty. The police, who had fought so many battles with the stormtroopers over the past five years, were suddenly all smiles. Many of them sported swastikas themselves. From all over Prussia, and indeed from every part of Germany within reach of the capital, party members converged on the Tiergarten, to prepare for their victory parade.

Brilliantly organized by Goebbels, the show began at 7.00 pm that evening. Somehow, the Berlin Gauleiter had managed to provide every marcher with a flaming torch; Hitler was so moved by the spectacle that he asked, 'How on earth did he conjure up all those thousands of torches in the space of a few hours?' Goebbels had also taken over every radio station, so that listeners in every part of the country that evening could hear nothing but live commentaries of the march. The Nazi supporters tramped through the Brandenburg Gate in massed columns, shoulder to shoulder, 16 abreast, to the thunder of drums and the blare of military bands, roaring out the *Horst Wessel Song*. Crowds packed windows and pavements, young men perched in the branches of trees, boys 'hung from the iron railings like bunches of grapes'. The Adlon and other hotels along the route had to lock their doors, as every room was packed full.

As they passed the French embassy in Pariserplatz, each band stopped, broke off from whatever they were playing, and with a preliminary roll of drums struck up a challenging old war song, *Siegreich wollen wir Frankreich schlagen!*', '*Victorious, we're going to thrash France!*' Ambassador André François-Poncet watched from behind the embassy's curtains. 'These torches,' he wrote later, 'form a single river of fire, and the waves of this swelling river build up to advance with great power into the heart of the capital.'

The painter Max Liebermann had his own view of the spectacle as he watched from his house alongside the Brandenburg Gate. Turning away in disgust, he told a friend: 'Pity one can't eat as much as one wants to vomit.'

Wheeling right after passing the Adlon, the marchers continued along the Wilhelmstrasse, past the British embassy and the presidential palace, where they saluted the old field marshal, beating time to the marches with his stick and apparently much moved by what he saw. A few yards further on, they broke into wild shouts of acclaim and great cries of 'Sieg Heil!' for Hitler, on the balcony of the chancellery. The battle for the soul of Berlin had begun.

At 9.10 pm on the evening of 27 February 1933, exactly four weeks after Hitler's accession, Werner Thaler, a 21-year-old typesetter, was passing the Reichstag building. Hearing the sound of breaking glass, he ran to two policemen patrolling nearby. 'Quick!' he shouted. 'Somebody's trying to break into the Reichstag!'

'For a moment,' wrote Fritz Tobian, historian of the event, 'all three of them looked on in paralysed astonishment. Then, as a man could be seen rushing from window to window waving a flaming torch, the three men started after him.' The policemen drew their pistols, and fired a few warning shots, then asked a passer-by to run to the police post at the Brandenburg Gate to call the fire brigade. But it was already too late. By the time the firemen arrived the building was well alight.

Hitler was dining with Goebbels at his apartment on the Reich-skanzlerplatz (now Theodor-Heuss-Platz, but from late 1933 till 1945 Adolf-Hitler-Platz). He was alerted by telephone. Looking out and seeing the reflections of the flames in the sky above the Tiergarten, he immediately cried 'It's the communists!' They set off at once for the blazing Reichstag, where they found Hermann Göring, immense in a camel-hair coat with his brown hat turned up at the front in the 'Potsdamer style', already inside the building giving orders, the first of which, characteristically, had been 'Save the tapestries!' The valuable Gobelin tapestries, which were in fact his personal property, were handed out to safety before anything else was touched.

Göring, who had been president of the Reichstag since the end of August 1932, was now living in the old Prussian presidential palace, which was connected to the building by an underground tunnel. He had been the first person on the scene after the alarm was raised. Like Hitler, he was quick to apportion blame, just as Bismarck had blamed the socialists for the assassination attempts on the Kaiser 55 years before. 'This is the start of a communist uprising!' he yelled. 'Not a moment must be lost!'

'Now we'll show them!' Hitler interrupted. 'Anyone who stands in our way will be mown down. The German people have been soft too long. Every communist must be shot. All communist deputies must be hanged this very night. All friends of the communists must be locked up – and that goes for the social democrats and the Reichsbanner as well!'

There is little doubt that Goebbels and Göring were responsible for organizing the fire. The arsonist, a simple-minded young Dutch communist named Marinus van der Lubbe, had been picked up by the SA earlier in the day after unsuccessfully trying to set fire to the old royal palace and two other government buildings. These first attempts were hopelessly amateurish and inadequate, but when it came to the Reichstag, van der Lubbe had clearly been given a helping hand. The fire which engulfed it so quickly had been started in various parts of the building, with such large quantities of chemicals and petrol that one man could not have carried them in, or ignited them simultaneously.

In the event, the communists were neither shot nor hanged – at least, not at that time. Only poor van der Lubbe was beheaded, after a swiftly staged show trial. But 4,000 leading communists were seized by the SA, along with a great many social democrats and liberals, including Reichstag deputies who were constitutionally immune from arrest. For the first time, the Nazi thugs rampaging through the streets of Berlin had official blessing. Truckloads of stormtroopers broke into homes, businesses and bars all over the city, dragging their victims away to the first 'wild' concentration camps, mostly disused warehouses and factories where they beat, tortured and in some cases murdered them. One of the most notorious centres was a disused eight-storey brick water tower at the corner of Kolmarerstrasse and Knaackstrasse in Prenzlauerberg, which is now preserved as a memorial.

Hitler's first comment on arriving at the blazing Reichstag had been: 'Good riddance to the old shack.' The 'old shack' was, of course, hardly ancient, being exactly 40 years old, but he put its burning to excellent use. Within a few hours, he had persuaded Hindenburg to declare a state of emergency and to suspend all civil rights, giving the chancellor virtually unlimited authority. This enabled him to suppress the activities of his opponents and win a free run for the Nazis in the new national elections a week later, which he needed to confirm and consolidate his power. Even then, he only just managed to scrape home with the support of Papen's Nationalist Party. He had to lock up large numbers of communist and social democrat deputies before he could get the required two-thirds majority in the Reichstag giving him dictatorial power 'to end the distress of people and state'.

It seemed appropriate that the new assembly should meet in the Kroll Opera House, a suitably theatrical setting where its members were reduced to the role of chorus under the baton of Hermann Göring. The Berliners soon took to describing it as 'Germany's most expensive choral group'.

Even with most of their opponents suppressed, terror squads on the streets, and thousands of voters imprisoned, the Nazis could only raise 31 per cent of the Berlin votes during the national elections. And in new local elections a week later, they received fewer votes than the outlawed KPD and the harassed SPD, winning only 86 of the 225 seats. Two days later, Hitler had the Prussian state government dissolved by presidential decree, and both state and city were brought under direct Reich control, ruled by a Reich commissioner.

The Nazi grip on Berlin itself was tightened when the SA

commander, Wolf von Helldorf, was appointed police president. Friedrich Lange, who had been governing mayor since the incorporation of Greater Berlin in 1920, was replaced by Julius Lippert, the leader of the Nazi group on the council and a former editor of *Der Angriff*. Lippert tackled his new job with ominous zest. One of his first orders was for the dismissal of all Jewish doctors working in the city's hospitals.

With his authority secured both nationally and locally, Hitler immediately turned his attention to the 160,000 Jews living in Berlin. On 9 March, SA strong-arm squads went into action without fear of interference. Working in gangs of between five and 30 men, they toured the streets, beating up any Jews they encountered until, as the *Manchester Guardian* reported, 'the blood streamed down their heads and faces, and their backs and shoulders were bruised. Many fainted and were left lying in the streets.'

Over the following days and weeks, the attacks intensified. On 15 March, three Jews were dragged out of the Café New York and taken to local SA headquarters. There, they were robbed of all their money, 'beaten bloody with rubber truncheons, and then turned out in the streets in a semi-conscious state'. Three days later, Siegbert Kindemann, a baker's apprentice, was also taken to SA headquarters. Before the Nazis came to power he had been attacked by SA thugs, who had been arrested, charged and convicted. Now, they took their revenge, beating him to death. Before they threw his body on to the street from an upstairs window, they took their daggers and carved a large swastika into his chest. This time, there were no arrests, and no convictions.

As the number of individual attacks mounted, the Nazi assault on the Jews, which was to have such an enormous effect on the life of Berlin over the next twelve years, was acknowledged as official government policy. On 1 April, Goebbels organized a nationwide boycott of Jewish businesses, stores, cafés, restaurants, lawyers and doctors. Committees were formed to co-ordinate and control the boycott and all other forms of Jew-baiting. They distributed lists detailing every Jewish business. SA men daubed the Star of David on Jewish shopfronts, along with the word '*Jude*' (Jew), swastikas, and slogans such as 'Jews Out!', 'Perish Judah!', 'Go to Palestine!' and so on. Party members were warned that they must constantly remind their friends and neighbours not to buy from Jews, and that they must break off friendships with anyone who continued to do so. 'It must go so far,' the order stated, 'that no German will speak to a Jew if it is not absolutely necessary, and this must be particularly pointed out.' The names of people who continued to buy from Jewish stores were published on notices posted in the streets by way of warning, exposing them to the threat of reprisals.

There were demands for the removal of all Jewish students from German schools and colleges: a new law laid down that they were to be treated as foreigners. On 7 April, Hitler issued a decree for the dismissal – euphemistically described as 'retirement' – of all civil servants 'who were not of Aryan descent'. The division of the population into 'Aryan' and 'non-Aryan' had begun, a division that was to be formalized by the Nuremberg Laws of September 1935, and refined into grades depending on the proportion of parents and grandparents who were Jewish.

Adolf Hitler had a fixation with Friedrich the Great. He clearly identified with him, and may even have thought himself a reincarnation of the Prussian king he so admired – somehow, he seems to have been able to overlook Friedrich's aberrations like smoking and drinking, to say nothing of homosexuality and Freemasonry. In the Huguenot Museum in the French cathedral on the Gendarmenmarkt, there is a bust of Friedrich in his forties which bears an uncanny resemblance to Hitler at the same age. The only thing missing is the moustache, but anyone bold enough to hold the end of a comb, say, under Friedrich's nose cannot fail to be impressed by the similarity. Whether Hitler ever saw that bust, no one can say, but he was certainly familiar with other likenesses. His most prized possession was a life-sized head and shoulders portrait of Friedrich, which he took with him wherever he went: it hung over his desk at all times, even in the succession of dismal concrete bunkers that were his field headquarters during the Second World War.

Hitler tried to emulate his hero in many ways, most notably in seeking to expand his territory by force of arms. He imagined he had somehow inherited Friedrich's military genius, and even called the 1939 Polish campaign his 'Silesian War'. His own genius, however, was disastrously flawed, and unlike Friedrich, he had not inherited a highly trained and superbly equipped army. He would have to build that for himself, which would take a little time. But there were other ways in which he could follow in Old Fritz's footsteps, and the one he found most agreeable was the idea of creating a great new city.

Hitler was unimpressed with Berlin. 'It is not a real metropolis,' he declared. 'It is nothing but an unregulated accumulation of buildings. The only monumental parts are Unter den Linden, the Palace and their immediate surroundings.' He was determined to erase most of it, and replace it with something that would stand comparison with or even surpass Paris and Vienna.

'As the Reich capital of a nation of sixty-five million,' he told the mayor and other civic dignitaries shortly after he became chancellor, 'Berlin must be raised to such a high level of urban planning and culture that it may compete with all the other capital cities of the world . . . The renewal of Berlin must be the very epitome of what can be accomplished with present-day means.' It could have been Friedrich himself speaking at the beginning of his reign.

Hitler's concept of 'present-day means', however, did not include modern architecture. Within weeks of seizing total power, in April 1933, he ordered a raid on Gropius's Bauhaus, which had moved to an abandoned telephone factory in the south Berlin district of Steglitz. Four months later, it was permanently shut down. Its creative stars fled: Walter Gropius himself, with Miës van der Rohe and Martin Wagner, moved to London, Bruno Taut to Moscow.

The Führer's choice to oversee his grand scheme, his Knobelsdorff, was a young architect who created a revolutionary design for the great party rally to be held on the Tempelhof field on the night of 1 May, Albert Speer. Speer's plan, involving enormous black, white and red banners illuminated by the beams of powerful searchlights, was a great success and formed the basis of his later designs for the Nuremberg rallies.

Hitler's 'renewed' city was not even to be known as Berlin, but as Germania. It was to accommodate ten million people, served by four airports. The Potsdam and Anhalt railway stations were to be torn down and relocated to the south of Tempelhof airfield, which would be linked to the Reichstag in the centre by a three-mile-long (5-kilometre) grand avenue, inspired by the Champs Elysées in Paris, but two and a half times as long and 70 feet (21 metres) wider. At the city end was to be a huge domed congress hall, designed by Hitler himself, which was to be the world's largest building, sixteen times bigger than St Peter's in Rome and capable of seating 150,000 people. For the southern end he had designed a vast triumphal arch, at 400 feet (122 metres) more than twice the height of the Arc de Triomphe in Paris, with the names chiselled into its sides of all the 1.8 million Germans who had fallen in the First World War. All, that is, but those who had been Jewish.

The idea of Germania continued to obsess Hitler right to the last. Even while the Allied bombs were falling on Berlin in the final days of the war, he would make his way by underground passage to Speer's office, to study the huge model of the city-to-be, which was due for completion by 1950. In the end, virtually the only large-scale projects in the original plan to be completed were the East–West Axis road and the Reich chancellery where he and his regime eventually perished. The model survived, however, and can still normally be seen in the Berlin Museum, which is housed in the former Kammergericht (Supreme Court), Berlin's first purpose-built administrative building, dating from 1734.

On 10 May 1933, it rained in Berlin. That night, however, despite the damp conditions, another torchlight procession made its way through the centre of the city and up the Linden. This time it was made up not of stormtroopers but of thousands of students. They gathered in Opernplatz, with the university on one side and the State Opera House and national library on the other. Awaiting them in the centre of the square was a pile of 20,000 books, collected during the day by students and stormtroopers from libraries and bookshops all over Berlin, on the orders of Dr Goebbels.

The books were by authors the Nazis disapproved of. These included eminent German writers such as Thomas and Heinrich Mann, Lion Feuchtwangler, Jakob Wassermann, Arnold and Stefan Zweig, Erich Maria Remarque, Walter Rathenau, Albert Einstein – in short, anyone who was liberal, or progressive, or Jewish, or in any way subversive. From around the world, there were names as diverse as H.G. Wells, Jack London, Upton Sinclair, Helen Keller, Havelock Ellis, André Gide, Marcel Proust, Emil Zola, and of course Sigmund Freud. They were all doused with petrol and set on fire with the marchers' torches, while students and storm-troopers pranced round the flames under the stony gaze of the statues of Wilhelm and Alexander Humboldt. At midnight, Goebbels arrived by car to announce that 'the phoenix of a new spirit' would arise from the ashes. Then he headed back to his ministry, leaving the dwindling crowd to grow more and more sodden.

The book-burning was not one of the Nazis' best-organized spectacles, but, perhaps more effectively than anything else, it signalled the beginning of Berlin's decline as a great European centre of culture. Following it, the departure of the finest creative and intellectual talent of all kinds turned into a mass exodus. Those who remained were controlled and regimented by the Reich Chamber of Culture under the direction of Goebbels, set up on 22 September 1933.

The dead hand of censorship, after a temporary absence during the Twenties, was back, and its grip on Berlin was tighter than anything known under the Kaisers. The music of Jewish composers, like Mendelssohn and Mahler, was banned. Jazz was officially frowned upon and eventually forbidden, though this did not prevent a number of 'swing clubs' springing up. For many young people, owning and playing American and British records became a form of anti-Nazi resistance, a seemingly harmless act of defiance that could, nevertheless, lead to arrest and imprisonment.

With the departure of so many of the best directors, writers and actors, the Berlin theatre lost both its edge and its audience. The greatest Nazi theatrical success in the 1930s was a heavy-handed farce, *Krack um Iolanthe*, the heroine of which was a sow. Hitler saw the production several times, and described it as 'epoch-making'.

Control of the press, radio and films was even more rigorous. Party functionaries were appointed to supervise all newspaper offices, where the editors were informed they were now salaried employees of the party. In 1928, Berlin had 147 independent daily and weekly newspapers. By the spring of 1933, it had none.

By summer, it had no political parties, either, other than the Nazis. The Communist Party, of course, had already been outlawed after the Reichstag fire. Shortly after the March elections, the Nazis had attacked the social democrats, confiscating all their property, banning their meetings, and dismissing their members from all official positions. The right-wing nationalists, supposedly the Nazis' partners in the coalition that had given Hitler power, were next to go, followed by the small People's Party. The Catholic Centre Party and the Bavarian People's Party dissolved themselves. A new law in July 1933 banned all parties other than the Nazis, and abolished all organizations such as the Stahlhelm and the Reichsbanner.

To drive home the message that no opposition would be tolerated, the SA had staged another large-scale terror raid in Köpenick that June, seizing well over 500 communists, social democrats and trade unionists and dragging them off to local SA barracks, the former Reichsbanner watersports centre, and the local prison, where they were tortured and beaten. Ninety-one of them were murdered, their mutilated corpses sewn into sacks and thrown into the river Dahme.

The only private army now left in Germany was the SA, and even that had but a short while to live. Now that he had total power, protected by his personal guard, the SS, and with his new secret police, the Gestapo, to control subversion, Hitler no longer needed the stormtroopers. Indeed, as the number of men commanded by Ernst Röhm swelled to 4.5 million, he saw them as the only force capable of posing a threat to his position. In 1934, the dangerously ambitious Röhm demanded a greater national role for the SA, even proposing that it should absorb the Reichswehr, a prospect that alarmed the army general staff. He also envisaged the creation of an SA Luftwaffe, thus earning the enmity of Göring, too.

Röhm was getting too big for his boots. The SA's unrestricted terror campaign was bringing anarchy to the streets of Berlin, reviving bitter memories of 1919 and 1920, something the military establishment were not prepared to stomach. Hindenburg and the army commander-in-chief, General Werner von Blomberg, warned Hitler that if he did not move against the SA leadership, the army would. Hitler acted, in a swift and deadly operation during one night, 30 June 1934, that has gone down in history as 'the night of the long knives'.

While Hitler flew to Munich to supervise the arrest and execution of Röhm, Göring took charge of the purge in Berlin. SS and Gestapo death squads grabbed SA leaders and took them to Gestapo headquarters in Albrechtstrasse or to the former army cadet school in Lichterfelde, now an SS barracks, where they were lined up in batches in front of firing squads. During 24 hours, the order to fire was given over a hundred times. Even some of the hardened SS marksmen found it too much. Those who cracked under the strain were promptly put in front of their own squads for summary execution.

Throughout the Reich, at least 1,000 people were murdered that night. By no means all of them were SA officers: the party took advantage of the opportunity to settle old scores with socialists, liberals, communists, and anyone who happened to have crossed it. The former chancellor General Schleicher was among the victims, gunned down in his own home along with his wife of 18 months.

By 1 July, the last serious threat to Hitler's power had been removed. The decapitated SA had been made harmless and brought back firmly under party control. Hindenburg and the generals congratulated him and thanked him for removing the threat of revolution. It was to be the old field marshal's last act. Two weeks later, he was dead. Hitler declared himself president as well as chancellor. He also assumed the title of supreme commander of the armed forces, and echoed Wilhelm II by demanding a personal oath from all officers and men:

> I swear by God this sacred oath, that I will render uncondi-
> tional obedience to Adolf Hitler, the Führer of the German
> Reich and people, supreme commander of the armed forces,
> and will be ready as a brave soldier to risk my life at any time
> for this oath.

The short life of the ill-fated German republic was over. The 15-year experiment with democratic government had been replaced by yet another absolute ruler, in a new empire, the Third Reich.

By 1936, Hitler's hold on Germany had been consolidated by a series of striking successes. The shame of Versailles was expunged with the ending of reparation payments and the beginning of rearmament, the return of the Saar from France, and the remilitarization of the Rhineland. A new treaty had leigitimized the building of a great new German navy – 'the happiest day of my life,' Hitler had said of the signing. The streets were clean and safe. Unemployment had almost disappeared. Industrial production had doubled between 1933 and 1935. To the man in the street, Hitler had brought peace and prosperity, national rehabilitation and the return of German pride.

German pride reached a new peak in August 1936, with the staging of the Eleventh Olympiad in Berlin. The First World War had put paid to the games that had been due to take place in the city 20 years before, and Germany had been barred from international competition until 1928. Now she resumed her place at the centre of the international scene.

The games had been assigned to Berlin following the 1932 Olympics in Los Angeles, but for a time after Hitler came to power it seemed the city's hopes would be dashed. He had previously denounced the whole Olympic movement as an invention of Jews and Freemasons, and was disposed to cancel the Berlin games. It was the stadium that finally changed his mind – he could not resist the opportunity of creating a new monumental construction. Inspecting the old stadium that had been built for the 1916 games, he declared it was too small, too insignificant. It should be replaced with something worthy of the new Reich. 'The proper solution of the problem,' he boasted later, 'demanded thinking on a grand scale.'

Convinced as always that only he was capable of thinking grandly enough, Hitler envisaged a totally new sports complex, bigger and more impressive than anything built for previous Olympiads, covering an area of almost 350 acres (140 hectares). The main arena was to be capable of seating 100,000, with a large open-air theatre alongside, to be named the Dietrich Eckart Theatre after his guru in his early days in Munich. In addition, the complex was to include a swimming pool with seating for 16,000, a hockey stadium that could seat 20,000, a vast Hall of German Sports, and an accommodation block with sleeping quarters for 400 female competitors. Male athletes were to be housed in several luxury barracks to be built by the German army in a wooded valley at Döbernitz, nine miles to the west, which would later revert to the military.

One feature that particularly appealed to Hitler was a huge bell that would be rung only twice, to signal the start and finish of the games. This was to be hung in a tall tower at the entrance to the main arena. But probably the most valuable area of the whole complex was what came to be known as the May Field, a huge expanse of some 27 acres (11 hectares) of turf, with low tiers of seats on two sides. This was to provide the dramatic setting for future Nazi Party mass rallies; at that time there was no suitable space for them in Berlin.

Building the new complex was a huge task – the demolition of the old stadium alone took nearly a year. To begin with, much of the work was done by hand in order to use the maximum number of unemployed: eventually, some 2,600 men, most of whom had previously been out of a job, were working flat out round the clock.

Costs sky-rocketed, but Hitler, typically, did not care. 'I can still see the faces of my colleagues,' he recalled nine years later, 'when I said that I proposed to make a preliminary grant of 28 million marks for the construction of the Berlin Stadium! In actual fact, the stadium cost us 77 million marks – but it brought in over half a milliard marks [500 million] in foreign currency!'

In the main, Berliners were enthusiastic about their new stadium. The extra employment it brought was welcome, but certain other developments in the city were not. Hitler decided to spend millions of marks widening and 'improving' the eight-mile-long (13-kilometre) east–west route from the old royal palace to the new Olympic complex, including the Unter den Linden, Charlottenburger Chaussee, Bismarckstrasse, Kaiserdamm and Heerstrasse. This was to become a great Via Triumphalis not just for sporting heroes but also for German armies returning victorious from war, a highway broad enough for troops to march twelve abreast down each carriageway. Fifty-foot-high (15-metre), green-painted flagpoles for carrying Nazi banners shot up like weeds along the entire length. People who lived along the route were given special grants to cover exterior repairs and redecoration.

As a result of the road widening, many well-loved old buildings had to go, which upset many Berliners. This was bad enough, but worse was to come. To make room for a forest of flagpoles and banners along the Linden, Hitler committed the ultimate sacrilege: he had many of the famous lime trees that gave the avenue its name cut down. Berliners were furious at this vandalism, and complained vociferously to their mayor. Surprisingly, even the normally complaisant Lippert found the courage to fill a large packing case with the hundreds of letters he had received from indignant fellow Berliners and send it, along with his own letter of complaint, to Hitler. Hitler, of course, simply ignored the whole thing.

Berliners, in fact, were extremely superstitious about their linden trees. They believed the words of a favourite old song by Walter Kollo, which had become the city's unofficial anthem: 'As long as the old trees still bloom on Unter den Linden / Nothing can defeat us – Berlin will stay Berlin.' As the trees came down, the whisper went round: 'No more lime trees in Unter den Linden . . . presently there will be no more Berlin.'

A horrific accident that occurred right in front of Goebbels's official town residence, the former palace of the marshals of the

Prussian court at number 20, Hermann-Göring-Strasse (formerly and now Ebertstrasse, running from Pariserplatz to Potsdamerplatz along the route of the communist wall) seemed to bear out everyone's worst fears. A tramcar loaded with passengers crashed through the roadway into the excavations for a new U-Bahn line beneath. 'You'll see,' said the local prophets of doom, 'that's where we'll all end up – at the bottom of a hole in front of Goebbels's house.'

Disturbed by the popular reaction, the city authorities hastily attempted to make good the damage to the Linden. They replaced the desecrated trees with several hundred four-year-old 16-foot (5-metre) American lime saplings from nurseries at Elmshorn in Holstein. Staked, sprayed, protected with railings, the new trees were neatly planted at intervals of 25 feet (8 metres), interspersed between new Biedermayer-style street lamps. Since the lamps were tall and ornate, each with four arms carrying the lights, the saplings looked weedy and stunted by comparison. Berlin wits were not slow to give the avenue a new name: 'Unter die Lanterne'.

During the months before the games, the reign of terror inflicted by the Nazis on Germany in general and Berlin in particular suddenly slackened. Even the persecution of the Jews was eased, and thousands of concentration camp victims were released. To the world's wishful thinkers, it seemed the regime was stabilizing at last: that it had no further need of the excesses that had marred its first three years. To the more hopeful citizens of Berlin, it even seemed to signal the possibility of a return to the 'Golden Twenties'. Nightclubs and cabarets reopened, expensive whores were back on the streets, loudspeakers along the entire length of the East–West Axis played jolly music. The whole city was en fête.

In truth, Hitler, ably assisted by Göring and Goebbels, had simply embarked on a huge public relations exercise, one of the biggest whitewashing operations of all time. And for a time, it worked. Visitors poured in from all over the world, and were duly impressed. They saw no discrimination on account of race or colour, they saw no persecution of the Jews (all the signboards and slogans had been taken down or painted over) and no repression of the Protestant and Catholic churches.

The visitors may have been fooled, but the Berliners approached the whole thing with their usual irreverence. The biggest cheer from the thousands lining the route to the stadium on the opening day was reserved for a lone cyclist, who somehow managed to penetrate the ranks of police and troops and calmly pedalled his way home from work, along the Via Triumphalis.

Two friends of the authors of this book also played their parts in keeping things down to earth. Maria Countess von Maltzan, always a rebel, talked her way into the VIP enclosure with her cabaret artist husband Walter Hillbring by posing as foreign dignitaries speaking a language totally unknown to man. After defeating the best efforts of 17 interpreters, they ended up watching the opening ceremony only a few seats away from Hitler himself. They enjoyed making fools of the system more than watching the spectacle in the arena.

Not far from Maria von Maltzan in the stadium were two well-dressed young Jewish men. They sat through the ceremony until the end, but when the orchestra started the *Horst Wessel Song* they found it too much to bear. 'We don't have to sit through this,' one whispered to his companion. The friend was Fritz Kalkstein, son of an old East Prussian Jewish family, who has lived in London for over half a century as Fred Kendall. Fritz had fled to Britain in 1935 to escape persecution and establish a home for his mother and sisters, who had remained in Berlin.

Taking advantage of the 'Olympic pause' in anti-Semitic activity, Fritz had slipped back into Berlin by train, via Holland. He had been met at Charlottenburg station by his Jewish friend, who had promised help in getting his family to safety. Needing somewhere safe to discuss their plans, the friend had obtained two tickets for the opening ceremony, reasoning that the one place that would be 100 per cent secure was the Olympic stadium. There, they would be surrounded by hundreds of international pressmen and thousands of visiting foreigners. Even if they were recognized as Jews, no one would dare to take any action against them.

The two men sat through the opening ceremony talking quietly, until the *Horst Wessel Song*. Then, drawing as little attention to themselves as possible, they left their seats and slipped out of the stadium. They reached their car without incident and were just about to drive off when they were halted by an officious SS man. Fearfully, they had no alternative but to do as they were told and stay where they were. The area was thick with SS and SA men, and there was clearly no possibility of escaping.

After what seemed hours, they watched Hitler and his entourage emerge from the stadium nearby and climb into their big, black Mercedes cars. The cavalcade moved off, and the officious SS man imperiously waved Fritz and his friend to follow: because they were also in a big, black, open Mercedes, he had assumed they were part of the official procession. For the whole length of the Via Triumphalis back into the city centre, they drove at a discreet two cars' length behind Goebbels, nervously acknowledging the cheers of the crowd. To their relief, they finally managed to turn off just before they reached the Reich chancellery.

It was just as well for Fritz Kalkstein and his friend that they did manage to escape; had they been forced into Wilhelmstrasse they might have found themselves trapped by the crowds that thronged the newly paved square in front of the chancellery to cheer themselves hoarse. Time after time, Hitler had to appear at the balcony overlooking the square to acknowledge their adulation, until it was time to leave and return to the Olympic stadium for the evening's great youth pageant.

For the two weeks of the games, Berlin turned into one enormous party. The members of the International Olympic Committee needed iron constitutions to keep up with the endless flow of rich food and German wines and, of course, speeches, speeches and more speeches.

Hitler confined his party-giving to one formal dinner on Wednesday 12 August, entertaining 150 guests in the new state dining room of the chancellery building. This may have been the principal formal occasion of the games, but it was the parties given by the three senior Nazi paladins, Göring, Goebbels and the future foreign minister Ribbentrop, that were the most keenly anticipated events in the social calendar. The three men were not only political rivals, but also bitter personal enemies: they could be relied upon to compete with each other in the extravagance of their entertaining.

As a former wine merchant, now married to the heiress to the Henkell sparkling wine fortune, Ribbentrop could be relied on to serve excellent food and drink at the dinner and dance he gave at his house in the exclusive suburb of Dahlem. But Ribbentrop was a prize bore, and his party was utterly conventional. Not so Göring and Goebbels, who were always much more adventurous.

Göring, in fact, had an unfair advantage, being able to host three different official parties since he held positions in the national government, the Prussian state government and the Reichstag. He began with an exotic luncheon for the IOC in his town residence, the Reichstag president's palace. He followed this with a dinner held in the State Opera House on the Unter den Linden on 8 August, which rivalled Friedrich the Great's victory celebration held there in December 1742.

Göring transformed the majestic old theatre for the occasion with tables for 2,000 guests, while singers and dancers from the Opera provided the entertainment. The colours for the evening were red and white, reflected in long banners hanging down all around the auditorium and stage. Over 100 periwigged footmen in pink livery and knee-breeches lined the stairs, holding glass lanterns on long poles. To maintain the colour scheme, the ladies were asked to wear white, as did Göring himself, his dress uniform ablaze with decorations and gold braid. Berlin had known nothing like this since the start of the First World War.

Göring gave his third and final party in his role as air minister and head of the Luftwaffe. He turned the gardens of his ministry building into a colourful carnival, complete with carousels, sideshows, taverns and dance bands. In response, Goebbels took over Pfaueninsel, the island in the Havel, for the final fling of the fortnight. He used his position as head of the film industry to have the island on the Havel decorated from end to end like an enormous movie set, and filled with pretty girls dressed as Renaissance pages in tabards and tights. The main entertainment was provided by the Berlin Philharmonic and dancers from the Opera. This was followed by dancing to no fewer than three bands, and an enormous firework display. After that, the whole thing degenerated into something approaching an orgy, with male guests pursuing scantily clad 'pages' through the undergrowth. It was a fitting conclusion to Berlin's biggest-ever social event.

CHAPTER 17

The Road to War

T HE EUPHORIA SURROUNDING the Olympic games lasted well into 1938, when Hitler brought Austria back into the German empire after an absence of 67 years. But when he began trying to take the Sudetenland from Czechoslovakia, the enthusiasm of the Berliners, at least, was muted.

When a motorized division of troops rolled through the centre of the city just as Berliners were leaving work on 27 September, Hitler expected a joyful demonstration to send them on their way. Instead, everyone turned away or looked on in mute disapproval. Hitler appeared on the balcony of the chancellery to review his troops, but when he saw that the square outside was virtually empty of spectators he marched back inside in a temper.

It was fitting that the crisis meetings Hitler held with Daladier of France and Chamberlain of Great Britain should have been in Bad Godesberg and Munich, and not in the capital. But there was much greater enthusiasm after the Munich agreement – 'delirious joy' William Shirer called it – compounded of relief at the news of peace, and pride in a bloodless victory over the Allies.

If the Berliners had been lulled by the Munich victory, they were in for a savage awakening six weeks later, when attacks on the Jews, which had dwindled during and since the Olympics, suddenly exploded again in the 'Kristallnacht' pogrom of 9–10 November. Supposedly in 'revenge' for the murder of a German diplomat in Paris by a distraught 17-year-old Jewish youth from Hanover, the nationwide action by the SA was initiated in Munich, where Hitler and his party henchmen were celebrating the anniversary of the failed putsch of 1923. Although the pogrom took place in every town and city in the Reich, inevitably the biggest and best-organized action was in Berlin.

Before the stormtroopers were let loose to wreck Jewish homes and businesses, and to burn down synagogues, Police President Count von Helldorf ensured everything was ready for them. Police squads isolated Jewish buildings, cut telephone wires, switched off electricity and gas supplies to Jewish shops to prevent untoward accidents, and set up barriers to divert traffic away from the areas where the mobs were to be let loose. Only when everything was prepared, at 2.00 am, did Helldorf give give the signal for the 'spontaneous' action to start. While the stormtroopers did their worst, the fire service stood by, just in case the fires spread from Jewish to Aryan properties.

By dawn, nine of the twelve synagogues in Berlin were ablaze, and already the death toll was mounting as Jews were beaten to a pulp, or leapt from upper storey windows, or were trapped in flames. With daylight, the mobs swarmed down the Linden, the Kurfürstendamm and Tauentzienstrasse, smashing plate-glass windows, hauling out furs, jewellery, furniture, silver – but only from Jewish-owned businesses. All day, the rampage continued as the looters moved on eastwards. 'In Friedrichstrasse in downtown Berlin,' reported the *Washington Post*, 'crowds pushed police aside in their hunt for plunder. Late in the afternoon fire broke out in Israel's department store near the Alexanderplatz, but firemen soon extinguished the blaze.'

The Berlin correspondent of the London *Daily Telegraph*, Hugh Carleton Greene, wrote: 'Mob law ruled in Berlin throughout the afternoon and evening and hordes of hooligans indulged in an orgy of destruction. I have seen several anti-Jewish outbreaks in Germany during the last five years, but never anything as nauseating as this. Racial hatred and hysteria seemed to have taken complete hold of otherwise decent people. I saw fashionably dressed women clapping their hands and screaming with glee, while respectable middle-class mothers held up their babies to see the "fun".'

Not all Berliners thought of the pogrom as fun, of course. Most were deeply ashamed. Many, even some in high positions like Colonel Hans Oster, chief of staff to the head of the Abwehr, Admiral Wilhelm Canaris, risked their own lives and property by offering shelter and protection to Jewish friends and neighbours. Walter Henry Nelson, who was then a boy living in the city as the son of a US consular official, describes how the janitor of his block cried, 'They must have emptied the insane asylums and penitentiaries to find people who'd do things like that!' Another Berliner, Hans Werner Lobeck, saw stormtroopers emerging from the wreckage of a Jewish-Hungarian restaurant, the 'Czardas' on Kurfürstendamm, near the still-smouldering synagogue on Fasanenstrasse. They were carrying dozens of bottles of looted Tokay wine, which they decided to give to 'some of the old Berliners' who were watching. 'A shudder went through the crowd, and it fell back,' Lobeck said. 'The people dispersed, leaving the SA men alone on the sidewalk.' The disapproval, for many Berliners, had nothing to do with race, only with civilized standards of behaviour. Kate Freyhan, a teacher in a Jewish girls' primary school, found her corner shop full of people watching children throwing cobblestones through the windows of the synagogue on the opposite side of the street. The young woman who owned the shop was indignant: it was disgraceful, the police just standing there and doing nothing. 'After all,' she declared, 'it is private property.'

When the immediate violence was over, all the active Jewish men in the city were rounded up and transported to Sachsenhausen concentration camp at Oranienburg, 18 miles to the north-west, where they were beaten up, tortured, starved, and held for several weeks. Hundreds of them died there. Meanwhile, Göring decreed that the Jews must make good all the damage caused, and pay an 'atonement fine' of one billion marks.

The trauma of that night and day of violence has remained with Berlin ever since. But of course, it did not mark the end of anti-Semitism, nor even its climax, only the beginning of a terrible new phase. The programme of 'Aryanization' of Jewish businesses was stepped up, with new regulations on 28 November for the winding up and dissolution of all Jewish enterprises. That same day, other regulations banned German or stateless Jews from certain parts of the capital. Those who were unfortunate enough to live within a forbidden area needed a police permit to cross the boundary, and were given warning that such permits would not be issued after 1 July, 1939. The ban covered most of central Berlin, and all places of entertainment or recreation. Jews were forbidden from owning cars. And ominous new plans were announced forcing Jews to sell or exchange their homes in fashionable districts and move into controlled Jewish quarters.

For Berlin, the great event of January 1939 was the opening of the great new Reich chancellery running from Wilhelmplatz along the entire length of Voss Strasse. For the past year, that part of the city had been dominated by frantic building work, as 4,500 men slaved day and night on the seemingly impossible task of completing the enormous project in less than a year. In the event, they finished early, with 48 hours to spare.

Hitler, meanwhile, unable to bear the noise and the upheaval, had moved out to stay with Goebbels in the English mock-Tudor mansion he had helped him buy on the near-island of Schwanenwerder, in the Havel just north of Pfaueninsel. He had described the old chancellery, the eighteenth-century Radziwill palace, as being 'only fit for a soap company'. Nevertheless, it had been incorporated into the new building, and he kept his private apartment in it.

'I need grand halls and salons,' he had told Speer, 'which will make an impression on people, especially the smaller dignitaries.' With the new chancellery, which was to be the last great public building to be erected in old Berlin, the end of the line started by Schlüter and Nering so many years before, Speer had done him proud.

Everything about the new building was on a grand scale. The Voss Strasse frontage stretched for 400 metres of yellow stucco and grey stone. Huge square columns framed the main entrance, where visitors drove through great double gates into an enormous court of honour. A flight of steps led them into a reception room; from there they could pass through double doors almost five metres high and flanked by gilded bronze and stone eagles, each clutching a swastika in its claws, and on into a large hall with floor and walls clad in gold-and-grey mosaic tiles. From this Mosaic Hall, more steps led up to a circular chamber with a high domed ceiling, and from there the visitor passed into a magnificent gallery lined with red marble pillars. At 146 metres, the Marble Gallery was twice as long as the Hall of Mirrors in Versailles, a fact that gave Hitler particular pleasure. Beyond the gallery was a great hall for state receptions. The whole concourse of rooms was some 220 metres of rich materials and colours, flamboyant, ostentatious, and grandiose.

The first ceremonial occasion in the new building was Hitler's annual New Year reception for the Diplomatic Corps on 12 January, when he startled everyone by spending several minutes talking to the Soviet ambassador. Six days later, he addressed 3,600 newly commissioned army lieutenants crammed into the Mosaic Hall, setting the tone that would dominate the rest of the year. 'I demand of you, my young officers,' he told them in a speech that could have come straight from Wilhelm II, 'an unconditional belief that one day, our German Reich will be the dominant power in Europe, that no other power will be in a position to stop us, let alone to break us . . . It is my unshakeable will that the German Wehrmacht becomes the most powerful force on earth.'

Not wishing to leave the navy out of all this, on 13 February he travelled to Hamburg to launch the Reich's first super warship. He named it, inappropriately, the *Bismarck*.

The remainder of 1939 became a continuous preparation for war. Tension was already mounting over Poland's rejection of German claims to Danzig, the ancient Hansa seaport that had been made a free city by the Treaty of Versailles. But Hitler was not yet ready to tackle the Poles. First, he had other affairs to settle. On 15 March, his troops marched into the remainder of Czechoslovakia. A week later, he personally led another army into the Baltic port of Memel, which had been sliced from East Prussia in 1919 and given to Lithuania.

With the whole of the media in the hands of Goebbels's propaganda ministry, even normally sceptical Berliners could not help but be impressed with Hitler's achievements. But for anyone who still doubted – and there were many in the capital – the Nazis staged a gigantic show in honour of his fiftieth birthday on 20 April. The celebrations started the night before, when he drove with Albert Speer along the length of the newly completed East–West Axis – the

Via Triumphalis of the Olympics with further widening at various points. The whole route was permanently lined with tall metal flagpoles – 'for hanging bigwigs in the future,' the Berlin wits suggested. As Hitler officially declared it open, bands played the traditional Badenweiler March and fireworks lit up the sky with an enormous swastika.

At midnight, a choir from the SS Life Guards sang in the courtyard of the new chancellery, while Hitler inspected his presents. These included a scale model of his planned triumphal arch, and dozens of model ships, aircraft and weapons, which he seized upon like a small boy.

Next morning, Berlin awoke to the sound of military units arriving for the grand birthday parade. Six army divisions, 40,000 men with 600 tanks, armoured personnel carriers, countless artillery pieces, rolled past the dais for four solid hours in an astonishing display of military might. Overhead flew wave after wave of bombers, fighters, and the new Stuka dive bombers. The spectators cheered and waved and applauded the show.

Before the parade started, Hitler received his three commanders-in-chief, Göring, General Brauchitsch and Admiral Raeder, together with the chief of staff of the OKW, the supreme command of the armed forces, in his study. He told them he intended to go to war that year.

By August, it was clear to everyone that war was inevitable. With the newspapers screaming of Polish provocations and threats, general mobilization was ordered on 15 August. The first quarter of a million reservists were called up for duty on the western front, just in case the French should decide to do anything stupid. The army general staff began moving out of Berlin's Bendlerstrasse to new headquarters in Zossen, some 25 miles (40 kilometres) south of the city, where they would be closer to the action when the war began. The railways were alerted to prepare for the immense task of moving men and equipment to the Polish border. And the pocket battleships *Graf Spree* and *Deutschland*, together with 21 U-boats, were got ready to sail.

The big worry for the Berliners, like most Germans, was that the old alliance between Britain, France and Russia would be repeated, and that they would once again be forced to fight a war on two fronts, surrounded by enemies. On Tuesday, 22 August, that worry was removed. That morning, the Berliners awoke to the news that their government was about to sign a pact with the Soviet Union. Germany was now blockade-proof. With a back door open for the import of food and raw materials from the Soviet Union, there was no way the British navy could strangle the Reich as it had done during the First World War. There would be no repetition of Berlin's turnip winter of 1917. Stalin, once the arch-enemy of the Nazis, had given them carte blanche to deal with the troublesome Poles. Without the help of the Soviet Union, the British would surely not intervene, and without the British, the French would certainly not fight. Hitler would be left alone to wage his 'Silesian War'.

Wednesday, 23 August, was hot and humid in Berlin. The conditions did not help the taut nerves of those waiting for confirmation that Ribbentrop and Soviet Prime Minister Molotov had actually signed the pact. It finally came at about 2.00 am on Thursday.

The crowds in the streets of Berlin later that day were as cheerful and good-humoured and noisy as if they had all won the national lottery. The cafes along the Linden and the Ku'damm were filled to overflowing with Berliners celebrating peace for their time. They joked and played pranks on each other, greeted friends and acquaintances with 'Heil Stalin' instead of the usual obligatory 'Heil Hitler'. Some young fellows even rang the doorbell of the Soviet embassy in the Linden, shouted 'Heil Moscow!', then ran off like naughty schoolboys, roaring with laughter. And in at least one mid-town Bierstube the band struck up the previously banned *Internationale*, bringing the entire clientele to its feet as though they had played *Deutschland Über Alles*. There would be no great war, everyone said: you could bet on it. And indeed, many people did just that. So confident were some diplomats at the Foreign Office that they were offering odds of 20 to one on peace, in bottles of champagne.

While the revellers on the Ku'damm were celebrating peace, preparations for war continued. At 7.00 pm that same evening, CBS correspondent William Shirer sat in his room at the Adlon and watched Luftwaffe personnel installing anti-aircraft guns on the roof of the giant chemical combine IG Farben's new head office, nearing completion opposite the hotel. German bombers had been flying over the city all day.

More anti-aircraft guns were now appearing all over the city, in squares, parks, sports fields, any open space. Even the red hard courts of the august Rot-Weiss Lawn Tennis Club in Dahlem, which boasted Göring, Ribbentrop and former chancellor Papen among its members, began sprouting guns. Indeed, the club had been practically taken over by the military: the floor of the ballroom in the clubhouse was covered with hay to provide bedding for recruits, and camp kitchens erected behind the building were 'seasoning the air with the aroma of potato, carrot, and suggestion-of-pork stew'. In spite of all this activity, however, keen tennis players still managed to get in a game or two.

Berliners started to sober up when the news came that Britain and France were standing firm on Poland and that both countries were starting to mobilize. Suddenly, the streets were full of marching men instead of partygoers. A never-ending stream of vehicles, civilian as well as military, including commandeered furniture vans and grocery trucks, rattled eastwards down the broad boulevards carrying troops and equipment, following the flights of Stukas and Messerschmitts heading for airfields close to the Polish frontier. This time, unlike 1914, there were no cheering crowds lining the streets. No women threw flowers. No one sang patriotic songs. The cafés were empty. The glum faces of the Berliners reflected their anxiety.

On the radio, Hitler's deputy, Rudolf Hess, spoke openly of war. 'If it comes,' he warned, 'it will be terrible.' His message was taken to heart by many people, including the children of a school in the north-eastern suburb of Pankow. Hearing the sound of a siren, they remembered their air-raid drill and immediately filed out of their classrooms to the shelters. But it was a false alarm – the 'siren' turned out to be a factory hooter.

The newspapers were now filled with stories of Polish atrocities against Germans living in Poland and Danzig. In screaming headlines, the *12-Uhr Blatt* accused the Poles of firing on three unarmed German passenger airplanes, and of torching German farmhouses in the Polish Corridor between East Prussia and the rest of Germany. The *Berliner Zeitung*, which had stood up against Bismarck so bravely back in the 1870s, loyally played its part: GERMAN FAMILIES FLEE, it proclaimed, accusing the Poles of massing troops on the German border. The Nazi Party's own *Völkischer*

Beobachter continued to whip up war hysteria on 27 August with the headlines: WHOLE OF POLAND IN WAR FEVER! 1,500,000 MEN MOBILIZED! NON STOP TROOP MOVEMENT TOWARD THE FRONTIER! CHAOS IN UPPER SILESIA! And to drive home the seriousness of the situation, German radio played continuous martial music, broken only by occasional announcements.

The Germans themselves, of course, had been mobilized for the past two weeks, though the papers omitted to mention this. Now, it was announced that what was called 'the organization of all measures for eventualities' had come into force. Berliners discovered that long-distance and international telephone services had been cut off, and that they could no longer leave the city by train or air. The whole national transport system was now under military control, and only foreigners or those whose journeys were of national importance were allowed to travel.

It was announced that Hitler had cancelled the next Nuremberg rally, billed as the great party congress of peace, which was to have been the biggest ever Nazi event, attended by over a million party members. (In fact, Hitler had given the cancellation order two weeks before, but it had not been made public at the time.) Then, ominously, on Sunday 28 August, a hot and glorious day when half of Berlin seemed to have made its way to the inland beaches at Wannsee and Müggelsee to brown in the sun and take their minds off the international situation, policemen began knocking on doors and handing out ration cards. As of Monday, people were informed, they would need the cards to buy food, soap, shoes, textiles, and even coal.

On Thursday, 31 August, there was a full-scale practice air-raid alert in the city. The long, undulating wail of the sirens soon cleared the streets. All traffic stopped as drivers and passengers joined pedestrians scurrying into cellars and basements marked out as shelters. Diners in restaurants were herded into back rooms for an hour and a half, until the all-clear sounded. They were warned that in a real raid they would have to take refuge in the cellars. All the street lights were turned off. People at home had to close their windows, which they had already covered with black paper, if they had been able to find any.

On almost every roof, soldiers with binoculars kept watch on planes flying overhead – though, since this was a rehearsal, the only planes they could see were from the Luftwaffe. The streets below them were silent and empty within a few minutes. Kerbstones and crossings, which boys of the Hitler Youth had been busy daubing with white luminous paint, glowed eerily in the dark. The only living souls – apart from horses tied to lampposts while their drivers took shelter – were grim-faced policemen, their gas masks at the ready.

After the appalling results of raids by the German Condor Legion in the Spanish Civil War and Japanese attacks on Chinese cities like Shanghai, everybody expected any modern war to start with aerial bombardment. So, in addition to holding practice drills, providing air-raid shelters for the general population was a top priority. Unfortunately, there was a grave shortage of skilled building workers: those who had not been called up were engaged on official projects. So, the authorities decided to make ordinary citizens responsible for constructing shelters in the cellars of their own buildings. Supervision was no problem: every building already had its own party *Hausleiter* (house leader) keeping an eye on the tenants and reporting their activities to the authorities. Officials from the Air Ministry inspected each cellar for suitability, and advised on construction. The tenants were then expected to start digging.

Friday, 1 September, dawned grey and sultry. Clouds hung low over the capital. At 5.11 am, in the vastness of his new chancellery study, Hitler signed the document that made Germany officially at war with Poland. It was, in fact, purely academic, since German bombers had begun their attack 40 minutes earlier.

The people received the news with numb apathy, going about their business as though nothing had happened. Few bothered to buy the news extras that hit the streets at breakfast time. Along the East–West Axis, Luftwaffe crews were setting up five heavy anti-aircraft guns to protect Hitler when he addressed the Reichstag at 10.00 am.

The general blackout in Berlin that night was not a rehearsal. The first proper air-raid alert came at 7.00 pm, when there was a rumour that 70 Polish bombers were approaching. In fact, two Polish aircraft had managed to get as far as the city, but they did no damage and were themselves unharmed. All the same, everyone dashed for cover. It may have been a reaction to the strain of their first real alert, but when the all-clear had sounded and people emerged from their cellars, many of them seemed determined to have a last fling before the shutters finally came down. Suddenly, the cafés, restaurants and beer halls were packed with people trying to drink Berlin dry.

That night, a new decree was issued, forbidding anyone from listening to foreign broadcasts, on pain of death. From then on, anyone caught listening to the BBC from London – which many Berliners had depended on since 1933 as their only reliable source of news – faced the executioner's axe.

On Saturday, 2 September, the Berlin railway stations were jammed with military personnel on their way to join their units, and with foreigners and their children trying to get out of the country. They were also crowded with small German children, all with blue tags around their necks marked with their names and home addresses. They were being evacuated to the safety of the countryside, away from the expected bombing.

Outside, Berliners were enjoying the last of their Indian summer, strolling through the sunlit streets as they did every weekend. But there were few smiling faces. Everyone was waiting anxiously to find out what Britain and France would do.

The waiting ended on Sunday, 3 September, another lovely sunny day, when the Berlin radio station interrupted a concert from Hamburg. For those who were not at home, clustered anxiously around their radio sets, there were loudspeakers fixed to lamp posts in many Berlin streets, so that everyone could hear the news first-hand. Shortly after noon, Liszt's *Hungarian Rhapsody* was faded and a man's voice said: 'Achtung! Achtung! In a few minutes we shall be making an important announcement.' Ten minutes later, came the news that Britain had declared herself at war with Germany.

The people in the streets, even the small crowd of about 250 gathered in front of the chancellery, listened in stunned silence. Four hours later, they learned that France, too, had declared war. There was no excitement, nor even any hate for the British and French, whose embassies still needed only a lone policeman each to guard them.

As always, Berlin was alive with rumours, most of them absurdly optimistic. Papen, it was said, was already in Paris negotiating a separate peace with the French government; German and French soldiers facing each other across the Rhine were already fraternizing and refusing to fight; the Soviet Union had delivered an ultimatum to Britain, threatening to join Germany in the war. On a more pessimistic note, it was said that Saarbrücken, for example, had been shelled by French guns and was now in ruins.

Berliners, however, had not yet lost their cynical sense of humour. Anti-Hitler jokes had always been popular in the city. Now, a new crop was whispered in cafés, told amongst friends. The latest concerned both Hitler and Goebbels. It seems they were out on a drive together in the countryside, when their car ran over a dog. Goebbels said he thought he ought to find the owner and apologize. 'Go ahead,' Hitler replied. 'I'll stay in the car. But see you come right back.' Over an hour later, Goebbels returned, smelling of drink and very much the worse for wear. Hitler was furious, and demanded an explanation. 'Well, it was like this,' Goebbels slurred. 'I found the house where the dog's owner lives. I knocked on the door, and when he opened it I said: "Heil Hitler, the dog is dead." "Come inside," said the man. "Let's celebrate!" '

But no one in Berlin was celebrating that night.

CHAPTER 18

'Lair of the fascist beast'

ERLIN HAD EMERGED PHYSICALLY un-
scathed from the First World War. And for the first twelve
months of the second, it remained undamaged as Hitler's
armies scored easy victories. First the Poles and then, after six
months of uneasy waiting in the west, Denmark, Norway, Holland,
Belgium, Luxemburg, France and the British Expeditionary Force
all collapsed. With each new success, Berliners were ordered to put
out the flags and put on a show of celebration. But their celebrating
was always half-hearted – at least, it was until the day in mid-June
1940, when local infantrymen came back from France.

Cheering crowds showered the returning heroes with confetti as
they marched triumphantly through the Brandenburg Gate, to be
reviewed by Goebbels and the commander of the Berlin garrison
from a stand erected outside the French embassy. As they continued
on up the Linden, its buildings draped with red and white pennants,
children broke through the police cordon to hand them little bouquets
of flowers. The city went wild. But the Berliners were celebrating

because the troops had come home to be demobilized. The war, they thought, was over.

After a year of rationing and shortages, Berlin was suddenly awash with good things. Soldiers returned from France and the other defeated western nations laden with luxuries for their wives and sweethearts: silk stockings, satin underwear, fur coats, perfume, toiletries. The shelves in every street corner Kneipe were stacked with fine cognacs and armagnacs from France, powerful Dutch geneva gin, Havana and Sumatra cigars. Bourgeois families dined on smoked hams and foie gras, washed down with the best French champagne and vintage wines. For most people, it was a summer to remember.

The autumn brought the Berliners back to earth with a painful jolt. The British had retreated across the Channel, but they had not capitulated. And the planned invasion had been thwarted by the RAF, whose light bombers had destroyed most of the barges assembled on the French and Belgian coasts, while their fighters had all but destroyed Göring's much vaunted Luftwaffe. Göring and Hitler had switched the German bomber attack from the British airfields to the cities. It was a disastrous decision, for not only did it allow the Spitfires and Hurricanes to keep flying, but it also brought reprisals.

On 24–5 August, German bombers attacked the heart of the City of London, destroying many historic buildings including the Christopher Wren church of St Giles, Cripplegate. The very next night, 103 RAF aircraft took off to bomb German cities for the first time, 89 of them headed for Berlin. Because of adverse weather conditions, the length of the journey, and the lack of sophisticated navigation equipment, only 29 actually reached the city. Their bombs caused little damage, but the fact that they had braved the 1,160-mile (1,867-kilometre) round trip to strike at Berlin itself was a chilling portent of what was to come.

The RAF came 38 more times between then and the end of October, gaining experience and improving accuracy with every raid. Berliners got used to spending their nights in the shelters, then struggling to work along rubble-strewn streets and shattered S-Bahn tracks. In a tacit admission of the effectiveness of the raids, Goebbels ordered the compulsory evacuation of all children under the age of 14. Some 90,000 were shipped out on special trains to the safety of the eastern and south-eastern provinces. Older children, members of the Hitler Youth or the League of German Maidens, stayed put, to play their part in the city's civil defence and rescue services. Later, many of them were conscripted into the Luftwaffe as anti-aircraft auxiliaries. Initially, they were supposed to work as messengers and general dogsbodies, but as the war progressed, more and more of the boys found themselves actually manning the guns, while the girls operated searchlights.

Despite its distance from Britain, Berlin was always going to be the prime target for RAF bombing. As well as being the administrative centre of Germany, it was also the powerhouse of the nation's war effort. It housed an enormous garrison, with more than 90 military headquarters, barracks and depots, as well as the ministries of all three armed services and their combined high command. With twelve main rail lines converging on it from all directions, it was the hub of the communications network for Germany and indeed the whole of northern Europe, a network that was vital to Hitler for the rapid movement of troops and materiel. And the internal waterways, which had been developed continuously since the time of the Great Elector, consolidated the city's position at the heart of the northern canal and river system.

More than half of Germany's entire electrical industry was located in Berlin. As well as the giant Siemens plant just to the west of the central area, there were also ten AEG plants in Henningsdorf in the north-west, Moabit in the centre and Oberschöneweide in the south-east, making a wide range of products from radio components and insulators to heavy generating equipment. Telefunken made radio and telecommunications equipment at Tempelhof, just south of the city centre, Lorenz was at Zehlendorf in the south-west, and Bosch just beyond it at Kleinmachnow.

At Spandau, on the western edge of the city, the Alkett factory produced tanks, self-propelled guns, and half of the Wehrmacht's field artillery. Auto-Union factories at Spandau and Halensee, on the western end of the Kurfürstendamm, also produced tanks, while the engines to drive them were built in the Maybach factory at Tempelhof. Rheinmetall-Borsig, in its new factory town in the north-west of the city alongside the Tegelsee, made heavy artillery as well as its more traditional lines in locomotives and rolling stock. DIW and the DWM plant at Wittenau in the north of the city both produced small arms, mortars and ammunition. And Berlin was Germany's third-largest centre for the manufacture of ball bearings.

The city was also an important centre of aircraft production. To the north, the Heinkel works at Oranienburg was busy turning out bombers, while at Johannisthal in the south-east, the Henschel works produced Junkers bombers as well as Henschel attack aircraft. The Dornier, Flettner and Focke-Wulf companies all had factories in the city making components or assembling parts of aircraft. In Reinickendorf was the Argus works, where the engines for the V1 flying bombs would later be made. And to the south at Genshagen was the largest Daimler-Benz aero-engine plant in Germany.

Along with these major works, there were also, of course, literally hundreds of smaller firms and factories turning out vital components. Many of them, as they always have been in Berlin, were located in the back courts of apartment blocks in the heavily populated central districts, turning the Mietskasernen in areas like Wedding and Kreuzberg and Prenzlauerberg into military targets.

Berlin was a navigator's and bomb aimer's delight, with the broad expanse of the East–West Axis running in a straight line from the Havel to the Spree, pointing like an arrow to its heart. The authorities did everything they could to frustrate Allied aircraft, going to great lengths to disguise the city. They erected dummy buildings in open spaces in and near the centre. They strung a canopy of camouflage netting, laced with strips of green cloth and false fir tree tops, along the whole length of the Charlottenburger Chaussee from the Brandenburg Gate through the Tiergarten, to hide the long stretch of concrete. Even the lampposts were dressed up as fir trees. For local motorists and pedestrians, it was like passing through 'an enormous, overgrown, green circus marquee'. At the centre of the avenue, the Siegessäule, the Victory Column, was draped in netting from head to foot. The buxom goddess on top was stripped of her gold leaf and painted a dull brown.

Many individual buildings and installations were also camouflaged. The Deutschland Halle, for example, the giant exhibition hall that was used during the war for storing grain, was covered in netting cleverly painted so that from the air it looked like a park with paths running through it. And the nearby Lietzensee, a useful signpost for aircraft heading for the city centre, was also covered with netting to stop it reflecting the moon like a mirror. The lake was planted with covered scaffolding structures intended to look like buildings on a housing estate. RAF pilots may have been deceived by this illusion, but the wild ducks that frequented the lake were not – they continued to swim around beneath the camouflage. Later in the war, when the RAF began using radar to locate their targets, Berlin's lakes were studded with cross-shaped sheets of metal to reflect the signal back again.

Elsewhere in and around the city, there were even more ambitious deceptions. There were no fewer than five dummy towns built around the edges of the city boundaries, while vacant lots just beyond Ostkreuz S-Bahn station were covered with replicas of government buildings, designed to trick raiders into thinking they were over the Wilhelmstrasse. To complete the illusion, huge piles of brushwood were kept on most of the dummy sites, ready to be set on fire after bombs were dropped, to simulate burning buildings. The Berliners, typically, did not place much faith in their decoy sites; they claimed that some British bombers peeled off from the main line of attack to drop wooden bombs on them.

Deception techniques, no matter how clever, are no shield against bombs, so the Berlin authorities did what they could to protect the city's treasures. Smaller public statues were first cocooned in paper and then entombed in brick sarcophagi. Ancient works of art that were too large or too fragile to be moved were surrounded with sandbags. The huge Pergamon Altar, housed since 1930 in its own building on Museum Island, was so heavily protected it ended up looking like a Wehrmacht command post. Other pieces, such as the Egyptian bust of Queen Nefertiti, and the 'golden treasure of Priam' from Troy, were crated and stored along with the Rembrandts and Renoirs in various cellars and bunkers. Among them was an increasing number of paintings, sculptures and treasures looted from the conquered territories.

Later, as the raids grew worse, the art treasures would be moved to the deep Kaiseroda potassium mine in Thuringia, some 200 miles (322 kilometres) south-west of Berlin. But Hitler kept the Winged Victory of Samothrace, an ancient Greek sculpture taken from the Louvre in Paris, in his study in the chancellery. It was a satisfying personal retaliation for Napoleon's removal of the Quadriga in 1806. The Quadriga itself was not removed for safe keeping, standing defiantly on top of the Brandenburg Gate throughout the entire war. Most of the raids in 1941 came in the six weeks following

12 March, when British bombers devastated the heart of the Linden, hitting the state library, the old royal palace, and many other buildings for several blocks on either side. The State Opera House was gutted. Its massive exterior walls were left standing, but direct hits by some 30 incendiary bombs created an inferno that reduced the auditorium to a mess of charred timbers and twisted girders. The great golden eagle of the Kaisers, which had been mounted on red velvet hangings behind the old imperial box, was discovered by stunned sightseers next morning, lying charred, discoloured and sodden under the ruins. As a matter of pride, the building was patched up and put back into partial use, only to be smashed again three years later.

After the first raid in March, Goebbels, in his capacity as Gauleiter, had a visit from Count von Helldorf. The police chief was worried about Berlin's ability to withstand really heavy bombing. There were, he said, simply not enough adequate public shelters. Goebbels had always regarded Helldorf as a pessimist, and listened impatiently. 'What London can put up with,' he told him, 'Berlin will have to bear, too.'

During the first two years of the war, Berliners tended to regard the flak defences of their city as something of a joke: 'Hermann's sleeping battalions' they called them – Hermann, of course, being Göring, who, as commander-in-chief of the Luftwaffe, was responsible for protecting the city from aerial attack. But during 1941 the situation changed dramatically. By the end of that year Berlin bristled with searchlights and flak batteries arranged in concentric rings around the city. Its inner defences, meanwhile, were dominated by three massive flak towers built during 1941: one in the Zoological Gardens near the Kaiser Wilhelm Memorial Church; one in Humbolthain park, some two miles (three kilometres) due north of the Unter den Linden; and one in Friedrichshain park, about one mile (1.5 kilometres) east of Alexanderplatz.

Designed by Albert Speer's office in the heavy *Ordensburgen* style (literally 'order castles'), the towers were to be the first buildings for Hitler's new city of Germania. Intended to remind people of mediaeval fortresses, they were bomb-proof and shell-proof, modern Crusader castles with walls of reinforced concrete more than 2.5 metres thick, their deep-cut window slits shielded by solid steel shutters eight to ten centimetres thick. They had their own water and electricity supplies and their own hospitals, and were kept stocked with enough food and ammunition to sustain a twelve-month siege. On top of each tower, projecting above the trees of the surrounding park, eight 128-mm guns were mounted in pairs – 'double-barrelled', Hitler called them, 'the most beautiful weapons yet fashioned'. Just below roof level, four more gun positions housed twelve multi-barrelled 20-mm quick-firing 'pompoms' and 37-mm cannon to give protection against attack by low-flying aircraft.

The zoo tower was the biggest of the three at 40 metres tall, the equivalent of a 13-storey building. Two of its five levels formed an air-raid shelter for 15,000 members of the public, and another was a secure warehouse for art treasures. The Humbolthain tower, though slightly smaller, could provide refuge for even more Berliners, as its lower floors were connected to one of the deepest stations on the U-Bahn system, Gesundbrunnen: 21,000 people could shelter there during raids.

Alongside each flak tower stood a slightly smaller communications and radar control tower. From the zoo communications tower, Luftwaffe controllers directed the air defence of the city, issuing orders to all Berlin's flak and searchlight units. Beside the radar dishes was an observation turret like a small penthouse, large enough to hold at least a dozen people, from which party notables could watch the progress of a raid, for all the world like Roman senators at the Coliseum.

Berlin's formidable defences were one of the factors that led the British to call a halt in the bombing from the autumn of 1941. By then, however, the Berliners had something else to worry about. Hitler had invaded the Soviet Union in June, expecting his armies to smash their way to Moscow before winter set in. By mid-September, with the first snowfalls, the attack had ground to a halt and German casualties were beginning to mount. Suddenly there were wounded and crippled soldiers everywhere in the city, and an increasing number of women in mourning black.

The air raids had brought misery to many Berliners, but most of all to the Jews. More than half of all the Jews in Germany were now living in Berlin, having left the small towns and villages where they felt isolated and exposed, to seek the anonymity of the big city and the comfort of being with their fellows. Underfed, overcrowded, and deprived of the right to pursue any profession or business, most were directed into compulsory labour in armaments factories or other essential war work. Although they were persecuted, the policy of extermination had not yet begun.

As British bombs made more and more people homeless, Albert Speer stepped up his seizure of Jewish-owned apartments to rehouse them. He also needed to find accommodation for the capital's growing army of civil servants and officials; larger and more luxurious homes in the more fashionable districts were especially sought after by leading party members. At the end of September 1941, he warned the Jewish community leaders who had to find new homes for those who had been evicted that he would shortly begin a further 'resettlement'. But this time, the resettlement took a different form.

On 15 October, as darkness fell, two Gestapo men arrived at each apartment to be vacated and ordered the family to pack one suitcase with essentials. They took them to the remains of the synagogue on Levetzowstrasse, still in ruins since it was burnt down during Kristallnacht. They were held there for three days before being marched in a long procession through the city to the railway station at Grunewald. Young children and the sick were driven in trucks. On 18 October, the first train left, carrying 1,000 Jews to be dumped in the working ghetto of Lodz, in eastern Poland. Over the next ten weeks, another 25 trains followed, carrying Berlin Jews to Lodz and other ghettos in Minsk, the capital of Belorussia, Kaunas, at that time the capital of Lithuania, Riga, capital of Latvia, and Smolensk, in Russia.

At the beginning of 1942, there were still 40,000 Jews in Berlin, most of whom were saved from deportation by their jobs in war industries. But on 20 January, a conference in a villa at Wannsee under the direction of Reinhard Heydrich set out the plan for the 'final solution' of the Jewish problem. The remaining Jews throughout Nazi-occupied Europe, including the Reich itself, were to be exterminated in special death camps to be built in the east. Jews working in munitions factories would be systematically replaced by foreign workers from the occupied territories. Berlin would at last become *Judenfrei*.

The final round-up began on 27 February 1943. Day after day, week after week, trains of cattle trucks pulled out of Grunewald station, heading east for the gas chambers and ovens of the extermination camps. The whole operation was run with a deadly bureau-cratic efficiency.

There was, however, one unusual hitch in the Nazi plan. During the initial round-up, some 4,700 Jewish men who were partners in mixed marriages were segregated from the others, and taken to a building in the Rosenstrasse, not far from SS headquarters in Burg-strasse. On the Sunday morning, their non-Jewish wives got together and set out to find them. They descended on Rosenstrasse, and crowded round the building where their husbands were being held. There they stood, refusing to leave, shouting and screaming for their men, hour after hour, throughout the day and the night and into the next day.

Worried SS leaders gathered in Burgstrasse, not knowing what to do. They had never been faced with such a situation. Would they have to machine-gun nearly 5,000 German women? All night the arguments raged, until at noon on the Monday a decision was reached: all men married to a non-Jewish wife could return home. 'Privileged persons,' the official announcement said, 'are to be incorporated in the national community.' The 4,700 Jewish men had been given back their lives. They remained in an uneasy state of limbo until the end of the war.

The Jews were not the only people to be persecuted in Nazi Berlin, of course. Socialists, communists, homosexuals, and committed Christians of all sects also suffered under the regime. They were harried, arrested, tortured and sent to concentration camps. Many of them, too, were exterminated, albeit not en masse, as were Jews and gypsies. Under a ruthless totalitarian regime, with secret police and informers more active even than in the days of Friedrich the Great and Bismarck, dissent was dangerous and active opposition suicidal. For the most part, Berliners did what they had done during centuries of repression stretching back to Friedrich Iron-tooth: they kept their heads down, got on with their lives as well as they could, and waited for better times. They relieved their feelings with their own brand of black humour, though even that could be extremely dangerous – a joke in the wrong place, overheard by the wrong person, could lead to the executioner's axe or the guillotine.

Understandably, resistance in Nazi Germany was never as strong as in the occupied countries of Europe. Nevertheless, there were a few brave souls who were prepared to risk everything to defy Hitler, and many of them were in Berlin. They included high-minded aristocrats with historic names like Moltke and Bismarck, churchmen like Pastors Dietrich Bonhoeffer and Martin Niemöller, perpetual rebels like Countess Maria von Maltzan, the young woman who had gobbledegooked her way into the Olympic stadium, army officers like Colonel Hans Oster, chief of staff to Admiral Canaris, head of the Abwehr (Military Intelligence), journalists, former trade unionists, shopkeepers and ordinary citizens with nothing to gain but freedom and nothing to lose but their lives. Many of them, including Helmuth James von Moltke, Dietrich Bonhoeffer, Hans Oster and Wilhelm Canaris, paid the ultimate price. But others battled on to the end.

Their activities were as varied as their personalities. Some spent their time planning the fine details of a new government ready to take over from the Nazis. Others plotted assassination attempts. The largest number devoted themselves to helping the victims of Nazism to escape or survive. Thanks to their efforts, some 1,400 Jews were able to submerge and stay alive in Berlin until 1945. Being Berliners, they jokingly called themselves 'U-boats'.

During the lulls in the bombing, the city entertained itself as well as it could. Food rationing meant severe restrictions for restaurants, but most of them kept going somehow. Dancing in public was banned, as it had been during the Kaiser's war, and there was a shortage of beer, which kept many traditional beerhalls closed for much of the time. But clubs and cabarets were still open, and theatres were packed every night.

Although many musicians had fled before the war, and the banning of works by Jewish composers reduced the available repertoire, Berlin still remained a great centre for music. The Berlin Philharmonic, its musicians exempted from military service, flourished under Wilhelm Furtwängler until the very last days of the war. The Staats Oper on the Linden might have been destroyed, but Herbert von Karajan continued to present his masterly interpretations of Wagner at the Deutsche Oper in Bismarckstrasse until that, too, was bombed out in 1943 and he moved into the Admiralspalast in Friedrichstrasse.

On less exalted levels, the UFA film studios churned out a steady stream of epic war movies, cheeky comedies and frothy romances. Championship soccer was still being played in the Olympic stadium, with players on special leave from the armed forces, and in good weather people still swam at the lidos, sailed on the Havel and the Müggelsee, or rowed on the Tiergarten lakes and the canals.

But maintaining a semblance of normality became steadily more difficult as the war progressed. The British Eighth Army's defeat of Rommel's Afrika Corps at El Alamein was followed by disaster on the eastern front at Stalingrad. And the air raids on Berlin started again in January 1943, with renewed force. The RAF had been re-equipped during 1942 with four-engined heavy bombers capable of carrying much greater bomb loads.

In February 1943, at a packed meeting of the party faithful in the Sportpalast, Goebbels declared a state of 'total war'. Everything was to be sacrificed to the war effort, and anyone who did anything that might possibly detract from it would lose his or her head. The RAF responded with its heaviest raid on the city yet, with 302 aircraft. 'Tonight you go to the Big City,' Air Marshal Sir Arthur 'Bomber' Harris had signalled to his crews in RAF Bomber Command. 'You have an opportunity to light a fire in the belly of the enemy and burn his Black Heart out.' By coincidence, it was the day after the Nazis had begun the final round-up of the city's Jews. Many Berliners, reeling from the impact of thousands of tons of high explosives and incendiaries, saw it as a fitting retribution.

Throughout the summer of 1943, the RAF raids on the city were light. But on 1 August, a week after an enormous raid had wiped out Hamburg, killing at least 41,800 people in a horrific firestorm, the RAF dropped leaflets on Berlin calling on all women and children to leave at once. They had done the same thing before the raid on Hamburg, so the implication was clear. Goebbels ordered the evacuation of all remaining children and adults not engaged in war work. Well over a million obeyed, pouring out of the city on special trains, mainly heading south. Many of them came back after a while – like true Berliners they preferred to face sudden death by bombing to slow death by boredom in the countryside.

In fact, the truly massive raids did not materialize until late November, when Harris launched what he called the Battle of Berlin, convinced that he could destroy the city and bring down the Nazi government, thus ending the war. Night after night, wave after wave of Lancasters, Stirlings and Halifaxes lumbered overhead, braving the flak and the German nightfighters to pound the city into smouldering ruins. In March 1944, they were joined by the B17s and B24s of the United States Eighth Air Force flying by day. But when the battle was called off for the summer, when the nights would be too short to offer the protection of darkness to the RAF bombers, the city, although battered almost beyond recognition, was still functioning.

By that time, Berliners' morale was close to breaking point. Added to the strain of the raids, there was continual bad news from all the fronts, where the German armies were being smashed in the field. In the east, the Red Army was grinding its way inexorably forward, a terrifying juggernaut for which the ultimate target was always Berlin, the hated 'lair of the fascist beast'.

But much of the fear – for many, indeed, the worst fear of all – came from within the city itself. It was the fear of 'them': the Gestapo, short for the Geheime Staatspolizei, the secret state police. Increasingly, danger came not from bombing but from denunciation and the summary conviction of the People's Court, presided over by the rabid Judge Roland Freisler. The execution shed at the Plötzensee prison was working like a factory production line, taking just two minutes to dispatch each victim. Today, it stands empty and silent, open to the public as a grim memorial to those who died there.

When members of the resistance group in the army general staff failed in their attempt to assassinate Hitler on 20 July, the court and the executioners had a field day. The chief conspirator, Colonel Klaus von Stauffenberg, was shot in the courtyard of the general staff building that same night. But the other ringleaders were rounded up and tortured in Gestapo headquarters in Prinz-Albrecht-Strasse, to extract the names of any other supporters. All told, Himmler's men arrested some 7,000 suspects. The central conspirators were denied the honour of death by beheading, and were hanged from meathooks hastily fixed from a roof beam in the execution shed. The rest were guillotined. The executioners were kept busy until the very last days of the war, killing close on 5,000 souls, 2,500 of them in Plötzensee alone.

By the end of July, Berlin and its industries were being kept going largely by women and foreign workers drafted in from all the occupied countries. With the Soviets advancing in the east and the western Allies pushing forward in France and Italy, the Germans were facing the realities of a major war on three fronts. Goebbels, who had been appointed city president a few weeks earlier, was given absolute power to squeeze the last drops from German reserves. He called up all boys between the ages of 16 and 18 for full military service, along with men between 50 and 60. He stripped factories and offices of able-bodied men who had previously been in reserved occupations and sent them to the fronts. Their places were taken by German women and girls, and by foreign workers, drawn from 26 different countries.

Some of the foreigners were supposed to be volunteers, others were forced labourers, some were prisoners of war. The largest contingent came from Poland, including thousands of women and girls. All told, by mid-1944 there were 800,000 foreign workers in Berlin, making up a quarter of the population.

On Sunday afternoons, the city centre was packed with 'volunteers' from the west or the Ukraine enjoying their rest day. Native Berliners were astonished at their noisy exuberance as they paraded along the Linden or the Ku'damm, behaving in a very exuberant and un-German fashion, shouting cheerfully to each other in a Babel of different languages, and swarming across the road without paying the slightest attention to the traffic signals which every good German always obeyed without question. They brought a reminder of better times, even a hint of the heady days of the Olympics. They also brought, to many Berliners who broke the ban on fraternization, the truth about the war in other countries.

In January 1945, Berlin was swamped with other arrivals from the east. Refugees began pouring in from Silesia, fleeing from the advancing Russians and bringing tales of the terror to come. By February, the Red Army was on the Oder, only 40 miles from the city. The western Allies, meanwhile, had started bombing round the clock again, the RAF by night and the US Air Force with 1,000 bombers and more during the day. The centre of the city was becoming little more than a heap of rubble, with electricity, gas and water services operating spasmodically at best.

After the collapse of his last gamble in the west, the Ardennes offensive, Hitler returned to Berlin and buried himself in the deep concrete bunker beneath the chancellery garden. It soon became clear that he was planning to die there, like one of his Wagnerian heroes, with the city of Berlin as his funeral pyre. Realizing the danger, the party bigwigs started fleeing to the west, hoping to meet the Americans and British before the Russians arrived. But for the three million ordinary citizens there was no escape: Goebbels forbade anyone to leave without special permission. The rule even applied to the 120,000 children under the age of ten who were still in the city.

Until mid-March, in fact, there was no co-ordinated plan for the defence of Berlin. It was protected only by a few thousand second-echelon troops and young anti-aircraft gunners, and by the Volkssturm Home Guard, which was described, accurately, as 'the last round-up of the old and the lame, the children and the dotards'. The Volkssturm, which had been formed in October 1944, had received little or no training. They had no uniforms, no steel helmets, and virtually no weapons. They were expected to hold off some 2.5 million of Stalin's toughest and most battle-hardened soldiers with a few old rifles, a reasonable supply of hand grenades and the new hand-held Panzerfaust anti-tank rocket, a crude but highly effective weapon that actually performed better than the American bazooka on which it was based.

The Red Army sat on the Oder for two and a half months, gathering their strength for their final, massive attack. The Berliners could only wait helplessly, digging trenches and throwing up barricades, until they chose to attack. But in the meantime, the Americans were powering in from the west at an astonishing rate. Suddenly, it seemed possible that they might actually beat the Russians to Berlin, and that the city would be spared the terrors of conquest by its ancient enemies, the Slavs. But the Americans decided to stop at the Elbe, less than 50 miles (80 kilometres) to the west.

The Red Army launched its great assault across the Oder on 16 April. On 20 April, Hitler's birthday, the first Soviet shells exploded in the city centre as over 1,000 Flying Fortresses of the US Air Force, followed by Mosquitoes from the RAF, made their last raid, leaving the Soviets to make the final kill. It was not a quick death. For a further eleven days, German troops battled bravely against overwhelming odds, obeying their orders to fight on to the end. A few thousand fanatical SS troops actually fought their way in from the west, to take part in the last stand in the heart of the city. Few, if any, of them were Berliners. Many were not even German. All were dedicated Nazis, determined to defend their Führer till their last breath. They were supported by brainwashed youngsters of the Hitler Youth, a few members of the Volkssturm, and the tattered remnants of the army and the Luftwaffe, bound by honour to fulfil their oath of allegiance.

They were released from that oath on 30 April, when Adolf Hitler committed suicide. Joseph Goebbels, named as his successor, followed suit with his wife next day, having first poisoned their six children in the Führer bunker. At 6.00 am on 2 May, the military commander, Lieutenant-General Helmuth Weidling, officially surrendered the city. It would be a further six days before the rest of Germany capitulated, but for Berlin, the war was over. So, too, was the Nazi regime.

The cost of Hitler's brief twelve years in power had been dreadful. The city, its life and culture all lay in ruins. But most terrible of all was the cost in human lives. Of the 160,000 Jews who had lived in Berlin in 1933, only 6,100 remained: 1,400 'U-boats' and 4,700 'privileged persons'. Another 90,000 had fled, but at least 55,000 had been murdered in concentration camps, and 7,000 had died, most of them by their own hands. More than 360 Allied air raids had killed at least 50,000 Berliners. Another 30,000 had died during the last battle.

CHAPTER 19

The Rape of Berlin

T HE TEUFELSBERG, the devil's mountain, rises abruptly out of the Grunewald, Berlin's 15.5 square miles (40 square kilometres) of forest. At 394 feet (120 metres), it is the highest hill in the region, the view from its twin peaks covering the entire city, both east and west, and sweeping on across the heathlands of Brandenburg. Its lower slopes are verdant with 10,000 young trees, plus a vineyard, possibly the most northerly in Europe. On one peak, looking uncannily like a gleaming white space station, stands an American radar installation.

In summer, hordes of Berliners jam their cars into the car parks at the base of the hill and scramble up the solid wooden steps zigzagging dizzily to the other, flat summit. From an area the size of three football pitches they launch their model airplanes and kites, filling the sky with a soaring mosaic of colours and shapes – squares, circles, boxes and polyhedrons, eagles, dragons and Berlin crows, a whole phantasmagoria of kites. In winter, those same Berliners slide merrily down the toboggan runs, or hurl themselves from the two ski jumps below the radar domes. And at Silvester, New Year's Eve, they climb the hill to let off a small fortune in fireworks. Yet, few of them give a thought to what lies beneath their feet.

In fact, the Teufelsberg is an artificial hill, a Trümmerberg, a rubble mountain. Beneath the thin layer of soil that supports the vegetation lies much of old Berlin: 18 million cubic metres of shattered masonry, the remains of walls, doorways, window frames, bathtubs, roofing tiles – fragments that once formed one of the world's great cities. There are two similar but slightly smaller burial mounds, Die Insulaner in the south-western district of Schöneberg and the Bunkerberg in Friedrichshain in the east, plus a dozen or more lesser heaps in various parts of the city. Together, they contain over 100 million tons of debris, cleared from the remains of Berlin after the end of the war.

When the Russians arrived, they found a city already pounded to pieces by the Allied bombing. And as they blasted their way to the centre, they destroyed most of what was left with their guns, rockets and tanks. An area of over eleven square miles (28 square kilometres) was reduced to a field of rubble. From the air, it looked like a wasteland of empty matchboxes. Of its 1.5 million homes, 612,000 were totally destroyed, with another 100,000 severely damaged. People lived in holes in the ground, in the skeletal remnants of apartment buildings, anywhere they could find some sort of shelter.

Under the rubble, thousands of dead bodies still lay buried; a hideous stench of charred remains and putrefying flesh hung over everything. There were over 3,000 breaks in the water mains, the sewerage system had broken down and raw sewage seeped into the drinking water supply, such as it was. Within a short time, typhoid, diphtheria, tuberculosis and dysentery were rife, while medical services were almost completely inadequate. Thirty of the city's hospitals had been destroyed and many others severely damaged. By August, 4,000 people were dying every day.

But at the beginning of May 1945, the biggest danger hanging over the city was the threat of starvation. When the newly appointed Soviet military commandant of Berlin, Colonel-General Bersarin, posted up his first proclamation on 28 April banning the Nazi Party and all affiliated organizations, demanding that the citizens obey orders, and imposing a night-time curfew, it stated that existing ration cards would be honoured. This provoked cynical laughter from the Berliners, who said they had forgotten when they last got anything at all. The city's food warehouses had been stripped by desperate German looters and then by the Soviets to feed their own men during the battle. There was no food in the city, and no way of getting any more in.

For weeks, the Berliners had to depend on Soviet field kitchens for hand-outs. They swooped on any dead or abandoned horses, butchering them on the spot and hacking them down to bare skeletons within minutes. The 91 animals and birds which had somehow survived in the zoo, including Siam, the male elephant, Knautschke, the male hippo, and Suse the female chimp, had to be protected by armed Soviet guards.

When the Soviets took over the city, they immediately confiscated all printing and copying equipment and ordered the registration of all typewriters. The first thing they used the printing machinery for, apart from proclamations and orders, was to produce new ration books for the entire population. Gradually, more food became available, but rations remained close to starvation levels for many months. They were graded into five separate levels, just as they had been under the Nazis, depending on the position and work of the holder.

To the Soviets, feeding the people of Berlin was not a charitable enterprise. Until 1 August, they carefully recorded every detail of their food distribution, and prepared accounts for payment by the city authorities in the future, either in cash, kind or industrial goods. And while they were ferrying in huge quantities of food to feed the people of Berlin, they were equally busy ferrying out every bit of industrial plant and machinery they could lay their hands on. The Germans, they argued, had destroyed Soviet industry, therefore the Germans must replace the lost plant with their own.

Knowing they could only keep the Allies out of their allotted sectors for a limited time, the Soviets worked feverishly to strip the western parts of the city while they still had total control. When President Truman asked that the western Allies be allowed in at once, Stalin fobbed him off by saying that would not be possible, since Marshal Zhukov and the other commanders had been summoned to Moscow for a meeting of the Supreme Soviet and a military parade. 'What is more,' the Soviet leader added, 'some districts of Berlin have not yet been cleared of mines, nor can the mine-clearing operations be finished until late June.' Despite warnings from some of his own advisers, and from Winston Churchill, who cabled him repeatedly and told him, on 12 May, that 'an iron curtain is being drawn down' on areas occupied by the Soviets, Truman continued to trust Stalin.

The Soviet leader managed to delay the Allies for eight weeks. During that time, the hastily repaired rail lines to the east were carrying away whole factories, often including the workers needed to reassemble them and put them into operation in the Soviet Union. By the time the Americans, British and French arrived, more than 90 per cent of Berlin's heavy industry had been spirited away. Ironically, this eventually worked in favour of West Berlin's industries; when they came to start up again, they all had to be re-equipped with modern, brand-new machinery.

The population of Berlin in May 1945 had shrunk from its pre-war 4.3 million to around 2.3 million, one-quarter of whom were over 60 years old. Only one person in ten was under 30, but there were 53,000 homeless, fatherless children living in the ruins like wild animals, and just as dangerous. Two-thirds of the entire population were women, and it was to them that the city owed its survival.

Tens of thousands of German soldiers were rounded up and marched away to captivity in the Soviet Union, depleting the number of able-bodied males still further. So it was the women who cleared the streets and the bomb sites. They were paid a pittance, but were placed on the second-highest grade for food rations, which was far more important than mere money.

Gangs of *Trümmerfrauen*, 'rubble women', worked endlessly, salvaging bricks and other materials from the ruins for rebuilding. For months, the pervading sound throughout the central districts was the ceaseless tapping of their hammers and trowels as they cleaned and stacked bricks. Today, a statue of a Trümmerfrau stands by Rixdorfer Höhe, 'Rixdorf Heights', a 230-foot-high (70-metre) rubble mountain in Neukölln's Hasenheide park, near the spot where Turnvater Jahn set up his open-air gymnasium in 1811. It is also near Tempelhof airfield, where the first 300 women started work on 1 May 1945, clearing the runway with their bare hands to allow Soviet supply planes to land.

It was the women, too, who suffered most when the Red Army arrived. The first wave of battle-hardened troops who fought their way into the city were, in general, well-disciplined and did not harm civilians, either men or women. But these troops were speedily followed by second-echelon men, support unit soldiers many of whom had been prisoners of the Germans, or were criminals. 'We opened up our jails and stuck everybody into the army,' Stalin said, explaining why the Red Army could not be ideal. And these brutalized individuals more than made up for any restraint shown by those who had preceded them.

Every woman in Berlin, it seemed, regardless of age or beauty, was considered fair game. The grunted 'Woman, come' became the prelude to nightmare for thousands and thousands of Berlinerin, some of whom were raped over and over again. Some 90,000 women sought medical treatment as a result of being raped. It is almost impossible to estimate how many others did not. There are countless examples, countless stories of women's experiences, of how they tried to escape, of the subterfuges they and their husbands used to try to avoid further assaults. Many of those who failed sought the ultimate solution by committing suicide.

Some women, however, managed to display a little Berlin humour, even under such dreadful circumstances. One young Berlinerin recorded a conversation with a friend on the subject in her diary. 'How often, Ilse?' she asked what she described as 'the inevitable first question'. 'Four times,' came the answer. 'And you?' 'No idea. I had to work my way up through the ranks as far as a major.'

Some attractive women made the best of the situation by finding themselves a Soviet officer as a protector. Others did everything they could think of to make themselves look ugly and unattractive. Russians, it seemed, did not like women in trousers. Suddenly, almost every woman was ransacking what remained of her husband's or father's wardrobe, to find pants she could wear. A surer, but not infallible, repellent was found to be a small child – few Russians were prepared to rape a woman with a child, since this was regarded by them as a desecration of motherhood. Berlinerin with small children were soon doing a brisk trade in hiring out their offspring to any neighbour who needed to go out of doors.

For nearly two weeks after the fall of the city, the Soviet authorities turned a blind eye to the sexual assaults, and to the looting and robbery that went on unchecked. Clearly they believed their men deserved 'a little fun', as Stalin described it, after their years of fighting. Then, suddenly, the party was over: from 15 May, discipline was restored, and any Red Army man who stepped out of line was liable to be shot. The number of rapes was reduced, but they did not stop. The memory of that dreadful time still haunts the older women of Berlin today.

On 2 May, they hoisted the red flag on Schadow's Quadriga *(AKG)*, while the Reichstag burned again *(Ullstein)*

In marked contrast to the victory parade of July 1940, vanquished German troops were herded into the ruins of Pariserplatz (AKG)

Below: The Brandenburg Gate, former symbol of triumph, was now a symbol of defeat, isolated amid the devastation (LBS)

Below: In the first days of Soviet occupation, losing a bicycle was one of the smaller dangers faced by Berlin women. More than 90,000 sought medical treatment after being raped *(AKG)*. But it was the women, like this 'Trümmerfrau' *(bottom left)* preparing bricks for re-use, who put the city back on its feet *(AKG)*, while the Tiergarten *(bottom right)* was turned into a huge vegetable patch to help feed the population *(Ullstein)*

Top: History's verdict on the Hohenzollerns – an ignominious end for the statues from Wilhelm II's Siegesallee *(LBS)*

Above: The Soviet blockade in 1947–48 was defeated by American and British airmen flying in supplies non-stop by day and night. Berliners turned out to greet the first aircraft, such as this US plane landing at Tempelhof *(Ullstein)*

Below: West Berliners' resistance to communism was led by their governing mayor, Professor Ernst Reuter *(AKG)*

Above: The communists were led by Walter Ulbricht *(LBS)*, who called in Soviet tanks *(top left)* to crush the East Berliners' uprising against his government on 17 June 1953 *(Ullstein)*

Above left: On 13 August 1961, the communists began sealing off the frontier between East and West Berlin with the Berlin Wall. Initially, doors and windows of buildings on the boundary line were bricked up *(AKG)*

Left: It was not long before the wall became a more formidable and permanent obstacle. It was constantly strengthened and 'improved' over the next twenty-eight years *(AKG)*

YOU ARE LEAVING
THE AMERICAN SECTOR
ВЫ ВЫЕЗЖАЕТЕ ИЗ
АМЕРИКАНСКОГО СЕКТОРА
VOUS SORTEZ
DU SECTEUR AMERICAIN

President John F. Kennedy received a rapturous welcome as he drove through West Berlin on 26 June 1963, to make his famous declaration, 'Ich bin ein Berliner.' With him were the governing mayor, Willy Brandt, and Federal Chancellor Konrad Adenauer – who almost managed a smile for the city he loathed *(Ullstein)*

Above left: For many years, the heart of old Berlin remained in ruins. The Gendarmenmarkt – renamed Platz der Akademie by the communists – was largely untouched until the mid 1980s, when it was transformed by a magnificent rebuilding programme *(above right)* to restore the French and German cathedrals and Schinkel's Schauspielhaus *(LBS)*

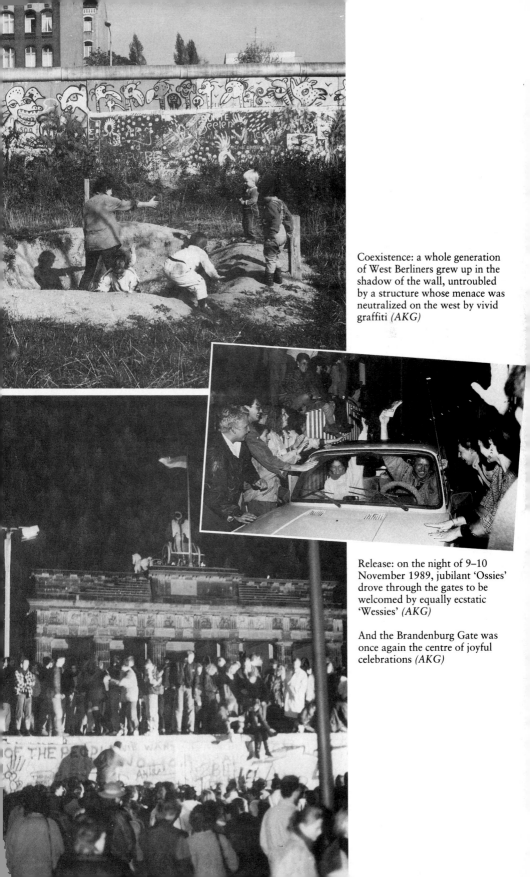

Coexistence: a whole generation of West Berliners grew up in the shadow of the wall, untroubled by a structure whose menace was neutralized on the west by vivid graffiti *(AKG)*

Release: on the night of 9–10 November 1989, jubilant 'Ossies' drove through the gates to be welcomed by equally ecstatic 'Wessies' *(AKG)*

And the Brandenburg Gate was once again the centre of joyful celebrations *(AKG)*

After reunification, the spectre of ancient dangers returned to haunt Germany. Federal President Richard von Weizsäcker – a former governing mayor of West Berlin and the first freeman of the reunited city – needed police protection against left wing agitators when he came to the Lustgarten on 8 November 1992, to speak against racial hatred *(Ullstein)*

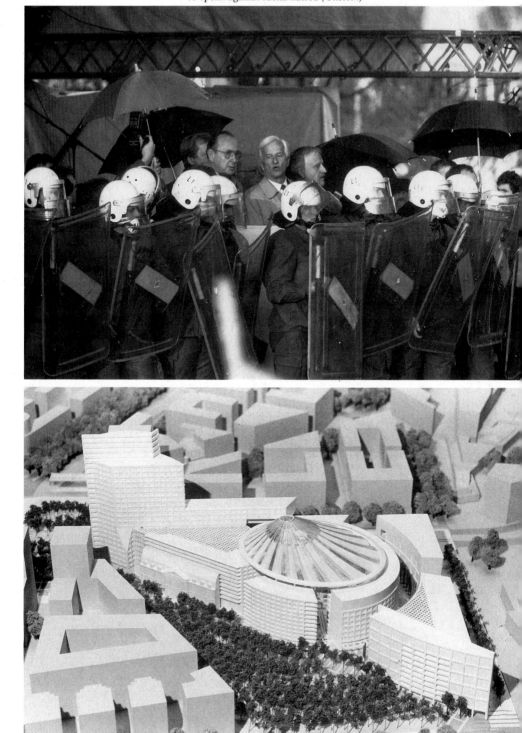

The future incorporates the past: the restored facade of the old Esplanade Hotel will be built into Sony's new development on Bellevuestrasse, off the new Potsdamerplatz *(Der Tages Spiegel)*

The order restraining Soviet troops from looting and robbery did not apply to those on official business: Berlin's biggest-ever armed robbery took place on the very day that it came into effect. During the war, the Nazis had looted the gold and currency reserves of all the countries they conquered, including parts of the Soviet Union. At one stage, the Reichsbank held in its vaults gold bars alone worth some $7.5 billion at today's value, plus vast amounts of coins, notes and bonds. After the bank was damaged by Allied bombing, most of the haul was moved to secret hiding places in southern Germany, but a considerable amount remained.

On 15 May 1945, Major Feodor Novikov of the GRU (Soviet Military Intelligence) appeared at the bank with a company of troops and two tanks. He ordered the officials to open the vaults, which by then contained little more than 90 gold bars and 4.5 million gold coins worth $50 million at present-day valuation. In addition, there were negotiable bonds worth $400 million, payable in gold or dollars. Major Novikov took the lot.

The Reichsbank's gold was never seen again, but for many years afterwards the bonds kept turning up in West Germany, Holland, Switzerland, Israel, Canada, Britain, the USA and elsewhere. As well as providing the Soviet Union with much-needed hard currency, the proceeds seem to have gone towards financing the operations of the GRU in the west.

Truman's insistence that he could do business with Stalin, and that he did not need to press for Allied troops to move in yet, allowed the Soviets to do far more than rape the women and remove gold, industrial plant and machinery. The longer Berlin remained entirely under Soviet control, the more they were able to ensure that the power structure they were installing would became permanent. They even decreed that Berlin should operate on Moscow time, and all clocks and watches had to be put forward two hours. This was one of the few things the Allies were able to change, but even that took several weeks.

While the final battle for the city was still raging, Red Army political officers and commissars had been selecting men almost at random in the various districts that they had taken and appointing them as mayors, in order to start creating some form of local administration. With effect from 1 May, the selection became more systematic. On that day, Walter Ulbricht, who had for long been groomed as leader of a communist Germany, arrived from Moscow with his ten-man 'Communist Action Group'.

Fifty-one-year-old Ulbricht was not an impressive figure. Small, bespectacled, balding, with a goatee beard and a reedy, high-pitched voice, he looked more like a fussy provincial postmaster than the future dictator of one of the world's most important communist countries. Born in Leipzig and trained as a cabinet maker, he had been actively involved in politics from the age of 19. He was a communist deputy in the Reichstag from 1928 to 1933, and district secretary of the Communist Party of Greater Berlin and Branden-burg from 1929. After the Reichstag fire, he fled, first to Prague and then to Paris. After a period of training in Moscow, he was sent to take part in the civil war in Spain, where he seems to have been involved in the liquidation of thousands of Catalan anarchists and socialists, ordered by the Comintern because they refused to take orders from the communists. Moving back to Moscow, he was quick to endorse Stalin's purges, on the grounds that they eradic-ated a dangerous fifth column.

In Moscow, Ulbricht and his second wife, Lotte, lived in the fading splendour of the Hotel Lux on Gorky Street, along with most of the senior foreign, and particularly German, communists. Their numbers dwindled as the purges ate their way ever deeper into Soviet society: one by one the distinguished émigrés disap-peared into the cellars of the Lubianka. But Ulbricht survived, to become, in 1938, the German Communist Party's permanent repres-entative on the Comintern.

Ulbricht combined a remarkable organizing ability with an extra-ordinary appetite for hard work: he was tireless, never seeming to flag, even after a 16-hour day. Totally humourless, apparently lacking any human emotion, he was the ideal apparatchik, a robot programmed to carry out the directives of Stalin. He was, however, a robot with ambition and a brain – he proved to be sensitive to every change in the party line, was responsive to the most subtle nuances of policy eman-ating from Moscow, and was a master of political infighting.

As soon as he arrived in Berlin, Ulbricht set about the task of creating the political framework for a communist 'democracy', which was to be the basis of a new German government. The Soviets intended to present the Allies with a *fait accompli*, a civilian administration controlled by them. 'It must look democratic,' Ulbricht declared, 'but we must be in complete control.' In an uncomfortable echo of the recent past, *Obleute*, 'supervisors', were appointed to oversee every block, street and apartment building, while the NKVD took over the role of the Gestapo.

The long process of de-Nazification began with the time-honoured rituals of denunciation. In some respects, little had changed but the doctrines; the Soviets even took over Sachsenhausen concentration camp and filled it with Nazis. Mass graves unearthed in 1990 contained some 10,000 bodies of people who had died there, mostly of disease and hunger: by comparison, more than 100,000 are known to have died there under the Nazis.

On 13 May, the Soviet military command appointed a new city council. Following Ulbricht's dictum that everything must look democratic, their choice as governing mayor, Arthur Werner, was a known non-communist. But his deputy, Karl Maron, who had been a leading member of the party until 1933, was one of Ulbricht's group from Moscow. Maron's first lieutenant was Arthur Pieck, son of Wilhelm Pieck, the chairman of the KPD, the German Communist Party. He was put in charge of the all-important department of personnel and administration.

The same pattern was stamped throughout the 20 borough councils. Only two of the mayors were communists, the rest were all either social democrats, liberals or conservatives. But in every case, the deputy mayor was a communist approved by Ulbricht, as were the police chief, the head of personnel and the director of education. Nine of the city council's 18 members were communists. So were six of the twelve department heads. When a new city police force was authorized on 19 May, Paul Markgraf, a former German army colonel who had been converted to communism as a prisoner of war in Russia, was appointed police president. By the time the new force was fully operational, 15 of the 21 divisional heads and 70 per cent of all station chiefs were party members.

While the communists were tightening their grip on the city, however, the illusion of democracy had to be maintained. The western Allies, after all, could not be kept out for long, and during the two months before their arrival, permission was given for new national political parties to be set up, or old ones reborn. The first, naturally, was the Communist Party, followed four days later by the Social Democratic Party, then by the conservative Christian Democratic Union, and finally the Liberal Democratic Party. So, within three weeks, all the major parties that were to dominate post-war German politics were founded in Soviet-controlled Berlin. The seeds of a new democracy had been planted; whether they would be allowed to germinate and bear fruit remained to be seen.

On a purely practical level, Berlin was already starting to creak back into life. The bus service started up again on 13 May, with the first U-Bahn trains running one day later. The S-Bahn and trams followed in a few days. The new ration cards were distributed on the 14th, though there was still precious little food to buy, and the curfew was lifted on 15 May. The first German newspaper, the *Berliner Zeitung*, appeared on 21 May, to join the Soviets' official news sheet, the *Täglischer Rundschau*, which had started publication a week earlier. The Berlin Philharmonic gave its first post-war concert on 26 May, in the Titania Palast cinema in Steglitz. It began with Mendelssohn's music for *A Midsummer Night's Dream*, 'Jewish' music that had been forbidden in its composer's home city for twelve awful years. The following day the Renaissance Theatre in Charlottenburg reopened, with the amazingly tactless choice of *The Rape of the Sabine Women* as its first production. The Deutsche Oper reopened in the virtually undamaged Theater des Westens on 15 June with a much more appropriate piece, Beethoven's great paean to freedom, *Fidelio*.

All over Berlin, makeshift theatres and cabarets were opening up, mostly run by women. Every little hall that could be patched up was pressed into service. Suddenly the city was crowded with actresses and performers – there seemed to be nearly as many as there were rubble women. Many were, of course, genuine professionals, but many more were attracted by the fact that under the Soviet administration, artists, like politicians and intellectuals, were entitled to grade-one ration cards, giving them more food than manual labourers. True Berliners have never been slow to grab an opportunity like that.

On 4 July, the first British and American troops arrived in Berlin to begin an occupation that was to last nearly 45 years. The French did not arrive until 12 August, though on 14 July an advance party had hoisted the Tricolour alongside the British Union Jack at the Siegessäule, the column erected in 1873 to commemorate Prussia's victories over Denmark, Austria and, of course, France. The Allies, incidentally, removed the relief panels depicting the Prussian victories from the base of the column, and in yet another round of the eternal game of tit-for-tat between France and Germany, the French shipped them off to Paris. Two were returned in 1984. The remaining four were discovered in Paris in 1986, and returned as a gift for Berlin's 750th anniversary celebrations.

The division of the city into sectors to be occupied and administered by the individual powers had been settled in London in September 1944. Initially, there were to be three – Soviet, US and British – but the British had given the French part of their sector, the boroughs of Wedding and Reinickendorf. The Soviet sector was the largest of the four, with eight of the city's 20 boroughs, comprising 45.6 per cent of the total land area, and 36.8 per cent of the population. The Americans had six boroughs, and the British four, including the Ku'damm and the west end.

The city was supposed to be run by the four-power Kommandatura, which had its first meeting on 7 July in the former offices of an insurance company in Dahlem. Its first order, issued four days later, confirmed all the arrangements already made by the Soviets, and said they would remain in force until further notice. The western powers had agreed to this as a matter of convenience, thinking they could make changes once they had had time to survey the situation and see what was needed. But the fact that decisions had to be unanimous gave the Soviets the power of veto, which meant in effect that nothing could be changed. Stalin's plan to establish the regime he wanted had worked. From then on, every time there was any disagreement, the Soviet commanders referred back to that first order, or simply did as they pleased. As friction increased, so the idea of joint administration foundered. Soon, each of the four powers went its own way in ruling its own sector.

The situation in the city Kommandatura was mirrored almost exactly in the four-power Allied Control Commission, set up to govern the whole of Germany. This was established in Berlin, in the stately buildings of the old Prussian High Court, more recently the Nazi People's Court where Roland Freisler had ranted and raved at the enemies of the regime until a British bomb silenced him for ever.

In the ACC, however, the intransigence of the Soviets was matched by an equal bloody-mindedness from the French. Stung by the 'insult' of not having being offered a seat either at Yalta or the forthcoming Potsdam conference, they were determined to press their own claims for vengeance and reparations, and to block any concessions to German unity or self-government.

The arrival of the Allies created fresh problems for Berlin, especially in the already desperate housing situation. They needed accommodation for their own troops, and were quite ruthless in requisitioning the few habitable apartments and houses and ejecting the occupants on to the street, sometimes at only an hour or two's notice. The same applied to public buildings, too. In the south of the city, the Americans threw the Berlin Philharmonic Orchestra out of the Titania Palast cinema, the only viable concert hall apart from the Theater des Westens, which they wanted as a forces club. Later, the Americans allowed the orchestra back into the Titania Palast for occasional concerts, but German audiences had to use the service entrance; they were not allowed to enter through the front door. Nevertheless, most Berliners welcomed the western troops, and despite strict rules banning fraternization, many of the younger women soon found themselves American, British or French boy-friends. 'Frat' quickly became another word for sex.

The black market, which until then had barely managed to get started, suddenly blossomed. Cigarettes became the main unit of currency, but the whole business operated on the barter principle. What the Berliners wanted, of course, was food from the Allied armies' supplies, and such 'luxuries' as coffee, chocolate, white bread, silk stockings and, naturally, cigarettes. In exchange, they offered the valuables they had managed to hang on to through the war – cameras, jewellery, fur coats, antique furniture and porcelain, paintings, and so on. Soon, the Alexanderplatz and the Tiergarten near the zoo established themselves at the centre of a trade that attracted some 4,000 people to each market every day.

While most people were content to trade in a small way to obtain the essentials of everyday existence, natural wheeler-dealers and fixers made fortunes from more serious transactions involving the new wonder drug penicillin, insulin, motor fuel, title deeds to buildings, and personal documents. One black market ringleader was found to be carrying diamonds worth nearly $300,000 when he was arrested, the equivalent today of well over $1.5 million or £1 million. At the other end of the scale was the new profession of *Kippensammler*, the collector of cigarette butt ends from streets, soldiers' clubs, army messes and cafés. The butt ends were processed in back-room factories into whole cigarettes, which sold for four marks each. Seven butt ends were needed to make one new cigarette, which in turn could buy a whole meal.

On 17 July, a conference of the Big Three opened in the Cecilienhof Palace in Potsdam. The Cecilienhof was the last of all the Hohenzollern palaces, built to house the crown prince and his family by Wilhelm II between 1913 and 1916. In fact, the prince moved back to it in 1923, when the revolutionary dust had settled, and was still living there in 1945. Despite the First World War, the Cecilienhof, named after the crown princess, was the final expression of Wilhelm's love of England: it is an exact replica of a mock-Tudor country house which would have been completely at home in the Surrey stockbroker belt.

As the conference of the Allied leaders began, there was already one change in the cast which had performed at Teheran and Yalta: Roosevelt had died on 12 April, and had been replaced as president of the USA by Harry S. Truman, a very different character. Stalin was still there, of course, as genial and as devious as ever. And at the start of the conference, Winston Churchill was still representing Britain. But Clement Attlee, the leader of the Labour Party, was already waiting in the wings, in Potsdam as a quiet member of the British delegation. It was Attlee, in fact, who had been responsible for drawing up the Allied plans for the partition of Germany. Halfway through the conference, a landslide defeat in the British General Election unseated Churchill, and Attlee took over.

The Potsdam conference lasted until 2 August 1945. The accord that had been present in the previous Big Three meetings was conspicuously missing. Instead, each of the three leaders – and in this respect, the substitution of Attlee for Churchill made no difference – was intent on furthering his own power and that of his country. Discord, not harmony, was the order of the day.

During the course of the conference, Truman had the unenviable task of telling Stalin that the western Allies had a new and terrible weapon, the atomic bomb. Stalin took the information very calmly. As it turned out, he was better informed than Truman about the tests at Alamagordo. What neither Stalin nor Churchill knew was that Truman had been briefed to avoid any semblance of a major peace conference: there was to be no new Versailles. Truman also still believed in Stalin's good faith, with the result that the Soviet dictator was able to get exactly what he wanted, a free hand in eastern Europe, without giving anything whatsoever in return. At the end of the conference, what Stalin, Truman and Attlee signed was not the peace agreement that the public expected, but what amounted to a declaration of the cold war.

CHAPTER 20

The Great Divide

B Y E A R L Y 1 9 4 6 , the first signs of regeneration could be
seen. The university reopened on 29 January, still in its old
building on the Linden but with a new name. Henceforth, the
Soviets decreed, it would be known not as Friedrich-Wilhelms but
as the Humboldt University, and it was firmly under Soviet control.
In the British sector, the old Technical High School was reopened
in April as the Technical University.

In the nineteenth century, the Technical High School had incorporated Schinkel's Bauakademie, where the great man had drawn up his
plans for the city and taught his successors. Into Schinkel's shoes now
stepped a new professor of architecture, Hans Scharoun, an eminent
architect with a Europe-wide reputation born out of his pre-war work
in developments at Siemensstadt and Charlottenburg. Like Schinkel,
Scharoun was in charge of the city's planning, until he became a victim
of the political arguments between the occupiers and the occupied. He
was also the first principal of the new Institute of Building Studies,
part of the Academy of Sciences. He fought to prevent city landmarks
being bulldozed, saving many for repair and eventual restoration. At
the same time, he drew up bold plans for a renewed city, which were
put on show in the remains of the old royal palace.

The political squabbles that cost Scharoun his job also scuppered any hopes of putting his grand design into practice. He was never able to become a second Schinkel in terms of scale, but he did leave his personal mark on the city before he died in 1972. Much of the radically modern Kulturforum in the Tiergarten is his work, including the state library and the splendid new Philharmonie, one of the finest concert halls in the world, acknowledged by musicians and audiences alike as having probably the best acoustics anywhere.

In 1946, however, the prospect of such fine new developments seemed an unlikely pipedream. The realities of life in Berlin were altogether harsher. The shortages enabled black market racketeers and criminals of all sorts to flourish. By early 1946, Berlin had become the crime capital of the world. Every day 240 robberies and five murders were reported. Gangs of criminals, deserters and displaced persons, including Poles, Czechs, Frenchmen, Spaniards, Russians and many other nationalities roamed the streets, all armed to the teeth. The most notorious, the Lehrter Bahnhof gang, was composed mainly of Russian deserters. Another gang over 100 strong held up a train at Anhalter Bahnhof in May and shot it out with military police like something out of the old Wild West. There were also stories of cannibalism and of a market in human flesh.

Things were no brighter on the political front. By failing to stand up to Stalin at a time when their forces were strong enough to make him listen, the Allies forfeited any hope of a proper four-power government covering the whole of Germany. The Americans and British had abandoned their own thoughts of splitting Germany up into a number of smaller states. And although the French still had hopes of at least separating the Rhineland and the Saar from the main body of the country, they had no support from their allies. But the Soviets went ahead and split Germany into two. Stalin had already annexed East Prussia and given Silesia and everything east of the Oder to Poland, which he was busily turning into a Soviet satellite. Now, he set about turning the Soviet zone into a separate communist state, with Berlin at its heart.

The first city-wide elections for a new municipal assembly were scheduled for the autumn of 1946, but already it was clear that the SPD, as always in Berlin, would draw the majority of votes, with the communists trailing in third place, behind the CDU, the Christian democrats. Ulbricht, who was by then heading the central committee, announced that he intended to reverse the 'mistakes' made in the 1918 revolution, when Liebknecht and the Spartakists had splintered the original Social Democrat Party, and in 1933, when the left's failure to unite had let in Hitler. There must, he declared, be an end to divisions among working people. Together, the parties of the left must follow a unique 'German road to socialism'. With the complicity of the leader of the SPD in eastern Berlin, Otto Grotewohl, Ulbricht and his fellow communists forced a shotgun wedding between the SPD and the KPD to form a supposedly new party, the SED, the Socialist Unity Party. Ulbricht was appointed its general secretary.

The merger did the communists little good. The SPD in the west repudiated it, and when the elections were held in October, polled 48.7 per cent of the total vote. The CDU came second, with 22.2 per cent, while the SED could only manage 19.8 per cent. Worse still, all eight boroughs in the Soviet sector elected social democrat mayors. The elections were the first free vote Berliners had been allowed for thirteen and a half years. For those in the eastern half of the city, there would not be another for a further 44 years.

The new city assembly and its executive council, the Magistrat, met in the Neues Stadthaus, a municipal office building in Parochialstrasse which had been less severely damaged than the nearby Red Town Hall. For several months, they avoided clashes with the Soviet military authorities. For much of that time, they had their hands full trying to combat the forces of nature: the winter of 1946–7 proved to be one of the most severe ever recorded in Europe, with blizzards sweeping in from the Arctic and temperatures of -30°C or more day after day, week after week. With an acute shortage of coal, power supplies were limited and 150,000 workers were laid off as over 1,000 companies closed down. Public transport ground to a halt. Some 700,000 Berliners found themselves relying on welfare handouts. The Magistrat opened public 'warming rooms', where the needy could escape from their patched-up, windowless, unheated homes, to huddle around an iron stove. Even so, more than 40,000 people had to be treated for hypothermia, and over 1,100 died of the cold.

Meanwhile, the division of both the country and the city was becoming steadily more certain. As the Soviets tightened their grip on the eastern part of Germany, the British and Americans merged the economies of their occupation zones at the beginning of 1947, naming the new entity 'Bizonia'. The French remained aloof, still deeply suspicious of any move towards the restoration of German unity.

The Soviets complained that the merger was a deliberate step towards establishing a separate German state in the west. They increased their pressure on Berlin, clamping down on all traffic approaching the city by road or rail. When the agreements for the occupation of the country had been made, the western Allies had seen no need to make special provision for access to Berlin, and the Soviet representatives had taken care to encourage their misplaced trust. The Allies discovered their error when they suddenly found they were limited to a single road and one rail line, from Helmstedt in the British zone, both of which could be blocked whenever it suited the Soviets. There was also one waterway, from Hamburg and the Elbe, along which the British carried coal and some food to Berlin, but the Soviets kept the barges once they had been unloaded, regarding them as reparation payments, so it was used less and less.

The situation was better in the air. Three corridors, each 20 miles (32 kilometres) wide, had been formally agreed in November 1945. They were supposed to be limited to military traffic, but for once the Soviet negotiators missed a trick, leaving a loophole in the agreement that allowed the Allies to use commercial aircraft registered in the USA, Britain or France. One legacy of this was that until 1990, scheduled civil airline flights to Berlin from the west were restricted to Pan Am, British Airways and Air France.

Inside the city, political opponents of the SED were harassed and threatened. Many were even kidnapped in the western sectors by the communist-controlled police force, to disappear into jails in the east.

The Soviet military authorities forced the new lord mayor, Otto Ostrowski, into agreeing to work with the SED on a joint programme. And when the social democrats voted Ostrowski out of office as a result, they vetoed the assembly's choice of a successor, Ernst Reuter, claiming that he was anti-Soviet. The assembly refused to appoint anyone else. Reuter's deputy, Louise Schroeder, a doughty old-time social democrat, took on the role of acting mayor, earning herself the honorary title 'Mother of Berlin'. But the position of lord mayor remained officially empty.

The Soviets were right to fear Professor Reuter – he knew them and their methods well. In the First World War he had been a prisoner in Russia, and had been converted to Marxism. During the Russian revolution, he met Lenin and Trotsky, and became commissar for the autonomous Volga German Soviet Republic, working directly under Stalin. Chosen to lead Germany to communism, he returned home at the end of the war as party secretary, first in Berlin, and then nationally.

Reuter's enthusiasm for communism, however, had faded by 1921. Thoroughly disillusioned, he quit the party and joined the SPD instead, serving on the Berlin city Magistrat as transport chief until the Nazis forced him into exile. He had spent the last eleven years in Turkey, only being allowed back into Berlin at the end of November 1946. When he saw the ruined streets, he was shattered. 'It's enough to stop your heart beating,' he said.

On 17 and 18 March, the Soviet authorities staged a 'People's Congress' in Berlin to mark the centenary of the 1848 revolution, during which a monument to the 'March dead' was to be unveiled in Friedrichshain park by Wilhelm Pieck, the chairman of the SED. Pieck had been Reuter's partner in leading the KPD in 1918, and so felt particularly bitter towards him for betraying the cause. In his speech at the unveiling, he denounced German politicians who, he claimed, were trying to split the country.

Reuter, meanwhile, was the final speaker among those addressing a crowd of 30,000 in front of the Reichstag ruins. With his famous black beret, the badge of the intellectual, pulled well down on his head, he spoke as passionately and skilfully as Goebbels – to whom his Marxist opponents compared him. He pointed to the communist coup that had taken place in Czechoslovakia three weeks before, and to the pressure then being applied by the Soviet Union on Finland. But, he said, 'if anyone asked "who will be the next?" we can answer him firmly and confidently: it will never be Berlin . . . the flood of communism will break against the dam of our iron will'.

That will was soon to be tested. Two days after the mass meeting outside the Reichstag, the Soviets walked out of the four-power Allied Control Commission for Germany. For a while, the city's Kommandatura went on meeting, but each time the four commandants got together the tension was greater. On 16 June, the Soviet representatives left the Kommandatura, too. The stage was set for a showdown.

The excuse came on 18 June, when the Allies announced the introduction of a new currency, the Deutschmark, in their zones, to replace the old Reichsmark. The Soviets refused to allow the new currency into Berlin, where unanimous four-power agreement was still necessary for such a measure. But five days later they tried to impose their own 'new' currency on the city and the rest of their zone. Because they had not been able to print new banknotes in time, the new Ostmarks were in fact old Reichsmark notes with small stickers attached to them with potato starch adhesive – 'coupon marks' or 'wallpaper marks', the Berliners scornfully dubbed them.

The western powers immediately introduced the new D-Mark in their sectors of the city, crisp new banknotes printed in America and rubber-stamped with a large B for Berlin; ten planeloads of the notes had been flown in some two weeks earlier. At Reuter's insistence, the Magistrat agreed that both currencies should circulate in the city, and passed a motion reasserting the fact that Berlin was not part of the Soviet zone, but a special territory under four-power supervision. They then called a meeting of the full assembly in the Neues Stadthaus at 4.00 pm that afternoon, to ratify their decisions.

The SED reacted in a way that stirred chilling memories of 1932 and 1933. An hour before the meeting, a communist mob occupied the Neues Stadthaus, while the police stood by and then disappeared. The meeting started two hours late, and in spite of barracking from the gallery, voted to confirm the Magistrat's decisions. When the assembly members tried to leave the building, they found it was surrounded by a savage mob. Those who tried to make a break for it were grabbed and beaten up. For Jeanette Wolff, a Jewish SPD representative, it was the SA all over again as she was beaten and called '*Judensau*' (Jewish sow), just as she had been before being dragged off to a Nazi concentration camp.

The new D-Mark, backed by massive American aid under the Marshall Plan, wiped out the black market in western Germany at a stroke. Suddenly, cigarettes were just for smoking, as confidence in money was restored and goods appeared from nowhere in the shops. The West German economic miracle was on its way. But whether Berlin would ever be allowed to share in it was another question. The very next day, the Soviets closed the land and water routes into the city from the west, and cut all electricity supplies from eastern power stations, convinced that this would force the Allies to abandon Berlin to them.

With food from the farms of Brandenburg denied to them, Berliners in the western sectors were reduced to the potatoes and other vegetables grown in their Schrebergärten, and in squares and parks turned over to agriculture. The Tiergarten, for instance, its trees blasted by bombs and shells and then chopped down for firewood, had already been ploughed up and turned into a huge market garden. But the parks and allotments could never hope to feed everyone. Food stocks in western sector warehouses would last less than a month, coal for only ten days. The electricity supply had to be limited to four hours a day, and two of those were in the middle of the night. Western Berlin was under siege, and if the Allies were not to be forced to surrender it, some way had to be found of feeding and heating it and providing power to keep it going.

The only way into or out of the city was by air, but it seemed inconceivable that 2.3 million West Berliners could be sustained solely by aircraft. For a start, they would need 4,500 tons of food and fuel alone every day, to say nothing of medical supplies, spare parts, machinery, newsprint, all the things that were necessary for supporting life. But for 462 days, American and British aircraft delivered all that and more, including all the coal to fire the city's power stations. Somehow, aircraft and aircrews were found – many of the latter airmen who had been dropping bombs on the city three years before – and facilities were created on the ground to receive and handle them.

The runways at Tempelhof and Gatow were strengthened and improved. The British turned the Havel lake into a landing strip, using Sunderland flying boats to ferry cargoes from Finkenwerde on the Elbe, to the delight of the small boys in the area, who gathered on the banks to watch the spectacular landings and take-offs. The boys – and girls – were even more delighted by many American and British crews who took to scattering precious chocolate bars and sweets from their aircraft as they came in to land, earning themselves the nickname 'the chocolate bombers'.

But two airfields and one lake were still not enough. So, in only three months, the Americans built a brand-new field from scratch at Tegel in the French zone, using just four bulldozers and 19,000 Berliners, 40 per cent of them women, working round the clock for DM 1.20 an hour plus a hot meal every shift. With so much rubble still piled up in the city, at least there was no shortage of hardcore for the runway and aprons. Flights into the new field, however, would be endangered by the tall transmitting towers of the Soviet-controlled Radio Berlin. When the Soviets refused to remove them, the French commandant, General Ganeval, a survivor of Buchenwald, simply demolished them. 'How could you do such a thing?' the Soviet commandant remonstrated furiously. 'With dynamite, *mon Général*,' was the reply.

The communist rent-a-mob returned to the attack on 26 and 27 August, molesting and threatening members of the assembly while the communist-controlled police and Soviet troops stood idly by. Two weeks later, on 6 September, they were back in greater strength than ever, this time actually helped by the police as they broke in and took over the chamber. Forced out of the Neues Stadthaus by the mob, the assembly reconvened in the students' union building of the Technical University on Hardenbergstrasse in the British sector. The 26 SED members, of course, stayed put in the Neues Stadthaus. Shortly afterwards, the assembly moved to Schöneberg town hall, in the American sector. The new location was a temporary arrangement, by courtesy of the borough of Schöneberg. It was to continue, as a temporary arrangement, for 42 years.

Most Berliners were shocked almost beyond belief by what had happened. Some 300,000 of them, an amazing one in seven of the entire population, gathered in front of the Reichstag on 9 September, to hear sober speeches from the leaders of all the western political parties. Among the speakers that day was the 35-year-old Willy Brandt, newly elected to the executive of the Berlin SPD, making his first major speech in public. But the man everyone had come to hear was Ernst Reuter.

'We Berliners are not a subject for barter, for trading off and for selling!' he announced to the world. 'People of America, England, France, Italy! Look upon this city and know that you must not abandon it or its people – that you cannot abandon them! . . . Help us during this time that confronts us, not just with the roar of airplanes, but with your steadfast, indestructible commitment to those ideals that alone can guarantee our future or indeed secure your own ideals as well.'

After his speech, Reuter and the other politicians led a march to the Allied Kommandatura, where they presented a protest against the suppression of liberties in the Soviet sector. Thousands of east

Berliners heading for home through the Brandenburg Gate met an example of that suppression when they found their way barred by armed communist police. The crowd, still high on the emotions generated by the meeting, pressed forward to break through the cordon. Some climbed to the top of the gate, and tore down the hated red flag fluttering over the Quadriga, hurling it to the ground, where it was torn to pieces. Soviet troops opened fire. The crowd stoned a Red Army jeep carrying the new guard for the Soviet war memorial just beyond the gate in the British sector. The Soviet guards had to be rescued by British military police. Twelve people were taken to hospital with bullet wounds. A 16-year-old boy, Wolfgang Scheunemann, became the first person to be killed on the Soviet Zone border when he was shot in the stomach while trying to shield a nurse.

Later that night, the Voice of America radio station broadcast a reply to Reuter's appeal: 'We have heard your voice, Berliners!'

At the peak of the airlift, or *Luftbrücke* (air bridge) as the Germans called it, aircraft were landing every 90 seconds and being turned round in an average of only six minutes. By the end, 277,264 flights had carried almost two million tons of supplies into Berlin, in the face of continual Soviet harassment along the length of the three air corridors. On their return journeys, the Anglo-American aircraft carried out Berlin's meagre exports of manufactured goods, plus more than 15,000 young children and about 1,500 tuberculosis patients. Seventy-nine people lost their lives during the airlift, most of them British and American airmen. It is impossible to say how many thousand lives were saved by it.

The airlift itself was a remarkable achievement, but the continuing resolve of the Berliners during the 13 months it lasted was equally remarkable. Housewives got up in the middle of the night to do their housework while there was electricity. They used candles for light and burned bits of wood scavenged from the ruins for heating and cooking. For news, they gathered in the streets to listen to the loudspeakers of broadcasting vans sent out by RIAS (Radio In the American Sector), the station started by the US Information Service in November 1945. The Soviet authorities offered people in the western sectors ration cards which would allow them to buy food in the east, where supplies were available from the fertile countryside of the Soviet sector. Barely 20,000 out of over two million inhabitants took up the offer, and many of those were people who worked in the east or had family there. The rest preferred starvation to submission.

As the blockade continued, Reuter coined a slogan to keep Berliners' minds concentrated: 'It's cold in Berlin, but it's colder in Siberia.' Berliners said that if they stood in the Potsdamerplatz, at the boundary of the Soviet sector, they could hear the water lapping on the Volga. As always, they sustained themselves with mordant humour. 'Aren't we lucky?' they joked. 'Just think what it would be like if the Americans were running the blockade and the Russians the airlift.' 'Don't get the jitters, Allies – we're right in front of you.' Coffee became known as 'Blumenkaffee', because it was so thin you could see the flower pattern at the bottom of the cup. With potatoes, eggs, milk and so much else arriving in powdered form, dehydration was the subject of many gags; a typical newspaper cartoon showed a stork delivering a flattened, tiny baby labelled: 'Dehydrated. Soak in warm water for 20 minutes.'

The epitome of blockade humour was to be found in a comedy series broadcast on RIAS. Called *Die Insulaner* (The Islanders), the programme was the Berlin equivalent of the British wartime hit series *ITMA*. Its star, Günter Neumann had something of the style of Britain's Tommy Handley, poking surreal fun at authority in a make-believe Berlin which had somehow become surrounded by water and peopled with devastating caricatures of Berlin types. It raised spirits and helped the Berliners to laugh at themselves and their oppressors through 148 episodes. When Neumann died in 1972, the Berliners erected a memorial to him on top of the rubble mountain in Kreuzberg that has been known ever since as *Die Insulaner*. It is, in many ways, a more fittingly Berlinisch monument to the airlift than the official one in Platz der Luftbrücke, in front of Tempelhof airport.

The blockade was lifted on 12 May 1949. But Berlin remained divided, split into two cities just as it had been 700 years before. Now, however, one city was the capital of a communist state, the other was an island, separated from the western state, which had decided to establish its capital in Bonn, on the Rhine. The communists had set up a separate city council for East Berlin on 30 November 1948 with its own governing mayor, Friedrich Ebert, son of the first president of the Weimar Republic. A week later, the people of

West Berlin voted in free elections; 64.5 per cent of them voted for
Ernst Reuter as their mayor.

The airlift had done more than help the West Berliners to survive.
It had changed the attitude of the western world to Berlin itself.
When the blockade started, the Berliners were still a defeated enemy
and the Allied troops were armies of occupation. By the time it was
lifted, they were friends and partners, united in the defence of
freedom. West Berlin had even gained a new university during the
time it was besieged: with American assistance, the Free University
had opened its doors in the former Kaiser Wilhelm Institute for
Scientific Research in Dahlem. Seventeen million Americans, meanwhile, had subscribed to pay for a replica of the Liberty Bell, which
was presented to the city in October 1950 as a gesture of solidarity.

Berlin was a special city again. Throughout the long years of the
cold war, it was to remain the world's focal point, the interface
where east and west remained in constant collision.

CHAPTER 21

Scum on Silver Bicycles

THE NEW GERMAN FEDERAL REPUBLIC chose two non-Berliners as its leaders: for president, Theodor Heuss, a respected academic, and for chancellor, Konrad Adenauer, the former CDU mayor of Cologne. The West Berliners had little confidence in either. Heuss travelled to West Berlin six weeks after taking the oath, to assure a crowd of 200,000 in front of the Schöneberg town hall that the links between the city and the new state remained close. But it was more than seven months before Adenauer could bring himself to visit the city he loathed. The West Berliners preferred to put their faith in their governing mayor, Ernst Reuter. He was the man that mattered in the city.

East Berlin, however, was still a capital city and the seat of government for the DDR, the German Democratic Republic. It was just like old times when the appointment of the 77-year-old Wilhelm Pieck as president and Otto Grotewohl as prime minister was celebrated with a torchlight procession through the Brandenburg Gate and up the Linden. And true to tradition, the rulers of the state took a direct role in running the city. Mayor Ebert may have been responsible for the day-to-day administration, but the man who called the tune on policy matters was Walter Ulbricht, who was confirmed as party secretary of the SED in July 1950.

In both Berlins, rebuilding was now the main priority. Barely a quarter of the rubble had so far been cleared – it would take twelve years in all to complete the Teufelsberg and the other Trümmer-berge. Bomb disposal teams were still working flat out to defuse and remove thousands of unexploded bombs. Most people were still living in makeshift homes, with boarded-up windows. Many bridges were still out of action, and few factories were yet in full working order. The city government in West Berlin recorded 300,000 unemployed; the East Berlin authority refused to admit it had any.

The West German government had declared the city a disaster area. To take charge of economic planning for recovery, Reuter brought back one of his old SPD colleagues from the Weimar era, Paul Hertz, who had been living in exile in New York. Hertz inaugurated a four-year investment programme, in conjunction with industrialists and aid-givers, notably the Americans, of course, and rebuilding began in earnest.

In the east, the SED announced plans 'to construct Berlin as a socialist capital', which meant industry came before homes. So, it seemed, did sport, already perceived as an area which could bring much-needed prestige and national pride to the people of the DDR. The youth of East Berlin was organized into work brigades to knock down the remains of the old guards barracks in Chaussee-strasse and build a new stadium on the site. They completed the task in only four months. The Walter Ulbricht Stadium, with room for 70,000 spectators, was opened on 27 May 1950. Not to be outdone, West Berlin reopened the Olympic Stadium three weeks later with a championship football match watched by 100,000.

Not all the building and clearance projects in the east were as well-received as the new stadium. Shortly after noon on a miserably damp 7 September 1950, the first explosive charges were detonated under the east wing of the old royal palace, the huge, rambling city Schloss that had grown out of Iron-tooth's Zwingburg. It was claimed, with some pride, to be the ugliest building in Berlin.

Despite protests that, although badly damaged, much of it could be saved, Ulbricht, Grotewohl and Ebert were determined that it should go. And so it came down, piece by piece, right through the winter, until there was no trace left standing.

The only part of the building that was saved was one doorway – 'Portal IV' – and the balcony above it, from which Karl Liebknecht had declared a socialist republic on 9 November 1918. This was carefully removed and kept in store, to be incorporated into the new Council of Ministers building to be erected on the side of the square, which was itself to be renamed Marx-Engels-Platz. Ironically, the balcony was also the one used by Kaiser Wilhelm II to announce the start of the First World War on 1 August 1914.

The whole square was cleared and paved. It was to remain empty for over 20 years, until work started on the Palace of the Republic, a graceless box of white marble and brown mirror glass, in 1973. When it was completed, the new palace contained an assembly chamber for the DDR parliament, an auditorium seating 5,000, a theatre, a night club, a bowling alley and several restaurants. But, like the republic it symbolized, it remained in use for only a few years after its completion in 1976. It was closed in 1990 because of asbestos contamination.

At about the same time as the old Schloss was destroyed, the West Berlin authorities demolished what was left of the Kroll Opera, on Platz der Republik opposite the ruins of the Reichstag: it had been too badly damaged for restoration, and with its recent history, as home to Hitler's puppet assembly, was not greatly mourned by anyone. But the destruction of the city Schloss made them determined to save Berlin's other great Hohenzollern palace, Charlottenburg, which had been just as badly damaged. Work began the following year, but it was a long, slow process lasting right through the Fifties and Sixties to restore its rococo glories and create one of Germany's most magnificent museums and art galleries. The first milestone along the way was passed in 1952, when Andreas Schlüter's masterpiece, the bronze equestrian statue of the Great Elector, was installed in the central forecourt. The statue, which had originally stood on the Lange Brücke outside the city palace, almost didn't make it. It had survived the war safely in storage, but when it was being brought back to Berlin by water in 1946 the barge carrying it was in a collision and sank in Tegel harbour. It was not recovered until 1949, but fortunately was not too badly damaged. By a stroke of good fortune, Schlüter's original drawings both for the statue and for its carved plinth had survived in the Bode Museum, so they could be faithfully restored.

Two years after the Great Elector's statue had been given its new position, work started on restoring the palace built for Friedrich the Great's brother, Prince August Ferdinand, in 1785–6, Schloss Bellevue. The elegant Bellevue, on the northern edge of the Tiergarten, had been used by the Nazis as a government guest house (Soviet Prime Minister Molotov had been one of the first to stay there, in 1940) but its new role was to be much more controversial. It was to be the official residence in Berlin of the Federal president.

Although the blockade had been abandoned, the Soviets and their East German puppets kept up the pressure on West Berlin with a continuous series of petty restrictions. In May 1952, they cut all telephone links between the two halves of the city. Two months later, they forbade West Berliners from staying anywhere in the DDR, apart from East Berlin. In January 1953, they stopped buses and trams crossing sector boundaries, though U-Bahn and S-Bahn trains still did so.

Ulbricht predicted that the DDR would experience an explosion of industrial activity and growth that no capitalist country would be able to match. But the explosion failed to materialize, which is not surprising since his recipe for success was the increasing Stalinization of all business activity. Small businesses, including private shops, pubs and bars, restaurants, workshops, were deemed politically inappropriate and were taken over by the state. The churches were suppressed, self-employed people and their families had their ration cards cancelled, and farms began to be collectivized. The net result was to drive more and more able East Berliners into the west.

Equally insane was Ulbricht's decision to follow earlier Soviet economic models and invest almost entirely in heavy industry. He turned down proposals to increase investment in light industry and consumer products on the grounds that they were politically incorrect: under socialism, heavy industry must be favoured.

By February 1953, it was clear that Ulbricht's policy was not working. The danger of bankruptcy loomed. There were acute shortages of the staples of life, such as meat, coal and the potatoes that are such a vital part of the Berlin diet. The rest of the Politburo began pressing for a swift U-turn in economic policy. Increasingly harried, Ulbricht turned to his mentor, Stalin, to bail him out. But in March, Stalin died, leaving a power vacuum in the Soviet Union with Beria, Bulganin, Khrushchev, Malenkov and Molotov all jockeying for power. The only message from Moscow was that Ulbricht should follow a new, more liberal economic policy.

In April, Ulbricht was forced to raise the prices of basic commodities. Then, on 28 May, the government announced rises in the 'norms', the regular work quotas on which all wages in the DDR were calculated. This meant that workers had to produce between 10 and 30 per cent more per day to earn the same money; in effect, it was a substantial wage cut.

Faced with a rising tide of anger from people who felt betrayed, the party leadership grew increasingly jittery. On 9 June, following Moscow's advice, they decided on a change of policy dubbed 'the New Course'. The Council of Ministers approved it on 11 June, but in typical totalitarian fashion, no one thought of telling the people. Resentment continued to grow. It increased on 15 June, when Otto Grotewohl refused to meet a delegation of workers protesting about the new norms.

The next day, 100 construction workers on East Berlin's most prestigious building project, the transformation of the old Frankfurter Allee into Stalin Allee, a two-mile-long boulevard lined with monumental blocks of workers' flats identical with those on the Lenin Allee in Moscow, downed tools. They marched on the House of Ministries in Göring's old Air Ministry building on Leipzigerstrasse, near Potsdamerplatz, their numbers swollen on the way by workers joining from other sites along the route. By the time they arrived, marching to an old workers' song, *Brüder, zur Sonne, zur Freiheit!* (Brothers – forward to the sun, to freedom!) there were 10,000 of them, and their demands had grown.

Now, they were demanding not only the scrapping of the new norms but also free elections, the reunification of Germany, the return of German prisoners of war still held in Soviet camps, and the removal of Walter Ulbricht and his cronies. 'Down with Gruntawohl and the Siberian Goat!' they shouted (Ulbricht was known as 'Goatee' or 'the Goat' because of his pointed beard). 'Goatee, belly and specs – that's not what the people want!' 'We want freedom, justice and bread – or we'll see the bosses dead!' they chanted.

Ulbricht and Grotewohl stayed out of sight behind barred windows and doors, but three minor ministers were sent out to talk to the crowd. They were shouted down. When Grotewohl announced later that the new norms had been cancelled, it was not enough. The workers wanted freedom, and they turned to their old familiar weapon to achieve it: they called a general strike for the next day, 17 June 1953. Unfortunately, with all the media in the DDR in the hands of the party, they had no way of spreading their strike call to the rest of the country. Later that evening, RIAS broadcast a news report of the day's events in the east, but the use of the words 'general strike' was forbidden by the US authorities. Not until 5.00 am next morning was there any specific reference to it. By then, it was too late for any concerted action in the rest of East Germany, though an estimated 300,000 people demonstrated in some 270 towns and cities.

In East Berlin, however, the word had already spread throughout the city. Early on 17 June, about 100,000 workers poured on to the streets. It was not long before violence flared. Windows were smashed, kiosks overturned, and the red flag was torn down from the Brandenburg Gate again and burned. Ulbricht called out the Volkspolizei, but many of them openly sympathized with the workers. By the afternoon of 17 June, he was forced to turn to the Soviet military commandant to put down what had become a popular uprising. The commandant declared martial law and sent in Soviet tanks, T-34s, the same type that had smashed their way into the centre of Berlin eight years before.

The tanks patrolled Alexanderplatz, the Lustgarten, the Linden, Leipzigerstrasse, Friedrichstrasse, Potsdamerplatz, all the main thoroughfares. The Berliners reacted with rage and anger, but they had no weapons apart from sticks and stones. Scores were killed. No one has ever been sure of the death toll, and all sorts of figures have been quoted. At the time, the East German authorities gave the numbers as 25 dead and 378 injured. Recently, using the archives of the Stasi, the former State Security Police, a West Berlin historian has estimated the number of deaths during and immediately after the uprising as between 100 and 200. There were also about 4,000 arrests, and some 1,400 people were sentenced to life imprisonment. Interestingly, the archives show that Soviet tank commanders were under orders to avoid casualties as far as possible.

One man they saved from becoming a casualty was Walter Ulbricht.

At about noon, the Soviet military commandant, Major-General Pavel T. Dibrova, ordered that he be smuggled out of the Central Committee building in a tank. He was taken to Kienbaum, a small village close to the Soviet military airfield, so that he could be flown out to Moscow if the situation got any worse.

It took the Soviets nearly two weeks to stamp out resistance, but the operation was not without its costs – the Red Army was forced to hold many courts martial on Soviet soldiers who had refused to shoot protesters, or who had tried to escape to the west, resulting in at least 16 death sentences.

Ironically, the uprising left Ulbricht even more securely ensconced in power. The two members of the Politburo who had been eager to overthrow him, Rudolf Herrnstadt, editor of the party newspaper *Neues Deutschland*, and Wilhelm Zaisser, the head of internal security, were supporters of the Beria faction in Moscow. On 17 June, the Soviet Presidium ordered Beria, the head of state security, to fly to Berlin to put down the revolt. He went, dithered awhile, then flew straight back to Moscow without really achieving anything. On 9 July, he was arrested and denounced as an enemy of the people. Ulbricht's opponents had backed the wrong horse, while he, though a staunch Stalinist, was at least the devil the Kremlin knew. The Soviets were in no mood to make changes until their own leadership battle was finally resolved. In any case, replacing Ulbricht would send the wrong signal to those difficult Berliners – it would never do for them to get the idea that the leaders of the SED had lost Moscow's confidence.

One effect of the uprising was to bring about the relocation of the party elite. Ulbricht, Grotewohl and company used to live mostly in Pankow, the northern suburb of Berlin favoured by foreign ambassadors and diplomats. But after 17 June a secret, walled estate, complete with watchtowers and armed guards, was built for them at Wandlitz, on the B109 road beyond Schönerlinde and Schönwalde. Here, amid the pine trees of Brandenburg, they lived a gilded existence with their luxurious villas and large swimming pools which few West Germans could equal. Here, they were safe from their fellow countrymen.

Reactions to the uprising among East German intellectuals were predictable but curiously muted. One significant exception was

Kurt Bartel, secretary of the Writers' Union. In a positive orgasm of fawning and self-abasement, he issued a pamphlet entitled *How Ashamed I am*. It was addressed to 'builders, painters, carpenters' – in effect, to those who had started the uprising. He began by thanking the Soviet army for wiping the city clean, and blamed the whole unfortunate episode on 'scum from the other side who stole on silver bicycles through the city, like swallows before the rain'. 'But you,' he told the builders, painters and carpenters, 'could go to sleep in your beds by nine that night, like good children. For you and for the peace of the world, the Soviet army and the comrades of the People's Police kept watch. Are you not ashamed, as I am? For you will have to build much and well and wisely in future before this shame of yours will be forgotten.'

East Germany's most famous writer, Bertolt Brecht, who had returned to the city in 1949, replied to Bartel's queasy literary effort. Brecht despised Bartel, not to mention Grotewohl and Ulbricht. The dislike was mutual. They did not care for him or his work. 'You call this art?' Grotewohl is said to have asked after a performance of Brecht's play *Mother Courage*. But Brecht and his Berliner Ensemble theatre company had become too famous for the party to touch, and in any case the playwright was always too slippery to be pinned down on any issue. He procrastinated endlessly, and never joined the Communist Party though his wife, the actress Helen Weigel who starred in the first performance of *Mother Courage*, was a dedicated member. Brecht was no hero: death on the barricades did not appeal to him at all. Nevertheless, he wrote a less than enthusiastic endorsement of the Soviet action for *Neues Deutschland* and, two-faced as ever, spitted the unfortunate Bartel on the sharp point of a poem:

> After the uprising of 17 June
> The secretary of the Writers' Union
> Had pamphlets distributed in the Stalin Allee
> Stating that the people
> Had forfeited the confidence of the government,
> And could win it back only
> By redoubled efforts. Would it not be easier
> In that case, for the government
> To dissolve the people
> And elect another?

The western powers made no more than token noises of disapproval during the uprising. No one could predict the outcome of the leadership struggle then taking place in Moscow, and no one wanted to take the risk of provoking the Soviet Union into actions that might escalate into a third world war. Their commitment to Berlin, it seemed, was limited to the western half of the city.

A few days after it was all over, Reuter announced that the Charlottenburger Chaussee, the avenue leading through the Tiergarten to the Brandenburg Gate, was to be renamed Strasse des 17. Juni as a memorial to those who had died. Ten weeks later, Reuter was dead himself, felled by a heart attack. His funeral procession was watched by hundreds of thousands of mourners.

Ernst Reuter's immediate successor as mayor was Otto Suhr, who was seriously ill for most of his time in office. But his true successor, Willy Brandt, was already standing by, ready to take office in 1958. Like so many true Berliners, Brandt was not a native of the city – he was born in the Baltic seaport of Lübeck, the illegitimate son of a poor shop assistant, in 1913. Exiled from Germany in 1934, because of his active role in the SPD, he took refuge in Norway, and when he was stripped of his German nationality became a Norwegian citizen. He covered the Spanish Civil War as a war correspondent. During the Second World War he fled from the Nazis again, this time to Sweden, where he worked for the German resistance against the Nazis. At the end of the war, he moved to Berlin as press attaché to the Norwegian military mission, regaining his German nationality in 1948, the year he became a member of the executive of the Berlin SPD. Reuter's greatest tests as mayor of West Berlin were the blockade and the 17 June uprising. For Willy Brandt, the crisis that would establish his greatness had yet to materialize.

Throughout the Fifties, the differences between the living standards of the two Germanies continued to widen. Year by year, they grew further apart, and nowhere was the difference more obvious than in Berlin. As a political and economic showpiece, West Berlin was given every help and encouragement from Bonn and Washington. Money poured in for reconstruction. New buildings appeared everywhere, while the old were restored and purged of all traces of war damage.

In 1957, the city celebrated the handing over of the 100,000th municipally funded new flat, in Kommandantenstrasse, Kreuzberg, close to the East Berlin boundary. The Congress Hall, the 'pregnant oyster' with its 600-ton cantilevered roof, a gift from America, opened on the spot where the old refreshment rooms of In den Zelten had entertained Berliners 100 years before. And an international building exhibition brought together more than 40 of the world's leading architects to create a striking new Hanseatic quarter to the north and west of the Tiergarten, replacing the fashionable residential district that had been totally destroyed in the air raids of November 1943.

By 1958, new luxury hotels were opening in the west end: first the Hotel Berlin, on the edge of the Tiergarten, then that ultimate symbol of western opulence, the Hilton, its tall tower block overlooking the zoo clearly visible from beyond the Brandenburg Gate. The major industrial plants, including great names like Borsig, Siemens, Osram, AEG, resumed production with the most modern new equipment. The Berlin International Film Festival, created amid the traumas of 1953, was establishing itself as a major annual event in world cinema. By 1960, work had started on Hans Scharoun's new Philharmonie, which was to be the centrepiece of the ambitious Kulturforum complex of museums, galleries and concert halls in Tiergarten, and on rebuilding the Deutsche Oper in Bismarckstrasse. The city was beginning to boom – it was like the Gründerjahre of the 1870s all over again.

But for East Berlin, as in the rest of the DDR, it was a different story. A few prestige projects, mostly of a cultural nature, were completed. In 1953 the old Sing-Akademie was reopened as the Maxim Gorki Theater, and Brecht's Berliner Ensemble moved into the reconstructed Schiffbauerdamm Theater; in 1955 the Staatsoper on the Linden reopened. But most of the ruins remained. Older apartment blocks and Mietskasernen in districts like Prenzlauerberg went unrepaired, while new housing was soulless and sub-standard. There were no luxuries for the ordinary East German, and few comforts. Food, clothing and other necessities were still in short supply.

From 1952, East Germany had been sealed off from the west with barbed wire and machine guns along the length of its frontier. Only in Berlin was there no physical barrier between the two states, since the four-power agreement stated quite clearly that all four occupying armies had the right of unrestricted movement throughout the entire city. Berlin had become the only open gateway through which those wishing to escape from the oppression and drudgery of life in the east could pass. From West Berlin, those not wishing to stay in the city were airlifted out to start afresh in the Federal Republic.

The display of naked military might on 17 June 1953 horrified many of those in East Berlin who had previously supported the regime. It also created a haemorrhage of refugees. Even before the uprising, 1,000 people a day were crossing to the west. In its immediate aftermath, over 320,000 people fled westwards. The permanent reception facility at Marienfelde, set up by the West Berlin authorities to house and process refugees was now handling 1,500 a day. Half of them were under 25, three-quarters of them under 45, East Berlin's most able and enterprising citizens.

Colleges, institutions, factories, farms, workshops and offices in the DDR were finding it increasingly difficult to operate because of lack of trained personnel. In Berlin, the situation was aggravated by 52,000 *Grenzgänger*, 'border commuters', people who lived in the east but worked in the west, where wages and conditions were so much higher. By 1961, a total of between two and a half and three million East Germans had fled to the west since the establishment of the DDR. Almost a million had crossed through Berlin.

Ulbricht and Khrushchev fumed at this public humiliation, and looked for ways of cutting off the escape route. In 1958, Khrushchev had issued an ultimatum to the other powers, demanding that they withdraw all their forces from Berlin within six months. The western powers stood firm, and faced him down, but it was another anxious time for West Berlin.

For the next three years, Khrushchev kept up the pressure, threatening to sign a separate peace treaty with East Germany which would end all occupation rights. When he met the newly elected President John F. Kennedy in Vienna in June 1961, Berlin was top of the agenda. Khrushchev tried to bully the young president into agreeing that West Berlin should be transformed into a 'demilitarized free city', as part of his proposed peace treaty. Bloodied but unbowed after his first confrontation with the belligerent Soviet leader, Kennedy refused to give way. He told Khrushchev US rights of presence and access to Berlin were 'intimately interlinked' with the security of western Europe, and that 'we are determined to maintain those rights at all cost and thus to stand by our commitments to the

276

people of West Berlin'. The cold war was reaching its most explosive time, and it was clear to the whole world that Berlin was the flashpoint that could ignite it.

Ulbricht, meanwhile, was still trying to stem the flow of refugees, which was not only damaging his industry but also making it more difficult to feed his country. So many people were deserting the collectivized farms that large areas of land were lying idle for want of labour. He imposed strict controls on East Germans travelling to Berlin, and on both West Germans and West Berliners entering East Berlin. But it was no use. The numbers of refugees crossing into West Berlin reached new records as fears grew that the border might be closed. When Ulbricht, unprompted, declared: 'No one has any intention of building a wall,' thousands more took the hint and fled. In July, 30,415 refugees arrived in West Berlin, of whom 51.4 per cent were under 25. In the first twelve days of August alone, another 21,828 followed. The situation called for desperate measures.

CHAPTER 22

The Wall

AROUND MIDNIGHT on Saturday 12 August 1961, all S-Bahn trains travelling from East to West Berlin stopped running. Passengers were forced to get out and walk. West Berliners returning home were allowed to pass through the check points, after their papers had been thoroughly scrutinized. Easterners were turned back. Around them, they saw East German troop carriers and armoured cars lining up along the sector boundary, backed by Soviet tanks. Behind them were convoys of trucks carrying rolls of barbed wire, steel and concrete posts, pneumatic drills and other tools. At 2.00 am, troops and men of the SED work brigades started unrolling barbed wire, tearing up cobblestones and paving slabs, and positioning tank traps, to block off streets running from east to west along the entire sector boundary.

The whole operation had been planned with military precision, under the direction of the member of the SED central committee responsible for state security, Erich Honecker. On Potsdamerplatz, protected by heavily armed People's Police and East German border guards, soldiers and workmen with pneumatic drills and jackhammers dug holes for concrete posts and strung coils of barbed wire between them. In front of the Brandenburg Gate, where the boundary bulged out into the Tiergarten in an arc 90 metres wide and 45 deep, the workers sank a row of steel posts into the ground and secured them with concrete. Over the posts, they slotted flat, prefabricated concrete slabs, each six feet (1.8 metres) wide with holes for the posts to go through. They poured wet mortar over the slabs, then repeated the process until they had a solid wall, seven feet (2.1 metres) high and six feet (1.8 metres) deep running right across the front of the gate. It took 53 hours of continuous work to complete this tank-proof barrier, with men working shifts and sustained by army field kitchens parked under the gate itself. All the time, they worked under a barrage of jeers and abuse from thousands of West Berliners, gathered to watch and protest, who frequently had to be restrained by West Berlin police.

In Bernauerstrasse, which lies between the boroughs of Wedding and Mitte, the houses on one side of the street formed the eastern boundary, while the pavement outside was in the west. The troops initially bricked up every doorway and window on the ground floor. Later, when they found residents on either side of the street were still calling to each other from the upper windows, and even jumping out of them or lowering themselves down on ropes, they bricked them up, too. They also had to brick up the porch of the Church of the Atonement further down Bernauerstrasse, which was inconvenient enough to lie across the border. Worshippers had to find another way in.

In two streets in Neukölln, the houses were in the west, but the pavement was in the east. Here, the troops erected the wall in the gutter, but posted notices reminding people that the pavements belonged to East Germany, and any 'provocation' on it would result in unnamed 'security measures'. In other places, the fence threaded its way between houses, apartment blocks and back yards.

The first barbed wire barrier was completed in a matter of hours, stretching right along the border of the Soviet sector and linking up at either end with the border fence that separated West Berlin from the DDR. Then work began on piling up concrete blocks to form a crude wall, at first only about five feet (1.5 metres) high, behind the barbed wire.

Willy Brandt was on a West German train between Nuremberg and Kiel when he heard news of what was happening. He flew straight back to the city, where he found the Allied military authorities in total disarray. He begged them to send patrols to guard the new internal border, but it took them nearly twenty-four hours to make up their minds, and two more days before they got round to sending an official protest to the Soviet commandant. The reaction from the Federal German government in Bonn was no more positive. Adenauer simply lay low, while Foreign Minister Brentano bleated about the need for greater east–west co-operation. Only Brandt spoke up for Berlin, forcefully and emotionally.

On the following Saturday, Brandt's efforts bore some fruit. US Vice President Lyndon Johnson flew into the city with General Lucius Clay, former US military commander in Germany and the hero of the airlift, and both joined Brandt in making stirring speeches to a great crowd, gathered in pouring rain outside Schöneberg town hall. The occasion ended in an emotional climax, with the tolling of the Liberty Bell. The following day, Johnson, Clay and Brandt greeted US troop reinforcements as they paraded through West Berlin in an impressive show of force. But by then, of course, the wall was an established fact.

For nearly 30 years, the wall was to be the dominant feature of Berlin's life. The fact that it was there not to keep others out but to keep East Berlin's own citizens in, was a curious throwback to the past, when one of the functions of the Hohenzollerns' city wall had been to prevent their soldiers deserting. As ever, most Berliners accommodated themselves to their new circumstances, and settled down to wait, patiently, for better times.

Throughout the autumn of 1961, the fence grew into a wall of concrete slabs, 13 feet (4 metres) high and 97 miles (155 kilometres) long, completely encircling West Berlin. Twenty-seven miles (43 kilometres) of it lay between the two halves of the city, the rest between West Berlin and East Germany. It cut off 62 city streets and 131 roads. Before the wall, there were 81 crossing points between the city sectors. Afterwards there were just eight, one of which was reserved for mail vans, another for the dead, whose coffins were allowed through in either direction every Wednesday. The rest could only be used by foreigners or by East Germans with special passes.

U-Bahn and S-Bahn crossings were all closed, with the exception of Friedrichstrasse station, where lines from the west ended in customs posts. Other stations on or near the boundary were closed down, their locked and barred entrances to stand untended for the next 30 years.

One single crossing was preserved for western diplomats, troops and foreigners in cars. It was in the middle of Friedrichstrasse, once one of the busiest streets in the world, and was to become internationally famous as 'Checkpoint Charlie'. This was the scene of the first real showdown between east and west on 23 October 1961, when US and Soviet tanks moved into position on either side of the barrier, their guns loaded and aimed at each other, after the DDR had tried to prevent members of the US military mission exercising their right of free passage. The confrontation lasted three tense days, before both sides backed off, each believing it had made its point.

For nearly two and a half years, West Berliners were barred from the east altogether. After Christmas 1963, however, they were allowed in for single days at holiday times. East German pensioners were then allowed out to visit families at any time. The East Berlin authorities claimed this was a humanitarian gesture, but more cynically minded Berliners pointed out that pensioners were a drain on the economy, and it was clearly hoped they would choose to stay in the west.

The refugees had now become escapers, fleeing from a prison camp. The first of them started jumping over the coils of wire, slipping through bomb sites, swimming across canals, that first morning before the barriers were completed. At that stage, no one was shooting at them, but the flow had been reduced from an average of 145 an hour down to 50. Only 800 crossed over that first day, but as work continued there was a rush of people frantic to grab what they knew could be their last chance. Between then and the end of the month, another 25,605 made it across, to set a final monthly record for August of 47,437. By December, the monthly figure was down to 2,420.

Quite a few of the escapers were border guards, policemen, and soldiers, often in company with those they were supposed to be trying to stop. It was not long before East Berliners among the troops and guards were replaced by men from other parts of the country, mainly Saxons, who could be better relied on to shoot at fugitives and not join them.

The first escaper died six days after the barbed wire went up: 47-year-old Rudolf Urban fell to his death while trying to climb down from the window of his top-floor apartment in Bernauerstrasse on 19 August 1961. Three days later, Ida Siekermann, aged 59, jumped to her death in the same street. Two days after that, the Volkspolizei, the 'Vopos', shot and killed their first victim, 24-year-old Günter Litfin, who was trying to swim to freedom across the Humboldthafen, on the Spree between the Charité Hospital and the Lehrter Bahnhof.

Sixteen more would-be escapers died before the end of 1961. But the death that really brought home the inhumanity of the East German regime to the whole world came a year later, on 17 August 1962. Two 18-year-old construction workers made a dash for the wall two blocks from Checkpoint Charlie, and tried to climb over it. They were spotted by the Vopos, who started shooting. One youth made it to the west, but the other, Peter Fechter, was hit as he tried to scramble over the barbed wire. He fell back into eastern territory, wounded and bleeding severely. For 50 minutes, the Vopos and border guards did nothing as he lay there, out of reach of the West Berliners who could only watch helplessly as his cries grew gradually weaker. Western photographers recorded the scene as he bled to death before finally being carted away.

Over the years that followed, the wall was strengthened and 'improved' with numerous refinements. One was having concrete piping laid along its top edge to stop grappling irons or fingers getting a grip; ironically, the pipes had to be bought from West Germany. What had started as a simple concrete structure grew eventually into a deadly complex, hundreds of feet wide in places, guarded by 300 watchtowers, an obscene scar across the face of Berlin.

Behind the wall itself, which was always just a few feet inside East German territory, was a bare track which not even the border guards were allowed to enter. Floodlights mounted on tall lamp standards were planted in this, to illuminate the rest of the strip, which incorporated an anti-vehicle ditch, a patrol track, a run for guard dogs on a guide wire, trip alarms, concrete bunkers to provide cover for the guards in case of trouble, and high concrete watchtowers, each within direct visual contact of the next, with powerful searchlights on top and machine-gun ports halfway up. On the eastern side, the border strip was closed by a high wire fence with built-in alarm systems, beyond which were 'Spanish horsemen' – steel girders welded into three-armed crosses to stop tanks or other vehicles.

Buildings alongside the wall in the east, including those in Bernauerstrasse, were razed and the land where they had stood cleared to provide a killing ground. For Berliners, the most obscene piece of vandalism after the sealing of the Brandenburg Gate came when the remains of Potsdamerplatz, once the throbbing heart of the city, were flattened. Erik Mendelsohn's Columbushaus, the pillared front of Schinkel's Potsdam Gate, the ruined circular tower of Kempinski's Haus Vaterland – all were bulldozed. A vast area including Leipzigerplatz, Ebertstrasse, the Wilhelmstrasse (renamed Otto-Grotewohl-Strasse!) and Wilhelmplatz (changed to Thälmannplatz), was transformed into a barren desert. But it was not entirely lifeless: it became a haven for a thriving rabbit population, a bizarre nature reserve. It also became one of West Berlin's principal tourist attractions, a regular stop on all coach and bus tours, with a large steel viewing platform for visitors, and a jumble of souvenir stores and refreshment stalls.

The fortifications did not stop the escape bids. By the time the wall came down, the West Berlin police had recorded 5,043 successful 'wall runners', of whom 565 were serving members of the East German armed forces. They came by every imaginable route: in the early days by crashing through the wall in heavy trucks; through tunnels – 57 people came through one that was over 135 metres long, 12 metres deep and only 70 centimetres in diameter; hidden in false tanks and panels of cars and trucks; in coffins; in hot-air balloons; in an improvised cable car; in counterfeit Soviet army vehicles, wearing home-made Red Army uniforms; even in a do-it-yourself motorized mini-submarine. One group hired a passenger boat for a river excursion, got the captain drunk, then locked him in his cabin and headed for the west at full throttle, under a hail of bullets from the banks. More than 5,000 escapers were caught. The guards are known to have opened fire 1,693 times. At least 80 people died in the attempt, the last as late as February 1989.

Despite Ulbricht's unintentional warning, the erection of the wall took most people in the west by surprise, including the Allied intelligence services. Even before the wall, Berlin was a hotbed of espionage, with no fewer than 90 western intelligence agencies of one sort or another located in the city. But once the wall was in place, it became the undisputed spy capital of the world. For writers of fiction, or even semi-fiction, like Len Deighton and John Le Carré, the wall was a gift from the gods. A whole generation of secret agents, from Harry Palmer to Quiller, and shadowy controllers like George Smiley, invested Berlin with the seedy glamour of the world of espionage.

For once, the reality almost matched the fiction, and people in the west became accustomed to seeing pictures of captured agents being exchanged between the girders of Glienicke bridge, which links Wannsee with Babelsberg and Potsdam. But this was deceptive: for the most part, real-life intelligence work is a humdrum business of collecting and collating small scraps of information, gleaned by sifting through dull reports and eavesdropping endlessly on intercepted radio signals or tapped telephone lines.

The best-known intelligence scam was 'Operation Gold', a joint CIA–MI6 operation to tap the main Soviet telephone cable through a tunnel under the border near the village of Alt Glienicke, on the south-west boundary of Berlin. Its success rested not on shadowy secret agents but on the skills of tunnellers, air-conditioning and electronic technicians, and telephone engineers seconded from the General Post Office in London. It was elaborate, laborious, and expensive. And ultimately it was totally useless. In the best tradition of the superior spy story, the KGB knew all about the operation from the start, through a mole in British intelligence, George Blake.

For the reading and film-going public, however, espionage was still thrilling and dangerous, a world peopled with beautiful women and men licensed to kill. So Berlin became a favourite film location, and its image in the rest of the world as an exciting city was kept alive.

Berlin's international profile was raised still higher when Jack Kennedy came to demonstrate his and his country's solidarity with the beleaguered citizens. A modern white knight straight from Camelot, he rode down the Ku'damm and along the Strasse des 17. Juni to the Brandenburg Gate in an open car, with a smiling Brandt and a sour-faced Adenauer, who clearly still found it impossible to feel any affection for the city.

Through it all, the Berliners looked on, a touch cynically, as they have done for 750 years. They appreciated Kennedy's visit, and packed the square in front of Schöneberg town hall (since renamed John F. Kennedy Platz in his memory) to listen and to cheer. But many of them chuckled at his famous declaration. He should have said: 'Ich bin Berliner' – *eine Berliner* is a jam doughnut, short for *Berliner Pfannkuche*, a 'Berlin pancake'.

On the other side of the wall, Khrushchev countered by visiting East Berlin six days later. After denouncing Kennedy's visit as 'adding poison to the international atmosphere', he justified the wall as East Germany's legitimate border, claiming that it helped 'normalize' relations and 'served the cause of peace'. The best way of bringing about German reunification, he said, was to abolish capitalism in West Germany and create a single socialist state. His audience was considerably smaller than Kennedy's, and far less enthusiastic.

Later, in a conversation with West Germany's ambassador to Moscow, Khrushchev made no secret of his part in the decision to erect the wall. 'I know the wall is an ugly business,' he said. 'It will disappear one day, too, but only when the reasons that led to its being built no longer apply... I am not going to deny to you that it was I who, in the final analysis, gave the order to go ahead and build it. Ulbricht had pressured me for some time and, in the final months, with growing urgency. But I wouldn't like to hide behind his back – it's far too narrow for me!'

Having to go cap in hand to the man who had vilified his idol must have been a bitter pill for Ulbricht, the unreformed Stalinist. But clearly, he knew he had to swallow it. The proof that he had done so came in mid-November, when the Stalin Allee was changed overnight into Karl Marx Allee, reverting to Frankfurter Allee a little further out. All the signs bearing Stalin's name were removed during one hectic night of hammering and chiselling. The great bronze statue of the man, which Ulbricht had ceremoniously dedicated in 1951, was smashed up and carted away, like the scrap metal it had suddenly become.

The wall did at least give Ulbricht the chance to stabilize his regime and concentrate on trying to build up the economy of East Germany. A seven-year plan announced in 1958 got into its stride at last, as the people, with little else to do in their prison, settled down to work. They were hampered by the centralized communist system and by shortages of both skilled labour and raw materials, but gradually they began to achieve results.

Over the years, East Berlin remained, as old Berlin had in the days of the Reich, not only the capital and the administrative centre, but also the DDR's largest industrial city. Its chief products were electronics, electrical engineering and machine tools, but it also manufactured motor vehicles and chemicals, and a wide range of consumer goods, especially furniture, wallpaper, textiles and clothing.

By the mid-Seventies, per capita income in the DDR was reckoned by the World Bank to be higher than that of Britain, while its output ranked it as number eight in the world's industrial nations. But the figures were hollow. They depended on a captive, heavily subsidized market, with inefficient industries propped up by the Soviet Union, which was still promoting the DDR as the standard-bearer for communism in Europe. Little of the proceeds was invested in the infrastructure, or in modernizing industrial plant. Instead, it went to fuel a growing bureaucracy, ever-increasing corruption, and the insatiable machinery of repression and military show.

For all their hard work, the standard of living for East Berliners remained well below that of the west. While the west celebrated its 250,000th new home since the war in 1964, most homes in the east were still unmodernized and poorly maintained. And although there was enough food to eat, there was neither the variety nor the quality that was to be found on the other side. Consumer goods, including clothing, were shoddy, scarce and expensive. But there were many who were happy to accept this as the price for building what they considered a better life, free from the materialism of the west.

There were compensations, too, especially when it came to leisure time. West Berlin, of course, had the Tiergarten at its heart and the Grunewald, Spandau and Tegel forests as its lungs. It had the Havel and several smaller lakes for swimming, sailing, fishing and water sports. It had the Deutsche Oper, the Philharmonie, the Theater des Westens, the Schiller Theater and a whole range of smaller playhouses. It had the consumer's dream palace of the reconstructed Ka-De-We department store and a new, if smaller Wertheim, and all the plush shops, cinemas, restaurants and night clubs of the

Ku'damm and Tauentzienstrasse. But there was always a feeling of claustrophobia – whichever way they moved, West Berliners were hemmed in by the wall.

Easterners, on the other hand, could get right out of the city, on empty roads, to the pine forests and lakes of the Mark Branden- burg, into real countryside. Sport in all its varieties was worshipped even more than it had been under Hitler, so facilities were excellent and the rewards for success considerable. And for entertainment in the city they had superb opera and theatre at bargain basement prices in the Staats Oper and the Komische Oper, at the Berliner Ensemble in the Schiffbauerdamm Theater, the Deutsches Theater and many others. They could attend concerts of the East Berlin Philharmonic Orchestra for a fraction of what it cost their western cousins to listen to Herbert von Karajan. They could enjoy spec- tacular revues at the Friedrichstadt Palast and musical comedies at the Metropol. There was even satirical cabaret, playing to packed houses at *Die Distel* (The Thistle), opposite Friedrichstrasse sta- tion. Life in the east was not always miserable and grey.

The wall became a ghastly tourist attraction for West Berlin. Thou- sands of westerners came to gawp at the east, as though through the bars of a cage. Yet from the point of view of the East German politburo, the whole exercise almost succeeded in its secondary purpose, coming close to throttling West Berlin's economic and social systems. The very rich took their money and their style and decamped for the less circumscribed pastures of Bonn and Munich. Some workers followed them, but many were determined to stay: with high wages and subsidized rents, they could enjoy petty bour- geois comfort and respectability. But, most dangerously of all for the city, the young began to drift away to the west, leaving behind a steadily aging population. Berlin was on the verge of sliding into a cosy, subsidized decline. The Senate – as the Magistrat had become, since West Berlin was now a self-contained West German *Land*, with its own parliament – had to introduce incentives, in conjunction with the federal government in Bonn, to lure both individuals and companies to locate and stay in the city. Investment grants and substantial tax breaks made it a more attractive island to live on, but it was still an island in a sea of hostility.

Yet, somehow, West Berlin survived. Somehow, even in its

truncated form, it managed to retain something of the old metropolitan flavour, something of the glamour that was lacking in other German cities. And gradually, young people started to move back. Young men, in particular, were attracted by another echo from the distant past: West Berliners were exempt from conscription into the armed forces (easterners enjoyed no such privilege, despite Allied protests that the call-up was a breach of the city's four-power status). Those who took advantage of this loophole tended, naturally, to be the awkward young. Many were political radicals, left-wingers and anarchists who rejected all forms of order, whose gods were Che Guevara, Ho Chi Minh and Mao Tse-tung rather than Marx, Lenin and Stalin. Their arrival shook up the staid political scene in West Berlin.

There was, inevitably, a great deal of animosity towards the new arrivals, but, like them or not, they were the saviours of the city. They injected new energy into aging arteries, preventing West Berlin from descending into *Kleinbürgertum*, that small-town mentality so totally alien to all that Berlin had ever stood for. Gradually, artists, writers, musicians, actors, began to return. Students wanted to be there. Film makers started to find it a more sympathetic milieu than Munich and Hamburg. Squatters occupied empty buildings and turned them into 'alternative' communities, infuriating more-solid citizens. Berlin began to buzz again. One could feel once more that famous Berlin tempo.

The race riots, anti-war and anti-authority demonstrations that tore America, Britain, France and other countries apart during the late Sixties were repeated in Berlin as young activists raised hell. Flower power in West Berlin was violent, though never as ferocious as it was in Paris. But the police, untrained in patience or tolerance, reacted with sickening brutality. Water cannons, indiscriminate baton charges, and ruthless beatings became a regular feature of the scene, as they tried to drive demonstrators from the streets.

A sociology student originally from East Germany, Rudi Dutschke, became the leader of what he dubbed the Extra-Parliamentary Opposition Group, which rejected all organized forms of government. They pelted US Vice President Hubert Humphrey with stones and bottles when he visited the city in April 1967. But things really boiled over when the Shah of Iran arrived a few weeks later. Faced with a barrage of tomatoes, eggs, bottles and cartons of milk, the police started shooting. They created a new martyr for the left when they killed a student called Benno Ohnesorg. More demonstrations and rioting accompanied his funeral.

On 15 April 1968, in a conscious attempt to emulate the assassination eleven days before of Martin Luther King in Memphis, USA, Dutschke was shot twice in the head as he walked down the Ku'damm. Dutschke survived after a five-hour operation, but his supporters took to the streets, their protests exploding into mass riots. Their main target was the right-wing Axel Springer newspaper group, which they accused of creating a climate of intolerance. The 20-storey Springer newspaper and printing complex, deliberately built right against the wall only a couple of hundred metres from Checkpoint Charlie, was protected by riot police and barbed-wire barricades, but demonstrators managed to invade the company garage and set fire to several vehicles. More than 1,000 people were arrested during the disturbances.

East Berlin, by comparison, remained a haven of calm. With the Soviet army still there in force, and memories of 1953 still vivid, Ulbricht's Berliners made no attempt to emulate the citizens of Prague in 1968. The troops and tanks which quelled the revolt in Czechoslovakia came from the East German army, as well as the Soviet.

By 1969, the revolutionary fire was beginning to die down in West Berlin, just as it was elsewhere in the world. The authorities in the two western universities made important concessions to the students, giving them an active role in the administration, and even an involvement in appointing teaching staff. The Extra-Parliamentary Opposition Group merged with other hard-left factions into a loose association calling itself the Alternative List. In the rest of Germany, it became the Green Party. The great swell of general unrest calmed down, to be replaced by small terror groups like the 'Red Army Faction', born in May 1970 when Andreas Baader and Ulrike Meinhof escaped from Tegel prison. Their use of violence revived memories of the Twenties for older Berliners, but their exploits seemed tame by comparison with what had gone on 50 years earlier.

International friction was easing, too. US President Richard Nixon visited West Berlin and called for 'action to end the tensions of a past age'. He was supported by Willy Brandt, who had moved on from his position as governing mayor in 1966 to become foreign minister of the Federal Republic, and immediately started seeking reconciliation with eastern Europe. In 1969, Brandt was appointed West Germany's first SPD chancellor. In his inaugural speech he called on the four powers to sit down and negotiate over Berlin. In 1970, they did so, with the ambassadors holding their first meeting in the same room in the former Berlin courthouse where the Nazi judge Roland Freisler had sentenced so many people to death.

The ambassadors initialled the Four-Power Agreement on Berlin on 3 September 1971, three months after Walter Ulbricht had finally been persuaded to stand down as leader of the DDR. He was replaced by Erich Honecker, a Saarlander who, although he had overseen the building of the wall, had a much more relaxed attitude to relations with the west. The agreement, which was timed to take effect from 3 June 1972, recognized the two cities and the rights of their citizens, and guaranteed access, communications, travel and visiting rights for West Berliners in East Berlin. One of its first fruits was the reopening of telephone contact between the two Berlins, albeit with only ten lines rather than the original 4,000. Calls from East to West Berlin, however, were charged at international, not local, rates.

The Four-Power Agreement was a truce rather than a settlement, but it worked. There were many frustrations along the way – it took till 1975, for instance, to reach an agreement to rescue people who had fallen into any of the waterways along the boundary between east and west, by which time five children had drowned. But it opened the door for other agreements and treaties to be hammered out over the following years, allowing the two Germanies, and the two Berlins, to coexist.

CHAPTER 23

Coexistence and Competition

BUILDING AND REBUILDING had been going on at a great pace all through the Sixties in both East and West Berlin, often with significant differences in attitudes. In 1961, on the same day as the new Coventry cathedral was consecrated in England, West Berliners dedicated a new Kaiser Wilhelm Memorial Church on Breitscheidplatz, at the beginning of the Ku'damm, as their monument to the horrors of war. Like the citizens of Coventry, they left the ruins of the bombed church standing, but added a new, modern church alongside, a squat, octagonal building, with walls of blue glass and concrete. On the other side of the ruined spire they erected a hexagonal bell tower, containing what must surely be the loudest carillon in the world. The three buildings were swiftly christened the Powder Compact, Lipstick, and Hollow Tooth.

Next door to the Memorial Church, the remains of the old Romanische Café were being cleared away. The pre-war haunt of Berlin's artists and intellectuals was replaced by a temple to commercialism, the Europa Centre. This complex of shops, offices, night clubs and cinemas, its 22-storey tower block topped with a giant three-pointed Mercedes star, constantly revolving and neon-lit, was a fitting symbol of much of 1960s West Berlin, with its emphasis on glitter and gloss. Originally, it had an open-air ice skating rink in the space between the tower block and the church, in imitation of New York's Rockefeller Centre, but this was replaced by another of the pieces of modern sculpture dotting the streets of the west end which offer Berliners endless scope for their wit. This one, a polished stone hemisphere officially called the Globe Fountain, is known to Berliners as the 'Wasserklops' – *ein Klops* is a meatball.

In the east, the demolition of historic buildings was usually to make room not for commerce but for officialdom. In 1962, they demolished what was left of Schinkel's Bauakademie on the far side of the empty square left by the razing of the old palace. It was replaced by a disastrous, eleven-storey building for the DDR Foreign Ministry, its bland façade decorated with abstract aluminium sculptures.

Meanwhile, just across the Spree, work had started on a new Alexanderplatz, which was to stretch far beyond its old confines as a symbol of the spaciousness of socialist planning. The remains of the old centre – 'the quivering heart of a cosmopolitan city' as Alfred Döblin described it in his 1929 novel, *Alexanderplatz* – home to police headquarters, gangsters, small shopkeepers, market traders, and thousands of ordinary Berliners, were completely swept away. In their place, the planners created a vast open area running right down to the river, past the Red Town Hall, which had previously been hemmed in by a tight web of narrow streets. Where the ancient Neuen Markt had stood for centuries, only the Marienkirche remained. The old church had been patched up immediately after the war, but was completely and beautifully restored in 1969–70, when the Neptune Fountain was placed nearby. The fountain, designed by the dreaded Reinhold Begas as a gift from the city to Kaiser Wilhelm II in 1891, had previously stood outside the royal palace, but had been preserved on Museum Island since 1951.

Around the edges of this lifeless empty space, the East Berlin city council erected lines of precast concrete apartment buildings and stores, including their showpiece Centrum department store, the biggest in the DDR, but a poor substitute for the old Hermann Tietz and Wertheim stores. Alongside, they threw up tall office blocks and the 400-foot (122-metre) tower of the Hotel Stadt Berlin. In the centre of the expanse of concrete, they placed an elaborate world clock, and in 1966 began work on a television tower, easily the tallest building in Germany at 1,198 feet – 365 metres, one for every day of the year. It was 214 feet (65 metres) higher than the Eiffel Tower, but, tactfully, was a little shorter than its Moscow equivalent.

Built with Swedish assistance, the tower has a huge sphere covered in brown-tinted glass halfway up its long, tapering stem containing, along with offices and technical equipment, a viewing platform and a restaurant. Berliners quickly dubbed the tower 'the giant asparagus', asparagus being a much prized delicacy in Berlin, where the start of its season is awaited as keenly as the first strawberries once were in England. But what particularly delighted them was that when the sun was setting in the west, its reflection in the glass of the sphere created an enormous golden cross, shining out across the territory of Walter Ulbricht, the man who had banned crosses from the roofs of East Berlin's churches.

Nearby, more clearance was under way. The old Fischer neighbourhood on Fischerinsel, the original heart of old Kölln, was pulled down to make way for six 22-storey apartment blocks. In contrast, West Berlin started a great urban renewal scheme in its central districts, preferring to renovate and restore old, characterful buildings, and saving its big municipal housing developments for new suburbs like the Märkische Viertel on the northern boundary of Reinickendorf, and Gropius Stadt in the south-east, each of which provided homes for 50,000 inhabitants. After some teething problems, the new suburbs have become model communities, clean and free from vandalism and – astonishingly for West Berlin – from the ubiquitous graffiti. East Berlin followed suit ten years later, with new satellite towns at Marzahn, Hohenschönhausen and Hellersdorf, on its eastern boundary.

Through the Seventies and into the Eighties, the two cities co-existed peacefully, but West Berlin drew further and further ahead as the lack of investment on the other side of the wall began to show. Ever more confident, the West opened an impressive new airport at Tegel, and a new International Conference Centre and exhibition grounds by the old radio tower in Charlottenburg. More luxury hotels opened around the Europa Centre, to house tourists and visitors flocking in to trade fairs and exhibitions, and executives arriving to do business with West Berlin's booming industries.

In East Berlin, Honecker decided that the best way to compete was to capitalize on the old city's historic buildings, which the west could not hope to match. In marked contrast to Ulbricht's efforts to wipe out all traces of Berlin's imperial past, Honecker set out to make use of it as a source of pride and national identity for his citizens. He began a massive programme of reconstruction and restoration along the Linden, with buildings like the Zeughaus and various palaces, and eased the way for the work already being paid for by the western churches to restore the Dom. The equestrian statue of Friedrich the Great, which had been banished 30 years before to Sans Souci in Potsdam as a despised symbol of feudalism, was brought back to its original place in the centre of the Linden at the end of November 1980. And work was started on the most impressive of all the restoration schemes, the reconstruction of the old Gendarmenmarkt, perversely renamed Platz der Akademie. Schinkel's magnificent Schauspielhaus, the former National Theatre, and the two domed cathedrals flanking it, were still in a state of total ruin, with self-seeded trees growing among the stones.

The work would take most of the Eighties to complete, outlasting Honecker and his regime, but the result has been a triumphant success. The square, which reverted to its original name in 1991, is once more the heart of the old Friedrichstadt. The Schauspielhaus, converted from its former role as a theatre, is now one of the most elegant concert halls in the world, and the twin churches stand guard on either side once more, as Friedrich the Great intended. The French cathedral, rebuilt with money from the Evangelical Church, now has a fine organ often used for recitals, and an excellent restaurant in its tower. It also houses a centre for the Calvinist French Reformed Church, and the fascinating Huguenot museum.

But the fine restorations stood out like new teeth in a mouth full of decay. Between and around them the ugly gaps of bombed sites remained, flanked by buildings still bearing the scars of war, their façades pockmarked and cratered by thousands of bullets, shells and shrapnel fragments. Even major streets like Friedrichstrasse were still surfaced with badly patched cobbles and rusting tramlines, and to walk around the railway station at night was to step back 50 or 60 years into some old *film noir*, with grimy brick walls dripping damp and great pools of darkness barely punctured by the inadequate glimmer of gas lamps. The girls who lurked in the dark corners waiting for customers had none of the brash confidence of their counterparts on the Ku'damm, with their expensive clothes and glossy make-up.

Prosperity brought a bloodless revolution to West Berlin. In 1975, the seemingly impossible happened: for the first time since its formation, except for the periods when it was banned by either Bismarck or Hitler, the SPD lost its position as the city's largest party. That year, as in every year since, more votes went to the conservative Christian Democrats. Until 1981, the SPD managed to hang on in coalition with the liberal Free Democrats, but then the CDU gained its first overall majority. In that year, the city elected its first CDU governing mayor since Walther Schreiber, who had briefly succeeded Ernst Reuter after his death in 1953.

Richard von Weizsäcker, a distinguished lawyer who had been president of the Evangelical Church, was a Berliner by birth. His father, although a staunch opponent of the Nazi regime, had been state secretary in the Foreign Office from 1938 till 1943. Under Weizsäcker's leadership, the two halves of the divided city were brought closer together in various ways. The Teltow canal, closed to shipping since the war, was reopened. A contract was signed for a pipeline to supply natural gas to West Berlin from the Soviet Union. The Federal German government was persuaded to cover the cost of plant in East Berlin to purify effluent flowing into West Berlin. The public transport authority in the west took over the increasingly decrepit S-Bahn system, providing not only the capital for desperately needed modernization but also all the electricity to run it. The take-over included paying the east DM 3 million for the ruined transport museum in the former Hamburger Bahnhof, the oldest railway station in the city, which like the S-Bahn was owned by the East's Deutsche Reichsbahn, although it was situated in the western district of Tiergarten. The old museum was incorporated into West Berlin's splendid Museum of Transport and Technology.

The station building has since been carefully restored and is now an exhibition hall and art gallery.

Weizsäcker was the first governing mayor to meet Erich Honecker and the state council of the DDR, to discuss closer co-operation. He continued working for *détente* and the destruction of the wall, stressing the common bonds between the two halves of city and country, when he was elected president of the Federal Republic in July 1984.

As industry flourished, West Berlin became a magnet for workers once more. This time, they came on sufferance, as *Gastarbeiter*, 'guest workers' with no rights of citizenship. The influx started modestly enough: in 1961, West Berlin had 20,000 non-German inhabitants, not counting military personnel of the three powers, of course. But from the start of the Seventies the numbers began to rocket. By 1975, there were 190,000. By the end of 1989, there were at least 297,000, a figure swelled by thousands of 'refugees' taking advantage of West Germany's liberal asylum laws. They were flown in to East Berlin from third-world countries on special cheap charter flights by Interflug, the DDR state airline, and given instant transit to West Berlin. This cynical operation was specially attractive for East Germany: it made money from flights and visas, and at the same time undermined West Berlin by pouring in penni-less souls who became a charge on the state, and whose presence might cause unrest among resentful German workers.

By far the largest individual group of immigrants was the Turks, and the city soon grew used to swarthy-skinned men with mous-taches and quiet, dark-eyed women in headscarves. By the end of the Eighties, 128,000 Turks made up 5.9 per cent of the population of West Berlin, or 3.7 per cent of the city as a whole. As a comparison, the Jews, the largest ethnic group in pre-Hitler Berlin, had accounted for 2.9 per cent in 1933. The next-largest groups were the Jugoslavs with 34,000, and the Poles, with 22,000.

The number of immigrants flocking into West Berlin during the Eighties was the clearest possible indication of its growing pros-perity. In stark contrast, by 1989, there were only 21,000 foreigners living in the whole of East Berlin, another damning indictment of the communist regime's failure. The Poles who came to Berlin every day by car and coach in the late Eighties – Berlin is less than an hour's drive from the Polish frontier at Frankfurt-an-der-Oder – did not even bother to stop in the east. They drove straight through to West Berlin to sell their bits and pieces in the Polish market on waste land off the Reichpietschufer, a stone's throw from the Potsdamerplatz.

Most of the foreigners, particularly the Turks, settled in the traditional workers' districts of Kreuzberg, Schöneberg and Wedding. In these districts, one in four of the entire population is an immigrant. They have created their own communities, just as the Huguenots and Jews did in their time. They have completely changed the nature of Kreuzberg in particular, where they have settled happily alongside the artists, punks and squatter communes in their garishly painted blocks, sharing the community facilities in the former Bethanien hospital, which is now an arts centre.

When President Reagan paid the ritual visit to Berlin in 1987 to make his 'Kennedy' speech, Kreuzberg was sealed off with barbed wire. The West German government in Bonn was so terrified of the natural bloody-mindedness of the Berliners that it arranged for a specially vetted, ticket-only audience of 35,000 to listen to him. To make doubly sure, they even bused in a large number of American servicemen and -women from Frankfurt. Slogans and graffiti were whitewashed out. The whole occasion was thoroughly sanitized, by the simple process of keeping real Berliners away from it. Dr Goebbels, who shipped in tens of thousands of Germans from outside the city for occasions like Hitler's victory parade on 30 January 1933, would have approved wholeheartedly.

The West German authorities were expecting a crowd of East Berliners to assemble on the other side of the wall. The week before, there had been a huge attendance for a rock concert held on the western side. Thousands of 'Ossies' had turned out to listen and to applaud. But few turned up for Reagan.

1987 offered a unique opportunity for the two halves of the divided city to co-operate in celebrating the 750th anniversary of the first recorded mention of Kölln. It was understandable that the two sides should have had different views on the various other anniversaries that had fallen during the Eighties: the fortieth anniversary of the Soviet 'liberation' of Berlin in 1985, for example, and of the formation of the SED in 1986, followed by the twenty-fifth anniversary of the building of the wall. By way of marking that less-than-glorious silver jubilee, the East Germans rebuilt their side of Checkpoint Charlie, replacing wooden huts with more permanent concrete structures. Only a year earlier, they had blown up the *Versöhnungskirche*, the Church of Reconciliation, which had been stuck in no-man's-land for many years, to expand the killing zone.

But although the 750th anniversary of Berlin was common to both sides, they could not bring themselves to share it, using it instead to compete with each other. As well as staging countless seminars, exhibitions and displays, they each embarked on a grand building programme to mark the event. The west held another International Building Exhibition, with architects from all over the world designing more new housing schemes. In the east, the existing restoration programme was tied in to the celebrations; a new carillon was installed in the French Cathedral, to mark the occasion, for instance. But Honecker, increasingly concerned with history, had another grand scheme up his sleeve: the construction of a whole new 'ancient' quarter around the Nikolaikirche, the oldest building in Berlin.

Work on the Nikolai Viertel began in 1981, with completion timed to coincide with the anniversary celebrations. The remains of old houses, shops and taverns from different parts of the city were collected together and rebuilt in the area between the Red Town Hall and the Molkenmarkt and Mühlendamm, the centre of the original Berlin settlement, to create a traffic-free zone with narrow, winding streets. Even for such a prestige project, money was not unlimited, and many of the houses, particularly those around the edge and facing the river, were built with textured concrete slabs precast to mimic traditional shapes. The result, nevertheless, has great charm, managing very successfully to recall Berlin's pre-Wilhelmine past without ever descending to the level of a theme park.

On both sides of the wall, the anniversary celebrations unleashed a hankering for more recent history, the cosy days of the Wilhelmine era. A sudden rash of 'old' taverns and Kneipen broke out all over the west, old barrel organs were found and renovated or copied, and Heinrich Zille came into his own, with new Zille bars and museums. In the east, where many Kneipen had closed down, few publicans had the funds to indulge in exercises like that – they had a hard enough time simply trying to keep their furniture repaired and finding paint to brighten up their walls. The Magistrat selected one street, Husemannstrasse in Prenzlauerberg, and pain-stakingly recreated it as a living museum of turn-of-the-century Berlin, with an old bar-restaurant on one corner, various shops along the way, and all the buildings freshly painted in that unique greeny-buff colour of the period.

Husemannstrasse was, and remains, an attractive piece of nostalgia well worth a visit. But it only served to highlight the awful condition of the streets surrounding it, where, as in much of East Berlin, stucco had cracked and fallen off in chunks, doors and windows had rotted and cast-iron balconies had been allowed to rust until they were beyond repair and had to be cut away. Tenants of the apartments in the unreconstructed Mietskasernen asserted their individuality by painting the walls around their windows, as far as they could reach, with what they had left of whatever coloured paint they had been lucky enough to find to decorate their kitchens and living rooms, creating a sad, defiant patchwork.

The 750th anniversary celebrations lasted throughout the year. They brought Berlin back to international attention as the heads of state of the occupying powers arrived to pay tribute. Queen Elizabeth of Great Britain, President Mitterand of France, and President Reagan of the United States all paid the usual visits to the wall, and mouthed the usual platitudes. The socialist Mitterand described Berlin as a bridge and a link between two worlds. Queen Elizabeth, the head of a diverse Commonwealth, said she hoped this Berlin which was the symbol of the division of Europe would one day be the symbol of its unity. Reagan, pointedly ignoring Honecker and his regime, called on President Gorbachov to open the Brandenburg Gate and tear down the wall.

Mikhail Gorbachov came to Berlin, too. He held a meeting of the Warsaw Pact there in May, but said nothing about the wall, or the division of the city. Eberhard Diepgen, the governing mayor of West Berlin, reminded him, calling for an end to the infamous order to East German border guards to shoot anyone attempting to escape. He also issued a more direct personal challenge to the reforming Soviet leader. 'Anyone who is serious about *détente* and disarmament should prove it first in Berlin,' he declared.

There was no immediate response from Gorbachov, who had then been in power for just two years, and was still consolidating his position. But he was already beginning the process of perestroika in the Soviet Union, and it was a process that, once started, would be impossible to control. Like the first trickle of water from a small crack in a mighty dam, it heralded a collapse that would sweep away everything before it, including the Berlin wall.

Through the rest of 1987 and 1988, there were more meetings and exchanges. Honecker paid a state visit to the Federal Republic, and a private one to his old family home in the Saarland. Diepgen met his East Berlin counterpart, Erhard Krack, at a church service in the east during the 750th anniversary celebrations, and a year later held talks with Honecker to agree on increased contacts and easier travel arrangements between the two Berlins. Chancellor Helmut Kohl raised the subject of Berlin during a state visit to Moscow, and Gorbachov confirmed that the special status of Berlin was sacrosanct.

To Berliners and interested observers alike, it seemed possible that there would be a steady easing of tensions which would culminate, naturally and after a few years of gradual convergence, in the eventual removal of the wall. No one was prepared to say, or even to hope for, anything more than that. Some were not even prepared to go that far: in January 1989 Honecker declared confidently that 'the wall will still stand in fifty and even a hundred years'.

Honecker and his cronies in the SED were appalled at the liberalization being introduced to the Soviet Union. They would have none of it. They even banned the Soviet magazine *Sputnik* from the DDR, when it started openly discussing political changes, and on 8 June 1989 they were the first to endorse the Chinese government's massacre of students in Tiananmen Square. As far as they were concerned, it had all been caused by Gorbachov, who had stirred up unrest during his visit to Beijing. Now, he was offering the German Federal Republic a permanent *détente* that would eliminate the front line in Europe, in exchange for West German money and technology. No front line, of course, meant eventually no DDR.

When he paid a state visit to Bonn in mid-June, Gorbachov received a welcome such as no foreign statesman, not even Jack Kennedy, had ever enjoyed. Delirious crowds cheered themselves hoarse and chanted 'Gor-by, Gor-by, Gor-by' whenever he appeared. At a press conference, he echoed Khrushchev's words from 26 years before: 'The wall can come down when the circumstances that led to its being built in the first place no longer apply.' But his idea of how those circumstances would be changed was quite different from Khrushchev's.

While Honecker was still stubbornly clinging to his outdated Stalinist line, other east European leaders were aligning themselves with Gorbachov. For some, it was already too late; in Poland the communist government was swept from power in elections that same month. The Czechoslovak government was looking decidedly shaky, and the Hungarians were looking around desperately for ways of demonstrating their commitment to democracy. On 27 June, they opened their frontier with Austria, and on 10 September announced that they would allow East Germans through, even without an entry visa for Austria or the Federal Republic. It was the decisive crack in the eastern European dam, and citizens of the DDR rushed to pour through it to freedom. By the end of September, more than 25,000 of them had already made it.

Week by week, the flood of refugees grew, now through West German embassies in Prague and Warsaw as well as Budapest. As the pressure of protest within the DDR built up, Honecker steadfastly denied that there was any problem, in spite of the fact that demonstrators were marching through the streets of East Berlin and Leipzig. When Gorbachov came to East Berlin again on 6 October for the ceremonies to mark the fortieth anniversary of the DDR, the aging German ruler was still adamant in rejecting his appeals to accept reform, despite Gorbachov's warning: 'He who acts too late will be punished by life.' More demonstrations followed, not only in Berlin and Leipzig, but in other towns and cities across the country.

As the clashes with the police and security forces became increasingly violent, even Honecker had to acknowledge what was happening. On 18 October, he was forced to resign, 'on health grounds', supposedly suffering from a terminal cancer which, at the time of writing, years later, has still not killed him. By one of those wry coincidences that dot Berlin's history, the Komische Oper was presenting the 350th performance of *Bluebeard* that night, in which the chorus, at the overthrow of the tyrant, sings: 'The people rule, the people march, following the old tradition.'

Honecker's successor, Egon Krenz, known to Berliners as 'Horse Face', was confirmed in office a week later, though for the first time ever in the DDR the vote was not unanimous. Few East Berliners had been aware of the famous line in *Bluebeard*, but thousands of them found great amusement in the fact that Krenz's appointment was announced on television during an interruption in a popular programme called *Everybody Dreams of a Horse*.

During the week between the two announcements, there had been a significant change in the atmosphere in East Berlin. The candlelit demonstration that took place the night Krenz was confirmed in office was entirely peaceful. The police turned up to watch as the procession gathered on the Alexanderplatz, but made no attempt to interfere. They simply stood by, carefully keeping in groups of four, wearing their ordinary uniforms, not riot gear. Their shields, batons and sub-machine guns were conspicuously absent. For those present that night – as the authors of this book were – it was an eerie atmosphere, tingling with expectancy and hope.

But no one that night, on either side of the wall, could foresee or even dare to hope for the amazing events that were to take place just a few days later, on 9 November. During the days between, there were more demonstrations, declarations from Krenz that the wall was 'a bulwark', and general confusion. On 7 November, the DDR government resigned. On 8 November, the entire politburo followed suit. The following day, a new politburo was appointed, most of them men who had just resigned. At their first meeting, they decided to heed the pleas from the Czech government in Prague to do something to stem the flow of refugees, which was causing chaos. One answer would be to issue passports to all East Germans who wanted them, allowing them to come and go as they pleased, which should at least stop the immediate mad rush and allow everyone time to think.

At the end of his daily press conference, after announcing the new appointments, the Berlin party chief, Günther Schabowski, was asked a question about travel arrangements. Almost without thinking, he reported the politburo's decision to issue passports and travel permits on demand. People would be able to use border crossing points between the two Germanies, he added, eliminating the need to travel through other countries. When asked when the new regulation would come into force he replied, 'Immediately.'

East Berliners took Schabowski at his word. His announcement was made at 6.57 pm, and was included in the evening news on television and radio. Within minutes, thousands of them were hurrying to the nearest checkpoint, brandishing their identity cards and demanding to be let through. A great line of Trabant cars formed at the single vehicle entry, Checkpoint Charlie, turning the air blue with the exhausts from their two-stroke engines as they queued to drive into the west.

The bemused border guards had received no orders, and did not know what to do. For a while they tried to turn people away, but as the crowds built up, laughing, singing, all insisting that they had heard an official announcement, they gave up. Some of the guards had heard the radio news, too, and decided it must be true after all. One by one, the barriers were raised, and the great exodus of 'Ossies' began, to be greeted on the other side by crowds of 'Wessies', who had also heard the news and hurried to be there, to open bottles of sparkling Sekt, the German champagne, and to join in the great celebration.

West Berlin rapidly turned into one enormous party, a party that was joined by countless millions around the world as television networks broadcast live pictures of the incredible scenes. And at the Brandenburg Gate, where there was no crossing, a young 'Ossie' crossed the barriers and hoisted himself on to the top of the wall itself . . .

The cold war ended, appropriately, not in pomp and ceremony but almost by accident, in a situation worthy of the highest farce. For once, the misunderstandings and bungling had produced the right result: the people of Berlin had spoken, and for once they were not to be denied.

In another of those odd coincidences, the date, 9 November, had a special significance for Berliners, and indeed for all Germans. It was on 9 November 1918 that the last of the Kaisers, Wilhelm II, had abdicated, leaving his defeated country a prey to revolution and, eventually, to Adolf Hitler. On 9 November 1923, Hitler had first come to national prominence with his failed putsch in Munich, and the anniversary of that event was celebrated every year as the Nazis' national party day. And on 9 November 1938, Hitler had unleashed the prelude to the Holocaust with his first pogrom, the Reichskristallnacht, designed to scare the Jews out of Germany. Now, that past was purged: 9 November became a day of hope for a brighter future.

CHAPTER 24

Berlin is still Berlin

THE PARTY LASTED for days. Hammers, crowbars, pickaxes appeared as if by magic, as the 'wall-peckers' started chipping away at the concrete of the hated wall. One young man was seen working with a hammer in one hand and a sickle in the other. They were all on the western side, where the surface was covered with layer upon layer of brightly coloured graffiti – writing or painting on *any* walls had always been strictly forbidden in the east, and in any case easterners had rarely been able to get close enough to the wall itself to touch it. Their wall had been painted in alternating shades of blue, expanses of pale colour designed to show up any intruder as a sharply defined target. Within hours, dozens of holes had been hacked right through the wall, and fragments were being offered for sale at 20 marks apiece. Grinning Ossies protested good-humouredly, 'You can't sell that – it's *our* wall!'

For weeks afterwards, the main streets of the west end were jammed with pop-popping Trabants and crowds of easterners swarming along the pavements, window shopping and simply enjoying the new Berlin Bummel before returning home again. The crowds were swollen by hundreds of thousands of visitors from the rest of both

Germanies, and tourists from other countries. Not since the Olympic games in 1936 had Berlin been so much at the centre of approving world attention. Naturally, being Berliners, the Wessies were soon grumbling at the size of the invasion and the inconvenience of it all, while the Ossies, recovering from their first openmouthed shock at the sight of so many consumer delights, grumbled at the price of it all.

Gradually, the initial excitement wore off, to be replaced by a more practical look at the problems of reunification – any lingering thoughts that the two halves could somehow continue their separate existences were very quickly swept aside. And once it became clear that Berlin would have to become one city again, so it followed automatically that the two Germanies could no longer remain apart. Whatever the politicians thought, whatever prudence and caution dictated, the people had spoken. What they wanted was 'Ein Volk, einig Vaterland', and they would not be denied.

Whether the rest of the country wanted Berlin as its capital was another question. For many Germans, the city carried too much emotional and historical baggage. And for many more, the old suspicion and dislike of the big city and its cocky, irreverent inhabitants, so unlike the stolid, respectable citizens of Bonn or Munich or the thousands of small towns in both parts of Germany, was reborn. The argument raged for over 18 months. Even when it became clear that there was a majority in favour of restoring Berlin to its position as the official capital of a reunited Germany, many still argued that the seat of government should stay in Bonn. It was not until 20 June 1991 that the Bundestag, after nearly twelve hours of heated debate, decided by only 337 votes to 320 that Berlin should be both.

During those 18 months, a great deal had happened in Berlin. For a start, dozens of new openings were punched in the wall. The first, on 10 November 1989, was Glienicke bridge, scene of so many exchanges of prisoners. Two days later, an even more significant new opening was created on Potsdamerplatz. West Berlin's governing mayor Walter Momper met East Berlin's lord mayor, Erhard Krack, on the border. They promised to co-operate, especially on travel. That afternoon, the federal president, former governing mayor Richard von Weizsäcker, made an official visit to the new crossing point.

On 22 December, a provisional regional committee representing both East and West Berlin and the two national governments, held its first meeting in Schöneberg town hall. Afterwards, another emotional gathering watched and applauded as Chancellor Kohl of the Federal Republic and the new premier of the DDR, Hans Modrow, together with the two mayors, opened up the Brandenburg Gate as a pedestrian crossing point. It was a fine Christmas present, and all over Berlin – both Berlins – church bells rang out joyously to celebrate it.

For the first time since the end of the war, Berliners could now travel the entire length of the old East–West Axis, and thousands took advantage of the opportunity, despite the winter rain. It was a journey that managed to encompass, either in fact or name, virtually every major point in Berlin's history: from Heerstrasse near the Olympic stadium, across Theodor-Heuss-Platz (originally Reichskanzlerplatz, then Adolf-Hitler-Platz) along the broad Kaiserdamm and Bismarckstrasse, widened by Albert Speer in 1936, crossing Ernst-Reuter-Platz on to the Strasse des 17. Juni, then passing through the Tiergarten via the Grosse Stern and the Siegessäule, built to commemorate Bismarck's three victorious wars, past the Reichstag to the Brandenburg Gate itself; and then, moving through the gate – even through the central span reserved in former years for the exclusive use of kings and Kaisers – passing what was left of Pariserplatz and the entrance to the former Wilhelmstrasse, at that time still unmemorably labelled Otto-Grotewohl-Strasse, with its bare mounds of earth marking the location of the old Reich chancellery and the Führer bunker, and on up the Linden past the restored glories of the Hohenzollern years to end at the Dom, the Lustgarten, and the Palace of the Republic standing on the site of Iron-tooth's Zwingburg. All day and for most of the night, Berliners promenaded up and down the Linden, smiling and nodding at each other as Berliners used to do in years gone by, reclaiming the old city as their own.

1990 started with a bang, or to be precise with thousands of bangs, as half a million people gathered around the Brandenburg Gate again, to see in the New Year with music and fireworks and exploding bottles of Sekt and, of course, dancing on the wall. Some revellers managed to climb to the top of the gate to the Quadriga, haul down the DDR flag and cut out the central communist emblem before running it back up the flagpole again. Someone else hoisted the twelve-starred blue flag of the European Community. And finally, as if to establish the international flavour of the celebrations, the maple leaf flag of Canada suddenly joined it. No one seemed to mind. It was, after all, a night that belonged to the world.

The rest of that memorable year passed in a madcap blur of rapidly accelerating change. On 15 January, a crowd of East Berliners stormed the headquarters of the Stasi, the still-hated secret police. It was the equivalent of the storming of the Bastille by the Paris mob in 1789, a declaration of revolution, after which there could be no turning back. Hans Modrow's government was shaken to the core: if the people could attack the Stasi, then clearly nothing was sacred any more. For two weeks, they dithered uncertainly, complaining in a bewildered way about the lack of order. Then they gave in, and announced a general election to be held on 18 March, the first free elections for the people of eastern Germany since 1933.

In effect, the elections were a referendum on reunification, and the people of the DDR made their feelings quite clear. Their new coalition government was led by a Christian democrat, a former professional viola player and descendant of the Huguenots, Lothar de Maizière, who declared for German unity as quickly as possible.

On 1 April, all Berlin's waterways were officially opened to unrestricted use. On 5 May, talks began between the two German governments and the four powers, to end the rights held by the victorious powers since 1945. The following day, the first free local elections in East Berlin gave most votes to the SPD, with the Socialist PDS (the new name for the SED) in second place. The SPD formed a coalition with the CDU, with a social democrat lord mayor, Tino Schwierzina. By 18 May, the two German finance ministers were able to sign an agreement to unify their currencies and economies on 1 July.

On 12 June, almost 42 years since the communists forced the West Berlin city council out of the Neues Stadthaus to take up temporary residence in Schöneberg town hall, the two administrations held their first joint session in the Red Town Hall. Next day, the official demolition of the wall started, appropriately in the divided Bernauerstrasse. Lother de Maizière had promised that the wall would come down fast, and he was as good as his word. On 22 June — coincidentally the 49th anniversary of Hitler's invasion of the Soviet Union — the foreign ministers of all four victorious powers and of both Germanies, together with the two mayors, watched as Checkpoint Charlie was dismantled. The wooden hut that had housed American, British and French military police for so long was lifted out in one piece by a giant crane, and carted ignominiously away.

According to the plan, it should have taken until the end of the year for the entire length of the wall to be removed and crushed. In fact, like everything else in that incredible year, it went much more quickly: the last piece was torn down on 13 November. All told, it amounted to over a million tonnes of rubble. Some of it was earmarked for use in constructing the new high-speed rail track, between Berlin and Hanover. The rest was sold to construction companies, as hardcore for the foundations of new buildings, the proceeds going into the city's reconstruction fund. A few short stretches of wall were left standing as memorials to its victims.

One stretch of wall, a little over three-quarters of a mile (1.2 kilometres) in length along the west bank of the Spree in Mühlen-strasse, Friedrichshain, has been left as an especially Berlinisch memorial, known since September 1990 as the East-Side Gallery. On the initiative of a Scottish gallery owner, Chris MacLean, 118 artists from 21 different countries were each given a segment of wall on which to paint their own pictures. The result is claimed, in true old Berlin style, to be the world's biggest open-air art gallery. Some pictures are particularly striking; most have a sharp, satirical edge, such as the one of Soviet premier Brezhnev locked in a mouth-to-mouth kiss with Erich Honecker, over the caption, 'My God, help me to survive this deadly love.'

On 1 July, two days after the two city councils named President Weizsäcker as the first freeman since 1946 of the united city of Berlin, the last frontier checks were abolished and full monetary, economic and social union came into force; the Deutschmark, the introduction of which had given the Soviets their excuse to divide the country, was now the sole currency. As a special concession to the Ossies, the exchange rate was set at 1:1, a ludicrously generous handout that was vital if they were not all to be turned into paupers overnight.

And still the breakneck pace towards unity did not flag. Full-scale negotiations began on 6 July, and the treaty was signed, in the old crown prince's palace on the Linden, on 31 August. Twelve days later, the foreign ministers of the four powers and the two Germanies met in Moscow, to sign the '2 + 4 Treaty', rescinding the rights of the victors of 1945 over Germany in general and Berlin in particular. At midnight on 3 October, Germany was reunited at last – and in Berlin, of course, not in Bonn. As the political leaders carried out the official ceremony in the Philharmonie, the federal flag was raised in front of the Reichstag to the sound of the national anthem, and more than a million people from east and west joined in yet another gargantuan party along the entire length of the Linden. Next day, no doubt nursing a massive collective hangover, the first all-German parliament since the Second World War convened for its first session in the Reichstag.

On 2 December the first free elections since 1946 (or even, by some reckonings, since 1933) were held for an all-Berlin city council. The differences between the two halves of the city were very clear. In the west, the conservative CDU collected 47.8 per cent of the vote, almost an overall majority; in the east they managed only 24.3 per cent, to give a city-wide figure of 40.4 per cent. The PDS, the former Communist Party, on the other hand, notched up 24.8 per cent in the east, but a mere 1.3 per cent in the west, to score a total of only 9.2 per cent. The SPD was more evenly balanced, but was still well below the CDU, returning an overall figure of 30.4 per cent. Even with the two halves rejoined, the old days of Red Berlin were still over. The new mayor was, once again, a Christian democrat, Eberhard Diepgen.

Even before the hangovers faded, it was obvious that there would be enormous problems in trying to stitch the two Berlins together again into a homogeneous whole. They represented two very different systems, at two totally different levels of progress; in many ways, they were more like two different worlds than two halves of the same city. But it was not until unification that the planners and engineers in the west realized just how serious the problems were. They discovered that most of East Berlin's utilities had not even been properly maintained for the best part of half a century, never mind modernized.

Since the days of the blockade, West Berlin had been forced to be self-sufficient in electricity, with nine modern power stations supplying all its needs, though it had no spare capacity. Its system provided a steady and uninterrupted supply of power, with no spikes or surges – a vital requirement for modern electronic appliances. In East Berlin, the main electricity transformer centre, housed in a wonderful, cathedral-like building, had been constructed in the 1920s, and was still using the same equipment. Indeed, one of the biggest headaches facing the electrical engineers was that the two systems were completely incompatible. In February 1992 the whole of the old eastern system suffered a major failure.

Gas supplies were little better. In the west, an alarm automatically sounds if there are more than two leaks per kilometre of gas main. In the east, 33 or more leaks in the same distance was regarded as quite normal. The engineers found some 500 miles (800 kilometres) of gas main urgently needed replacing. The task was so urgent and so huge, that they called in help from all round Europe: among the companies contracted to repair and replace the damaged mains was British Gas, a successor of the company that installed Berlin's first gasworks, back in 1826.

Unrepaired war damage, as well as increasingly heavy traffic on the roads, meant that 25 per cent of all East Berlin's main sewers were in desperate need of emergency repairs, with raw sewage leaking into the city's shallow water table through thousands of cracks. First estimates of the cost of bringing the system up to an acceptable standard were DM 2–3 billion. In addition, they discovered that up to 40 per cent of households were not even connected to the main sewerage system, while 25 per cent still had no plumbing.

The telephone service was another major problem. Most East Berlin exchanges were as much as 60 years old, and while in the west there were far more phones than people, in the east there was only one phone for every ten people. The only efficient communications operation was that run by the Stasi, which had its own private telephone network as well as facilities to tap and record 20,000 calls simultaneously. There was a standing order that in case of riots or other attacks, the Stasi exchange was to be defended to the death: every employee had an automatic rifle, marked with his or her name, locked in a rack in the basement.

Business users, starved both of phones and of lines, soon developed ways of overcoming the problem of contacting the west. Bicycle couriers flourished: one company started out with seven riders in 1989, and had 500 two years later. The second way, used by many Ossie businessmen, was to save up their calls, then jump into their Trabis and drive across the old border to find an empty public telephone kiosk in the west. For the more successful, mobile phones, never before seen in the east, became essential, though a radio call to West Berlin cost as much as a conventional call to Egypt. The telephone company is working flat out to lay new lines and to replace the old electromagnetic and operator-controlled exchanges with state-of-the-art digital equipment. But, like everything else, it will take time. At the time of writing, the wait for a new domestic line is about two years.

Roads, railways, postal services, social services, all contributed to the difficulties, not to mention housing, where one in five of all East Berlin homes was considered uninhabitable. It will take another 40 years to complete the renewal programme – and in the meantime, there remains a shortage of 200,000 homes.

The influence of the west can already be seen in the old city centre, with glittering international names, names like Gucchi and Yves St Laurent, Ralph Lauren and Hugo Boss, appearing on and in smart new shops along the Linden. They are replacing government bureaus and the spartan, somehow ersatz, offices of east European and Soviet airlines. They are also, less happily perhaps, replacing the shops selling culture to the masses at heavily subsidized prices – books, music, records, artworks. The old Opera Café, in the old Prinzessinpalais where Jules Laforgue had read French newspapers to the aging empress, has been transformed into the Opernpalais, containing three excellent restaurants and a luxurious piano bar.

But the effects of reunion can be seen in other places and in other ways, too, as the radical young of the two halves of the city merge effortlessly and spread themselves into new quarters in the old east. The removal of the deadening pressure to conform has released an enormous burst of creative – and anarchic – energy in young Ossies. Prenzlauerberg, by tradition always the liveliest district of East Berlin, was soon rivalling Kreuzberg as a centre of the arts world and the alternative society. More centrally, part of Oranienburger-strasse, where it links with the northern tip of Friedrichstrasse, suddenly transformed itself into the focal point of the youth scene, with simple, cheap cafés and bistros, lively clubs, and the astonishing Tacheles multimedia arts centre created by some 50 artists, from both east and west, who moved into the ruins of an old department store in 1990.

Further along Oranienburgerstrasse, at the heart of what was the old Jewish quarter, the nineteenth-century New Synagogue, the biggest in Berlin until it was burnt down by Nazi thugs during Kristallnacht, has been magnificently restored to its Byzantine splendour, complete with its ornate silver and gold dome. There is a thriving Jewish community centre and mostly vegetarian restaurant alongside.

Friedrichstrasse, particularly near the Gendarmenmarkt, is already beginning to take its place again as an elegant, up-market centre. Locals now regard the new Grand Hotel Maritim, a sumptuous and solid establishment built in reproduction turn-of-the-century style by an international group in the last days of communism, as the best hotel in Berlin, displacing, at least for the moment, Kempinski on the Ku'damm and the Inter-Continental on Budapesterstrasse, near the zoo. At the southern end of the Gendarmenmarkt, Hilton have taken over the equally smart but more showy Dom Hotel, and are restoring it to its former glory, though it is hard to believe it was ever as glamorous as this. Further north on Friedrichstrasse, near the railway station, the Zille Museum, and the tower block of the International Trade Centre, is the Hotel Metropol, once the resort of the communist elite. The Metropol, where the bedroom suites were clearly designed for ministerial business, is fast transforming itself into a first-class international hotel, with an efficient but notably friendly management consisting largely of Ossies.

More and more visitors to Berlin will choose to stay in the old east. There is still a thrill in stepping out on a bright, chill Berlin morning into what was once a forbidden city, a kind of communist Lhasa. And there is a thrill, too, in being able to walk the length of the Unter den Linden before breakfast, surrounded by so many reminders of the city's eventful past. Of course, this has always been possible for a foreigner, but previously it involved passport and monetary controls and a feeling that one was stepping into an alien world. The world still feels slightly alien, because of the absence of traffic jams – at least for the moment – but the views are stunning.

The west, however, is fighting back strongly. To the east of the zoo, for example, any hotel with available land, such as the Inter-

Continental, or the excellent Hotel President on An der Urania, is busy building extensions or special conference centres. And just about every hotel in what was West Berlin is refurbishing and refitting frantically in a collective show of confidence in the city's future.

For the foreseeable future, Berlin is likely to remain the world's biggest building site. Over the next 15 years, the federal government is planning to spend an incredible £850 billion on construction projects in the former East Germany. A considerable proportion of it will be in Berlin, where accommodation will have to be found for all the ministries and government departments that will be moving from Bonn – though as recession tightens its grip, renewed opposition from other German Länder is already extending the timetable for the moves well into the twenty-first century.

All around the Reichstag, in the old Tiergarten district that was almost completely destroyed in the war, there is to be a brand new government quarter, including a new federal chancellery, presidential office and Federal Council building. It will encompass the old In den Zelten, where the Huguenots set up their refreshment tents in the eighteenth century, where the revolutionaries of 1848 gathered to march on the royal palace, and where Christopher Isherwood and his friends danced the night away as the Golden Twenties faded into the terrible Thirties.

The Reichstag itself, which will eventually house the Bundestag, is to be completely refurbished to a plan by the British architect Sir Norman Foster, winner of a competition that was open to all German architects and ten invited international superstars. Foster's first imaginative concept put the whole of the old building on an open podium beneath a great canopy, higher than the Reichstag's vanished dome, supported by 25 stainless steel columns, each 50 metres high. The final design, however, reflects the more cautious mood of Germany brought on by recession: the dramatic canopy has gone, and the exterior will look much as it has always done. But the interior will be gutted and replaced, with a circular assembly chamber at its centre, under a smaller canopy where the dome used to be. Wide spaces and much use of glass symbolise more open government, but some lessons from the past have been well-learned — the design allows for secure underground tunnels to and from the new presidential palace, chancellery and Federal Council building.

But federal and city government expenditure is likely to be dwarfed by private spending by big business. Already, there is so much building going on in the city that at least one of Germany's biggest contractors has told clients they will have to take their places on a waiting list. And when work begins on the really major projects, Berlin's waterways will come into their own again, since its roads will be totally inadequate to cope with the flow of materials.

Inevitably, many architects and building companies complain of indecision and delays in the planning system, though the problems of rebuilding Berlin have been under consideration for nearly 40 years. There was an international competition for the centre of the city, under the title 'Capital Berlin', as far back as 1957–8. There have also been accusations that certain sites in the east have been sold off too cheaply, but this tends to ignore one of the major problems faced by any developer buying land in the former East Berlin: who actually owns it? First the Nazis, then the Soviet occupation authorities, followed by the East German government, all took over land without considering that ownership might one day have to be sorted out in Federal Republic courts. There is a further factor, all too rarely admitted. Berlin city officials believe that nearly one-third of the land now on offer in East Berlin was once owned by Jews, many of whom died intestate in concentration camps. All this is obviously the substance of which developers' nightmares and lawyers' dreams are made.

Even the simplest and, on the face of it, least intractable land ownership question can still prove fraught with difficulties. The case of Equitable Life of New York, the insurance giant, is but one example. Their real estate investment subsidiary has planned an eight-storey office and retailing complex on the site of their old headquarters close to Leipzigerstrasse, which they acquired in 1886. They plan to spend DM 180 million on the project, but cannot yet prove that they are the rightful owners. Even East Berlin's most famous new landmark, the TV tower, is built on land that appears to have no fewer than eight different owners.

There are sinister rumours, too, that not all the companies investing in East Berlin are respectable multi-nationals. The Mafia is said to be buying its share of the city's real estate. It would be interesting to know if it suffers the same legal hassles that have faced so many

314

other companies, or whether, if things become too difficult, its executives make any owners an offer they can't refuse. . .

In East Berlin, there are at least three prime sites for commercial development. In Friedrichstrasse, the main development is in the hands of New York companies, giving rise to local fears of Manhattan-on-the-Spree, with skyscrapers disrupting the old city's unique skyline. Part of this project is the Friedrichstadt Passagen, reviving one of old Berlin's most exclusive shopping arcades on the edge of the Gendarmenmarkt, with its two elegant cathedrals and the reconstructed Schinkel Schauspielhaus. It will encompass 120,000 square metres of shops, offices and apartments, and represents an investment of a staggering DM 1.4 billion, about £580 million or $875 million.

A little further down Friedrichstrasse, on the site of Checkpoint Charlie, will be the American Business Center, a complex covering four city blocks and involving five different buildings. One of them is being designed by Philip Johnson, the 86-year-old New York architect who was responsible for the Lincoln Center and the AT & T Building in New York, and London's tallest building, the controversial Canary Wharf skyscraper. The whole complex will provide 100,000 square metres of shops, restaurants, offices and apartments. It is intended to provide a home for US companies wishing to establish headquarters in Europe.

One block east of the Gendarmenmarkt lies Hausvogteiplatz, before 1933, the centre of Berlin's – indeed, of Germany's – rag trade, which was dominated by Jewish textile merchants. Now, a new Jewish consortium, led by Azra Harel with French partners, are hoping to revive the old tradition by transforming Hausvogteiplatz into a European fashion centre again, around a Berlin branch of the great Paris store, Galeries Lafayette.

But the biggest and most important commercial site in all Berlin is the Zentrale Bereich (central area), the wasteland around the former Potsdamerplatz, which Governing Mayor Walter Momper accurately described as 'where the old heart of Berlin used to beat'. A master plan, drawn up for the city by a firm of local architects, Hilmer and Stattler, echoes the classic Berlin formula for the Mietskasernen: city blocks six stories high. The site includes Leipzigerplatz, part of Potsdamerstrasse, and the area running down from Potsdamerplatz towards Pariserplatz and the Brandenburg Gate, including the western side of the former Wilhelmstrasse, happily no longer saddled with the name of Otto Grotewohl, but now called, somewhat uneasily, Toleranzstrasse. In this part, mounds of earth show where Hitler's chancellery stood, and the bunker where he and Goebbels met their end, undoubtedly the most controversial site in the whole of Berlin.

Elsewhere on the flattened former no-man's-land there is nothing to be seen of lost landmarks like Mendelsohn's Columbushaus, Kempinski's Haus Vaterland, Schinkel's gatehouses, the Café Josty, Wertheim's department stores or any of the grand hotels. Only part of the old Grand Hotel Esplanade remains, an isolated semi-ruin on Bellevuestrasse, in the west, close to the Philharmonie and the Kulturforum. Since 1985, the remains of the hotel have been known as the Filmhaus Esplanade, part of the Berlin Film Academy, but in June 1991 the Senate sold the building and the surrounding area to the Japanese electronics giant Sony, which is to redevelop it with an ambitious scheme designed by Murphy Jahn that will include a vast hotel as well as its new head office in Germany.

Some time before the wall came down, when it was still difficult to attract investment to Berlin, the governing mayor of West Berlin, Walter Momper, promised Daimler-Benz, the biggest company in Germany, a prime position in the centre of Potsdamerplatz if it would relocate its headquarters to the city. The company bought a large site, shaped like an ill-cut wedge of cheese south of the Sony site, and commissioned 14 international architects to compete for its design. Among them were some of the most distinguished names in the business, architects like Sir Richard Rogers, Arata Isozarki, O.M. Ungers, Richard Meier, and so on. The competition was won by Genoan-born, Paris-based Renzo Piano, who, unlike some of the others, stuck to the rules of the master plan, which called for 'a reconstruction in contemporary style of the old urban configuration'. Around a rather anonymous 22-storey office block, he offers low-rise blocks with internal courtyards, each twinned with another block, a subtle modern variation of the traditional Berlin pattern. He also includes a new theatre to stand beside the Kulturforum, linked to it by means of a shared entrance.

The building boom is by no means limited to the east, or to the former border strip. Spandau, on Berlin's western edge, has been chosen as Berlin's rail gateway to western Europe, courtesy of the new high-speed trains. Santiago Calatrava, the young Spanish engineer famous for his dynamic, soaring bridges, has been asked to design the new station. His proposal is similar to the station he has recently built in Zurich, with gull-wing platform canopies supported by beams as slim and elegant as bird bones. The whole thing gives the impression that it might just flap its wings and take off. By the end of the century, Berliners will be able to step aboard a train at Spandau and speed down to Paris or Toulouse at around 200 miles per hour (322 kilometres per hour), arriving in the French capital in under four hours, and Toulouse less than two and a half hours later.

Another, but altogether more controversial, project in West Berlin is Sir Richard Rogers's 19-storey tower, the Brau und Brunnen building, for a triangular site on Joachimstalerstrasse between the Zoo station and the Kaiser Wilhelm Memorial Church. The lower levels will be occupied by a series of shops, cafés and offices, then between the twelfth and sixteenth floors there will be the bedrooms of a four-star hotel, reached from a lobby at street level. Above them will be two floors of conference suites and more offices, and then a rooftop restaurant with views across the city. It is a striking scheme, but cannot be welcomed by the nearby Inter-Continental Hotel, whose guests can at the moment eat in its own rooftop restaurant, while enjoying unrivalled views across the city to the east and west, views such as Eduard Gärtner might have painted 150 years ago. If the new tower goes up to its full 19 stories, breakfast at the Inter-Continental will never be quite the same again.

The intentions of the Brau und Brunnen scheme are good. They aim to lift an area that is becoming increasingly tacky, with gift shops, fast-food restaurants and the kind of retail outlets for the gimcrack and trashy that appear around main railway stations everywhere. Like New York's Times Square or London's Piccadilly Circus a short time ago, this part of Berlin's west end is in urgent need of a face lift. The controversy arises because any grandiose building project in Berlin harks uncomfortably back to the Hitlerian or communist past. The shadow of Hitler's planned Great Hall, and of the monolithic grey blocks of the Stalin Allee loom over every development, including Sir Richard Rogers's tower. Having got rid of the Hohenzollerns and Hitler and Honecker, Berliners don't want any new architectural horrors imposed on them.

Dr Hans Stimman, the Senate's building and housing director, understands this view and, indeed, shares it. He has stated that Berlin is a European city existing within a European tradition: it is not Manhattan or Chicago. Set as it is on the flat Prussian plain, 'it does not need tall buildings, but it does need architects who understand the traditional streetscape'. Naturally, such opinions are anathema to architects and developers, who are already complaining about interference from Dr Stimman. Not only is he seeking to control the height and density of new buildings, he also wants a say in details of architectural design that they feel are none of his concern.

Of course, Berliners want gleaming new buildings designed by the current crop of international stars of the architectural world. But at the same time, they demand that those stars remain true to the spirit of Berlin's Wilhelmine past, which Berliners are looking on more and more as some sort of architectural golden age – which it never was. But however heavy and ornate, however ugly it sometimes became, Wilhelmine Berlin possessed its own distinctive style, and above all it was built on a human scale. There were no skyscrapers, no high-rise blocks of apartments then. Berliners could still feel themselves to be the centre of their world. Will they still feel the same 20 years from now?

Finally, what of the Berliners themselves? Physically the wall has disappeared, with the scar on the landscape healing over remarkably quickly. But in many other ways, it is still there. It still exists in the heads of people who lived with it for over 40 years, and who are still reeling from the revelations of just how corrupt their former rulers were, and how far the tentacles of the Stasi spread. It exists as a totally different approach to life; it has been said that West Germans spend money and save time, while East Germans do exactly the opposite. It exists in the attitudes of the two communities to each other: envy and resentment on one side, and a snobbish disdain on the other. To the rich, the poor are lazy and feckless; to the poor, the rich are idle and spoilt.

Many Wessies strongly resent being asked to pay for the mistakes of the communist government with massive hand-outs. But it can be as hard to accept charity as to give it: many Ossies strongly resent being patronized, as they see it, by arrogant Wessies who think everything from the west is good, and everything from the east bad. *Die Distel*, the political cabaret that still operates alongside Friedrichstrasse station, greets visitors with a sign reading: 'Welcome to the BDBZ.' The initials stand for *Bundes-deutsche Bezatsungs-Zone* – the Federal German Occupation Zone. The sign speaks for many in the east who want to hold on to the good things in their own social history and lifestyle, to their own more old-fashioned values, to little things like the fact that there was a guaranteed kindergarten place for every single child in East Berlin.

Ossies with gardens that were alongside the wall now find themselves cheek by jowl with Wessies who were on the other side. Among the many complaints they have about their new neighbours is the fact that they bring their dogs to their weekend cottages and wreck the gardens. But what dogs! The Wessies' dogs, they accuse, are Rottweilers and Dobermanns, aggressive brutes. 'No East German has dogs like that,' they say. 'We stick to dachshunds and spaniels.' Such Ossies do not want to be 'assimilated' into West Berlin; rather, they want to contribute towards the creation of something new and different, a product of both cultures.

In time, the differences – and the suspicions that go with them – are bound to fade. And, eventually, something new and different will be created. It will take years, of course, and there will still be differences in the standards of living – but then, there always were. Berlin always had a mixture of poverty and prosperity, and as it happens they were generally divided between the east and the west, just as they are now. As always in Berlin, everything is new but nothing is ever new. Whatever happens in the future, the old city motto will still hold true: *Berlin bleibt doch Berlin*, Berlin is still Berlin.

Bibliography

The authors consulted the following books in the writing of this book. Unless otherwise stated, publication was in London.

ADLON, HEDDA, *Hotel Adlon*, Barrie Books, 1956.

ALTMANN, ALEXANDER, *Moses Mendelssohn*, Routledge and Kegan Paul, 1973.

ANDREAS-FRIEDRICH, RUTH, *Berlin Underground, 1939–1945*, Latimer House, 1949.

——, *Battleground Berlin: Diaries 1945–1948*, New York, Paragon House, 1990.

ANONYMOUS, *A Woman in Berlin*, Secker and Warburg, 1955.

ARNOLD-FOSTER, MARK, *The Siege of Berlin*, Collins, 1979.

BALFOUR, ALAN, *Berlin: the Politics of Order, 1737–1989*, New York, Rizzoli International, 1990.

BARRACLOUGH, GEOFFREY, *The Origins of Modern Germany*, Oxford, Basil Blackwell, 1979.

BECKER, FRITZ, *Cookbook from Berlin*, Münster, Wolfgang Hölker, 1988.

BERGER, JOACHIM, *Berlin, Freiheitlich and Rebellisch*, Berlin, Goebel, 1987.

BIELENBERG, CHRISTABEL, *The Past is Myself*, Chatto and Windus, 1968.

BOTTING, DOUGLAS, *In the Ruins of the Reich*, Grafton Books, 1986.

BOYD, BRIAN, *Vladimir Nabokov: the Russian Years*, Chatto and Windus, 1990.

BRECHT, BERTOLT, *Poems 1938–1956*, Eyre Macmillan, 1976.

BÜLOW, PRINCE BERNHARD VON, *Memoirs* (4 vols), Boston, Little Brown, 1931–2.

CARR, WILLIAM, *A History of Germany 1815–1985*, Edward Arnold, 1987.

CECIL, LAMAR, *The German Diplomatic Service, 1871–1914*, Princeton, NJ, Princeton University Press, 1976.

CHANNON, SIR HENRY (ed. ROBERT RHODES JAMES), *Chips: The Diaries of Sir Henry Channon*, Weidenfeld and Nicolson, 1967.

CHARMAN, TERRY, *The German Home Front*, Barrie and Jenkins, 1989.

COBURG, GÖTZ VON (ed.), *The Wall and How It Fell*, Press and Information Office, Land of Berlin, 1990.

DARNTON, ROBERT, *Berlin Journal, 1989–1990*, New York, W.W. Norton, 1991.

DELMER, SEFTON, *Trail Sinister*, Secker and Warburg, 1961.

DIETRICH, RICHARD (ed.), *Berlin: Neun Kapitel seiner Geschichte*, Berlin, Walter de Gruyter, 1960.

EHRENBERG, ILYA, *Truce, 1921–33*, MacGibbon and Kee, 1963.

——, *Men, Years, Life*, MacGibbon and Kee, 1963.

ENGELMANN, BERNT, *Berlin, eine Stadt wie keine andere*, Munich, Bertelsmann, 1986.

——, *In Hitler's Germany*, Methuen, 1988.

EVERETT, SUSANNE, *Lost Berlin*, Bison Books, 1979.

FLANNER, JANET, *Janet Flanner's World*, Secker and Warburg, 1980.

FLANNERY, HARRY, *Assignment to Berlin*, Michael Joseph, 1942.

FLENLEY, RALPH, *Modern German History*, Dent, 1968.

FLÜGGE, GERHARD, *Das Dicke Zillebuch*, Hannover, Fackelsträger, 1991.

FRIEDRICH, OTTO, *Before the Deluge*, Michael Joseph, 1974.

GELB, NORMAN, *The Berlin Wall*, Michael Joseph, 1986.

GRUNBERGER, RICHARD, *A Social History of the Third Reich*, Penguin, 1974.

HAFFNER, SEBASTIAN, *Germany's Self-Destruction: The Reich from Bismarck to Hitler*, Simon and Schuster, 1989.

HART-DAVIS, DUFF, *Hitler's Games: the 1936 Olympics*, Harper and Row, 1986.

HAUS, WOLFGANG, *Geschichte der Stadt Berlin (Meyers Forum Bd 6)*, Mannheim, BI Taschenbuch Verlag, 1992.

HENDERSON, SIR NEVILE, *Failure of a Mission*, Hodder and Stoughton, 1940.

HORST, DIETER (ed.), *125 Jahre Schutzmannschaft Berlin*, Berlin, Haupt and Koska, 1973.

HÜRLIMANN, MARTIN, *Berlin: Königresidenz, Reichshauptstadt, Neubeginn*, Zurich, Atlantis, 1981.

HURST, LINDSAY, *Royal Porphyria*, Southampton Medical Journal, Vol 5, No 2, Autumn 1988.

ISHERWOOD, CHRISTOPHER, *Christopher and His Kind*, Eyre Methuen, 1977.

——, *Goodbye to Berlin*, Eyre Methuen, 1987.

——, *Mr Norris Changes Trains*, Eyre Methuen, 1987.

KUBY, ERICH, *The Russians and Berlin*, Heinemann, 1968.

KURTZ, HAROLD, *The Second Reich: Kaiser Wilhelm and his Germany*, Macdonald, 1970.

LAFORGUE, JULES, *Oeuvres Complètes: Berlin, la Cour et la Ville*, Paris, Mercure de France, 1930.

LORENZ, CHRISTA (ed.), *Parzelle, Laube, Kolonie: Kleingärten zwischen 1880 und 1930*, Berlin, Märkisches Museum, 1988.

LUUK, ERNST (ed.), *Berlin Handbuch: Das Lexikon der Bundeshauptstadt*, Berlin, FAB Verlag, 1993.

JACKSON, ROBERT, *The Berlin Airlift*, Wellingborough, Patrick Stephens, 1988.

KARDORFF, URSULA VON, *Diary of a Nightmare: Berlin 1942–45*, Hart-Davis, 1965.

KURTZ, HAROLD, *The Second Reich, Kaiser Wilhelm II and his Germany*, Macdonald, 1970.

LEONHARD, WOLFGANG, *Child of the Revolution*, Collins, 1957.

MAAS, JOACHIM, *Kleist*, Secker and Warburg, 1983.

MCELVOY, ANNE, *The Saddled Cow: East Germany's Life and Legacy*, Faber and Faber, 1992.

MACKINNON, MARIANNE, *The Naked Years: Growing Up in Nazi Germany*, Chatto and Windus, 1987.

——, *The Alien Years*, Lewes, Sussex, Book Guild, 1991.

MALLORY, KEITH and OTTAR, ARVID, *Architecture of Aggression: Military Architecture in Two World Wars*, Architectural Press, 1973.

MALTZAN, MARIA, GRÄFIN VON, *Schlage die Trommel und fürchte dich nicht*, Berlin, Ullstein, 1989.

MANDER, JOHN, *Berlin: The Eagle and the Bear*, Barrie and Rockliffe, 1959.

MANN, GOLO, (trans. Marian Jackson), *The History of Germany since 1789*, Chatto and Windus, 1968.

MASSIE, ROBERT K., *Dreadnought: Britain, Germany, and the Coming of the Great War*, Jonathan Cape, 1992.

MASUR, GERHARD, *Imperial Berlin*, New York, Dorset Press, 1970.

MELZER, RALF, *Berlin im Wandel: August 1989 bis Oktober 1991*, Press and Information Office of the Land of Berlin, 1992.

MILLAR, PETER, *Tomorrow Belongs To Me*, Bloomsbury, 1992.

MOSSE, GEORGE L., *Nazi Culture: Intellectual, Cultural and Social Life in the Third Reich*, W.H. Allen, 1966.

NELSON, WALTER HENRY, *The Berliners*, Longmans, 1969.

OLIVEIRA, A. RAMOS, (trans. Eileen E. Brooke), *A People's History of Germany*, Gollancz, 1942.

OVEN, WILFRED VON, *Mit Goebbels bis zum Ende*, 2 vols, Buenos Aires, Dürer-Verlag, 1949–50.

PALMER, ALAN, *Frederick the Great*, Weidenfeld and Nicolson, 1974.

READ, ANTHONY and FISHER, DAVID, *The Deadly Embrace: Hitler, Stalin and the Nazi-Soviet Pact, 1939–1941.* New York: W.W. Norton, 1989.

——, *Kristallnacht: Unleashing the Holocaust*, Michael Joseph, 1989.

——, *The Fall of Berlin*, New York: W.W. Norton, 1992.

REIMANN, VIKTOR, *The Man Who Created Hitler: Joseph Goebbels*, Kimber, 1976.

RIBBE, WOLFGANG, *Geschichte Berlins*, 2 vols, Munich, C.H. Beck, 1987.

SCHNEIDER, RICHARD (ed.), *Historic Places in Berlin*, Berlin, Nicolai, 1992.

SEMMLER, RUDOLF, *Goebbels: The Man Next To Hitler*, Westhouse, 1947.

SHÄFER, HANS DIETER, *Berlin im Zweiten Weltkrieg: Der Untergang der Reichshauptstadt in Augenzeugenberichten*, Munich, Piper, 1985.

SHARP, TONY, *The Wartime Alliance and the Zonal Division of Germany*, Oxford, Clarendon Press, 1975.

SHIRER, WILLIAM L., The Nightmare Years, 1930–1940, New York, Bantam Books, 1985.

——, *The Rise and Fall of the Third Reich*, Secker and Warburg, 1960.

——, *Berlin Diary: An inside account of Nazi Germany*, New York, Bonanza Books, 1984.

SIMMONS, MICHAEL, *Berlin, the Dispossessed City*, Hamish Hamilton, 1988.

SINCLAIR, ANDREW, *The Other Victoria: The Princess Royal and the Great Game of Europe*, Weidenfeld and Nicolson, 1981.

SMITH, HOWARD K., *Last Train from Berlin*, New York, Knopf, 1942.

SOMMER, ERICH F., *Das Memorandum*, Munich, Herbig, 1981.

SPEER, ALBERT, *The Slave State*, Weidenfeld and Nicolson, 1981.

——, *Inside the Third Reich*, Sphere, 1971.

STERN, CAROLA, *Ulbricht: A Politial Biography*, Pall Mall Press, 1965.

STRATENSCHULTE, ECKART D., *East Berlin*, Berlin, Information Centre, 1988.

STROHMEYER, KLAUS (ed.), *Berlin in Bewegung*, 2 vols, Reinbeck bei Hamburg, Rowohlt, 1987.

STUDNITZ, HANS-GEORG VON, *While Berlin Burns*, Weidenfeld and Nicolson, 1964.

SUTCLIFFE, ANTHONY (ed.), *Metropolis 1890–1940*, Mansell, 1984.

TUSA, ANN and JOHN, *The Berlin Blockade*, Hodder and Stoughton, 1988.

VAN DER VAT, DAN, *Freedom Was Never Like This: A Winter's Journey in East Germany*, Hodder and Stoughton, 1991.

VASSILTCHIKOV, MARIE, *The Berlin Diaries, 1940–1945*, Methuen, 1987.

WETZLAUGK, UDO and KOZIOL, CHRISTIAN, *Berlin: Outlook*, Berlin, Berlin Information Centre, 1985.

INDEX